Use R!

Use R!

This series of inexpensive and focused books on R will publish shorter books aimed at practitioners. Books can discuss the use of R in a particular subject area (e.g., epidemiology, econometrics, psychometrics) or as it relates to statistical topics (e.g., missing data, longitudinal data). In most cases, books will combine LaTeX and R so that the code for figures and tables can be put on a website. Authors should assume a background as supplied by Dalgaard's Introductory Statistics with R or other introductory books so that each book does not repeat basic material.

More information about this series at http://www.springer.com/series/6991

Moshe Arye Milevsky

Retirement Income Recipes in R

From Ruin Probabilities to Intelligent Drawdowns

Springer

Moshe Arye Milevsky
Schulich School of Business
York University
Toronto, ON, Canada

ISSN 2197-5736 ISSN 2197-5744 (electronic)
Use R!
ISBN 978-3-030-51433-4 ISBN 978-3-030-51434-1 (eBook)
https://doi.org/10.1007/978-3-030-51434-1

This Springer imprint is published by the registered company Springer Nature Switzerland AG
The registered company address is: Gewerbestrasse 11, 6330 Cham, Switzerland

Fames est optimus coquus . . .

Preface

This book is primarily intended for use as a supplementary college or university textbook, typically for a 12-week elective course on *computational problems in personal wealth management*, with a focus on retirement income planning. That is how I have used this material and content. The key differentiator of this book is the algorithms or more precisely the computer *recipes* embedded within every chapter. In other words, this book will also teach you (i.e. students) how to write and execute (simple) scripts in the **R** language. These are small self-contained pieces of computer code that will enable you to reproduce and replicate most of the numbers displayed. So, the readers should be able to confirm everything they read. Now, since this is an advanced textbook (i.e. course), it assumes a basic familiarity with personal financial concepts such as the calculation of mortgage schedules, income taxes, life insurance products, pension systems, life annuities, and the growing universe of investment funds and vehicles. The book also assumes a basic understanding of financial economics and accounting such as the personal balance sheet and income statement, the relationship between risk and return, life-cycle smoothing as a normative model, and individual risk management principles, all of which are covered in a basic course on financial economics or a rigorous course on personal finance. (Well, at least that is what I teach in a third-year course at a business school!)

More specifically, the intended audience and readership for this book—or what I would target as the ideal students for the course on which it's based—are "retirement quants" in training. These are (future) professionals within the financial services industry, individuals who will be part of a *wealth management* team and asked to solve (and report outcomes of) complex retirement income problems for *real live* people. But, these students aren't necessarily experts in multi-factor portfolio theory, advanced derivative pricing, or actuarial science. And, even if the student (or reader) happens to be a rocket scientist in a prior life, they might not have a sense or appreciation for the types of computational problems *real live* people will encounter around retirement. In other words, even a Ph.D. in mathematics will benefit from being exposed to the types of problems that are interesting and relevant within the retirement income space.

My main pedagogical objective is first and foremost to get students—who might find the entire topic of retirement income planning to be distant and perhaps even boring—interested, motivated, and fully engaged. I would also like to get the reader to the point at which they can (1) generate numerical answers to common questions in the retirement income arena, (2) reproduce numbers commonly used and reported by the industry, and (3) properly understand the embedded assumptions. Of course to get them (or from here on, you) to this nirvana stage you also have to know enough about products, strategies, and the relevant *retirement* institutional details. That is assumed prerequisite knowledge. So this book is definitely not the place to learn about the time value of money, or the difference between a stock and a bond, life annuity vs. life insurance, or marginal vs. average tax rates. There are (many) other great introductory books that cover all that background material. I'll provide some references when the time is right, but this is an advanced book (and course).

My intended audience is broader than college and university students, though. For example, you might have *Certified Financial Planner* (CFP) or *Chartered Financial Analyst* (CFA) designation or have one of the many specialized insurance or investment designations. Regardless of your formal title, the letters after your name or professional affiliation, if you are in the business of providing retirement income services—or selling retirement income products—then I think you should have a deeper understanding of retirement income calculations and their embedded assumptions. I'll get to what I mean by *assumptions* as this book shifts into high gear. But remember that the devil is always in the details.

To be more specific and very honest, I find that many professionals in the retirement income business could benefit from a deeper understanding of (i.) basic demographic and actuarial calculations, (ii.) life-cycle financial economics, and (iii.) more importantly, how to generate and replicate the numbers they rely on for guidance. So, this textbook also helps fill a particular gap in skills in addition to knowledge. Moreover, I believe that the **R** language—which I'll elaborate on in a moment—is the ideal tool to help navigate and master the computational challenges that arise from merging finance, economics, and actuarial science. As this book progresses, you will hopefully see why **R** is ideal for the task. Each one of the chapters of this book will include snippets of code in **R**, which are basically functions of no more than 10–15 lines, which you can use with a free compiler that is widely available and already used by many professionals in the industry. Moreover, to keep the focus on computations and answers, the occasional heavy-duty mathematics (or anything requiring calculus) will be relegated to the very end of the chapter, once the code and examples have been fully developed. They are there if you want them, and advanced material or the exact source of the formulas and equations will be referenced at the very end of the chapter with ample citations. In some sense, this book teaches you how to "cook" in the **R** language, but with all the examples and case studies motivated by real-world problems in the *retirement income* industry.

To be very clear, despite the cookbook nature this tome is not intended for consumers or do-it-yourself investors. Indeed, there are many (many) aspects of retirement income planning that I am not addressing—partially because there isn't much in the form of interesting recipes or savory cooking to them—but which are *very* important when it comes to making personal decisions. So, although this book has the word retirement in its title, you will not hear about gerontology, mental health during retirement, long-term care, nursing homes, legacy and estate planning, or how frequently to visit the grandchildren, etc. In particular, real-world estate planning problems can quickly escalate into complex beasts that depend on tax and legal jurisdictions. Alas, I can't hope to capture all the administrative details and country-specific nuances and want to avoid turning this book into a collection of retirement rules and pension regulations. Rather, the tools introduced in this book can be leveraged to think broadly about retirement tradeoffs, strategies, and products. In sum, I hope to make *retirement income* engaging, interesting, and intellectually challenging *even* for readers who are decades away from that stage of their own life.

Since my intended audience is mostly practitioners and students (a.k.a., future practitioners) and not my fellow academics or scholars, I will use a more casual and informal voice throughout the book and within the various computational modules. I also apologize in advance for the occasional lame attempts at jokes and my sense of humor which might not appeal to everyone. Nevertheless, I do find that it helps lubricate material that can often get quite dry (especially for new students). Also, as far as the writing style is concerned, although I assume you are interested in all of this for your (future or current) clients, I will refrain from starting every second sentence with the tedious "assume that your client" wants this or that. Rather, I'll address you, the reader, who is likely interested in these matters for personal reasons as well. Think of it this way: We are having a conversation.

Now to the confessions. Academics who continue to publish books and articles for decades are often accused of writing the same thing over (and over) again. Sure, there might be a different twist or perspective to each new iteration, but the message is the same. As a practical matter, the current book fills a missing gap for my own teaching needs. But to be honest, there *is* a bit of overlap with prior work. *So, what is new here?* Well, this work sits somewhere between two other books I published in the first and second decade of the twenty-first century. Over ten years ago, I published a book called *The Calculus of Retirement Income: Financial Models for Pension Annuities and Life Insurance* (Cambridge 2006). As the title suggests, it's a rather technical book that reflected my research interests at the time. It obviously requires a bit of calculus and is missing a number of important topics. And, although I am gratified by the number of practitioners (and researchers) who use the book, it was also devoid of any computational tools. Also, that book is a bit dated, having emphasized concepts that aren't as relevant (e.g. tontine allocations) and ignored concepts (e.g. sequence-of-returns) that are central to the current dialogue in retirement income. That said, *this* book project started off a few years ago as a revised second edition to *that* book, but soon morphed into something very different.

At the other intellectual extreme is my book *The 7 Most Important Equations for Your Retirement: The Fascinating People and Ideas Behind Planning Your Retirement Income* (Wiley 2012), which is an attempt to give a very broad overview of the history and background of the field. Despite the weighty title, it really has no formal mathematics other than as pictures or graphics. It has been my bestselling book (again, I'm gratified) but it certainly isn't a textbook. I definitely can't really assign it as a university or college textbook (or I might lose my academic tenure!)

So, the current work—*Retirement Income Recipes in* **R**—sits between these two bookends. To be clear, there are a number of other books that have been written by academics and are aimed at a similar audience. Three related books (which I properly cite in the next chapter) are by William F. Sharpe, Wade D. Pfau, and Michael Zwecher. All of these were published in the last decade and focus on very similar topics and problems.

Again, to differentiate this work from most other works, the main objective here is to create a pedagogically coherent textbook so readers (students) develop and have access to *computational tools* that can easily be used to replicate all results. At the end, you should have the skills to answer these questions yourself—with your own numbers, assumptions, and beliefs—and not just refer to answers generated by someone else. In fact, even if you have no interest in learning a (new) computer programming language, the modules and chapters will contain quite a number of quotable numerical examples and cases (so you can pretend you did the coding yourself). Indeed, a number of well-known public figures have recently been advocating (very loudly) that everyone should learn how to code—earlier than later—and I think **R** is a great program in which to learn that skill.

Why **R**? The honest answer is that I have (only recently) learned how to use **R**, although I did work with its predecessor **S** in graduate school, during the 1990s. I am particularly enamored with its (1) data-manipulation abilities as well as its (2) graphic and plotting capabilities. And, like all new marriages, I want to display my newfound love to the world at large. On a serious note, I think you will see and appreciate as the book evolves the ease with which answers can be computed quickly and transparently. I will start slow and devote the first chapter/module to explain the basics of **R**. It's only halfway through the book that you will see the full power of the **R** language—when it comes to simulations and table manipulations—which again is open source and completely free. That said, I'll be the first to admit that in theory this book could have been written with Maple, Matlab, Mathematica, or even Excel. In fact, I have used them all. But, for the purposes of this work, the former high-powered packages would be overkill and the latter (Excel) would involve programming in Visual Basic (VB), leading to umpteen (incompatible) software versions and platforms. I should note that a strong competing alternative was to "cook" in Python, with many of the same benefits as **R**, which is very popular in the industry. Truth be told, it was a tough choice and perhaps the academic snob in me prevailed.

In fact, to be very clear, I'm *not* leveraging the full statistical power of **R** within the context of data visualization (ggplot) or multivariate analysis. I'm also *not* claiming my scripts are the most *efficient* way of computing the relevant numbers. I'm sure there are cleverer ways to shorten the code's verbiage. Rather, I created the scripts in a way that would be most pedagogically helpful and illuminating. They are all bite-size pieces that should be easy to understand and teach some coding along the way.

Finally, the readers who are old enough, and have some computer programming background, might remember a book that was published in the late 1980s called: *Numerical Recipes in C: The Art of Scientific Computing*, published by Cambridge University Press. It included a very large collection of code snippets which computed everything from numerical values for messy integrals to linear and non-linear optimization routines. These recipes or algorithms—or at least their spirit—made their way into many commercial segments of code and it was a bible of sorts for the computational (scientific) community. My plan is to develop similar code snippets and pieces, but to build an actual textbook around the code with a coherent pedagogical structure. The book will start with simple questions (calculations) and expand to more complicated problems as the chapter modules evolve. But no matter how complex the algorithm or the computation, I promise there will always be a *real live* problem in the background to motivate the topic and keep it focused. One of my guiding principles when writing was to place myself in the shoes of the reader (i.e. you) and continuously ask myself: "So why am I doing this exactly?" Anyway, I hope you enjoy *using* this book as much as I enjoyed *writing* it.

Toronto, ON, Canada
15 September 2020

Moshe Arye Milevsky

Acknowledgements

There are a number of distinct groups I would like to thank—and without whom this book would have been quite hard if not impossible to create. The first group consists of my fellow co-researchers and co-authors over the last decade, who helped me design, create, and think-thru the underlying *chemistry* involved in these retirement income recipes. They are my esteemed colleagues and friends: Narat Charupat, Jan Dhaene, Steven Haberman, Huaxiong Huang, David Promislow, Raimond Maurer, Kristen Moore, Steven Posner, Ermanno Pitacco, Chris Robinson, Thomas Salisbury, Mike Sherris, Virginia Young, and last but very much not least, the great Menahem Yaari. I fondly recall many hours debating, discussing, and (quite often) arguing about how to model various aspects of retirement income.

The second group of thanks goes to the research assistants, graduate students, and (even) undergraduates who subjected themselves to my advanced course on personal finance and/or helped stress-test many of these recipes. They are: Talon Becker, Alysa Bui, Julia Carrello, Batur Celik, Benjamin Gahtan, Navtej Gill, Faisal Habib, Vivian Huynh, Gaon Kim, Victor Le, Chamera Sivakumar, Ariel Sosnovsky, Pamela Zachcial, and especially Joe Bisk who did a very thorough technical review of the manuscript, as did Will Selden (who is definitely not a student.) This group also includes my dear daughter Natalie, who created a solutions manual for many of the problems at the end of the chapters, and (very patient) editor at Springer Nature, Laura Briskman. Laura Briskman, who quite remarkably replied to every one of my emails within 24 hours.

The third group are the hundreds and possibly thousands of real-world *retirement income* practitioners I have met over the years, who focused my attention on the relevant problems and issues. I can't name them, but the especially prominent (and very helpful) ones would include Alexandra Macqueen and Jason Pereira who have served as soundboard. Over the years, they asked (and challenged me to answer) great questions and inspired me to continue cooking up these recipes.

The final thanks goes (tongue in cheek) to COVID-19 which forced me (quite literally) to stay home during the early 2020, implicitly allowing me to complete the bulk of the work on this manuscript. And, while I am fully aware that COVID-19 caused much damage, destruction, and death around the world, I can truly say that without that *pause* in the rest of my life, this book would have never been completed.

Contents

About the Author

Moshe Arye Milevsky is a tenured professor of finance at the Schulich School of Business and a member of the Graduate Faculty in Mathematics and Statistics at York University in Toronto, Canada, where he teaches courses on wealth management, insurance, and retirement planning. He has written over sixty-five peer-reviewed articles and this is his 15th published book. His prior work: *King William's Tontine: Why the Retirement Annuity of the Future Should Resemble Its Past*, was awarded the Kulp-Wright Book Award from the *American Risk and Insurance Association.*

He is an Associate Editor of *Insurance: Mathematics and Economics*, as well as *The Journal of Pension Economics and Finance*. He is also a Fellow of the *Fields Institute for Research in Mathematical Sciences*, where he was previously a member of the board of directors and active in their scientific and commercial activities.

In addition to his scholarly work, he is a well-known industry consultant, keynote speaker, and fin-tech entrepreneur, with a number of U.S. patents. He was named by *Investment Advisor Magazine* as one of the 35 most influential people in the U.S. financial advisory business during the last 35 years and received a lifetime achievement award from the *Retirement Income Industry Association.* He recently joined forces with Guardian Capital Group (Canada) to help implement many of the ideas contained in this book.

Acronyms

ALDA	Advanced life deferred annuity
APV	Actuarial present value
ARIG	Annualized real investment growth
CLT	Cohort life table
COLA	Cost of living adjustment
CRRA	Constant relative risk aversion
DB	Defined benefit
DIA	Deferred income or life annuity
EPR	Effective periodic rate
EPV	Economic present value
FC	Financial capital
GBM	Geometric Brownian motion
GLWB	Guaranteed lifetime withdrawal benefit
GMIB	Guaranteed minimum income benefit
GPP	Gold-plated pension plan
HC	Human capital
HMD	Human Mortality Database
IDDR	Intelligent drawdown rate
ILA	Immediate life annuity
LRP	Lifetime ruin probability
MM	Moment matching
PC	Period certain (for annuities)
PV	Present value (for cash-flows)
QLAC	Qualified longevity annuity contract
RCLA	Ruin-contingent life annuity
RPI	Reference portfolio index
SoR	Sequence-of-returns
SPIA	Single premium income annuity
TLA	Temporary life annuity
VA	Variable annuity
WDT	Wealth depletion time

List of Figures

List of Tables

Chapter 1
Setting Expectations and Deviations

This brief chapter provides an overview and outline of the book, with a particular emphasis on the specific topics covered and the recipes described within each individual chapter.

1.1 The Big Idea in the Book

At the risk of getting far ahead of myself on the very first page, I'll start by introducing the critically important random variable: T_x, which will make many appearances throughout this book. It denotes the *stochastic* (that is, random, unknown) number of years you will live assuming you are currently x-years-old, chronologically. I use the word *chronologically* deliberately, because x only indicates the number of times you have circled the sun, really. It says nothing about your health, your frame of mind, or whether you live in a city ravaged by a mysterious virus. In fact, you might be a very healthy x-year-old female, or perhaps an unhealthy x-year-old male, all of which make a big difference to your longevity prospects. So, while x might be the one *explicit* parameter accompanying T_x, there are many other *implicit* parameters that will impact your remaining lifetime, most of which I'll get back to later on. For now, let's focus attention on T_x.

The variable T_{65} would represent the (stochastic) remaining number of years a typical $x = 65$-year-old will live, and $(65 + T_{65})$ represents the (stochastic) age at which this 65-year-old will die. Now, the realized value of the random variable T_{65} could be as high as 35 years, since he or she might live to age 100. Or, the realized value of T_{65} could in theory be very close to zero, as it's possible that he or she might die in the next instant of time. Technically, the random variable T_x is defined over the range: $(0, \omega - T_x]$, where the Greek letter ω is the maximum age to which a person can live. Currently, ω is thought to be around 120, give or take a few years. For the record, the world's oldest person in modern history was the French woman

M. A. Milevsky, *Retirement Income Recipes in R*, Use R!,
https://doi.org/10.1007/978-3-030-51434-1_1

Jeanne Louise Calment, who died at the age of 122 years plus 164 days (in August of 1997).

Although, I should note that some doubts have been cast on her age claims, and I refer interested readers to the article cited as [1] for more information on J.L. Calment and her record-breaking ω. The important point to emphasize here is that T_x is a continuous non-negative random variable, which allows for many possible candidates for the *probabilistic structure* of T_x. Either way, the *expected* remaining number of years this 65-year-old will live is denoted by $E[T_{65}]$ and the standard deviation is denoted by $SD[T_{65}]$. Now, once a candidate has been selected for the underlying *probabilistic structure*, one can write down an expression for the *probability density function* (pdf), the *cumulative distribution function* (cdf), and the survival probability $\Pr[T_x \geq t]$, all as functions of the above-noted explicit and implicit parameters. I'll get to all of that in due time. In sum, this is **Human Longevity**, and one critical side of the retirement income "equation."

Now let's move on to a completely different random variable. Think of someone at or near the (chronological) age of 60, 65, or 70, who has accumulated financial capital (a sum of money) and intends to spend that money during their retirement, a.k.a. their golden years. Now, if they are not careful and spend too much money too quickly their money won't last very long. On the other hand, if they are too cautious and don't spend very much (or anything) the money will last for a very long time. Of course, they might not be alive to enjoy the nest egg if their T_x value comes up short. So, let the new random variable L_ξ denote the longevity of the portfolio, or the length of time their capital will survive, assuming this person is spending ξ of their *initial* nest egg each year. Now, like the random variable T_x, its realized value will depend on a variety of implicit parameters, first and foremost the rate of return on the portfolio relative to ξ. I'll get to all of that later, but for now I'll retain the spending rate ξ as the (only) explicit parameter to mirror the notation and set-up for the remaining lifetime T_x random variable. Now, the realized value of L_ξ could be 10, 50, or even 100 years. It really depends on how much this (retiree) is spending, ξ, as well as how exactly it's invested. In fact, technically speaking, the realized value of L_ξ could be infinite. After all, if you don't spend very much—and portfolio returns are consistently positive—the money could last forever. That, in sum, is **Portfolio Longevity**, and the other side of the retirement income "equation."

With this pair of random variables (T_x, L_ξ) introduced, the main practical objective of this book is to develop *recipes* that help retirees—or more likely their financial advisors—ensure that $L_\xi \geq T_x$. Money should last as long as you do. So, for example, if a realization of $L_{0.04}$ was 23 years, but the realization of T_{65} was 32, you outlived your money, which obviously isn't a very good outcome. Remember, the realizations of both L_ξ and T_x are unknown in advance. And, while L_ξ might be under your control (to some extent), your remaining lifetime T_x is harder (although not impossible) to control. Nevertheless, they are both *random* variables which means that technically speaking the mathematical statement: $L_\xi \geq T_x$ doesn't make much sense. Rather, one can compute the expected value: $E[L_\xi - T_x]$, or perhaps the probability $\Pr[L_\xi - T_x]$, or some other function of $f(L_\xi)$ and $g(T_x)$, and compare them.

Now, lest I place too much emphasis on the rigid and fixed L_ξ as the only metric that matters, I'll admit there are many (many) questions this sort of framework raises. First and foremost, it's silent on how to account for the innate human desire to leave bequests or an inheritance for the next generation. Second, it provides little guidance on how to select a proper ξ and perhaps modify those withdrawals as time goes on. Indeed, I'll get to all these details eventually and offer alternative ways of summarizing whether a particular strategy is sustainable in retirement. Nevertheless, all chapters of this book chip away at various computational and mathematical aspects of both L_ξ and T_x. Those two variables are the critical intellectual threads that link all 15 chapters in this book.

1.2 Outline of the Book

In the next Chap. 2, I begin the formal journey by providing a very brief set of instructions on how to download and install the **R** programming language, the **R**-studio front-end as well as how to create and plot the output of basic functions. Chapter 2 is the first of three Chaps. 2, 3 and 4 that are primarily focused on getting-to-know the software. I should warn (the advanced **R** user) that most of the material and functions discussed are (extremely) rudimentary. So those readers who want a proper and more-detailed introduction to **R**, I would suggest the books cited as [5] and [2], the latter one being especially helpful for readers who are interested in a crash-course on basic probability and statistics.

With some basic **R** functionality under our belt, Chap. 3 dives right into the *economic* foundation of retirement income planning, which is the so-called *life-cycle model of consumption and saving*. I emphasize the word economic because that is how an academic financial economist thinks about retirement planning, via the process of consumption. This chapter leverages very basic functions in **R** to compute and plot the optimal spending (decumulation, drawdown) rate as a function of some key financial variables. This (toy) model helps set the tone for how to think about retirement income planning in a rational and smooth manner. It also provides the conceptual foundation for how to model the above-mentioned, L_ξ random variable, which implicitly assumes a given spending plan or drawdown rate.

The subsequent Chap. 4 provides some further instructions and details on working with **R**, which is the second of two chapters on the basics of the programming language. In particular, it explains how to import and manipulate statistical data by drawing on (hypothetical) numbers for a comprehensive personal balance sheet based on the life-cycle model that was introduced in Chap. 3.

Chapter 5 gets to the core of the L_ξ random variable by formally and properly defining portfolio longevity. This chapter also explains how to simulate forward-looking investment returns (a.k.a. Monte Carlo simulations) in **R**. It demonstrates how portfolio longevity relates to the infamous 4% rule of retirement income planning. Continuing along the L_ξ theme, Chap. 6 illustrates how portfolio longevity is influenced by (and correlated with) the so-called *sequence of returns* effect, which is a phenomenon that is much discussed among financial practitioners. This particular chapter leverages the statistical power of **R** and regression methodology to quantify the impact of various investment sub-periods on portfolio longevity.

Chapter 7 moves on from portfolio longevity L_ξ to human longevity T_x, by starting with discrete time increments. This chapter introduces and explains the detailed structure of cohort life tables around the world, which are freely available from the Human Mortality Database (HMD.) These *cohort* life tables are fundamental building blocks in actuarial science and demographics but they might not be as familiar to researchers and modelers in finance and economics who often work (only) with *period* tables. I'll obviously explain the difference between the two. Continuing with the focus on T_x, the subsequent Chap. 8 moves from discrete time mortality tables to continuous time, and focuses attention on some well-known laws of mortality. Specifically the chapter dwells on the (famous) Benjamin Gompertz law of mortality introduced almost 200 years ago (to the date), a model that (still) fits the data quite nicely, even in the 21st century. The chapter computes moments (via the cdf, pdf) of T_x and explains how to calibrate distributions and compute various statistical quantities of interest, all in **R**, of course. The two Chaps. 7 and 8 are the core material on modeling longevity and are slightly longer than the other chapters, but (in my opinion) are one of the key differentiators of this book relative to other books on *retirement income* planning, authored by research oriented practitioners and academics such as [3, 4] or [6].

With both L_ξ and T_x introduced and well-understood, Chap. 9 merges the concepts of human longevity together with portfolio longevity to compute the so-called *lifetime ruin probability* (LRP). This number is a forward-looking estimate of the chances (or risk) you will outlive your money, that is, experience a portfolio longevity that is shorter than your human longevity. Formally, it is defined using the Greek letter varphi: $\varphi = \Pr[T_x \geq L_\xi]$. This chapter offers a variety of analytic and simulation-based algorithms to compute this probability. Note that the opposite of the LRP is $1 - \varphi = \Pr[T_x < L_\xi]$, which is the probability of dying with leftovers (a.k.a. retirement success, not outliving your money). And, while I stop short of arguing that φ should be minimized in any control-theoretic sense, or that LRP is even a good risk metric, the fact is that the φ number is extremely popular in the financial industry. Every retirement income software calculator offers a rudimentary estimate of the φ number. Given its centrality and importance to practitioners (although derided by academics), the entire Chap. 9 is focused on φ and its pitfalls.

Chapter 10 moves from modeling life and death to financial products that can actually insure against outliving wealth. It starts by discussing how to value (versus price) longevity-contingent claims in a simple one-period discrete time framework. By longevity-contingent claim I simply mean a financial product that pays the owner or policy holder more, the longer they live. Think of a defined benefit pension annuity, for example, in which the longer you live, the more income you receive. If you think about these products from a longevity perspective, the random payout from any longevity-contingent claim is positively correlated with your own human longevity T_x. Therefore, if you add such a product or investment to your investment portfolio you could (in theory) extend the longevity of your own portfolio L_ξ, at least under suitably defined conditions. This chapter also gives me the opportunity to carefully introduce and explain the idea of *mortality credits* and how they can enhance portfolio investment returns. This chapter slowly transitions from (easy) discrete time to (calculus based) continuous time, and offers a variety of useful **R**-based pricing formulas for many types of life annuities. These are relatively simple life annuities (often called academic annuities) that don't offer any market-contingent or investment-contingent features. (I'll get to those later in the book, in Chap. 14) In some sense this chapter is a core component of *Retirement Income Recipes in R*, because it combines the T_x and L_ξ variables into one financial product. The algorithms, functions, and codes introduced in Chap. 10 are used (over and over) again in the subsequent chapters.

Moving on from comparing T_x to L_ξ, or valuing life annuities, Chap. 11 gets to another key idea of the book, which is the concept of *intelligent drawdown* rates. It takes an economic approach on how to determine a proper value of the withdrawal rate ξ. Up to this point in the book (and for the first ten chapters) I assume that withdrawal rates are *exogenous*. In this chapter I *endogenize* the spending rate using a utility-based approach, all of which will be carefully explained. Chapter 12 continues with the same philosophy of *intelligent drawdowns* and focuses attention on longevity risk pooling, the benefits of longevity-insured pensions, and the optimality of a *pensionized* balance sheet. In some sense, Chaps. 11 and 12 are the (most) practical chapters in the book, because they delineate an actual *retirement income* strategy, as opposed to valuing life contingent cash-flows or computing assorted risk metrics.

Finally, as I wind down the book, Chap. 13 returns to the x inside T_x. This chapter digs deep into what economists and demographers label: *mortality heterogeneity*, which is basically the idea that people with the same age might have very different life expectancies. I do this by introducing the concept of *biological age*, *risk-adjusted ages* and how they differ from *chronological age.* The chapter documents the extent of *mortality heterogeneity* and its importance to retirement income planning. This chapter discusses the dispersion of true ages around the world. Within the context of *mortality heterogeneity* this chapter also introduces the so-called compensation laws of mortality and their relationship to the aging process, some of which might be a bit advanced for first-time readers. Along the same lines, Chap. 14 introduces, describes, and values more exotic annuities, such as those embedded inside variable annuities. The two final technical Chaps. 13, 14 are then followed by a very brief concluding Chap. 15, which is a wish list of more advanced topics that could (in theory) be part of a book sequel.

1.3 How to Teach with the Book

This is how I would suggest using the book in a classroom setting, and how I have actually used the material in my own teaching—for a 4th year undergraduate (elective, finance) business course. I begin the semester with a brief (first) lecture where I motivate *retirement income* planning as a distinct and separate branch of wealth management. I pose a bunch of (quantitative) *retirement income* problems that naturally lead to mathematical and statistical thinking. I take the opportunity to carefully explain *why* I have decided to use **R** as opposed to Excel or some other software package. I wrap up the first lecture by instructing students to spend the next 2 weeks reading Chaps. 2, 3, and 4 on their own, and after installing **R** I ask them to solve a subset of problems at the end of these three chapters to ensure they can work with **R** and know what's coming down the line. Think of this as a first home assignment, and a first cut. Don't be surprised if—after taking the time to download and install **R**—some students decide that this isn't their cup of tea (and wont be an easy A).

The next meeting (for the survivors!) takes place after everyone is fully functional in **R**, perhaps after having been helped by a TA. I focus on *portfolio longevity* L_ξ, which covers 2 weeks of class using the material in Chaps. 5 and 6. This is supplemented with outside reading material on sustainable withdrawal rates, most of which are referenced in the two chapters. I consider this to be the first formal module of the course. The next (second) module is on *human longevity* T_x, which uses another 2 weeks, covered in Chaps. 7, and 8. This brings us to week number 5 or 6 in the term, where I am first able to merge the concepts of human longevity with portfolio longevity and assign a full-blown Monte Carlo simulation of success and failure rates in Chap. 9. This is the third conceptual module and we are now at the half-way point of the semester. I then move on to the fourth module on valuing life annuities in Chap. 10, which often takes a week or two to absorb, especially for students with no actuarial background. The next fifth module is on *intelligent drawdown rates* and the concept of *pensionization*, covered in Chaps. 11 and 12. This can take 2–3 weeks to explain and discuss since it requires some (rational) utility theory, which can be supplemented with outside reading on life-cycle economics. The sixth module is focused on mortality heterogeneity, in Chap. 13, which gets into the topic of *biological ages*. To complete the teaching component, the seventh module takes me another 2–3 weeks to cover. It starts off with exotic *FinSurance* products, including tontines and other non-guaranteed pooling schemes. I begin with Chap. 14, but then use material in Chap. 15 for further reading. Finally, after all the material has been covered, students are assigned a group project (which is a substantial portion of their grade) in which they use **R** to value a particular *retirement income* product, or analyze a strategy, such as tax efficient withdrawal schemes, or staggered annuitization plans, etc. There is no final exam for the class—or for the reader of this book either!

References

1. Collins, L. (2020, February 10th). Was Jeanne Calment the oldest person who ever lived? or a Fraud? *The New Yorker Magazine*.
2. Crawley, M. J. (2015). *STATISTICS: An introduction using R*. Wiley: Hoboken.
3. Pfau, W. (2019). *Safety-first retirement planning: An integrated approach for a worry-free retirement*. Retirement Researcher Media, Amazon.
4. Sharpe, W. F. (2017). *Retirement income scenario matrices*. Available at: https://web.stanford.edu/~wfsharpe/RISMAT/
5. Zuur, A. F., Ieno, E. N. & Meesters, E. H. W. G. (2009). *A beginner's guide to R*. New York: Springer Nature.
6. Zwecher, M. J. (2010). *Retirement portfolios: Theory, construction, and management*. Wiley: Hoboken.

Chapter 2
Loading and Getting to Know R

The objective of this chapter is to carefully explain how to download and install **R** together with **R**-studio, which is the front-end I'll be using. This chapter will teach you how to run and compile basic calculations, create some basic functions, and plot some basic figures. If you are already familiar with and/or have worked with **R**-studio, then you can skip ahead to the next chapter.

2.1 Functions Used and Defined

As in all chapters, this particular chapter uses a number of (simple, native) **R**-based commands or functions that are built into **R** and custom-made (user-defined) functions. Here is a list of the functions used in this chapter.

2.1.1 Sample of Native R Functions Used

- `c(.)` and `rbind(.)`, used to combine or bind data.
- `plot(.)`, used to generate very simple plots.
- `points(.)`, used within plots to place data.
- `exp(.)`, exponential function.

2.1.2 User-Defined R Functions

- `RGOA(g,v,N)`. This is an abbreviation for Regular Growth Ordinary Annuity, which is a type of present value factor that discounts growing cash-flows.

M. A. Milevsky, *Retirement Income Recipes in R*, Use R!,
https://doi.org/10.1007/978-3-030-51434-1_2

2.2 Where and How to Download R-Studio

Most of the hands-on numerical work in this book will be conducted and displayed in the **R-Studio** programming environment, which is open source and free. Technically, to get this software on your computer, you must first download and install the core **R** program and then add on **R-Studio**. You can either google **R** and **R-studio** or download them from the following locations:

```
https://cran.r-project.org/
https://rstudio.com/products/rstudio/download/
```

Figure 2.1 is a screenshot of the (first) website where you can download **R.** The developers of **R** are constantly improving and updating the software and website, so this particular screenshot might not be exactly what you will see. Also, in addition to downloading the most recent version of **R**, make sure to download the proper version for your operating system, which might be *Linux*, *Mac*, or *Windows*. Note that all of the code, functions and work displayed in this book were created within a *Mac* Operating System, and in particular the screenshots are from a *Mac*. This means that if you are using *Linux* or *Windows*, the look and feel might be just a bit different, especially when it comes to saving files and working with outside data.

Once you have **R** installed, the next step is to install the free version of **R-Studio** Desktop, which some people abbreviate as RStudio, or simply the open source studio version of **R**. And, as with **R** itself, make sure to download the (free and) most recent version of the package appropriate for your operating system. But, you certainly do *not* have to install the commercial (expensive) version to use any of the codes, algorithms, or recipes developed in this book. You can download R-Studio here: https://rstudio.com/products/rstudio/download/.

Now, once you have properly downloaded, installed, and finally launched **R-Studio**, you should see (something similar to) Fig. 2.2, which is a screenshot from my personal computer where all the work for this textbook was written. Note once again (and for the last time) that it's based on a *Mac* operating system, which means

Source accessed 1/Dec/2019: https://cran.r-project.org/

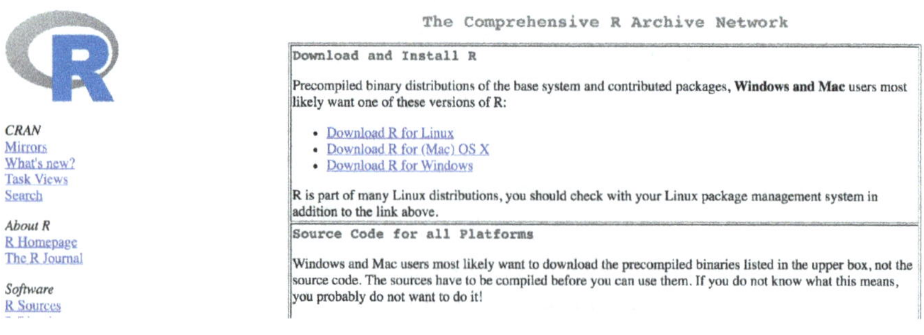

Fig. 2.1 The CRAN website where you can download R (Public screenshot. The R logo is ©2016 The R foundation. (https://www.r-project.org/logo/))

Source: Author's screenshot of R-studio user interface.

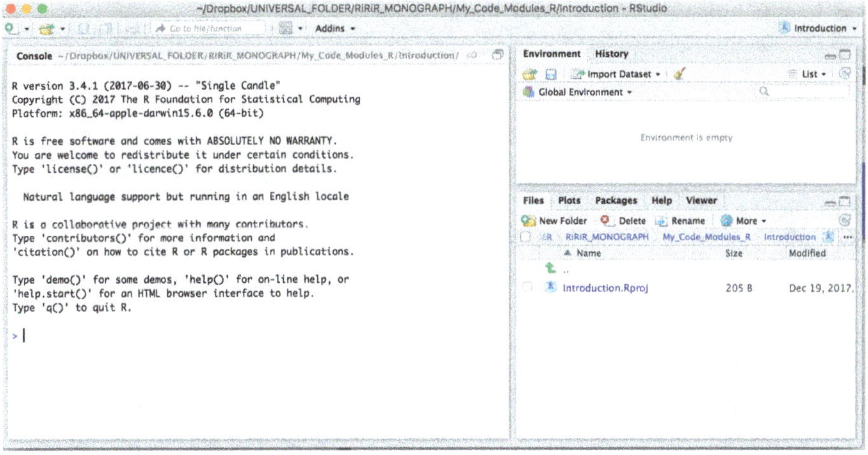

Fig. 2.2 The (very) basic R-Studio user interface

that your *Windows* or *Linux* set-up might look just a bit different, especially when it comes to the exact placement (and naming) of file directories. Also, if-and-when you update the software for **R** as well as **R-Studio** the version number listed on the very top-left corner of the screen will change as well. So, as long as you are seeing *something* similar to (my own) Fig. 2.2, then you should be okay and ready to go.

Notice that there are three boxes or regions on your screen, which should all be rather plain and empty when you first get started in **R**. But they will fill up quickly. The left-hand side contains the console where you will be doing (most of) your typing. The upper right-hand box (environment) is where (among other items) your user-defined functions will be stored, and the lower right-hand box is where you will see any generated plots and figures. There are many other items and objects that appear in the right-hand boxes, but at this (very) early stage I wouldn't worry or concern myself with them. Overall, this book will take a need-to-know approach to commands, functions, and operations in **R**.

2.3 Using and Playing with R

Start by typing the following text in the command line. To be clear, enter one line at a time and hit enter between each line. Each time you hit the enter button, another line should come up with a (greater than) > on the left-most side. So, you don't actually type the > sign, it shows up automatically. Basically, we are commanding **R** to assign the number 10 to the variable y, the number 20 to the variable x and then (eventually, will be) asking **R** to add them together by typing $(x + y)$. Note also that **R** is case-sensitive, so `x` isn't `X`. This is all rather basic, but the way to make those variable assignments is by using the combined <- symbol, rather than the more familiar and defining = symbol.

```
> y <- 10
> x <- 20
```

A bit of software history might help here. The **R** language originated from an older **S** language, and when that was first developed, the symbol <- was really the only way to make an assignment. This quirk is a remnant from an (even) older computer language called **APL**, and (very) old computer terminals that had a dedicated <- button. More recently the **R** developers have added the ability to use the (more familiar) equal sign to define and create variables, but it can get a bit confusing when it comes to calling and using functions. This is why I prefer to use the (older) approach and notation. Yes, it takes a bit of getting used to, but it will become second nature after a few iterations. Either way, let's get back to the basic addition, subtraction, multiplication, and division of $x = 20$ and $y = 10$. The output you will see in the command line should look like the following.

```
> y <- 10
> x <- 20
> x+y; x-y; x*y; x/y
[1] 30
[1] 10
[1] 200
[1] 2
```

I used the semicolon to separate the operations, but could just as easily have typed each one on a separate line and you might try the same. Take some time, let loose and play around with different values and different arithmetic operations. For example, you can define the variables x and y to be a sequence of numbers, not just a single number, by typing `x <- 1:10` and then `y <- 21:30`. This time around when you add the two together, **R** will actually add the two sequences and report the sum of the vectors. See the following for example:

```
> x <- 1:10
> y <- 21:30
> x+y
 [1] 22 24 26 28 30 32 34 36 38 40
```

And, since both x and y are vectors that are now stored in **R** with the above-noted elements, I don't have to type them in (or define them) every time I want to use them. For example, I can multiply them together element by element, or combine them with `c(x,y)` command. Also, try `rbind(x,y)` and see the difference.

```
> x*y
[1]  21  44  69  96 125 156 189 224 261 300
> c(x,y)
[1]  1 2 3 4 5 6 7 8 9 10 21 22 23 24 25 26 27 28 29 30
```

I would encourage you to experiment with these basic operations on scalars and vectors. Note that as long as the length of the vectors x and y are the same, you should be able to add, subtract, multiply, and divide them without any problems. But be forewarned that if one vector is longer or shorter than the other, **R** will reluctantly co-operate (with a mind of its own) as well as display an error message.

```
> x <- 1:10
> y <- 20:30
> x+y
 [1] 21 23 25 27 29 31 33 35 37 39 31
Warning message:
In x + y : longer object length is not
a multiple of shorter object length
```

Look closely and you will see that there is some clever internal logic to what **R** is doing here. First, it displays an error message because the y vector is longer than the x vector by one additional element. Nevertheless, **R** actually (tries to follow your request and) adds the individual elements despite the clear mismatch. But, at the very end, there is no corresponding 11th element in x that can be added to the final $y = 30$ value. So, **R** then cycles back and picks the first $x = 1$ value, which it then adds to the $y = 30$ value and adds the augmented number 31 to the summed-up vector. This results in an output of (yes) 11 items, even though the x vector only had 10 elements.

My point here is to illustrate a number of things about **R**. First of all, it tries very hard to do what it's told, even if you (the user) aren't being very precise. After all, you really shouldn't be adding two vectors of different lengths. But, at the same time, it makes the (rather arbitrary) determination that the final element in the combined vector should be created by using the first element. This is why **R** warned you about the mismatch, but still produced some reasonable output. The key takeaway is to keep this in mind as you continue to use **R** with ever-growing levels of complexity. Keep a close eye on those error warning messages!

2.4 Command-Line vs. Stand-Alone Scripts

Generally speaking there are two distinct ways in which to interact with and/or input items into **R**. First, you can type them into the command line, which is what I actually did over the last few pages, and then hit the enter button to compile or run your command. In fact, when you are in the command line (mode), you can use the

Source: Author's screenshot of R-studio user interface

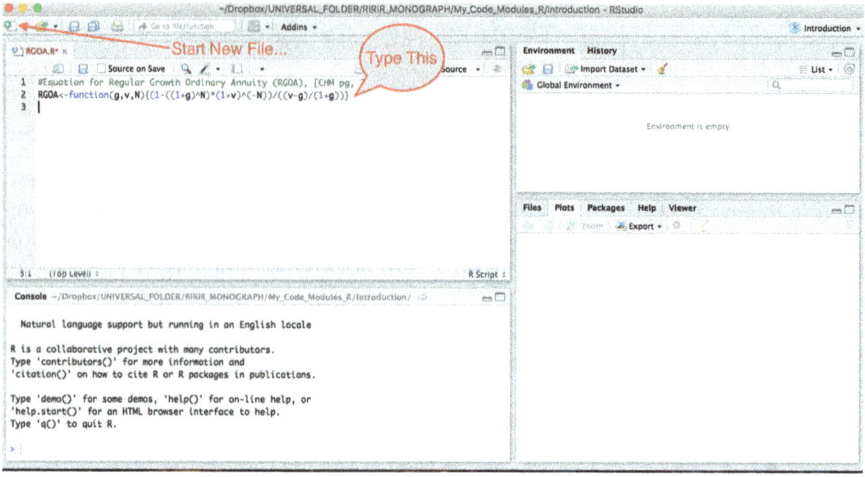

Fig. 2.3 Where to create scripts and code in R-Studio

top (and bottom) arrow button on your keyboard to recall or reuse material that was previously entered. This can save time when you want to make a small modification to a previous command or (more likely to) fix an inadvertent error.

But for longer commands, operations, and calculations this command-line process can get quite tedious. So, another way to (type and) compile is by creating and saving (longer) multi-line scripts. This will be very useful and important when I create the first user-defined function in the next section. Figure 2.3 shows where (and how) to create and run these scripts in the **R-studio** environment. Notice the new (extra) box in the upper left-hand corner. You start with a blank (empty) page or file, then type in the material or commands you want to run, highlight them, and actually click on the run button to compile. You can save the file for future use, or modify and create several versions of the script and save them separately. Like everything else in **R**, this will (only) become clear once you play around with this feature, but I'll provide an example of how this works by introducing our first user-defined function in the book.

2.5 The Present Value (PV) of an Annuity

As I noted in the first introductory chapter, this book isn't the place to learn about basic financial concepts such as the time value of money, or how to compute present and future values. Rather, at this stage I will take for granted that you understand the very specific and important meaning of *present* versus *future* values. I will simply write down the expression for the present value factor (i.e. per dollar) of a growing (ordinary) annuity, which is expressed mathematically as:

$$\text{RGOA} := \sum_{i=1}^{N} \left(\frac{1+g}{1+v} \right)^i = \frac{1 - (1+g)^N (1+v)^{-N}}{(v-g)/(1+g)}, \quad v \neq g. \tag{2.1}$$

This formula is the basis for 95% (ok, perhaps only 90%) of modern finance theory and is "proven" in any basic textbook, for example, my own [2], or the (comprehensive) textbook on the mathematics of finance [1]. In particular, book [1] is an excellent resource for students who are new to the mathematics of the time value of money (TVM), ordinary annuities versus annuities due, valuing perpetuities, etc. Either way, the important point here is that the sum of the N terms on the left-hand side of Eq. (2.1) is equal to the closed-form analytic representation on the right-hand side. Note that in this formula, the variable v represents an arbitrary valuation rate (e.g. 3%), used for discounting cash-flows and the variable g represents an arbitrary growth rate (e.g. 2%), used for increasing cash-flows. It's easy to get the (order of the) two of them confused if you are new to the field of finance. Also, carefully note that the right-hand side of Eq. (2.1) assumes that $v \neq g$, that is, the growth rate is not equal to the valuation rate. If in fact $v = g$, then the denominator and numerator are equal to zero and the expression is indeterminate. This (obviously) doesn't mean that the present values don't exist when $v = g$. Rather, in that case the left-hand side can be easily identified as a sum of ones, or simply N. Technically, the expression in Eq. (2.1) converges to N as $v \to g$. I'll leave that particular factoid as an assignment question at the end of the chapter and will provide numerical examples for other values of $v \neq g$, once I create the first script and user-defined function in **R**.

But, before we get to the first recipe, let me be very clear in terms of the definition of the growth rate g. If you are receiving cash-flows of \$1 per year at the end of the year (a.k.a. ordinary annuity), and those cash-flows are growing at 4% per year, then I assume the growth begins immediately. The first cash-flow you are receiving and discounting is assumed to be: \$1.04 (and not \$1). Some readers (and many students) often find this confusing, and believe that the first cash-flow (at the end of the first period) is only \$1, and that growth only begins at the end of period two. Please compare the following:

$$\texttt{How I Define Growth} \rightarrow \frac{1.04}{(1.05)} + \frac{(1.04)^2}{(1.05)^2} + \frac{(1.04)^3}{(1.05)^3} + \ldots + \frac{(1.04)^k}{(1.05)^{(k)}}$$

$$\textbf{Not } \texttt{How I Define Growth} \rightarrow \frac{1}{(1.05)} + \frac{1.04}{(1.05)^2} + \frac{(1.04)^2}{(1.05)^3} + \ldots + \frac{(1.04)^{k-1}}{(1.05)^{(k)}}$$

Now sure, you can assume any cash-flow you like (when you write your own text book) but as far as the definition (in this book) is concerned, the growth begins immediately and the powers of (k) are matched. This is why I emphasize the word *regular* growth in the notation and definition. And, on the off-chance you specifically want to model cash-flows that start growing at the end of the second period (i.e. the above set-up), well that (to me) is a *delayed* growth ordinary annuity

(DGOA). Mathematically it is simply: RGOA$/(1+g)$, to unwind the extra growth. There is no correct way to define it, or truth of the matter, but simply the convention I adopt in this book, which consistent with is continuous time (which I'll get to.)

Back to my numerical example, if you add up 50 of these (discounted) regular growth cash-flows, and use $N = 50$ in the formula in Eq. (2.1), the present value of the annuity at a $v = 4\%$ valuation rate is RGOA $= 25.87551$, and at a $v = 7\%$ valuation rate it is RGOA $= 15.8935$. Indeed, you will be able to confirm these numbers in **R** in just a minute. Finally, before we get to user-defined functions, note that when the cash-flow growth rate $g = 0$, then RGOA collapses to the much simpler and perhaps more familiar expression:

$$\sum_{i=1}^{N}\left(\frac{1}{1+v}\right)^{i} = \frac{1-(1+v)^{-N}}{v}, \tag{2.2}$$

which is readily available and used in any financial or business calculator.

2.6 Creating Your First Function in R

Given the centrality and importance of the formulas displayed in Eqs. (2.1) and (2.2), they will be the first expressions coded up in **R**. To do this easily and properly, create a new blank script (in the upper left-hand corner), as shown in the screenshot of Fig. 2.4. It displays how and where to run the script that defines the RGOA function. To be specific, enter this precise text as a new script:

```
RGOA <- function(g,v,N){
(1-((1+g)^N)*(1+v)^(-N))/((v-g)/(1+g))
}
```

There are a few important things to note and remember about the syntax of functions, all of which will come in (very) handy in the next few chapters. First, on the left-hand side you start by defining the name of the function, which in this case is RGOA. You then inform **R** the number and name of the arguments in the function, which in this case is `g,v,N`. Then, you must open up a curly left bracket and write down the mathematical formula itself. Be careful with all the parenthesis and brackets, and then end your function with another right curly bracket. This is the universal structure of user-defined functions in **R**. Now, it would be more accurate (and clean) to define this function with a formal `if` statement that conditions on whether $v \neq g$, otherwise you might (by mistake) use the function when $v = g$. In future chapters I will define and build these sorts of conditional functions. If you are an advanced user (who has coded before), then go ahead and include the `IF` statement in RGOA. I'll return to this later, but for now when $v = g$, the answer is N.

Source: Author's screenshot of R-Studio user interface

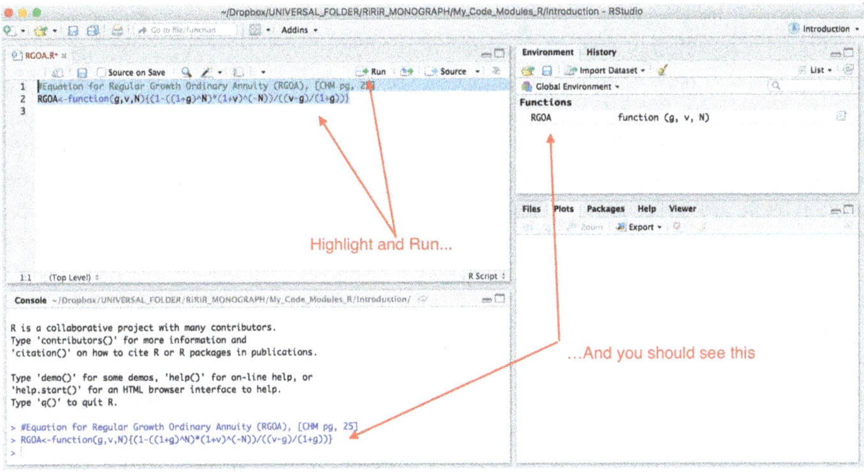

Fig. 2.4 Where to find and locate user-defined functions in R-Studio

Either way, after writing the script, you should compile and store (or save) the function so that it both appears as a new function in your **R** workspace and it's saved for possible future use. By this point your workspace should look very similar to Fig. 2.4. Once this function has been defined and created within **R**, you can use the function over and over again with different values, or with multiple values at the same time. Here are some examples which you should try yourself, at the very least to confirm that the book's first (and most important) function RGOA is doing exactly what it should. If your numbers are different from what you see here, then carefully check your brackets to make sure you didn't miss anything and then compile or run the RGOA function again.

```
> RGOA(0.02,0.05,30)
[1] 19.75032
> RGOA(0,0.05,30)
[1] 15.37245
> RGOA(0,c(0.01,0.02,0.03,0.04,0.05),30)
[1] 25.80771 22.39646 19.60044 17.29203 15.37245
> RGOA(0,0.05,1:30)
 [1]  0.95238  1.85941  2.72324  3.54595  4.32947  5.07569
 [7]  5.78637  6.46321  7.107822 7.72173  8.30641  8.86325
[13]  9.39357  9.89864 10.37965 10.83777 11.27406 11.68958
[19] 12.08532 12.46221 12.82115 13.16300 13.48857 13.79864
[25] 14.09394 14.37518 14.64303 14.89812 15.14107 15.37245
```

The present value of an annuity of $N = 30$ cash-flows of \$1, which are growing at 2% and discounted at 5%, is exactly \$19.75032 according to the RGOA formula.

But when the growth rate is $g = 0$, the present value is a (much) lower \$15.37245, which hopefully should be intuitive.

Notice a few things about the output displayed above. First, you can invoke or call the `RGOA` function with arguments that are vectors, not only scalars. This allows you to obtain present values for a whole range of parameters. For example, using the sequence `c(0.01,0.02,0.03,0.04,0.05)` instead of one single number in the formula will result in a collection of present values under a range of valuation rates v from 1 to 5%. I can also apply the same idea (multiple input values) with the third and final argument N, in the `RGOA` function.

There are a number of other examples presented with a variety of input values for the growth rate g, namely `c(0,0.02,0.04,0.06)` instead of one single number. The valuation rate is assumed to be $v = 5\%$ and the number of periods (years) is $N = 35$. Finally, in the next box, I ask **R** to multiply the present value factor `RGOA`, by the number \$50,000. Financially, this represents the present value of your salary (a.k.a. your human capital) assuming you currently earn \$50K per year, plan to work for another 35 years, and assuming you discount all cash-flows at 5%. Of course, this ignores income taxes, financial and mortality risk, as well as many other frictions. Nevertheless, under these parameters, the PV of your \$50,000 salary, assuming a 5% valuation rate, and growth rates of $g = 0\%, 2\%, 4\%, 6\%$ over a period of $N = 35$ years results in:

```
> RGOA(c(0.0,0.02,0.04,0.06),0.05,35)*50000
[1]   818709.7 1083647.1 1479984.5 2085088.2
```

The interpretation is that your human capital (HC) is worth between \$818,700 and \$2,085,000 depending on the growth rate assumed for your salary which is currently \$50,000. So, growth projections (for anything) really do matter. I'll return to the concept of human capital within the context of the life-cycle model, in the next chapter. My only point here is to show you how to use and combine the `RGOA` function with other operations.

2.7 A First Look at Sustainable Withdrawal Rates

This textbook is really all about retirement income and the later stage of the life-cycle, so this is as good a place as any to delve into the topic. And, despite the fact I haven't yet introduced any functions directly related to the two central longevity variables: L_x and T_x, mentioned in the prior chapter, I can utilize the `RGOA` function to take an initial stab at computing sustainable spending rates.

Assume for the moment that you retire at some unspecified age with exactly (and only) \$100 saved in your retirement account. This money is invested in a risk-free (i.e. safe, non-volatile, predictable) account earning exactly v. In other words, the funds would continue to grow at v per period (remember, this is an investment rate of return) if you didn't withdraw any money from the account. But of course, you (are retired and) plan on extracting or spending a fixed constant amount every year until the funds are exhausted. The question I would like to address here is: *How much can you afford to withdraw every year, if you would like to deplete your nest egg in exactly N years?* The answer to that question can be very easily computed in **R**, using the RGOA function, assuming (and that is a big assumption) that you know v with certainty forever. Technically, the present value of the unknown retirement income annuity should be equal to \$100. In **R** this can now be solved with one line, assuming four different values for v, as follows:

```
> 100/RGOA(0,c(0.01,0.02,0.03,0.04),10)
[1] 10.55821 11.13265 11.72305 12.32909
> 100/RGOA(0,c(0.01,0.02,0.03,0.04),25)
[1] 4.540675 5.122044 5.742787 6.401196
> 100/RGOA(0,c(0.01,0.02,0.03,0.04),35)
[1] 3.400368 4.000221 4.653929 5.357732
```

For example, examine the very last line in the text box. The interpretation is as follows. If you invest the \$100 into a savings account earning: $v = 2\%$ per year, and at the end of the year withdraw exactly \$4.000 dollars, and then continue to invest the remaining (\$100 × 1.02 − \$4.000), at the same $v = 2\%$, etc., the account will be depleted after exactly $N = 35$ years. The present value of the $N = 35$ cash-flows of exactly \$4.000 is equal to \$100 at a valuation (a.k.a. investment, interest) rate of: $v = 2\%$. But, if the valuation rate is (a lower) 1%, the sustainable withdrawal rate is only 3.40 per year (per \$100). And, if valuation rate is $v = 3\%$, the sustainable withdrawal rate is \$4.65 per year.

These numbers are obviously based on very simplistic assumptions regarding investment returns, inflation rates, and human mortality, but it's the first (of many) to visits this important topic. And, given their centrality to everything that follows in this book, I'll type and display these numbers as a stand-alone table.

Here is yet another way to interpret the numbers in Table 2.1. If you start retirement with \$$W$ dollars, for the sake of argument, and you invest that money in a fund or account that earns exactly $v = 2\%$ every single year, and withdraw exactly $(0.04)W$ every year, then the portfolio longevity of your money will be exactly 35 years. Note the impact of retirement horizon N, on the sustainable withdrawal rate. I'll return to the related concept of portfolio longevity again (and again), starting in Chap. 5, but for now the above is simply another example of how to use the RGOA function.

Table 2.1 Nest egg of \$100. How much can you withdraw?

Years of retirement income	$v = 1\%$	$v = 2\%$	$v = 3\%$	$v = 4\%$
$N = 10$ (Very short)	\$10.558	\$11.132	\$11.723	\$12.329
$N = 25$ (About average)	\$4.5406	\$5.1220	\$5.7427	\$6.4011
$N = 35$ (Quite long)	\$3.4003	\$4.0002	\$4.6539	\$5.3577

Note: assuming no uncertainty in investment returns v

2.8 Continuous-Time Present Values

Until now all cash-flows were assumed to be discrete, that is, in lumps at fixed points in time. In Table 2.1 cash-flows occur at the end of the year, and investment returns are credited at the end of the year. The RGOA function is designed in *discrete time.* Occasionally (and especially in later chapter) I will present valuation formulas and recipes for cash-flows that occur in *continuous time*. These cash-flows will then represent a rate, for example, \$$c$ per year, in which at every instant Δt, the cash-flow is $c\Delta t$. This isn't the proper place to get into the Calculus of the matter, so I refer interested readers to book [2], for in-depth coverage of these matters. The relevant factor equivalent to RGOA from Eq. (2.1) is written and denoted as:

$$\texttt{RGOA.CT} := \int_0^T e^{-rs}\, ds \;=\; \frac{1}{r}\left(1 - e^{-rT}\right), \tag{2.3}$$

where r is the continuously compounded valuation rate (instead of v in discrete time) and T is the time horizon in years (instead of N in discrete time.) Coding up this rather simple expression in **R** can be done quite easily using the `exp(.)` function, and is left as an exercise. Now that you learned how to calculate these values, let me show you how you can plot them on a graph to help visualize the various possibilities.

2.9 Very Basic Plots and Figures

```
> plot(RGOA(0.025,0.01,1:40))
```

One last thing worth noting and explaining at this early stage is how to generate (very) basic plots and figures in **R**. For example, if you want to visualize how the RGOA function looks as a function of N, assuming fixed values of $g = 2.5\%$ (growth rate) and $v = 1\%$ (valuation rate), type the above expression into the lower-left command line. You will immediately see in the lower-right box on your screen the relevant figure. In this case, the simple plot command (without any added bells or whistles) will generate the image seen in Fig. 2.5. It's crude, not very pretty, but does the job quickly.

However, there is a slightly longer and more elaborate way in which to generate (still very simple) plots in **R**, but one that gives you (much) more control over what you see, such as the title, labels, as well as the axis. Here is the recipe.

Source: Generated by Author

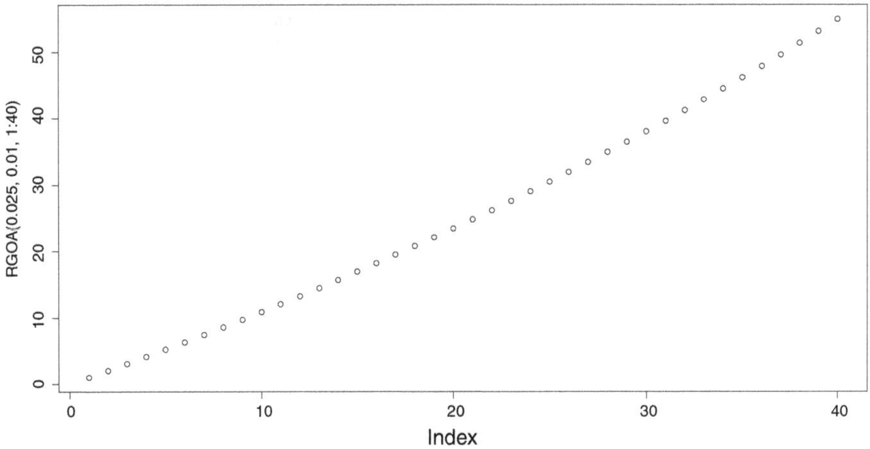

Fig. 2.5 Basic plot of present values of growing annuities as a function of time

```
plot(c(1,40),c(1,55),type="n",xlab="Periods",ylab="PV")
title("Regular Growth Ordinary Annuity")
for (i in 1:40){
points(i,RGOA(0.025,0.04,i),pch=16,col="red")
points(i,RGOA(0.025,0.01,i),pch=1,col="blue")}
```

The cooking process involves getting **R** to create an empty plot in which the x-axis dimensions `c(1,40)` and y-axis dimensions `c(1,55)` are specified explicitly. The empty plot's axis are labeled with `xlab="Periods"` and `ylab="PV"`. In fact, if you (only) run the first line of the following script, then you will see an empty graph. The second line in the script will place the title in the relevant location. Then, and this is the key part, you ask **R** to start a loop in which the index `i` ranges from a value of $i = 1$ to $i = 40$. Within this loop, the figure is created point-by-point by adding the relevant value of the RGOA function in which $N = i$. Look carefully at the `points(.)` syntax to see exactly how it works. The `pch` command controls the type of symbol to display, and the `col` command controls the color. This graph structure and syntax will be used over (and over) again in the subsequent chapters, although eventually I'll get to something called `ggplot`, which is yet another way of plotting in **R**. Nevertheless, do spend some time (playing around and) understanding what each command in **R** does.

Anyway, when you run and compile this longer script, the output will appear in the same lower-right panel as a new box. You should see (something like) Fig. 2.6 which displays a (somewhat) nicer version of the PV of annuities for different time periods under two different valuation rates. Notice the axis labels, the title, and the different colors (if you are reading this online). In sum, you now have two ways to plot simple user-defined functions, which you have learned how to create.

Source: Generated by Author

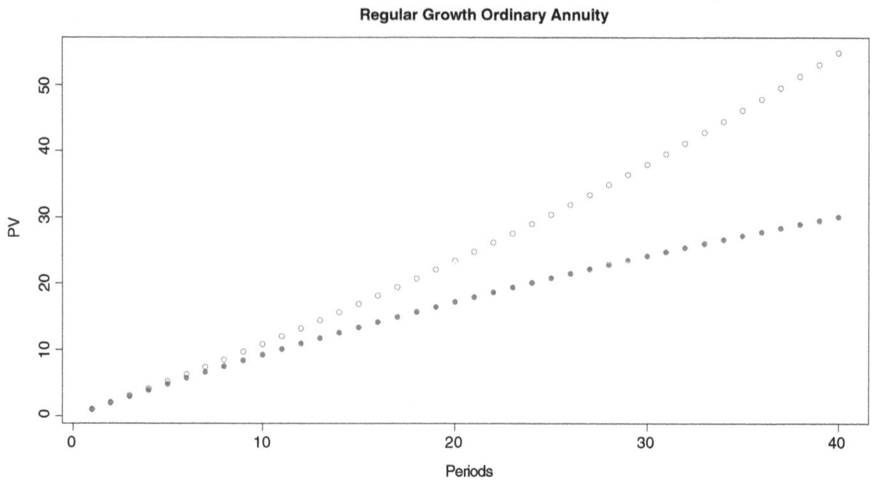

Fig. 2.6 PV with valuation rate of 1% (blue, top) versus 4% (red, bottom)

2.10 Final Notes

1. At this (early) stage, **R** might seem like just another clunky calculator, and everything I have demonstrated and computed could very easily be done with a financial or scientific calculator. The greatest advantage to using **R** is within the data input and manipulation capabilities, which will come later. So, have patience and you will see (some of) the power of **R** in the next few chapters.
2. For now, don't worry about all the different buttons, codes, screens, and keys in R-studio. Many of them will not (ever) be used in this book, and to be very honest I still don't know what many of them do.
3. I will introduce (many) more shortcuts and functions as they are needed. Generally speaking my approach is to take and present concepts on a need-to-know basis.
4. In this chapter I used the word valuation rate v (exclusively) to denote the very critical rate at which all cash-flows are discounted. This number is often called the interest rate within the concept of present values, and eventually I will (present and) work with a vector v_i in which the discount rate depends on the period in question. (Think term structure of interest rates.)
5. Although the command-line inputs to **R** begin with the > symbol, I will suppress them from here onward, since it should be clear from the box around the text.
6. Finally, for readers and students who are absolutely itching to learn about all the different functions and capabilities of **R**, I would suggest getting the book referenced as [3], which is actually sitting on my desk as I write this.

Questions and Problems

2.1 Compute and report values of RGOA assuming $N = 20$, for a growth rate of $g = 1\%, 2\%, 3\%$ under $v = 4\%$. Notice the pattern. What happens when you plug in $g = 4\%$? Why do you get this result?

2.2 Write a function that computes the present value of an ordinary annuity (similar to the RGOA function) that only starts growing after $M \leq N$ periods. Call it RGOA.DM. So, for the first M periods there is no growth and then cash-flows start growing by g per period, until time period N. Evaluate this function with parameters $M = 10$ years, $N = 20$ years, $g = 2\%$, and $v = 3\%$ and compare with the value of RGOA in which $g = 2\%$, $v = 3\%$ and explain the difference.

2.3 Write a function that computes the future value of an ordinary annuity, and call it RGOA.FV. Evaluate this function with parameters: $N = 20$ years, $g = 2\%$, and $v = 3\%$. Note that you should now have three user-defined functions appearing in the upper-right hand corner of your **R-studio** workplace.

2.4 You are $x = 65$ years old and entitled to an income (cash-flow, pension) of \$1000 per months for the rest of your life. Assuming $v = 3\%$, what is the present value of that pension if you live to age 95? What is the present value if you live to age 100? What is the extra cost of those 5 years?

2.5 Assume that you have 100 "units" of something (think of dollars, euros, yen, or people who are infected with a virus). Every day that number grows (think of interest rates) by 30%. At the end of the first day you have 130 units, at the end of the second day you have $100 \times (1.3)^2$ units, etc. In how many days will you have 300 million units?

References

1. Brown, R. L., Kopp, S., & Zima, P. (2015). *Mathematics of finance* (8th ed.). Toronto: McGraw-Hill Ryerson.
2. Charupat, N., Huang H., & Milevsky M. A. (2012). *Strategic financial planning over the life-cycle: A conceptual approach to personal risk management*. New York: Cambridge University Press.
3. Zuur, A. F., Ieno, E. N., & Meesters, E. H. W. G. (2009). *A Beginner's guide to R*. New York: Springer.

Chapter 3
Coding the (Simple) Financial Life-Cycle Model

This chapter continues the introductory process of learning to work and compute within **R-studio**. The pedagogical objective is to build a set of (simple) **R**-functions that implement various aspects of the financial life-cycle model, which (in the opinion of this author) is the core foundation of *retirement income* planning. In particular, recipes are provided for the optimal consumption (or savings) rates, the optimal multiple of salary that should be accumulated at any age, as well as the optimal amount of financial capital (a.k.a. nest egg) required at retirement. Emphasis here is on the word *optimal*. In other words, I solve for them and they aren't imposed exogenously (i.e. from outside). Being that we are just starting the journey, this chapter assumes no income taxes or pre-existing pensions, and absolutely no randomness in (1) investment returns, (2) salary and wages, or (3) mortality and longevity.

3.1 Functions Used and Defined

3.1.1 Sample of Native R Functions Used

- `IF{}, ELSE{}`. These two statements are used within user-defined functions to condition computations, syntax familiar to anyone who has ever programmed.
- `round`. This function will be used to round off some calculations.

3.1.2 User-Defined R Functions

- `SMCR(x,f,w,g,v,R,D)` computes an optimal smooth consumption rate, as a function of financial and demographic parameters.

M. A. Milevsky, *Retirement Income Recipes in R*, Use R!,
https://doi.org/10.1007/978-3-030-51434-1_3

- `OLCF(x,x0,f0,w0,g,v,R,D)` computes the optimal amount of financial capital that should be accumulated at any age, using the same parameters.
- `FCMW(x,x0,g,v,R,D)` computes optimal financial capital as a wage multiple.

3.2 A Quick of the Model

A common approach to retirement planning, which is quite popular among practicing financial planners, is to begin any conversation by asking about a client's retirement goals and dreams. For example, they might inquire: *how much money would you like to have at retirement?* or an alternative question might be: *what fraction of your (final) salary would you like to have in retirement?* It's quite innocuous and natural to begin any *get-to-know-you* conversation with a discussion of financial goals, dreams, and desires. However, to be very clear, this is *not* the computational approach taken in this chapter, this book, or for that matter by most financial economists steeped in (classical) economics. Rather, the approach I adopt is to (very carefully) examine the totality of financial resources you (or your family) have and the constraints you face. That financial and economic information—not goals and dreams—is then used to compute the highest and smoothest *standard of living* you can achieve. The focus is on maintaining a standard of living over your entire life, as opposed to a sum of money (e.g. \$one million) at an arbitrary age, or an arbitrary percentage (e.g. 70% of my final salary) over your retirement years. Now, sure, the end result of this financial life-cycle model approach discussed in this chapter might indeed be a sum of money that is close to \$1 million at age 65, or 70% of your pre-retirement salary. But that is a by-product of the optimizing process, not an exogenous goal. Hopefully the distinction between (what I'll call) the financial life-cycle approach and the financial planning approach will become clear as I provide numerical examples and (plenty of) recipes. For readers interested in a longer discussion of the financial life-cycle model, see the technical textbook [1] or the lighter book [2].

I'll start with some general notation and terminology that I'll be using in this chapter (and for much of the book). Your salary or wage in period j is denoted by the letter (w_j), and your total spending or, as economists like to call it, consumption is denoted by (c_j). Both of these quantities are measured in dollars (not percentages) and take place at the end of period j, which in most examples will be years. Note that even when j is measured in years, the period number (for example, $j = 3$) is distinct from chronological age (for example, $x = 25$). Also, all valuation rates are quoted as effective periodic rates (EPR). For the most part, this chapter will focus on computing the following four items. The first is the optimal (flat) smooth consumption rate: c^*. The second is the optimal savings rate as a percent of your wage: $s^*_j := (w_j - c^*)/w_j$, in period j, which is assumed to be during your working years. The third is the optimal trajectory of financial capital F^*_j over your financial life-cycle, and in particular its value in period j. F_j^* is the optimal amount of wealth you should have in period j. Finally, I'm ultimately interested in the optimal retirement spending rate $(c_j^*)/F_j^*$, once your wage income is zero, i.e. $x \geq R$. All these values will obviously depend on your retirement age R (in years), the overall length of life D (in years), and the valuation rate v. The objective here is to simply standardize notation, as opposed to postulating any financial or economic theories.

3.3 Human Capital vs. Financial Capital Over Time

Your economic net worth at any age x is the sum total of your financial capital F_x and your human capital H_x, minus any liabilities. Recall from the prior Chap. 2 that the value of human capital at age $x < R$ is the present value of wages (w_j) from age x until retirement age R. This can be written explicitly as:

$$H_x = \sum_{j=1}^{R-x} \frac{w_j}{(1+v)^j} = w \sum_{j=1}^{R-x} \frac{(1+g)^j}{(1+v)^j} = w \times \texttt{RGOA(g,v,R-x)}, \tag{3.1}$$

where, to be very clear and to align with the frequency of discounting, the first payment (cash-flow) is at the very end of age x (your first year in the workforce), which is exactly at age $x + 1$ and the last payment is exactly at age R. In contrast to human capital H_x, financial capital F_x, as its name implies, is the sum total of all our physical, monetary (i.e. non-human) capital, which evolves year-over-year according to the following equations of motion:

$$\begin{aligned} F_1 &= F_0(1+v) + w_1 - c_1 \\ F_2 &= F_1(1+v) + w_2 - c_2 \\ F_{(R-x)} &= F_{(R-x-1)}(1+v) + w_{(R-x)} - c_{(R-x)} \\ F_{(R-x+1)} &= F_{(R-x)}(1+v) - c_{(R-x+1)} \\ F_{(D-x-1)} &= c_{(D-x)}/(1+v) \\ F_{(D-x)} &= 0 \end{aligned} \tag{3.2}$$

Pay very careful attention to the evolution of financial capital F_x, and in particular the subscripts. In the above formulation you are assumed to enter the labor force—that is, you start working and earning a wage—at the age of x, which is time period $j = 0$, but you only get paid at the end of the year. You retire at age R, which is time period $j = R - x$, and you die at time period $j = D - x$, one instant after you consume your last (supper) denoted by $c_{(D-x)}^*$. When you enter the labor force your financial capital F_0 may be zero, positive, or even negative, if you have debts. Regardless of its magnitude or sign, this number grows at the valuation rate of v, per year. You are then paid your first wage at the end of the year, at time period $j = 1$ in the amount of w_1. Then, you consume an amount c_1, and start period $j = 2$, etc.

This process might seem extremely unrealistic and abstract at this stage, but the point here is to set notation and terminology as opposed to assuming that anyone actually behaves this way. Most importantly, and perhaps most unrealistically, I assume that $F_{(D-x)} = 0$, which is the time at which you die (known with certainty), your financial capital is zero. Notice also that 1 year before you die, $(D - x - 1)$, the amount of financial capital you have is exactly enough (in discounted terms) to finance consumption $c_{(D-x)}$ in the next year.

3.4 Solving for Optimal Consumption: c_x^*

Denote current age by x, pre-existing investable financial capital by f, current wage (i.e. salary) by w, projected growth rate of wages by g, valuation rate by v, retirement age by R, and total lifespan (i.e. the year you die) by D, then the optimal *flat* and smooth consumption rate is obtained via:

$$\texttt{Optimal}\quad\texttt{Flat}\quad\texttt{Consumption} = \frac{w\,\texttt{RGOA(g,v,R-x)} + f}{\texttt{RGOA(0,v,D-x)}}, \tag{3.3}$$

where $w\,\texttt{RGOA(g,v,R-x)}$ represents the discounted value of human capital, which I could have also abbreviated by H_x. Here is an example. Suppose valuation rates are $v = 3\%$ in real (inflation adjusted) terms, you are just about to celebrate birthday $x = 25$, and have just received your annual paycheck of $w_0 = \$50{,}000$, which is expected to grow at a real rate of $g_w = 1\%$ per year. For the sake of argument, assume that you spent your entire paycheck on a wild birthday party, and woke up (hung over) the next morning (broke) realizing that you are indeed about to turn 25 and should start planning for your financial future. After careful thought you have determined that you would like to enjoy a *constant* real standard of living for the rest of your life, which you estimate to be: $(90 - 25) = 65$ years. To be clear, I'm assuming $c_j^* = c_{j-1}^*$, which is a personal choice. What is your optimal consumption rate per year in dollars (denoted by the symbol) c_{26}^* and the optimal savings fraction (as a percentage of wages) at the end of the first year of savings s_{26}^*? Using the notation introduced earlier, the value of human capital at age $x = 25$, is

$$H_x = 50{,}000 \times \texttt{RGOA}(0.01, 0.03, 40) = 50{,}000 \times (27.45072) = \$1{,}372{,}536$$

Now, I deliberately set up the question so you have no financial capital, and therefore your economic net worth is $W_x = \$1{,}372{,}536$ as well. As stated, you would like to spend economic net worth evenly over the next 65 years of life, so:

$$c_x^* = c^* = \frac{1{,}372{,}536}{\text{RGOA}(0.0, 0.03, 65)} = \frac{1{,}372{,}536}{28.45289} = \$48{,}239$$

This leads to the optimal savings rate as a fraction of wage, at (year-end) of:

$$s_x^* = \frac{50{,}000(1+0.01) - 48{,}239(1+0.0)}{50{,}000(1+0.01)} = \frac{2261}{50{,}500} = 4.48\%$$

At the end of your 25th year of life, just before your 26th birthday, save \$2261 and enjoy the rest. Note that although your consumption rate c^* is constant over life, the amount of money you save s_x^*, or the fraction of salary that you save $(w_x - c_x^*)/w_x$, is age dependent. So, saving a constant 5%, or 10%, or 20% of your salary is not an optimal strategy because it won't produce a constant and smooth consumption profile. Although your salary increases each year by 1%, you continue to spend the exact same amount every year, and the additional income goes into savings (so the amount you put away into savings increases every year).

3.5 Coding Up the Smooth Consumption Rate

The new `SMCR` function depends on seven (7) explicit variables. They are: `x,f,w,g,v` and the horizon variables `R,D`, which represents current age, current financial capital, current wage, the projected wage growth rate, the valuation rate, the anticipated retirement age, and the terminal age horizon. Note that this function assumes periodic rates for the wage w that are aligned with g and v. So, if the wage is annual, then so are the g and v values. But if you want consumption to be solved for and reported monthly, all variables must be converted and stated accordingly. For the most part I'll work with annual cash-flows and discount rates. Also, when using **R**, do make sure to input them in the proper order. In fact, one of the easiest (and most common) mistakes made when using these (and other) vector-based functions is to inadvertently mix-up or re-order the input variables. Anyway, back to consumption, the function you should code up is as follows:

```
SMCR<-function(x,f,w,g,v,R,D)
{(w*RGOA(g,v,R-x)+f)/RGOA(0,v,D-x)}
```

Notice that this new function `SMCR` is itself a function of `RGOA`. Remember that $v \neq g$, for `RGOA` to work. Also, the number of consumption time periods $(D - x)$ (think years) can't be equal to zero or the entire expression makes no sense. Later on, as we move along to more advanced chapters (and soon enough) I'll make sure to place these restrictions inside the actual functions, but for now I simply note the warnings and move on. Either way, after adding this (second, new) function to your library, your screen should look (something) like Fig. 3.1.

Source: Author's screenshot of R-studio user interface

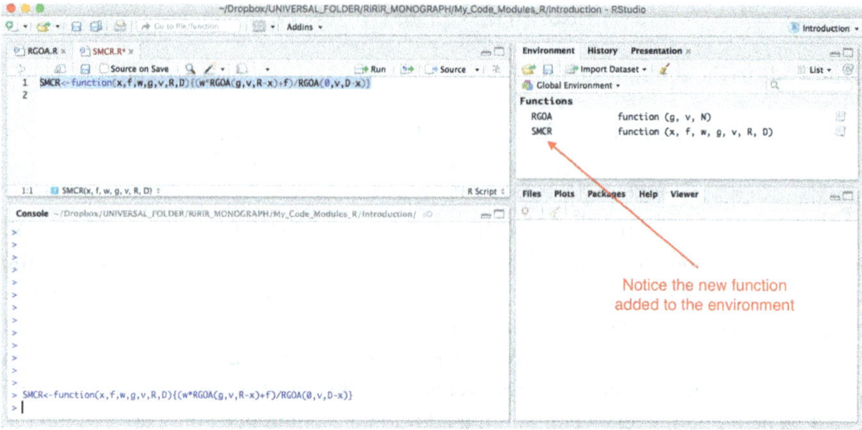

Fig. 3.1 New SMCR function stored in **R-Studio** environment

Here are some additional examples using the new SMCR function directly. Assume you are $x = 30$ years old, have no savings ($f = 0$), earn $w = \$60{,}000$ per year, plan to retire at age $R = 65$, and live until $D = 95$. Let's solve for the optimal (flat, constant) consumption rate under $v = 4\%$ and two different wage growth rates: $g = 0\%$ and $g = 1.5\%$. I'll also compute the savings rate, in dollars, per year.

```
 SMCR(30,0,60000,0,0.04,65,95)
[1] 48591.67
 60000-SMCR(30,0,60000,0,0.04,65,95)
[1] 11408.33
 SMCR(30,0,60000,0.015,0.04,65,95)
[1] 60594.68
 60000-SMCR(30,0,60000,0.015,0.04,65,95)
[1] -594.6765
```

Here is the interpretation of the numbers. If you don't expect your salary to (ever) grow, which means that $g = 0$, and you will earn $w = 60{,}000$ from age $x = 30$ to retirement age $R = 65$, then you should consume \$48,592 per year and save a constant \$11,408 per year, which is: $(w - c)$. But, in contrast to the first two lines in the above box, if you expect the wage growth rate to be $g = 1.5\%$ per year, then a number of things happen in the calculation. First, the optimal (flat) consumption rate is higher by almost \$11,500 per year (because your real wages will grow) and in the first year you don't have to save any of your salary. The negative in front of the 595 in the last line of the box means that you should borrow 595, add it to your wage of 60,000, and consume a total of 60,595. Later in the chapter I'll return to the negative number and borrowing.

3.6 An Optimal Savings Rate Depends on Age

There are a number of other interpretations and insights one can glean from playing around with this `SMCR` function. Although the consumption rate c^* is measured and reported in dollars per period (usually years), I am (more) interested in what fraction of wages should be saved at any point in time. The savings rate as a fraction of wages is simply:

$$s = \frac{w - c}{w} \tag{3.4}$$

In general, I would rather avoid defining new (mostly redundant) functions, so I will work with this expression directly and provide some numerical example. The input variables are age $x = 35$, financial capital $f = \$10{,}000$ (that is, you already have some money saved up at age 35), initial wage $w = \$60{,}000$, real wage growth rate $g = 1\%$, real valuation rate $v = 4\%$, and life to age $D = 95$. The key here is that I would like to examine how the planned retirement age influences the optimal savings rate as a fraction of your wage. I'll let: $R = 62$ as well as 67 and 72. Plugging in:

```
 (60000-SMCR(35,10000,60000,0.01,0.04,62,95))/60000
[1] 0.1796809
 (60000-SMCR(35,10000,60000,0.01,0.04,67,95))/60000
[1] 0.0877581
 (60000-SMCR(35,10000,60000,0.01,0.04,72,95))/60000
[1] 0.008350215
```

Here is the interpretation. If you (are 35 today and) plan to retire at the age of 62, then your savings rate must be 18% of your current wage. But, if you are willing to work another 5 years and instead plan to retire at the age of 67, then your required savings rate drops by half, to 9% of your salary. Why? Well, there are three things that are taking place when you add the extra 5 years of work. First, you are obviously working (and saving) for longer, so you don't need to save as much. Second, you only have to finance (that is pay for) 5 fewer years during retirement, which also reduces the amount you have to save in any given year. Third, the income you earn in those last 5 years is higher than the income you earned in any of the previous year (in your final work year you are making about 37% more that you were in the first year). Connect the three and your optimal savings rate as a fraction of your wage drops by almost 50%. And, if you plan to wait and work for another 10 years, instead retiring at age 72, your optimal savings rate (today) is less than 1%. Notice how changing the retirement age R by just a few years in either direction has an enormous impact on the optimal amount of savings required to finance your standard of living. Here is another example assuming you want to be hyper-careful and plan at age $D = 100$.

```
 (60000-SMCR(35,10000,60000,0.01,0.04,72,100))/60000
[1] 0.02655927
 (60000-SMCR(35,10000,60000,0.01,0.03,72,100))/60000
[1] 0.07844759
 (60000-SMCR(35,10000,60000,0.01,0.02,72,100))/60000
[1] 0.1430286
```

In this case the optimal savings rate as a fraction of your wage, is a 2.66% at the age of $x = 35$, when the valuation rate is $v = 4\%$, and as high as 14.3% when the assumed valuation rate is $v = 2\%$. The point here is to emphasize and demonstrate two things. First, the earlier you start saving the less you have to save (which should be obvious to anyone at this stage). The second point is to emphasize how sensitive the savings rate is to the assumed valuation rate, which is effectively the (safe, guaranteed) interest rate the consumer will earn over their life-cycle. Debating whether "Joe Saver" (at the age of 35) should save 2 or 14% is really a debate about valuation, discount, and investment rates.

3.7 Visualizing the Savings Rate

It often helps to draw some figures and observe the rising and then declining financial life-cycle effect visually. So, assume you plan to retire at age $R = 67$, live to $D = 97$. Note that is 30 years of retirement spending, and further assume that you have no financial capital today so ($f = 0$). You earn a wage of: $w = \$60{,}000$, which increases by $g = 1.0\%$ (in real terms) per year. Here is a visual of the fraction of your salary that should be saved if you start saving at various ages. I'll use the `plot` function built into **R**, which I introduced and used in Chap. 2.

```
plot(c(34,46),c(0.04,0.40),type="n",xlab="Start at age",
ylab="Percent")
title("Optimal Savings Rate")
grid(ny=8,lty=20)
for (i in 33:46){
  points(i,(60000-SMCR(i,0,60000,0.01,0.04,67,97))/
  60000,pch=16,col="red")
  points(i,(60000-SMCR(i,0,60000,0.01,0.03,67,97))/
  60000,pch=16,col="blue")}
```

Figure 3.2 displays a plot of the optimal savings rate assuming one starts saving at different ages (the x-axis) under two different valuation rates as generated by the code. To be very clear in how to interpret this figure, the assumption is that you don't start saving (anything) until the noted age on the x-axis. The left-most point assumes you start saving at age 34, and the right-most point assumes you wait to

Source: Generated by Author in **R**

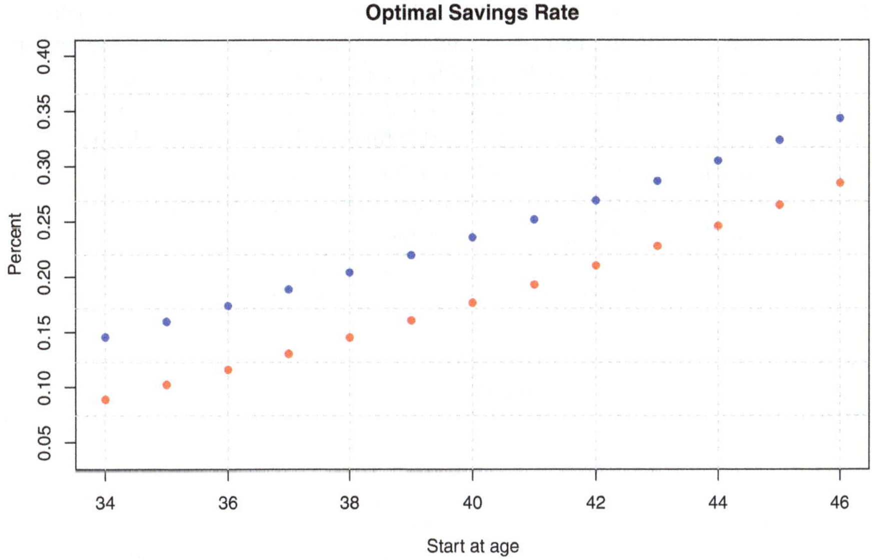

Fig. 3.2 Optimal savings rate when $v = 3\%$ (top) and $v = 4\%$ (bottom)

age 46. In some sense the main message is obvious yet again. The earlier you start the less (as a fraction of wage) you have to save, but this is yet another opportunity to use the basic SMCR function to arrive at that insight graphically.

3.8 Optimal Trajectory of Your Financial Capital

The fundamental budget constraint of life-cycle finance (assuming no bequest) is that *if* you are behaving optimally the present value of your lifetime consumption $PV(C)$ must be equal to the sum of your financial capital FC and human capital HC. This implies that: $FC = PV(C) - HC$, and I can create a formula (or recipe) for the optimal amount of financial capital you should have at any age. In fact, this is exactly how I solved the (earlier) numerical example in which I computed F_{25}^{*} in Sect. 3.4. To do this within **R**, I define a (new) function OLCF which depends on eight variables. They are current age x, initial age (you started working/saving) $x_0 \leq x$, initial financial capital f_0 at age x_0, initial wage w_0 at age x_0, the growth rate of wages g, the valuation (discount, interest) rate v, the retirement age R, and the lifetime horizon (i.e. exact age at time of death) D.

```
OLCF<-function(x,x0,f0,w0,g,v,R,D){
  if (x<=R){SMCR(x0,f0,w0,g,v,R,D)*RGOA(0,v,D-x)-
      (w0*(1+g)^(x-x0))*RGOA(g,v,R-x)}
  else {SMCR(x0,f0,w0,g,v,R,D)*RGOA(0,v,D-x)}}
```

Notice here for the first time, the `if` and `else` structure, which breaks up the function into pre-retirement ($x \leq R$) and post-retirement ($x > R$). If you are currently post (after) retirement, then financial capital must be equal to the present value of consumption, which is that final line in the code, after the `else` command. But before retirement, there is an additional component that comes from ongoing wages and human capital. Remember that this function is a forward-looking forecast (and in future modules will incorporate randomness), which is why it requires the two ages R and D for the input. Here is an example of the (optimal) amount of financial capital you should have at a given age.

```
> OLCF(36,35,10000,60000,0.015,0.04,65,95)
[1] 15074.09
> 10000*(1.04)+60000*(1.015)
-SMCR(35,10000,60000,0.015,0.04,65,95)
[1] 15074.09
```

The second calculation (line) confirms the first and should help understand what the user-defined function is actually doing. The optimal financial capital at age $x = 36$ is the future value of the original financial capital $f_0 = 10{,}000(1.04)$, *plus* the future wage \$60,000(1.015), *minus* the flat consumption rate from the `SMCR` function. Here are few more examples where I (only) modify the current age, which allows me to track and measure the evolution of financial capital over time, from age $x = 45$ until age $x = 95$.

```
 OLCF(45,35,10000,60000,0.015,0.04,65,95)
[1] 118545.8
 OLCF(55,35,10000,60000,0.015,0.04,65,95)
[1] 404248.9
 OLCF(65,35,10000,60000,0.015,0.04,65,95)
[1] 972260.3
 OLCF(75,35,10000,60000,0.015,0.04,65,95)
[1] 764128.5
 OLCF(85,35,10000,60000,0.015,0.04,65,95)
[1] 456042.5
 OLCF(95,35,10000,60000,0.015,0.04,65,95)
[1] 0
```

Notice that (for these parameters) at age $x = 65$ you accumulate \$972,260 (i.e. the nest egg) and spend it all by age $x = 95$. I will now code up a script that will generate the entire picture of financial capital, from initial age $x = 30$ to final age (red) $D = 90$ or (blue) $D = 100$, assuming the prior noted parameter values. The syntax of the script itself should be familiar by now. It starts by creating the frame (only) and then completes the actual values and numbers by looping from age $x = 30$ to age $x = D = 100$.

Source: Generated by Author in **R**

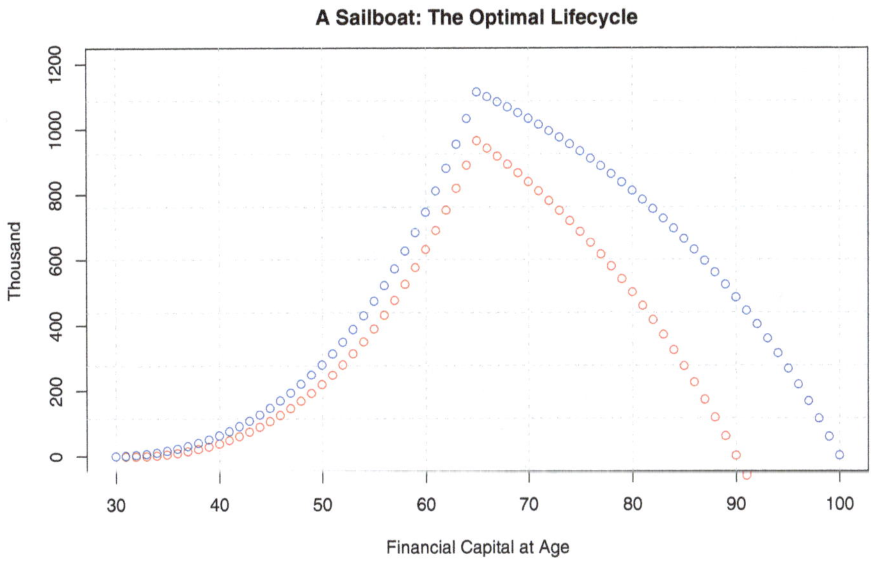

Fig. 3.3 Human life-cycle of financial capital from age 30 until death

```
plot(c(30,100),c(0,1200),type="n",
xlab="Financial Capital at Age",ylab="Thousand")
title("A Sailboat: The Optimal Lifecycle")
grid(ny=8,lty=20)
for (i in 30:100){
points(i,OLCF(i,30,0,60,0.015,0.04,65,90),col="red")
points(i,OLCF(i,30,0,60,0.015,0.04,65,100),col="blue")}
```

Figure 3.3 displays the projected (forecast, expected) financial capital from age 30 until death. Notice how financial capital climbs steeply in the beginning, peaks at retirement, and then declines to zero by the date of death. Notice the *convex* structure of the graph during the working (wage-earning) years, and then the *concave* structure after retirement, when funds are withdrawn and depleted from the account. I call this the *sailboat plot* for obvious reasons.

3.9 Optimal Financial Capital as a Multiple of Wages

It sometimes helps to think of financial capital in units of wages instead of dollars. This enables us to answer questions such as: *What fraction of your salary should you have accumulated at any age?* The crude approach to this question would be to explicitly compute:

```
SMCR(25,0,60000,0.015,0.04,65,95)
[1] 64783.62
OLCF(35,25,0,60000,0.015,0.04,65,95)/(60000*(1.015)^10)
[1] 0.01434026
OLCF(45,25,0,60000,0.015,0.04,65,95)/(60000*(1.015)^20)
[1] 1.577817
OLCF(55,25,0,60000,0.015,0.04,65,95)/(60000*(1.015)^30)
[1] 4.903434
OLCF(65,25,0,60000,0.015,0.04,65,95)/(60000*(1.015)^40)
[1] 10.29244
```

By the age of $x = 45$ you should have 1.58 times your salary in financial capital, by age $x = 55$ it should be a multiple of 4.90 and at retirement (age $x = 65$) you should have 10.29 times your (then) wage. These numbers (as you can see) were obtained by computing F_x^* and dividing by w_x. This is the brute-force way.

3.10 Pushing the Analytics Further

Let's dig just a little bit deeper into the computation of this important ratio. Is it possible to obtain this number without deriving the wealth F and the wage w, separately? To answer this question (and eventually build a proper function) one must consider four input ages. The initial (entering the work force) age x_0, the current age x, the estimated retirement age R, and the estimated end of the life-cycle (death age) D. Note that: $x_0 \leq x \leq R \leq D$. Remember once again the following (fundamental) economic relationship that holds at all times:

$$FC_x + HC_x \geq c\,\texttt{RGOA(0,v,D-x)}, \tag{3.5}$$

where c is your (current) consumption, a.k.a. standard of living and v is the valuation rate. Equation (3.5) reminds us that the discounted value of your (planned) lifetime consumption must not exceed your lifetime resources. The inequality comes from the fact that some people might want leave a legacy or bequest, but at the very least they must have the right-hand side (RHS) of Eq. (3.5) on their personal balance sheet. The plan now is to leverage equation (3.5) to extract additional insights into the wealth (F) to wage (w) multiple. The (discounted) value of human capital is

$$HC_x = w_x\texttt{RGOA(g,v,R-x)}, \tag{3.6}$$

where w_x is current wage at age x. I can combine equations 3.5 and 3.6, which leads to the following relationship, assuming no bequest or legacy motives).

$$FC_x = c\,\texttt{RGOA(0,v,D-x)} - w_x\,\texttt{RGOA(g,v,R-x)} \tag{3.7}$$

This isn't new. The above equation was the basis for the OLCF function defined earlier. I can now scale this equation by either w_x or by c to obtain a ratio in units of consumption or units of wages. It will be

$$\frac{FC_x}{w_x} = \left(\frac{c}{w_x}\right) \texttt{RGOA(0,v,D-x)} - \texttt{RGOA(g,v,R-x)}, \tag{3.8}$$

in terms of wages w_x, and correspondingly, in units of consumption:

$$\frac{FC_x}{c} = \texttt{RGOA(0,v,D-x)} - \left(\frac{w_x}{c}\right) \texttt{RGOA(g,v,R-x)} \tag{3.9}$$

You can think of the (first) expression: c/w_x as one minus your savings rate, and (the second) expression w_x/c as its inverse. Either way, we now have a nice relationship for wealth multiples. Here are some examples. Assume you are age 40, planning on retiring at age 65, living to age 95. You are saving 10% and spending 90% of your wage. What multiple of my salary should I have saved up, as depending on the assumed wage growth rate g? The following script provides the answer.

```
 (0.9)*RGOA(0,0.03,95-40)-RGOA(0.020,0.03,65-40)
[1] 2.020366
 (0.9)*RGOA(0,0.03,95-40)-RGOA(0.015,0.03,65-40)
[1] 3.321937
 (0.9)*RGOA(0,0.03,95-40)-RGOA(0.010,0.03,65-40)
[1] 4.528066
```

Here is the interpretation. Assume the above parameters, you should have 2× to 4.5× times your (after tax) wage saved by the age $x = 40$, with the exact multiple depending on the wage growth rate assumptions. If you are more optimistic about growth rate prospects ($g = 2\%$), then all you need to have saved up in financial capital is a mere 2× your wage. Your retirement nest egg should have twice your annual salary. We can also turn this relationship on its head and imply the wage growth assumption as a function of current wealth multiples. Someone who has (only) saved up twice his or her annual wage at the age of 45, and plans to retire at $R = 65$ and live to age $D = 95$, is implicitly assuming his or her wage will grow by $g = 2\%$, at least according to the life-cycle model.

3.11 A Cleaner Financial Target: Wage Multiples

Although it might appear as if we have extracted (or milked) everything possible from this *wealth-to-wage ratio*, I can push the algebra just a little more and arrive at a more convenient expression for this multiple, which I'll then code up in **R**. Recall that (optimal, flat, real) consumption itself, set early on at the initial age of x_0, should be equal to the following:

$$c = \frac{w_{x_0}\,\texttt{RGOA(g,v,R-x}_0\texttt{) + f}_0}{\texttt{RGOA(0,v,D-x}_0\texttt{)}}, \tag{3.10}$$

where f_0 is initial financial capital, which I now set to zero ($f_0 = 0$) for simplicity. If I then substitute c from Eq. (3.10) into Eq. (3.7), I arrive at yet another way of writing the value of financial capital:

$$FC_x = w_{x_0}\,\texttt{RGOA(g,v,R-x}_0\texttt{)}\,\frac{\texttt{RGOA(0,v,D-x)}}{\texttt{RGOA(0,v,D-x}_0\texttt{)}} - w_x\,\texttt{RGOA(g,v,R-x)} \tag{3.11}$$

Dividing this expression by the current wage w_x, result in:

$$\frac{FC_x}{w_x} = (\frac{w_{x0}}{w_x})\,\texttt{RGOA(g,v,R-x}_0\texttt{)}\,\frac{\texttt{RGOA(0,v,D-x)}}{\texttt{RGOA(0,v,D-x}_0\texttt{)}} - \texttt{RGOA(g,v,R-x)} \tag{3.12}$$

Recall the relationship between wages over different ages can be expressed in term of the wage growth factor. That is: $w_x = w_{x_0}(1+g)^{x-x_0}$. So, when $w_{x_0} = 100$, the growth rate: $g = 0.015$, the age difference: $x - x_0 = 15$ years, then $w_x = 100(1.015)^{15} \approx 125$.

This then leads to the (final) expression:

$$\frac{FC_x}{w_x} = (1+g)^{x_0-x}\,\texttt{RGOA(g,v,R-x}_0\texttt{)}\,\frac{\texttt{RGOA(0,v,D-x)}}{\texttt{RGOA(0,v,D-x}_0\texttt{)}} - \texttt{RGOA(g,v,R-x)} \tag{3.13}$$

At first glance this might appear to be yet another way of writing equation (3.8), with no additional benefit or insight. But upon close examination of Eq. (3.13), readers will notice that there is no explicit mention of consumption c, whereas this input variable was on the right-hand side of Eq. (3.8). Thus, the above representation of the optimized F_x^*/w_x doesn't require explicit knowledge of optimal consumption. It's implicit, and this equation will be used to define a new formal function. The financial capital (a.k.a. wealth) as a multiple of wages, denoted by (`FCMW`) at any age $x \geq x_0$, requires as input your initial working age x_0, and the usual (g, v) as well as (R, D) pairs, but not your current wage, or savings rate or spending rate.

```
FCMW<-function(x,x0,g,v,R,D)
{((1+g)^(x0-x))*RGOA(g,v,R-x0)
*RGOA(0,v,D-x)/RGOA(0,v,D-x0)-RGOA(g,v,R-x)}
```

For the record, we now have four user-defined functions in the library. They are `RGOA`, `SMCR`, `OLCF`, and `FCMW`. Let's generate some numbers for the new function. Suppose $R = 65$, $D = 95$, which means working to age 65, and spending 30 years in retirement, and that $g = 1.5\%$. Assume you enter the labor force and start saving at age $x = 30$. Here are the values:

```
 FCMW(30,30,0.015,0.04,65,95)
[1] 0
 FCMW(40,30,0.015,0.04,65,95)
[1] 0.7366027
 FCMW(50,30,0.015,0.04,65,95)
[1] 3.121397
 FCMW(60,30,0.015,0.04,65,95)
[1] 7.408494
 FCMW(65,30,0.015,0.04,65,95)
[1] 10.37093
```

Under a $v = 4\%$ valuation (interest) rate, you will retire at age $x = R = 65$ with 10.4 times your salary in total savings (a.k.a. financial capital). At the age of $x = 60$ you should have 7.4 times your wage saved up, and at age $x = 50$ you should have 3.1 times your wage in financial capital. Conceptually, the main objective in the last few pages has been to move the discussion from questions of *how much money should I have?*, to questions about wealth and salary multiples. For safety purposes (and to check our algorithm and derivations) I'll reproduce these numbers using the standard brute-force method as well. I'll compute the financial capital, via the `OLCF` function and then scale by current wage. Here are the numbers.

```
 OLCF(40,30,0,60000,0.015,0.04,65,95)/(60000*1.015^10)
[1] 0.7366027
 OLCF(50,30,0,60000,0.015,0.04,65,95)/(60000*1.015^20)
[1] 3.121397
 OLCF(60,30,0,60000,0.015,0.04,65,95)/(60000*1.015^30)
[1] 7.408494
 OLCF(65,30,0,60000,0.015,0.04,65,95)/(60000*1.015^35)
[1] 10.37093
```

In other words, you get the same answer for a wage of \$60K, \$6K, or \$1, when focusing on multiples. But, note the critical assumption that the consumption plan was set (in stone) at age $x_0 = 30$.

So, we basically have two convenient (reduced form) expressions for the wealth-to-wage multiple. The first is based on Eq. (3.8), and the second is the newly defined `FCMW` function. Which method should you use? Well, if you are closer to the (younger) x_0 age, and trying to estimate the optimal level of financial capital as a multiple of wage or salary at a future age x, (think of it as a target) then I would use the above-designed `FCMW` function. It's forward looking and gives you a plan of action, a benchmark of sorts. On the other hand, if you are somewhere in between the initial age at which you entered the work force x_0 and the projected retirement age R, trying to figure-out if your current wealth multiple is on-track, then I would use Eq. (3.8) for a quick *how am I doing* test. Recall that Eq. (3.8) can be expressed as:

$$\frac{FC_x}{w_x} = (1 - S)\,\texttt{RGOA(0,v,live)} - \texttt{RGOA(g,v,work)}, \tag{3.14}$$

where S is your current savings rate as a fraction of your wage (salary), the `live` input denotes the number of years of life you are planning, and the `work` captures the number of years you plan to continue working. Remember, of course, that both representations involve assumptions about retirement ages, wage growth rates, and valuation rates.

3.12 Debt: The Meaning of Negative Numbers

One final matter worth discussing and noting is that very often—and especially at younger ages—you will find that the output from the `FCMW` function, or the `OLCF` function, is a negative number. The multiple can be negative and the amount of financial capital is negative. Here is an example. Plan to age $D = 95$, assuming wage growth of $g = 2\%$, and initial starting age of $x_0 = 25$. The output will be:

```
 FCMW(30,25,0.02,0.04,65,95)
[1] -0.5760173
 FCMW(35,25,0.02,0.04,65,95)
[1] -0.6662685
 FCMW(45,25,0.02,0.04,65,95)
[1] 0.6079801
 FCMW(55,25,0.02,0.04,65,95)
[1] 3.86436
 FCMW(60,25,0.02,0.04,65,95)
[1] 6.269581
 FCMW(65,25,0.02,0.04,65,95)
[1] 9.22064
```

What does it imply for planning? Well, early in life it is optimal to take on debt. That is what the negative number implies. Your financial capital is negative. But then, between the age of $x = 35$ and $x = 45$, the relevant `FCMW` value flips from negative to positive and you now have positive financial capital.

```
plot(c(25,65),c(-2,11),type="n",xlab="Age",ylab="Multiple")
title("Financial Capital as Multiple of Current Wage")
mtext("2 percent wage growth from age 25 ",side=3,line=0.3)
grid(ny=15,lty=20)
for (i in 25:65){
points(i,FCMW(i,25,0.02,0.04,65,85),pch=20,col="black")
points(i,FCMW(i,25,0.02,0.04,65,100),pch=20,col="blue")
}
text(40,7.75,"Plan to Age 100 (blue)",col="blue")
text(40,6.25,"Plan to Age 85 (black)",col="black")
abline(h=0,col="red")
```

This plot is embellished with a few more items and (new) commands. In particular, notice the `grid` function which creates vertical and horizontal lines in the figure, notice the `abline` command which places a horizontal line, in red, at the coordinate of `h=0`, as well as the `text` that is placed as the given coordinates. Once again for those readers who want more detail on exactly how to use or modify these commands, the best option these days is to simply google the command and **R**, and the rest will follow.

Figure 3.4 displays the optimal financial capital as a multiple of wages starting at age 25, projecting forward (or more precisely, discounted) at 4% valuation rate with a 2% wage growth assumption. The (g, v) parameters aren't recommendations of forecasts, and I'll get to my preferred values in the next section. For now, I selected (rather high) values of both numbers to highlight the impact of the optimal wealth-to-wage multiple, and in particular the fact the early in life it's negative. Debt is optimal.

To contrast the situation displayed in Fig. 3.4, I also generated a more conservative figure (and perhaps more realistic) using only a 1% wage growth rate for g and a 3% valuation rate for v. Although economic interest rate forecasts take us far beyond the mandate of this book (and comfort zone of the author), my sense is that even 3% might be a bit too high given the current (abnormally low) interest rate environment. Nevertheless, Fig. 3.5 illustrates the financial capital as a multiple of wages under those values, and as you can see the two curves never go under zero. For this person (or rather under these set of assumptions) borrowing is not optimal.

Source: Generated by Author in **R**

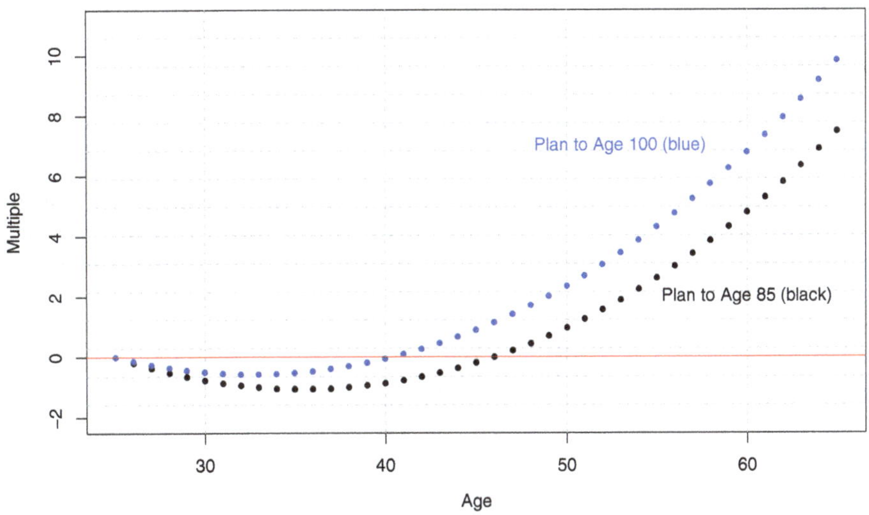

Fig. 3.4 Multiple with $g = 2\%$ and $v = 4\%$: young debt

Source: Generated by Author in **R**

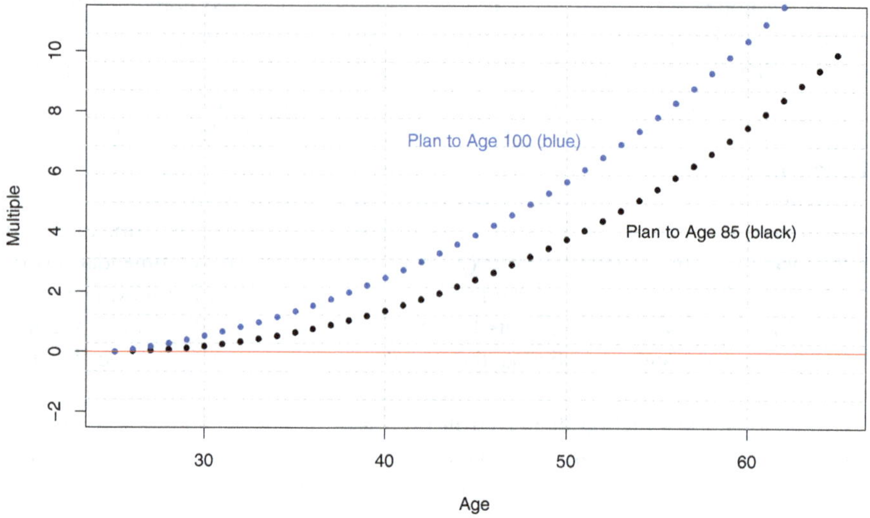

Fig. 3.5 Multiple with $g = 1\%$ and $v = 3\%$: don't borrow

To wrap up the topic of debt, I should note that these debts are *net* and not *gross* values on the personal balance. In other words, if you happen to have physical assets (e.g. your house) that are worth more than your debts (e.g. your mortgage), this particular formulation of the financial life-cycle model would consider you to have no debts.

3.13 A Stake in the Ground with Some Estimates

As we approach the end of this chapter, and the formal content on the financial life-cycle model, in this section I'll offer my *best estimates* for your optimal wealth-to-wage ratio, under a variety of planned retirement ages. Table 3.1 is a summary of those estimates, assuming—and quite critically—a wage growth rate of $g = 1\%$ in real terms, and a valuation rate of $v = 2.5\%$ in real terms. Both of these parameters make a (big) difference on the numerical results, but I'm reasonably confident they are suitable and appropriate for the purposes of retirement planning. The following script generates the numbers in the table, although for the sake of space I only reproduce the relevant section for the first row of the table.

Table 3.1 What multiple of your salary should you have saved up?

	Retire at age: $R = 62$		Retire at age: $R = 67$	
Currently:	$D = 85$	$D = 100$	$D = 85$	$D = 100$
$x = 35$ (Still young)	1.41	2.18	0.50	1.35
$x = 50$ (Middle age)	5.61	7.65	3.22	5.46
$x = 62$ (Getting close)	10.99	14.14	7.28	10.75

Note: assuming wage growth rate: $g = 1\%$ and valuation rate: $v = 2.5\%$

```
round(FCMW(35,25,0.01,0.025,62,85),digits=2)
[1] 1.41
round(FCMW(35,25,0.01,0.025,62,100),digits=2)
[1] 2.18
round(FCMW(35,25,0.01,0.025,67,85),digits=2)
[1] 0.50
round(FCMW(35,25,0.01,0.025,67,100),digits=2)
[1] 1.35
```

The only difference or addition you might notice in the script is that I have added the command `round` in front of the `FCMW` command, which as its name suggests rounds the value of the function to only two `digits`. This is done for convenience, and you can select any number for the `digits` that you would like. Quite frankly, the important numbers are the first digit or two. For example, if you are $x = 35$ year old, and have been working for 10 years (since the age of $x_0 = 25$, plan to retire early at the age of $R = 62$, and assume that the end of your financial life-cycle will take place at age $D = 85$, then according to the output from `FCMW` function, you should have 1.41× your wage saved up in financial capital. But, if you want to be safe and plan to a (much longer) terminal horizon of age $D = 100$ years, you should (obviously) have more saved up, and according to the `FCMW` function it should be 2.18× your current wage (at age 35.) Notice how the planned retirement age R, and the terminal horizon D, impact the optimal wealth-to-wage multiple. From within the table itself, notice how the optimal multiple increases with age, and by the time you get to $x = 62$ years of age, your so-called nest egg should have between 7 and 14 times your salary, with the precise amount depending on whether you plan to retire early (i.e. immediately) or wait until age $R = 67$.

Considering the fact I used reasonable parameters for future wage growth and valuation rates, it's interesting to note that none of these multiples are anywhere near 20, which is often quoted as a proper retirement target. Of course, the beauty and convenience of displaying the actual **R** script is that if you (the user) don't like any of my assumed parameter estimates for g or v, and would like to use your own numbers, simple cut-and-paste into the command line with your preferred assumptions.

3.14 Final Notes

- Although I noted this at the very beginning of this chapter, the financial life-cycle model I have presented here is an abstraction from reality; a very high level abstraction. Few people have any idea how much money w they will earn over the course of their entire working year, or the rate at which their current wage will grow g, or even the valuation rate v that will apply in the future. Likewise, the assumption of a known age of death D is ridiculous, and even retirement age R itself might be endogenous (that is determined optimally) as opposed to imposed exogenously, and perhaps even random (e.g. a virus forces you to retire). Rather, the point of this entire chapter is to set the stage for how this book thinks about the **objective** of retirement income planning, that is to maximize a smooth stream or flow of consumption.
- Another important omission that wasn't addressed in this chapter involves pension entitlements from government, states or corporations. Using our language and notation, many consumers are entitled to a guaranteed income between the ages: (R, D). Whether this income is financed by (other) taxpayers or by required deductions from wages w_x, the fact is that your liquid financial capital (outside the pension system) doesn't have to be as high or large to finance a smooth, constant standard of living. I'll return to the topic of pensions and how they impact optimal savings rates and ratios, after we delve into the topic of mortality, longevity, and risk pooling.
- Nevertheless, even with all of these disclaimers and warnings, I did offer some guidance on optimal *wealth-to-wage multiples* that should be accumulated at various ages. These can be used a possible guide or benchmark for a healthy personal balance sheet which is something I'll return to in the next chapter.

Questions and Problems

3.1 Build an expanded version of the `SMCR` function, which you can label `SMCR.PN`, which assumes that you are entitled to a government pension (for example, Social Security) of π times your final wage w_R. So, for example, if you final wage is $w_R = 100{,}000$ per year, you might be entitled to a guaranteed pension of $\pi = (0.60)$ of you final 100,000 salary between the ages of (for example) $R = 65$ and $D = 95$. So, please compute some values for the `SMCR.PN` function.

3.2 Continuing the above line of thinking, assume the same π pension rate, now create a new function `OLCF.PN` for the amount of financial capital you should have accumulated at any age x. Compute this multiple assuming you enter the work force at age $x_0 = 25$, earn $w_{25} = 50{,}000$ in your first year of work, it grows by $g = 1\%$ per year until you retire at age $R = 62$. Assume you (plan to) live to age $D = 95$, the valuation rate is $v = 2.5\%$, and the pension rate is $\pi = 35\%$ of your final salary. Of course, there is an implicit assumption here that you are entitled to keep your entire wage w_x and that you don't pay any tax (or pension contributions) which go towards funding the entitlement of π.

3.3 Create a function `FCWM.PN`, which computes the multiple of your wage that you should have saved up at any age x, assuming you are entitled to a pension of π at retirement. Assuming the same $g = 1\%$, $v = 2.5\%$ numbers (which were the basis for the above table), please locate scenarios (i.e. values of w, R or D) where there is no need to accumulate (or save) any money for retirement, because the pension of $\pi = 60\%$ will be enough to finance a constant smooth consumption plan.

3.4 You earn $w = \$100{,}000$ per year, the valuation rate is $v = 4\%$, wage growth rate is $g = 0$, you are $x = 35$ and have nothing saved $f = 0$. Please locate values of (R, D) that result in $F_R = \$1{,}000{,}000$. In other words, find situations in which you really do need one million dollars to retire.

3.5 Similar to question (3.4), assume ($R = 65$, $D = 100$) but modify the wage growth rate g and the valuation rate v, and locate parameters for which you need one million dollars to retire.

References

1. Charupat, N., Huang H., & Milevsky, M. A. (2012). *Strategic financial planning over the life-cycle: A conceptual approach to personal risk management*. New York: Cambridge University Press.
2. Milevsky, M. A., & Macqueen, A. C. (2015). *Pensionize your nest egg: How to use product allocation to create a guaranteed income for life* (2nd ed.). New Jersey: Wiley.

Chapter 4
Data in R: The Family Balance Sheet

The technical objective of this chapter is to learn how to import and analyze (large) sets of data within **R-studio**. This really is the primary purpose and core strength of **R**, statistical data manipulation. The chapter begins by explaining how to import a simulated dataset of numbers representing a hypothetical family balance sheet (FBS). The underlying variables are consistent with the financial life-cycle model presented in the prior chapter. Then, using some (simple) statistical tools in **R**, the chapter investigates and discusses the following questions. Does the typical family (individual) in this dataset have a healthy FBS? What fraction of the population as represented by the dataset could be considered to be financially secure? What fraction of the population might be at risk of not maintaining their standard of living during retirement?

4.1 Functions in This chapter

4.1.1 Sample of Native R Functions Used

- `range(.)`, `max(.)`, `min(.)` computes range of numbers in a dataset.
- `mean(.)` computes the mean of the numbers in the dataset.
- `length(.)` computes the number of elements in the dataset.
- `cor(.)` computes the correlation between two vectors in the dataset.
- `segments(.)` used for plotting.
- `rm(.)` used to remove and clear variables.

M. A. Milevsky, *Retirement Income Recipes in R*, Use R!,
https://doi.org/10.1007/978-3-030-51434-1_4

4.1.2 *User-Defined R Functions*

- This chapter does not include or add any new user-defined functions, but instead focuses on implementing the above-noted (and other) built-in functions.

4.2 Importing the Family (Personal) Balance Sheet Data

I created a sample dataset named `SIMPBS.csv` which is freely available for download from the book's resource center and at the website, www.MosheMilevsky.com. Once you have located, downloaded, and stored the csv file in the relevant directory on your computer, you can import the data itself into **R**. Before you do that, I would suggest you open and examine the original file itself (in csv format) using a basic text editor, so you get a feel for what the data looks like before importing into **R**. This particular file is small enough in size so reviewing it with a basic editor shouldn't be a problem. (Note: you can also import with `read.csv` command.)

Follow the sequence of screenshots presented and depicted in Figs. 4.1, 4.2, 4.3, and 4.4. For those who are new to this (and **R**) I'll carefully explain each one of the relevant commands in the next few paragraphs. But if you have done this before, feel free to skip ahead to the next section. As I warned in prior chapters, your particular screen and user interface might not look exactly the same as these figures, especially as **R-Studio** upgrades and revises the front-end. That said, I'm sure you can locate the relevant buttons and commands on your version and I'll now go through this step-by-step. To begin the importing process, click the *Import*

Source: Author's screenshot of R-studio user interface

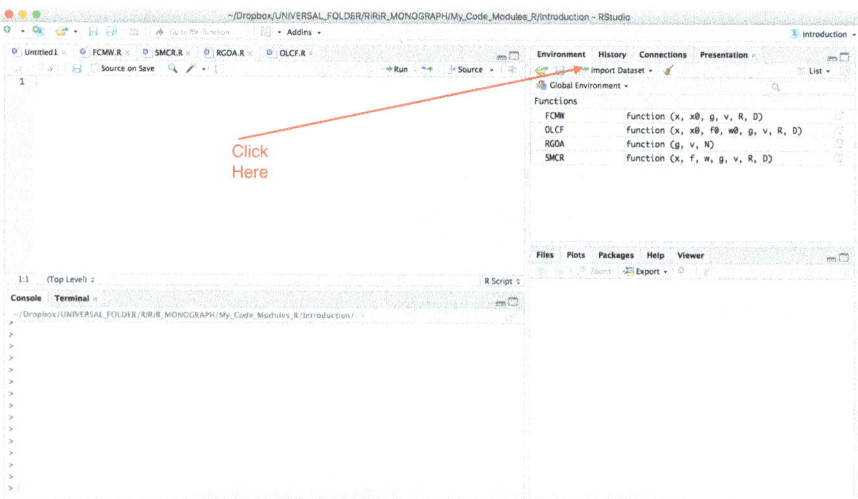

Fig. 4.1 The first step for importing data in R

Source: Author's screenshot of R-studio user interface

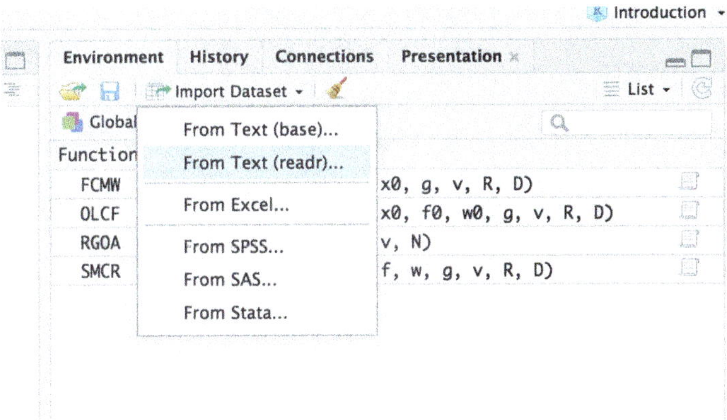

Fig. 4.2 The second step for importing data in R

Source: Author's screenshot of R-studio user interface

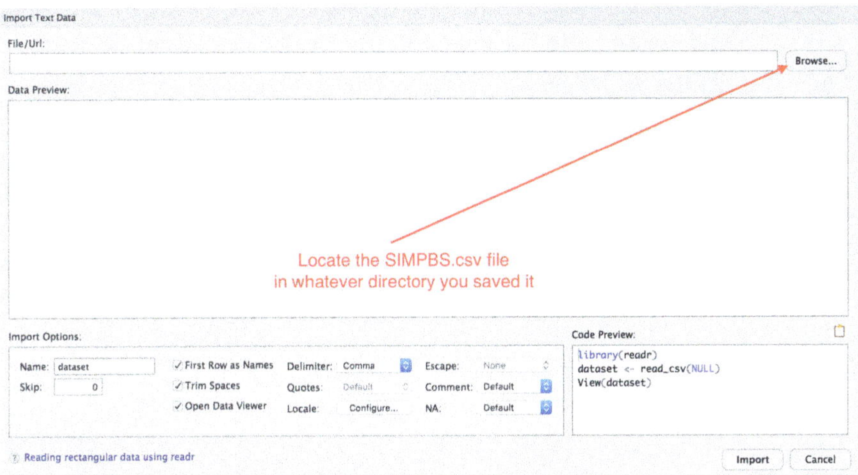

Fig. 4.3 The third step for importing data in R

Dataset button located in the top-right quadrant of **R-studio** as shown in Fig. 4.1. (Note that depending on your operating system, Windows vs. Mac, you might need to download `fpp2` or `farver`, first.) The button should be on top of the panel with the four user-defined functions created in the prior chapters. The next step, once you can access the dropdown menu, is to click on the *From Text (readr)* button, which is second from the top, as shown in Fig. 4.2. As you can see from the list in Fig. 4.2, you can also import data from Excel, as well as SPSS, SAS, and Stata, all of which are very popular (and competing) statistical software packages. I personally find csv the easiest (and least corruptible) format to use. In fact, if you are planning on importing data from other statistical packages, I would recommend converting (exporting) to csv format and then importing to **R**.

Source: Author's screenshot of R-studio user interface

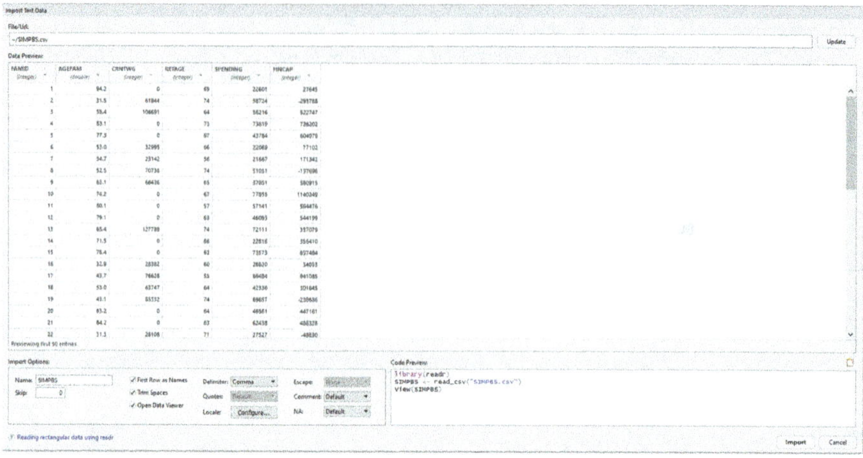

Fig. 4.4 Initial examination: last chance to review before importing

Source: Author's screenshot of R-studio user interface

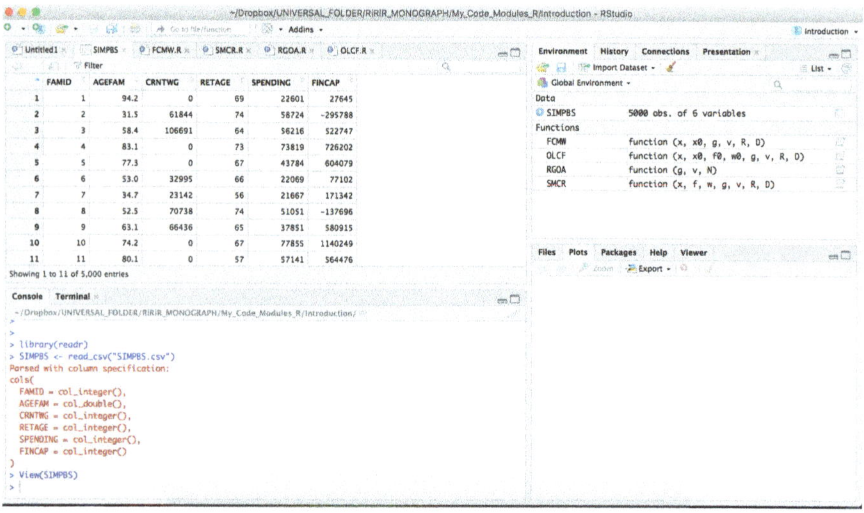

Fig. 4.5 A Glimpse of your data in the R-studio environment

Locate the usual and familiar browse button on the right-hand side of the screen and then navigate to the relevant directory that contains your copy of the SIMPBS.csv file, as shown in Fig. 4.3. Remember, that is the location where you stored the csv file on your local machine. You should now see something very similar Fig. 4.4, which is your last chance to review the data before you import (lower right corner button) into **R**. Finally, you should see Fig. 4.5 which tells us that the data is now in **R-studio** and is ready to be used.

The first thing you will notice in the left-hand corner of your screen, depicted in Fig. 4.5, is the top end of the actual dataset, and in particular the six (6) data columns denoted by `FAMID`, `AGEFAM`, `CRNTWG`, `RETAGE`, `SPENDING`, and finally `FINCAP`. The first column `FAMID` is a short descriptive label within **R** for the identification number (ID) of each of the 5000 anonymous (hypothetical) families that were surveyed. The ID number ranges from $N = 1$ to $N = 5000$, which won't be used for any of the statistical analysis.

Moving on to the actual data, the second column denoted by `AGEFAM` represents the age of the oldest person in the family, which one might think of as the head of the household (a.k.a. breadwinner), although in today's multi-generational and multi-income family units this designation might not be accurate or even correct. Nevertheless, I have assumed this number to be the age of the family unit itself, within the context of a financial life-cycle model. Perhaps it's more accurate to think of this family as one single person whose age is `AGEFAM`, and the data to be part of a *personal* balance sheet versus a *family*. Moving on, the third column `CRNTWG` is the survey response to the question: *what was the total wage earned by this family in the past year?* and is measured in dollars (or Euros, etc.) You will notice from the small visible portion of the dataset that there are some zeros in that column, which is quite natural if the family (i.e. the head of the household) is retired, or perhaps unemployed. The fourth column `RETAGE` captures the response to a question regarding retirement age. So, this is either the age (remember R from the prior chapter) at which the wage earner would like to retire or the age R at which they did retire, assuming their current age is above R. The fifth column `SPENDING` captures the response to the question: *how much did this family unit spend last year?*, echoing the consumption rate c_x in the prior chapter. The sixth and final data columns `FINCAP` measure the financial capital of the family, similar to the F_x variable in the financial life-cycle model. Both `SPENDING` and `FINCAP` are measured in dollars (or Euros, if you like, since this is all hypothetical.) I will now proceed to explore the data in **R**, and in particular explain the syntax used to obtain simple statistical summaries.

4.3 Exploring Your Data in R

The dataset (within **R**) is stored under the name of `SIMPBS`, which was the original name of the imported csv file. At this point, if you prefer, you can change the name to anything by typing `ANYTHING<-SIMPBS`. This will create a second copy of the dataset with the `ANYTHING` name, and you should probably delete the original duplicate copy with the `rm(.)` command. Later on, I'll rename some individual columns and ranges of data, but for now I'll continue to work with `SIMPBS`. I'll investigate the range of the five main statistical variables in the dataset. The command `range(.)` computes the highest and lowest number, and by using the `$` in front of the name of the column itself, it forces **R** to focus on the range of a particular column vector. The exact syntax is as follows:

```
 range(SIMPBS$AGEFAM)
[1] 30 95
 range(SIMPBS$CRNTWG)
[1]       0 242656
 range(SIMPBS$SPENDING)
[1] 19338 79140
 range(SIMPBS$FINCAP)
[1] -665492 1583767
```

Again, note very carefully the use of the `$` to extract a particular column (or vector) from the data file (or matrix.) The range for the age of the family unit in our data is from $x = 30$ to $x = 95$. The range of the current annual wage is from $w_x = 0$ to $w_x =$ \$242,656. The range of consumption spending is from $c_x =$ \$19,338 to $c_x = \$79,140$ per year. Finally, the financial capital of the family unit ranges from $F_x = -$\$665,492 (that is a lot of debt!) all the way to $F_x =$ \$1,583,767, which is the "richest" person in our data. The next step is to compute some simple arithmetic averages using the `mean()` function.

```
 mean(SIMPBS$AGEFAM)
[1] 62.10694
 mean(SIMPBS$CRNTWG)
[1] 36665.67
 mean(SIMPBS$FINCAP)
[1] 370262.2
 mean(SIMPBS$SPENDING)
[1] 49296.29
```

The average age of the (oldest person in the) family unit is 62, the average wage is \$36,666 per year, the average financial capital is \$370,262, and the average annual (consumption) spending is \$49,296, which interestingly enough is more (i.e. higher) than the average wage. On average these $N = 5000$ families spend more than they earn, although the word average should be used and interpreted with extreme caution. So, let's dig a little bit deeper and compute some *conditional* averages. In particular, I can ask **R** to (only) examine rows of data in which a particular column satisfies some conditions. In particular, I will compute the mean of the financial capital vector, but condition on ages that are above a particular value. Pay very careful attention to the syntax, as these commands are now getting longer and messier.

```
mean(SIMPBS$FINCAP[SIMPBS$AGEFAM>=40])
[1] 431072.9
 mean(SIMPBS$FINCAP[SIMPBS$AGEFAM>=50])
[1] 504935.5
```

```
mean(SIMPBS$FINCAP[SIMPBS$AGEFAM>=60])
[1] 530460.4
```

Note the `[.]` (square brackets) to condition on a subset of the `FINCAP` column vector, and the `>=` to condition on `AGEFAM` being greater than (or equal to) 40, 50, and 60. Here's how to interpret these three numbers. The arithmetic average financial capital (F_x) of those family units who (oldest person) is age $x \geq 40$ is \$431,073. This number is greater than the average financial capital (F_x) for the entire collection of $N = 5000$ family units, which was \$370,262. Intuitively, the `$AGEFAM>=40` condition excludes the younger families under the age of $x = 40$, whose financial capital is lower as per the predictions of the life-cycle model. The same calculation conditional on age $x \geq 50$ leads to an average financial capital of \$504,936 and when $x \geq 60$, the average financial capital is \$530,460. None of these results or numbers should come as a surprise. The older families have more financial capital. You saw this (theoretically) in Chap. 3, and now you see it demonstrated in the data. Of course, there are fewer families at older ages, which I will now explain how to count in **R**. The following command (and syntax) allows you to count the number of data points subject to certain restrictions. Run the following command.

```
length(SIMPBS$FINCAP)
[1] 5000
length(SIMPBS$FINCAP[SIMPBS$AGEFAM<=40])
[1] 761
length(SIMPBS$FINCAP[SIMPBS$AGEFAM<=40
& SIMPBS$CRNTWG >=50000])
[1] 425
length(SIMPBS$FINCAP[SIMPBS$AGEFAM<=40
& SIMPBS$CRNTWG < 50000])
[1] 336
```

The `length(.)` command counts the number of data points in the `SIMPBS$FINCAP` vector, which is obviously the full $N = 5000$ number of rows in the `SIMPBS` dataset. Using the same `length(.)` command, the number of data points in the `FINCAP` vector, where the `AGEFAM` value is less than or equal to 40, is equal to 761. In contrast, the third line in the above command sequence counts the number of data points in which the age of the family is $x \leq 40$, *and* the wage is greater than \$50,000 per year. That number is 425, which is less than 761 families under the age of 40. Stated differently, there are $(761 - 425) = 336$ family units with an annual wage lower than $w = \$50{,}000$ per year. That fact is confirmed by the final calculation in the box, where the conditioning is reversed from `(>=50000)` to `(<50000)`. Note again the role of the `&` in combining the two conditions. All of this will be (extremely) useful later on. Whenever you want to compute the fraction or percentage of data that satisfies certain conditions or meets various criteria, you will likely be using one of the `[]`, `&`, `$` commands.

So, take one last look at the syntax and the order in which the commands are placed, just to ensure it's clear.

4.4 Measuring Simple Correlations

This type of data conditioning can also be used with other commands, and in particular I'll now introduce the `cor(.)` function to measure the statistical correlation between two vectors in our dataset. Run the following commands in **R**, and be careful (again) with the syntax and order.

```
 cor(SIMPBS$AGEFAM,SIMPBS$FINCAP)
[1] 0.3381752
 cor(SIMPBS$AGEFAM[SIMPBS$AGEFAM<=75],
          SIMPBS$FINCAP[SIMPBS$AGEFAM<=75])
[1] 0.6473859
 cor(SIMPBS$AGEFAM[SIMPBS$AGEFAM<=65],
          SIMPBS$FINCAP[SIMPBS$AGEFAM<=65])
[1] 0.5643653
 cor(SIMPBS$AGEFAM[SIMPBS$AGEFAM<=55],
          SIMPBS$FINCAP[SIMPBS$AGEFAM<=55])
[1] 0.3619244
```

The first calculation computes the overall correlation between financial capital (F_x) and age x, in the entire dataset. That number is +33.8%, and positive, which is consistent with the fact that older people have more wealth. But, when you think about it, the number is somewhat low. But, if you condition on `AGEFAM` being 75 or less, and include families in the working-age range, the correlation doubles to 64.7%. That should make (more) sense, and is consistent with the life-cycle model. As people get older and move into retirement they should be depleting wealth and drawing down financial capital. In fact, if I reverse the conditioning statement and only focus on older families, the correlation between financial capital (F_x) and age is negative. See the following commands.

```
 cor(SIMPBS$AGEFAM[SIMPBS$AGEFAM>=55],
          SIMPBS$FINCAP[SIMPBS$AGEFAM>=55])
[1] -0.3975008
 cor(SIMPBS$AGEFAM[SIMPBS$AGEFAM>=75],
          SIMPBS$FINCAP[SIMPBS$AGEFAM>=75])
[1] -0.7817783
 cor(SIMPBS$AGEFAM[SIMPBS$AGEFAM>=85],
          SIMPBS$FINCAP[SIMPBS$AGEFAM>=85])
[1] -0.7751278
```

Think back to Chap. 3, or the book [1]. Remember the sailboat picture of financial capital over the life-cycle. The optimal (F_x) variable peaks at retirement and declines from that point onward, so the correlation (eventually) becomes negative. In sum, older people have *more* financial capital than the very young, but very old people might have *less* than those who are merely younger.

4.5 Plotting the Data

Let's visualize the data by plotting the average, maximum, and minimum amount of financial capital (F_x) on the family balance sheet, conditional on age. I can do this by creating a loop from age $x = 30$, the youngest age in the dataset, to age $x = 95$, which is the oldest age listed. (Technically the loop is from 30 to 94, as you can see in the actual syntax, because the data is aggregated into 1-year buckets.) This loop then implements the `mean(.)`, as well as the `max(.)`, `min(.)` command on the `SIMPBS$FINCAP` column, conditioning on the relevant age via the command `SIMPBS$AGEFAM<i+1` and simultaneously `SIMPBS$AGEFAM>=i`. In words, it computes the highest, lowest, and average values of financial capital of all the families whose ages are greater than or equal to (i) and less than ($i + 1$). This might sound more complicated than it really is, so review the attached script and then compile the results in **R**.

```
plot(c(30,95),c(-450,1500),type="n",xlab="Age",ylab="X 1000")
title("Financial Capital by Age (in the SIMPBS Dataset)")
grid(ny=15,lty=20)
for (i in 30:94){
  y.max<-max(SIMPBS$FINCAP[SIMPBS$AGEFAM<i+1
  & SIMPBS$AGEFAM>=i])/1000
  y.min<-min(SIMPBS$FINCAP[SIMPBS$AGEFAM<i+1
  & SIMPBS$AGEFAM>=i])/1000
  y<-mean(SIMPBS$FINCAP[SIMPBS$AGEFAM<i+1
  & SIMPBS$AGEFAM>=i])/1000
  segments(i,y.min,i,y.max,pch=20,col="black")
  points(i,y,pch=20,col="black")}
abline(h=0,col="red")
```

Notice from the script that the relevant `point` is placed at the age (i) on the x-axis, and the relevant `mean(.)`, `max(.)`, and `min(.)` on the y-axis. The `pch=20` command and the `col=black` command tell **R** what symbols and colors to use in the plot. The `segments(.)` command creates vertical lines at the relevant coordinates. Figure 4.6 displays the results. In addition to the plotted data and range itself, I have added a horizontal (red, for those who see this in color) line on the x-axis, so readers can see how (at younger ages) many of the `FINCAP` values are less than zero. That, again, is debt. In sum, before you move on, make sure you understand how each and every one of the commands in the above script impact and change the final figure. For the sake of some diversity

Source: Generated by Author in **R**

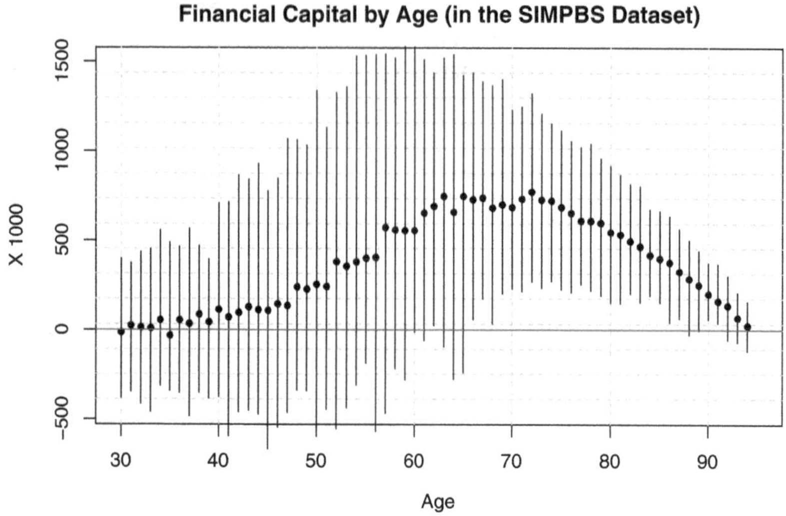

Fig. 4.6 Data: range and average financial capital (in \$1000) by age

and experimentation, change the `pch=20` to `pch=15` and see what happens. Or, change the title by replacing the text within the `title(.)` command, or modify the dimensions of the plot region by increasing or decreasing the numbers inside the `plot(c(30,95),c(-50,850)` command, etc.

4.6 Are These Households on Track for Retirement?

Recall that previously, in Chap. 3, I developed some simple mathematical expressions for the optimal amount of financial capital (a.k.a. wealth or nest egg) that individuals should have accumulated at various ages in the life-cycle, if they want to maintain their existing standard of living for the rest of their life. In particular I created an equation for the optimal ratio of wealth to wages at any age x, as a function of (only) the retirement age R and the life-cycle horizon D. In this section I will compare the ratios within the data (think: empirical) to the ratio predicted by theory. First though, I will simplify and clean-up the syntax by reducing the size of the names of the relevant vectors. Look at the following set of commands, and consider what side of the `(<-)` is easier to type and work with. Needless to say, I would rather work with two letter names versus the mess on the right-hand side.

```
SP<-SIMPBS$SPENDING[SIMPBS$AGEFAM<=40 & SIMPBS$AGEFAM>=30]
WG<-SIMPBS$CRNTWG[SIMPBS$AGEFAM<=40 & SIMPBS$AGEFAM>=30]
AG<-SIMPBS$AGEFAM[SIMPBS$AGEFAM<=40 & SIMPBS$AGEFAM>=30]
RG<-SIMPBS$RETAGE[SIMPBS$AGEFAM<=40 & SIMPBS$AGEFAM>=30]
FC<-SIMPBS$FINCAP[SIMPBS$AGEFAM<=40 & SIMPBS$AGEFAM>=30]
```

The above-listed commands will extract the relevant variables for those families between the age of $x = 30$ and $x = 40$ and store their annual spending `SP`, annual wages `WG`, current age `AG`, desired retirement age `RG`, and financial capital `FC` as separate vectors. If you want, run some summary statistics, such as `range(.)` or `mean(.)`, to get a feel for this particular subset of the larger dataset. The point here is to simplify the syntax with a (much) shorter name and to then compare against model values. In particular, recall the discussion of optimal wealth to wage multiples in Chap. 3, Sect. 3.11. Now let's compare life-cycle theory against life-cycle data. First, I'll compute the average amount of financial capital as a multiple of wage for each one of the family units in the [30, 40] age range, and then I'll compute what it should be according to theory.

```
mean(FC/WG)
[1] 0.6262815
MDL<-(SP/WG)*RGOA(0,0.03,95-AG)-RGOA(0.015,0.03,RG-AG)
mean(MDL)
[1] 1.507644
MDL<-(SP/WG)*RGOA(0,0.025,95-AG)-RGOA(0.01,0.025,RG-AG)
mean(MDL)
[1] 4.513412
```

The `mean(FC/WG)` is the average salary multiple in the dataset. The `MDL` variable is the theoretical optimal salary multiple the families *should* have according to the financial life-cycle model. Now, the theoretical value (multiple) for each family obviously depends on their desired retirement age `RG`. This is why I report the average as computed by `mean(MDL)`. What story does this tell? Well, it's not a pretty one. On average, families between the age of $x = 30$ and $x = 40$ (in the dataset) have 62.6% of their annual wage w_x accumulated in financial capital F_x. But, according to theory, assuming they would like to maintain a smooth constant standard of living until the age of $D = 95$, and assuming they want to retire at the age they specified in the `RETAGE` vector, they should have (much) more financial capital relative to their wage. Depending on assumptions for g and for v, it should be between 150 and 450% of their wage, not 60%. This group is significantly off track, if they want to retire at the age they specified.

4.7 Final Notes

- To be very clear, the data on which this entire chapter is based is simulated, and isn't real. It is (obviously) inspired by the financial life-cycle model and is quite similar to real-world datasets used by researchers, but the numbers themselves are fictitious. For those who are interested in how the $N = 5000$ rows were constructed, this is what I did. First, I randomized family age $x(i)$, annual wages $w_x(i)$, and (planned) retirement dates $R(i)$, for $i = 1..N$. After that, I computed the optimal amount of consumption $c^*(i)$ and financial capital $F^*(i)$ that should be spent and accumulated according to the financial life-cycle model. Finally, I added some (random) noise to the consumption and financial capital numbers and canonized the dataset.

- Real life is (obviously) messier than simulated data and in reality empirical researchers have to contend with missing data, non-sensical numbers, responses that are inconsistent, subjective valuations of financial capital and a variety of other concerns. This is why (in practice) it's much harder to test whether the financial life-cycle model is a good description of how people actually behave in practice. For one thing, consumers face a substantial amount of uncertainty in the parameters currently assumed to be constants. Also, many consumers (especially if they have children and grandchildren) would like to end the financial life-cycle at age ($x = D$), with more than $F_D = 0$, which is what I assumed during last few chapters. Nevertheless, the numbers computed do provide a reliable lower bound for how much families and individuals should have accumulated at various points and ages over the life-cycle.
- This chapter is the last of the introductory chapters in **R**, and from this point onward I'll pick up the pace and use a variety of **R** functions and scripts without spending too much time explaining the micro-steps and minutia in great detail. If you see a new command and you aren't quite sure what it does, how exactly the syntax works, then google. Or, get one of the books such as [2], [4], or even [3] listed in the references.

Questions and Problems

4.1 Assume that the real projected growth rate of wages is $g = 1.0\%$ and that real valuation (or interest) rate is $v = 2.5\%$. What fraction of the entire group *do not* have enough financial capital to maintain their standard of living? Please use the functions and metrics I designed previously to support your answer.

4.2 What fraction of the working population (sample) will not have enough to maintain their standard of living? Segment by age buckets.

4.3 What fraction of the population have 20% less than what they need to maintain their standard of living? (Call this financial distress.)

4.4 Assume a $g = 2\%$ growth rate and $v = 4\%$ valuation (interest) rate. Does the situation improve? Please describe.

4.5 For the age groups between $x = 30$ and $x = 40$ that was analyzed in the last section, can you locate a set of g and v parameters in the financial life-cycle model that will actually fit the observed 62.6% salary multiple that families had accumulated on average?

References

1. Charupat, N., Huang H., & Milevsky, M. A. (2012). *Strategic financial planning over the life-cycle: A conceptual approach to personal risk management*. New York: Cambridge University Press.
2. Crawley, M. J. (2015). *Statistics: An introduction using R* (2nd ed.). West Sussex: Wiley.
3. de Vries, A., & Meys, J. (2012). *R for dummies*. West Sussex: Wiley.
4. Zuur, A. F., Ieno, E. N., & Meesters, E. H. W. G. (2009). *A beginner's guide to R*. New York: Springer.

Chapter 5
Portfolio Longevity: Deterministic and Stochastic

This chapter formally introduces the notion of *portfolio longevity* (PL) within the context of retirement income planning. It explains how to define, measure, and simulate PL in a simple deterministic as well as stochastic (random) environment. This chapter also explains how to generate (simple) Monte Carlo simulations of forward-looking portfolio returns and its connection to asset allocation. Finally, the PL metric is used to analyze the (infamous) 4% rule of retirement income planning, and concludes by discussing some of its shortfalls.

5.1 Functions Used and Defined

5.1.1 *Sample of Native R Functions Used*

- `log(.)` computes the natural (not base 10) logarithm.
- `rnorm(N,mu,sigma)` simulates N normally distributed random numbers.
- `summary(.)` provides a statistical summary of the data.
- `hist(.)` creates a histogram graphic.
- `points(.)` adds points to a figure.
- `matrix(nrow=N,ncol=M)` creates a matrix with M columns and N rows.

5.1.2 *User-Defined R Functions*

- `PL(v,c,F)` computes portfolio longevity (PL), in units of years, assuming initial wealth F, withdrawals c under a constant fixed return v.
- `DTRJ(t,v,c,F)` computes the deterministic trajectory of a retirement portfolio.

M. A. Milevsky, *Retirement Income Recipes in R*, Use R!,
https://doi.org/10.1007/978-3-030-51434-1_5

- `PLSM(F,c,nu,sigma,N)` computes a vector of random portfolio longevity (PL) values, assuming normally distributed investment returns.

5.2 Constant Spending Is (Only) a Good Start

One of the main outcomes from Chaps. 3 and 4 is that it's quite natural for consumers (and retirees) to plan for a smooth, constant, and undisrupted standard of living over the course of their life. In fact, when there is no uncertainty whatsoever about investment returns, inflation, longevity, healthcare, etc., then the optimal utility maximizing default spending plan is indeed a constant dollar (or Euro or Yen) value per year. The proper spending rate was computed via the `SMCR(.)` function. Once the individual was retired, that is, $x \geq R$, it depended entirely on the assumed investment return (v) and the assumed lifetime horizon (D). (Remember, after retirement there is no wage to worry about.) For example, at $x = 70$ years old, with a total of $\$1M$ in financial capital, planning to $D = 95$, the optimal flat consumption rate is:

```
 SMCR(70,1000000,0,0,0.02,70,95)
[1] 51220.44
 SMCR(70,1000000,0,0,0.02,65,95)
[1] 51220.44
 SMCR(70,1000000,0,0,0.02,60,95)
[1] 51220.44
```

Notice that regardless of whether you retired at age $R = 60$, or $R = 65$ or just now at $R = 70$, the flat consumption rate that you can achieve under a $v = 2\%$ interest rate is \$51,220 per year. Of course, you personally might prefer to tilt your consumption up (you must start lower) or down (you can start higher), but the \$51,220 is the baseline for the initial conversation about sustainable spending rates. Now, within the context of this particular chapter and the concept of portfolio longevity, it helps to think of sustainable spending rates from a different direction. Namely, solving for the time (or age) horizon to which a particular standard of living is sustainable under an assumed interest or discount rate.

5.3 Portfolio Longevity: Under the Mattress

Imagine or assume that you begin your retirement years with a nest egg (a.k.a. financial capital, a.k.a. investment portfolio, a.k.a. money) of exactly $F = \$100{,}000$ and plan to withdraw exactly $c = \$5000$ (in real inflation-adjusted terms) at the end of every year until the money runs out. Once again, for now, ignore income taxes as well as all possible uncertainties. If your funds were invested in a simple bank account earning $v = 0\%$ (i.e. zero) interest, then it would last for exactly $F/c = 20$ years. At the end of the first year you would have \$95,000 remaining, at the end of the second year it would be \$90,000, etc., all the way to zero after your final withdrawal at (the end of) year twenty. This is all rather trivial, but another way to present and explain this is by stating that under that strategy and set of assumptions, portfolio longevity (PL) would be 20 years. Mathematically this can be expressed as:

$$PL = \frac{F}{c}, \tag{5.1}$$

which is as simple as any equation can get. For a given fixed amount (F) today, the more (c) you spend or consume per year, the lower the portfolio longevity. So, if you spend $c = 4$ per initial $F = 100$, the PL value is 25 years, but if you spend a mere $c = 2$, the PL value is 50 years. The inverse ratio of (c/F) is often called the initial withdrawal rate (IWR) in the retirement income literature and is expressed as a percentage. So, for example, an IWR of 5% would be equivalent to $c = \$5$ per $F = \$100$ or $c = \$50$ per $F = \$1000$, etc. Either way, at the end of the PL horizon, as defined by Eq. (5.1) there is nothing left. To get an intuitive sense of the PL value as a function of c, Fig. 5.1 plots the relationship between the IWR and portfolio longevity when money earns zero interest, a.k.a. the valuation rate $v = 0\%$. Here is the (by now familiar) script, looping and placing `points(.)` from values of 2 to 8, which generates Fig. 5.1, where the `cex=3` increases the size of the points.

```
plot(c(2,8),c(10,50),type="n",xlab="Initial Withdrawal Rate
(IWR) per Initial $100",ylab="Years")
grid(ny=15,lty=20)
for (i in 2:8){points(i,100/i,pch=20,col="black",cex=3)}
text(2.5,27,"25 Years")
abline(h=25,col="red",cex=3)
```

A horizontal line (in red, for those who can read in color) is placed at a PL value of 25 years, which (very) roughly speaking is the life expectancy of a typical consumer at retirement. (I'll get back to life expectancy and how to model random lives in Chaps. 7 and 8.) A casual examination of Fig. 5.1 reveals that any IWR values that are 4% or lower will yield a PL value that exceeds human life expectancy (good), but IWR values greater than 4% will lead to PL values that are lower than human life expectancy (bad.) In those cases the money runs out before life does. I'll return to the number 4% again (and again) later in the chapter. Needless to say, placing your nest egg under the mattress is an extremely simplistic way of financing (and thinking about) withdrawals, but should help introduce an intuitive concept: *the longevity of your money.*

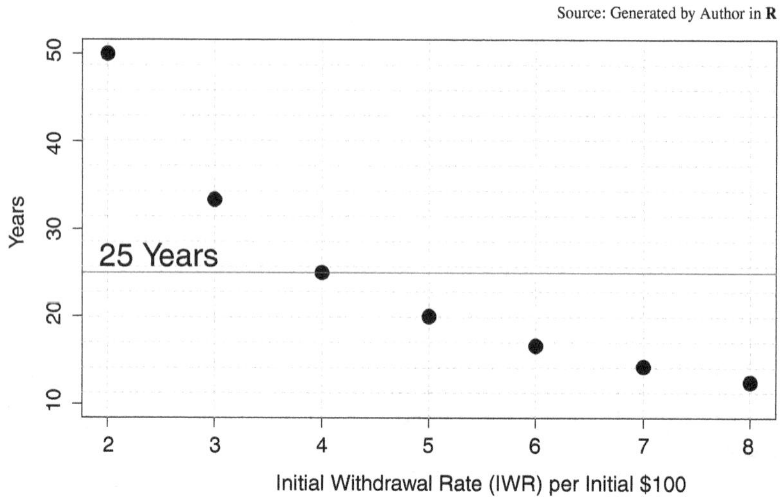

Fig. 5.1 How long does the money last when it's under your mattress?

5.4 Portfolio Longevity: Fixed Interest Rates

Moving on, what if $v > 0$ and the account (portfolio) earns interest, dividends, and (positive) returns over time? In that case the funds should last for more than $F/c =$ 20 years. But how much longer? Well, at the end of the first year of retirement you will have: $F(1+v)-c$ in your portfolio. At the end of the second year you will have $(F(1+v)-c)(1+v)-c$, etc., until the money runs out. So, what is the longevity of a portfolio earning a fixed interest rate of v, subject to a fixed initial withdrawal rate (IWR) of c/F? Note that the PL value could be infinite if v is high enough. After all, if you are withdrawing (very) little and earning a (very) high rate of interest, you could do this forever. So, one possible answer to the question *how long will it last?* is infinity. Keep that in mind. For now, if withdrawals $c > 0$ and investment earnings $v > 0$ take place *continuously*, then L will satisfy the following equation:

$$PL = \begin{cases} \frac{1}{v} \ln\left[\frac{c/F}{(c/F)-v}\right], & v < c/F, v \neq 0 \\ \infty, & v \geq c/F, \end{cases} \tag{5.2}$$

where ln[.] denotes the natural logarithm, and assuming both $F > 0$ and $c > 0$, for obvious reasons. Contrast equation (5.2), and its two branches, with the simple $PL = F/c$ expression in Eq. (5.1) for the zero ($v = 0$) interest case. The derivation (proof) of this formula will appear in the next section, after I provide some numerical examples and code up the script in **R**. But for now, you will have to trust me that the *limit* of Eq. (5.2) converges to Eq. (5.1) as $v \to 0$. Here is an example. If $F = \$100$, the annual withdrawal consumption rate is $c = 5$ and the continuously compounded interest (investment) rate is $v = 4\%$, portfolio longevity is: $PL = (1/0.04)\ln[(5/100)/((5/100) - 0.04)] = 40.236$ years. Compare this to:

$PL = 20$ years from Eq. (5.1), when the interest rate is zero. In this case, the extra non-zero earnings provide you with another 20 years of portfolio longevity, and the first 20 years of income is from principal. Here are numbers based on the top branch in Eq. (5.1), where the natural logarithm is `log(.)`.

```
 (1/0.04)*log(7/(7-4))
[1] 21.18245
```

Note that if the withdrawal (consumption, spending) rate is increased to \$7 per year, the portfolio longevity *PL* drops by almost half to $PL = (1/0.04)\ln[7/(7-4)] = 21.182$ years. The money runs out after 21 years and $(0.182) \times 52 = 9.5$ weeks. Here is a more conventional way of presenting and explaining the exact same information. The present value of a \$7 annuity (in continuous time) at a valuation rate of $v = 4\%$ (in continuous time) for a period of 21.182 years is exactly \$100. A standard business calculator will yield similar results. Input $PV = 100$, an (effective annual) interest rate of $e^{0.04} - 1$ and cash-flow of -7 and the resulting number of periods should be (approximately) 21 years. It's *approximate* because Eq. (5.2) assumes continuous cash-flows and your calculator will be assuming annual cash-flows. Either way, let's code up this simple formula in **R**.

```
PL<-function(v,c,F)
{if (c/F <= v) {999}
else {
  if (v==0){F/c}
  else (1/v)*log( (c/F)/(c/F-v) )}}
```

Note that one has to be very careful around points at which Eq. (5.2) branches or changes structural behavior, which is why there are two `IF, ELSE` conditions. First, if the interest rate is $v = 0$, then we already know the answer is (F/c). Second, if the interest rate $v \geq c/F$, then another problem occurs, namely the upper branch of Eq. (5.2) is undefined. So, in theory we must define the function to be the lower branch, infinity, but that creates some numerical problems which is why I use the number 999. Make sure you understand the logic of the script, and be forewarned that the number 999 is completely arbitrary. Again, the proper (theoretical) answer is infinity (since the log is undefined) and I could have asked **R** to return a text symbol of infinity. Rather, I coded it this way purely for (numerical) convenience, which will become evident in a moment. For now, here are some numerical examples.

```
 PL(0,4,100)
[1] 25
 PL(0.01,4,100)
[1] 28.76821
 PL(0.02,4,100)
[1] 34.65736
```

```
 PL(0.03,4,100)
[1] 46.20981
 PL(0.035,4,100)
[1] 59.41262
 PL(0.0395,4,100)
[1] 110.9374
 PL(0.04,4,100)
[1] 999
```

In all seven cases I am assuming an initial portfolio (a.k.a. nest egg) value of $F = \$100$, and consuming or withdrawing a fixed, $c = \$4$, for as long as it lasts. The only parameter or functional argument that changes is the interest rate v, which starts at the very top at $v = 0\%$, and converges towards 4%. Notice the trend, and in particular what happens as the interest (valuation, investment) gets very close to the value of $v = 4\%$. When the $v = 3.95\%$ the portfolio will last (a.k.a. longevity or horizon) for almost 111 years, which exceeds the lifetime of most humans. But, when I plug $v = 4\%$ into the PL function the response from **R** is 999, which (again) is arbitrary. The true answer is ∞. Why? Because the \$100 portfolio will generate exactly \$4 every year in investment earnings, which will be (exactly) consumed. In fact, the path or trajectory of your portfolio (think of F_t over time) will never veer or deviate from \$100.

Note that this PL function is versatile enough (and properly defined) to produce reasonable results even when $v < 0$. Now, one might question why anyone would invest their precious nest egg of F in a portfolio that shrinks over time. But, this really isn't as odd or surprising as it might sound initially. In recent times real (inflation-adjusted) returns on cash have been negative, so many retirees are indeed seeing their portfolio shrink in real values. Here are some numbers to illustrate.

```
PL(0,4,100)
[1] 25
 PL(-0.01,4,100)
[1] 22.31436
 PL(-0.02,4,100)
[1] 20.27326
```

I am assuming this individual begins with $F = \$100$ at retirement and plans to spend \$4 per year in real terms. And, as inflation rates are realized and reported the retiree increases nominal withdrawals from the portfolio in order to maintain a constant real standard of living. So, just to make sure this is clear, if inflation happens to be 2.5% in the first year of retirement, then in the second year they would consume or withdrawal $4 \times 1.025 = \$4.1$ per year in nominal terms, but the same \$4 in real terms. Of course, the formula and PL function assumes that everything takes place in continuous time, but hopefully the main idea is clear. According to the output displayed above, if the real rate of return earned on the portfolio is $v = -2\%$, and the withdrawals are $c = \$4$ per year, the longevity of the portfolio is a mere

20.3 years. Notice how the PL value shrinks as v declines. Compare the PL with a portfolio longevity value of 25 years when $v = 0$. Later on in the chapter when I introduce the concept of *stochastic* portfolio longevity and random returns, this idea of "shrinkage" will make an appearance again (and again).

5.5 Plotting the Cone of Portfolio Longevity

In this section I'll plot the value of PL, on the y-axis, as a function of the initial withdrawal rate (or amount per \$100) on the x-axis, under a variety of assumed interest rates v. Think of what follows as a generalized or expanded version of Fig. 5.1. The script syntax should be very familiar by now, so I won't dwell too much on the syntax. Figure 5.2 displays the portfolio longevity metric for various withdrawal rates, using the loop structure from $c = \$1$ to $c = \$9$ in increments of $c = \$0.10$ assuming valuation rates from 0% (bottom of curve) to 3.25% (top of the curve.) The figure itself is truncated at PL=50 years.

```
plot(c(1,9),c(10,50),type="n",
xlab="Initial Withdrawal Rate (IWR) per Initial $100",
ylab="Years")
grid(ny=15,lty=20)
for (i in 10:90){
y1<-PL(0.0,i/10,100)
y2<-PL(0.0325,i/10,100)
segments(i/10,y1,i/10,y2,lwd=2,col="red")}
abline(h=25,col="blue")
text(1.6,29,"25 Years",col="blue")
```

Figure 5.3 is generated by the exact same **R** script, but also includes negative values for v, which I previously called "shrinkage" cases. The figure illustrates how the initial withdrawal rate affects PL assuming the interest rates are between $v = -2\%$ and $v = 3.25\%$, instead of the (only) positive values in Fig. 5.2. Notice again how the PL values decline non-linearly with increasing withdrawal rate (remember $1/w$ from the $v = 0$ case), but look at the gap between the highest (top of the cone) and lowest (bottom of the cone) values. At larger IWR values (to the lower right corner) the decline or reduction in portfolio longevity values isn't as steep and the interest rate v doesn't make as big a difference. Intuitively, when you are consuming or withdrawing \$10 per year (for example), earning 1 or 2% doesn't make that big a difference in PL. But, to the left, at lower IWR values, the rate v makes a bigger difference. And, at a relatively low enough initial withdrawal rate, the portfolio longevity can be infinite (technically 999 in my code). In that region the interest rate (range) makes a bigger difference. Oddly enough, the less you (decide to) consume and withdraw, the more important the investment assumption (v) becomes in determining portfolio longevity.

Source: Generated by Author in **R**

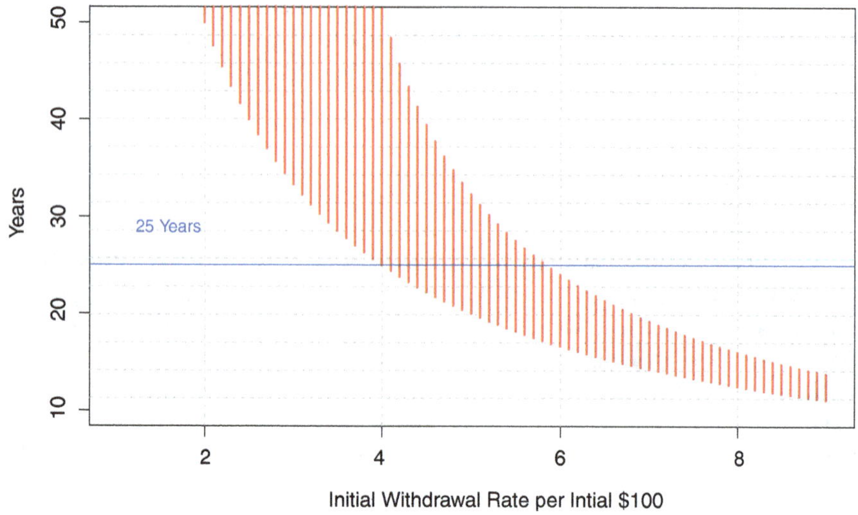

Fig. 5.2 Portfolio longevity (PL) under $v = 0\%$ to $v = 3.25\%$ real investment return

Source: Generated by Author

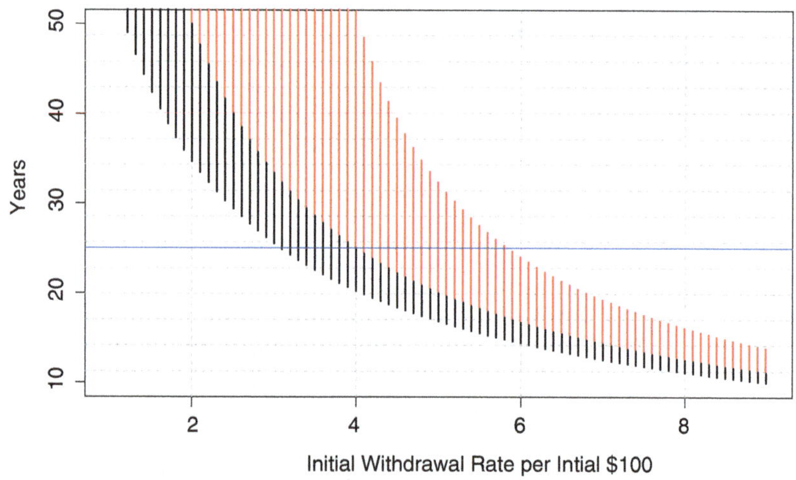

Fig. 5.3 Portfolio longevity (PL) under v=-2% to v=3.25% real investment return

5.6 Early Calculus: Deriving the PL Formula

Although my objective and plan is to keep the first few chapters of this book devoid of any advanced mathematics and calculus, in this section I would like to provide a brief sketch of the "proof" of Eq. (5.2). This will come in handy for the next section, where I discuss the trajectory and path of financial capital after retirement.

To start, if portfolio longevity is PL years, then by definition the present value of the consumption withdrawals c over that time period, must be equal to the initial value of the portfolio F. Using continuous-time notation, this implies that:

$$F = \int_0^{PL} c\,e^{-vt}\,dt = \frac{c}{v}\left(1 - e^{-vPL}\right), \tag{5.3}$$

which actually holds even if $PL = \infty$, in which case $F = (c/v)$, which is the present value of a perpetuity. Re-arranging equation (5.3) and isolating the PL value leads to:

$$e^{-vPL} = \left(\frac{c - Fv}{c}\right) \Longrightarrow PL = \frac{1}{v}\ln\left[\frac{c/F}{c/F - v}\right], \tag{5.4}$$

which is valid as long as $c/F > v$, otherwise we (obviously) can't take logarithms of $(c - Fv)/c$. Notwithstanding these restrictions, this is precisely the expression for portfolio longevity (PL) as defined in Eq. (5.2). In fact, as noted earlier, solving for portfolio longevity is nothing more than using a business calculator to solve for N when the present value of the annuity is: F, period cash-flows are $-c$ and the interest rate per period is v. The only difference is that the above formulation is in continuous time, closed-form analytic, and offers a number of intuitive insights that aren't available from a simple business calculator.

While operating in continuous time, it's worth noting that the derivative of (deterministic) portfolio longevity PL, with respect to (*w.r.t.*) the variable c, can be expressed as:

$$\frac{\partial PL}{\partial c} = -\left(\frac{1}{c^2/F - v}\right), \tag{5.5}$$

which is negative so long as $c^2 > c > vF$. In words, as the consumption withdrawal rate c is increased the longevity of the portfolio declines—which is somewhat obvious—so long as the PL value itself isn't infinite. Otherwise the definition of the derivative doesn't make much sense. Either way, here is a numerical example. Start with the usual baseline wealth value of $F = \$100$, and assume a (rather large, but convenient) consumption withdrawal rate of $c = 10$. In that case, according to Eq. (5.5), the denominator is $(1 - v) \approx 1$ and the left-hand side is approximately -1. What does this mean? Well, at that point (when $c = 10$) increasing withdrawals by \$1 (only) reduces portfolio longevity by less than a year. Of course, the PL value itself isn't very high, either.

5.7 Initial Withdrawal Rate vs. Ongoing Withdrawal Rate

Many practitioners in the financial industry, and especially writers in the popular media, tend to confuse the computation and definition of the *initial* withdrawal rate, and how it differs from the *ongoing* withdrawal rate. The IWR and the ongoing WR (or simply WR) are very different numbers. To understand the difference between the two it helps to start with an equation for the evolution of wealth over time, a.k.a. the trajectory of your portfolio. While this (again) involves a touch of calculus, it's relatively easy to show that the change in the value of your retirement portfolio (during the retirement years) satisfies the following ordinary differential equation:

$$dF_t = (vF_t - c)dt, \quad F_0 = F, \tag{5.6}$$

where the portfolio value F_t is expressed in continuous time. In any small increment of time dt, the portfolio grows by $vF_t\,dt$, which is the investment rate of return, but declines by $c\,dt$, which is the consumption withdrawals rate. This process starts at $F_0 = F$ and continues (in theory) forever, or at least until the portfolio is exhausted or depleted. This ordinary differential equation (ODE), which is one of the very simple ones, can be solved explicitly as:

$$F_t = Fe^{vt} - c\left(\frac{e^{vt} - 1}{v}\right). \tag{5.7}$$

To be very clear, the equation is defined over the entire range of $t \geq 0$, and could potentially become negative, that is, $F_t < 0$. What that means is that you continue to consume and withdraw c per year, but you are now *borrowing* at a rate of v. Naturally, I will only use this function—for the purpose of projected wealth—in the region where $t \leq PL$. Either way, I can now code up the trajectory of the financial capital F, in **R**, and compute specific values of the portfolio at various points and times in retirement. Here is the script, which is the **R**-version of Eq. (5.7).

```
DTRJ<-function(t,v,c,F){F*exp(v*t)-c*(exp(v*t)-1)/v}
```

For simplicity (and to keep things neat) I have ignored the "problem" of what happens after $t = PL$, but could have "fixed" that by placing yet another `IF, ELSE` statement that forces the function value to zero, once the portfolio has been depleted. Here is a numerical example.

```
round(DTRJ(c(0,5,10,15,20,25,30,35),0.02,4,100), digits=2)
[1] 100.00  89.48  77.86  65.01  50.82  35.13  17.79  -1.38
```

The portfolio starts off at a value of \$100, earning a real inflation-adjusted 2% per year and subjected to consumption withdrawals at a rate of \$4 per year, all in continuous time. So, at time $t = 0$ the portfolio value is (obviously) $F_0 = \$100$. Then, 5 years later at time period $t = 5$, the portfolio value is $F_5 = \$89.48$, slowly declining until it hits a value of $F_{30} = \$17.79$ in year $t = 30$. Remember though, the consumption withdrawals continue at a rate of $c = \$4$ per year, regardless of the shrinking portfolio value. Finally, the portfolio "goes negative" somewhere between year 30 and 35. Where exactly? The following command gives the answer:

```
PL(0.02,4,100)
[1] 34.65736
```

The portfolio longevity is 34.65 years. The mathematical trajectory continues downward, which explains the (negative) value of $F_{35} = -1.38$ years, as far as the mathematics is concerned. Although, from an economic perspective the nest egg is empty. This then offers a good opportunity to distinguish between the initial consumption withdrawal rate (IWR) c/F, and the ongoing withdrawal rate (WR), c/F_j. In the above-noted case, when you have $F_{30} = \$17.79$ remaining in year $t = 30$, and are withdrawing a constant fixed $c = \$4$ per year, that's equivalent to $22.5\% = (4/17.79)$ of the value of the portfolio. That then is the ongoing *withdrawal rate*, whereas the initial withdrawal rate was a mere 4%. The following command displays similar results for an initial withdrawal rate of 3%, and the table summarizes the results (Table 5.1).

```
DTRJ(15,0.02,3,100)
[1] 82.50706
 3/DTRJ(15,0.02,3,100)
[1] 0.03636052
 DTRJ(25,0.02,3,100)
[1] 67.56394
 3/DTRJ(25,0.02,3,100)
[1] 0.04440239
```

Many retirees might be surprised to learn that implementing a 4% strategy, that is, withdrawing 4% of the initial portfolio value and adjusting those dollar values by inflation will eventually lead to a situation (in year 25) in which they are withdrawing as much as 11.38% of the (real) value of the portfolio. Most would rather adhere to withdrawing 4% of the contemporaneous value of the portfolio (not 4% of the original amount). But, to be clear, that strategy won't result in a constant real consumption withdrawal—nor was that the original *Bengen 4%* rule, for that matter. Indeed, there are many different ways to define 4%.

Table 5.1 Initial withdrawal rate (IWR) vs. Withdrawal rate (WR)

	IWR = \$3/\$100 = 3%		IWR = \$4/\$100 = 4%	
	In 15 years	In 25 years	In 15 years	In 25 years
Portfolio Value (F_j)	\$82.51	\$67.56	65.01	35.13
Withdrawal Rate (c/F_j)	3.63%	4.44%	6.15%	11.39%

Note: assuming real withdrawals of c per year, and $v = 2.0\%$

5.8 Life is Random: Simulating Portfolio Longevity

Everything I have presented to this point in the chapter (and in this textbook, for that matter) has assumed that the valuation (a.k.a. interest, investment) rate v is fixed, known and constant over the entire retirement horizon. Otherwise the expression for portfolio longevity, and in particular Eq. (5.2), make no sense. Although one might be tempted to use the equation with an expected value of $E[\tilde{v}]$, but even that assumption has its own problems (a.k.a. sequence-of-returns) which I'll delve into in Chap. 6.

The issue I now address is as follows. What happens (in the real world versus the textbook) if the portfolio return $\tilde{v}$ is random, a.k.a. stochastic? After all, does one really know what return their portfolio will earn in any given year, month, or even day? Even if the funds are invested or allocated to a cash bank account earning zero nominal returns, one is never certain about inflation and the real $\tilde{v}$ value. Think of it this way. If the capital F is allocated to a diversified portfolio—which is quite common for retirees—during the first year of retirement the portfolio might earn $\tilde{v}_1 = 6\%$ (real), while in the second year it might earn $\tilde{v}_2 = 1\%$ (real) but in the third year it might earn $\tilde{v}_3 = -5\%$ (real), which is a loss. Alas, the portfolio itself might decline—or what I previously labeled shrink—even without consumption withdrawals (c). In this (real life) situation the portfolio longevity is *stochastic* and critically depends on the future (unknown) portfolio investment returns. And yet, while it's impossible to pinpoint the exact date at which the portfolio will be exhausted, it's possible to analyze the statistical distribution of portfolio longevity via Monte Carlo simulation techniques. The **R** language is well-suited for this sort of task. Yes, there are other native languages that might be faster and more efficient, **R** gets the (pedagogical) job done. Now, within the retirement income "literature" generally speaking there are two approaches for simulating portfolio longevity and Monte Carlo simulations.

1. Collect a long enough series of historical financial returns (e.g. index funds, mutual funds, or ETFs) and then scramble or *bootstrap* them. Think of a big urn with numbers written on pieces of paper. You draw them one out at a time, then replace them in the urn and draw again.
2. Make some economically plausible but forward-looking *analytic* assumptions about the distribution of returns, calibrate the model to historical returns, and then generate forward-looking random numbers probabilistically using that distribution.

To the uninitiated ear (and eye) these two approaches might sound (and look) quite similar, but there are deep philosophical differences between them. For example, the first approach places an (undue) amount of emphasis on history without any regard for whether that particular outcome is likely to repeat itself in the future. For example, if fixed-income bonds returned 30% in one of the prior $N = 50$ years, then it's simulated with a frequency of $1/50$. In contrast, the second approach would likely discard the 30% as a possibility, or at least one with a $1/50$ chance, when current interest rates are at historical (and abnormal) lows. After all, how much lower can bond-yields drop when they are already at 0%? In contrast, the second approach would *postulate* some sort of formal model for the evolution of future returns, one that is motivated (and inspired) by historical returns, but not necessarily held hostage to those numbers. The additional advantage of the second approach is the ability to obtain closed-form analytic expressions for the statistical quantities of interest, at least when simplifying assumptions are made about the return generating process. Indeed, the debate in this matter—*how to properly design a retirement income simulation?*—can get heated at times, and I'll return to this matter later on. For now I'll use the analytic (i.e. second) methodology, and at the risk of enraging fans and advocates of the first approach, I will start with an (extremely) simplifying assumption: normally distributed continuously compounded returns.

5.9 Normal Numbers

Getting **R** to simulate or generate random numbers is extremely easy (although again, not necessarily as fast as other languages). Here is an example of how to generate $N = 25$ random numbers that are normally (i.e. gaussian, bell-curved, etc.) distributed with a mean value of 3% and a standard deviation of 20%. At this point in the narrative I won't delve on exactly how **R** generates these numbers, but instead refer the interested reader to advanced material on Monte Carlo simulations, such as the book cited as [9]. For now, type `rnorm(.)` in the command line using the following syntax.

```
v<-rnorm(25,0.03,0.20)
v
 [1]  0.001470724 -0.049536054  0.081968218  0.007595034
 [5] -0.004212151  0.374103915  0.014192556  0.034780243
 [9] -0.267013480  0.321024066  0.246950585 -0.141261295
[13] -0.114878223  0.168271758  0.101573676 -0.142078856
[17]  0.178961316 -0.151984803  0.254120678  0.082672077
[21]  0.124891360  0.159017064  0.342147262  0.481518068
[25]  0.141713450
summary(v)
     Min.   1st Qu.    Median      Mean   3rd Qu.      Max.
-0.267014 -0.004212  0.082672  0.089840  0.178961  0.481518
```

The first argument in the `rnorm(.)` function represents the number of random numbers you are generating, the second argument is the mean and the third argument is the standard deviation. I have also asked **R** to assign (store) those random numbers in the variable, which is now a vector with $N = 25$ numbers. I then asked **R** to display and summarize those 25 numbers, which range from the lowest value of $\tilde{v} = -26.70\%$ to the highest value of $\tilde{v} = 48.15\%$. Notice that although I generated (i.e. requested) a mean return of 3% in the second argument of the `rnorm(.)` function, the *sample* mean of the 25 numbers was a (much higher) 8.9%. Indeed, that is random life when you generate (only) 25 numbers and is a cautionary tale for those who might be tempted to use the last 25 years of financial history to glean lessons about the true expected return from "the market." Yes, the sample average was 8.9%, but the return generating process assumed an average of only 3%. To this point, the next script generates another $N = 25$ numbers, and as expected the results are different.

```
v<-rnorm(25,0.03,0.20)
v
 [1]  0.3233489  0.1647857  0.4212850 -0.0238082 -0.2189103
 [6] -0.0491405  0.0494793 -0.0176773 -0.0523655 -0.2854436
[11] -0.1294552 -0.1892473  0.0916617  0.0989590  0.3379296
[16] -0.0359028  0.2196778 -0.0658511 -0.2729773  0.1169073
[21] -0.0739073 -0.1369118 -0.1213295  0.2479007  0.3444865
summary(v)
    Min.  1st Qu.   Median     Mean  3rd Qu.     Max.
-0.28544 -0.12133 -0.02381  0.02974  0.16479  0.42129
```

In this case, although the maximum and minimum values aren't that far or different from the prior $N = 25$ numbers, the sample mean is now 2.97%, which is quite similar to the (theoretically) requested mean of 3.00%. In fact, with a requested standard deviation of 20%, these two numbers are remarkably close. And, while all of this comes down to elementary statistics and the nature of true randomness, a quick and short refresher can't hurt. While on the topic of statistical summaries, notice that although the mean was 2.9%, the median was negative! Half the numbers fell under −0.2.38%, and a total of 14 (out of 25) numbers were negative. You can blame the 20% standard deviation for that. Moving on, let's visualize and plot our random numbers.

5.10 A Histogram of Investment Returns

To generate a (very simple) histogram, enter this at the command line: `hist(v)`, and Fig. 5.4 will display the resulting histogram. I should warn you that your v will be different than mine, because every simulation run generates a different vector. Your `mean(v)` might be quite far from 3%, as I noted above. This (obviously) implies that the histogram you see in Fig. 5.4 might look quite different from mine, but it should have a similar structure—that is, not quite *normal* looking. But, with 25 data points what do you expect?

Now I'll do it again by generating $N = 50{,}000$ numbers, which will take a bit longer to create in **R**, and I'll add some additional syntax that makes a (prettier) picture. Once again, this script will simulate $N = 50{,}000$ random numbers that are normally distributed with a mean (average) value of 3% and standard deviation of 20%. In fact, I'll bypass the v altogether and place the `rnorm(.)` command inside the `hist(.)` command. I also ask **R** to plot the histogram with 75 bins (or breaks), as opposed to the default values. Finally, I force **R** to display the results over the

Source: Generated by Author in **R**

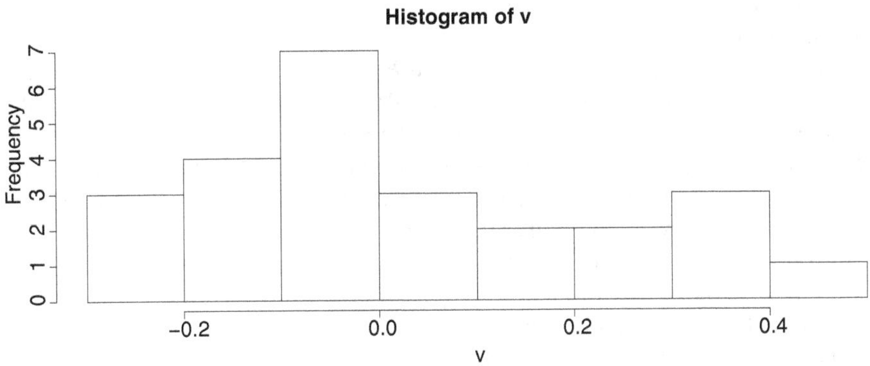

Fig. 5.4 Histogram of 25 simulated normal investment returns

Source: Generated by Author in **R**

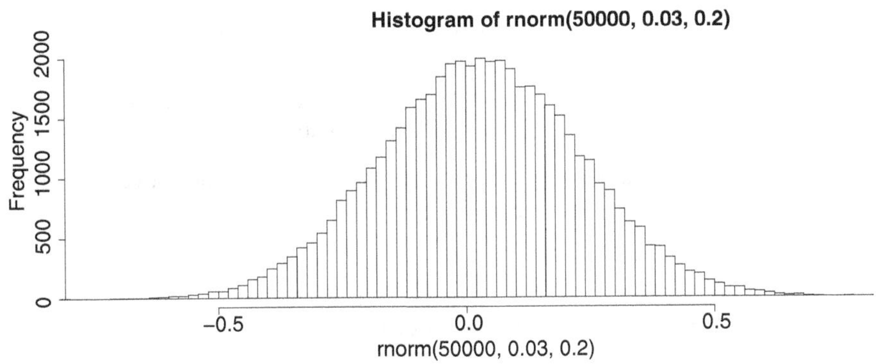

Fig. 5.5 Histogram of 5000 simulated investment returns

range of −75 to +75%. The end result is Fig. 5.5 which, you must admit, is prettier (and more normal-like) compared to Fig. 5.4.

```
hist(rnorm(50000,0.03,0.20),breaks=75,xlim=c(-0.75,0.75))
```

5.11 Simulation Algorithm for Portfolio Longevity

The next step is to use these random investment return elements to simulate portfolio longevity values recursively. The general idea can be expressed using the following algorithm.

1. Start with an initial portfolio value: $F_1 = F$, and a desired (fixed) consumption withdrawal rate: c.

2. Simulate one single (random, normal) continuously compounded investment return for the first year, denoted by: $\tilde{v}_1$.
3. The portfolio value at the end of the first year is then defined equal to: $F_2 = (F_1 e^{\tilde{v}_1}) - c$, where the subscript 2 on the F_2 reminds and alerts us to the fact it's the end of the first year of retirement withdrawals, and the very beginning of the second year, which is age $(R + 1)$ using the notation from prior chapters.
4. Generate a second investment return (uncorrelated with the first one) and continue the process for the second year, defining $F_3 = (F_2 e^{\tilde{v}_2}) - c$, thus moving the portfolio forward by another year, to age $(R + 2)$.
5. More generally, $F_j = (F_{j-1} e^{\tilde{v}_j}) - c$, which is defined recursively, only so long as the portfolio itself is still *alive*.
6. But, and this is the most critical part, if-and-when the value of $F_j <= 0$, the process is terminated and stops after j periods. So, for example, if this happens when $j = 2$, the portfolio longevity is declared to be 2 years, that is, it ran out (and was ruined) before the 2nd year. We exit the loop resulting in *one single value* of portfolio longevity: $PL(1) = j$. In the first simulation run, the portfolio was ruined in year j.
7. Then, start another (second) simulation run with $F_0 = F$ and we obviously get a different value of $PL(2)$, because the portfolio's longevity will be different, depending on the realized investment return. Generate as many $PL(i)$ values as you want (for example, N) and then do some statistics.

What follows is a (rather long) script in **R** that implements the above algorithm, or our first (serious) retirement income recipe.

5.12 The First Visit to Monte Carlo

Create a new function, which I highly recommend that you construct as a script and then compile, whose syntax is as follows:

```
PLSM<-function(F,c,nu,sigma,N){
  path<-matrix(nrow=N,ncol=100)
  PLV<-c()
  for (i in 1:N){
    return<-exp(rnorm(100,nu,sigma))
    path[i,1]<-F
    for (j in 2:100){
      path[i,j]<-path[i,j-1]*return[j]-c
      if (path[i,j]<=0) {break}
      }
    PLV[i]=j}
  PLV}
```

While the above script is a bit longer than (my internal, pedagogical limit of) ten lines of code, I have taken the liberty of writing the script and breaking down the command in a manner that will be easier to understand and absorb at first reading. The user-defined function `PLSM(.)` depends on the initial value of the portfolio F, and desired spending rate c, as well as the assumed mean and standard deviation ν, σ, and finally the total number of simulation runs N. Notice that this particular user-defined function begins by defining a new variable called `path`, which is set up as a `matrix` with `nrows=N`, that is, the number of separate `PL` values that will be generated, and `ncol=100`, which is completely arbitrary, reminiscent of the 999 value in the original `PL` function and can be modified if needed. That represents the number of years after which the retirement portfolio is assumed to have lasted *forever.* For any given trajectory, the algorithm stops, or exits, if it reaches a longevity of 100 years. There are various reasons this might happen. The consumption withdrawal rate c might be relatively low, or the realized (random) investment returns $(v_1, v_2, v_3 \ldots)$, etc., might have been quite high and the portfolio continued growing after retirement. Either way, if-and-when it reaches a $PL = 100$, it stops and begins another run. Enough with the explanations and hopefully the code itself is intuitive and consistent with the 7-step algorithm presented above. Now, let's generate some portfolio longevity numbers, using the function with the five input parameters, which will also help you understand the structure of the simulation in **R**. Here we go.

```
PLSM(100,7,0.03,0.20,50)
 [1]   35 37 14 16 16 19 14 12 100 10 21 31 12 16 13 13
[17] 15 13 27 29 88 16 11 17 62 36 25 100 17 15 12 100
[33] 39 11 19 12 16 19 100 14 100 15 27 24 48 17 13 12
[49] 14 17
```

The simulation generated a total of $N = 50$ portfolio longevity values. Each of those values is the result or output from a single portfolio trajectory, assuming an initial value of $F = \$100$ and an annual consumption withdrawal of $c = \$7$. In five (out of 50) scenarios the portfolio trajectory lasted for a full 100 years and the algorithm exited, reporting a value of `PL=100`. In the other 45 (that is 90% of) scenarios, the portfolio was ruined, exhausted, and depleted before reaching the 100 year milestone. Notice that the earliest (lowest) longevity value listed in these 50 values is 10 years. That means that the money (nest egg, portfolio) lasted for only a decade of retirement. Notice the many values of 11, 12, and 13. The lesson here is obvious, despite the minuscule ($N = 50$) sample. Withdrawing $c = 7$ when you expect to earn 3% isn't very sustainable, which doesn't require a simulation.

But what is interesting is the range of values. Notice how a full 10% of the time (again, only 50 runs) the portfolio lasted for 100 years. I'll return to the range (and the randomness) in the next chapter, when I discuss the (so-called) sequence-of-returns. Here is another run with a (more conservative, lower) withdrawal rate of $c = 5$, from a starting value of $F = \$100$. This time I generated a large sample of $N = 5000$ runs, together with some summary statistics.

```
sample1<-PLSM(100,5,0.03,0.20,5000)
summary(sample1)
   Min.  1st Qu.  Median    Mean   3rd Qu.    Max.
    7.0     20.0    30.0    44.6     66.0    100.0
```

Notice that the portfolio's expected (continuously compounded) return remains $E[v] = 3\%$ per year, with a standard deviation of $\sigma = 20\%$ per year. Why and how I selected these particular parameters are important questions, but I'll defer them to a later point in the chapter. But, to make a long story short, they are fitted to historical values of real (after-inflation, after-fee) investment returns of a *to-be-specified* diversified portfolio. Back to the results, as you can see, in this particular simulation run the smallest (minimum) value for the portfolio's longevity L was 7 years (ouch!) and the maximum value was (again) 100 years. Remember, once again, that the 100 is an artificial upper bound. A few other things to notice is that median portfolio longevity was 30 years. That is to say 50% of the $N = 5000$ simulations, or 2500 scenarios exhibited longevity of less than or equal to 30 years and 2500 scenarios exhibited longevity of more than 30 years. Yet another summary statistic worth noting is the 1st quartile which was 20 years. One quarter of the simulated results exhibited portfolio longevity of 20 years, or less. The 3rd quartile was 66 years. So, stated differently, 50% of the portfolio longevity outcomes fell between 20 and 66 years, which is a range of 46 years—and explains why retirement income planning and the appropriate consumption withdrawal rate is such a complex topic.

In contrast to the *median* value of 30 years, the *mean* value was higher and equal to 44.6 years. The additional 14.6 years of portfolio longevity compared to the *median* value might seem odd or confusing at first glance. But recall that the mean value is (highly) influenced by large outliers in a random sample. In this case the many scenarios with 100 years as the portfolio longevity skewed the calculation of the mean towards the higher number. In fact, technically speaking, the expected or mean longevity could be infinite. I'll return to this (rather subtle) topic later on.

```
length(sample1[sample1==100])/5000
[1] 0.2046
```

Finally, this particular simulation run experienced a total of 20.46% scenarios in which the longevity values were equal to 100. This was computed in the above-noted script by counting, via the `length(.)` command, the number of elements in the `sample1` vector that are exactly equal to 100, and then dividing by the $N = 5000$ simulation runs. Stated from the opposite (and more positive) perspective, in 79.54% of the generated scenarios the portfolio was exhausted or depleted prior to the 100-year mark. This (very important) number is occasionally referred to as the failure rate or ruin-probability of the retirement portfolio. Although, I should emphasize once again that this number depends quite critically on the initial withdrawal rate w as well as the portfolio investment parameters (ν, σ). To conclude this particular

Source: Generated by Author in **R**

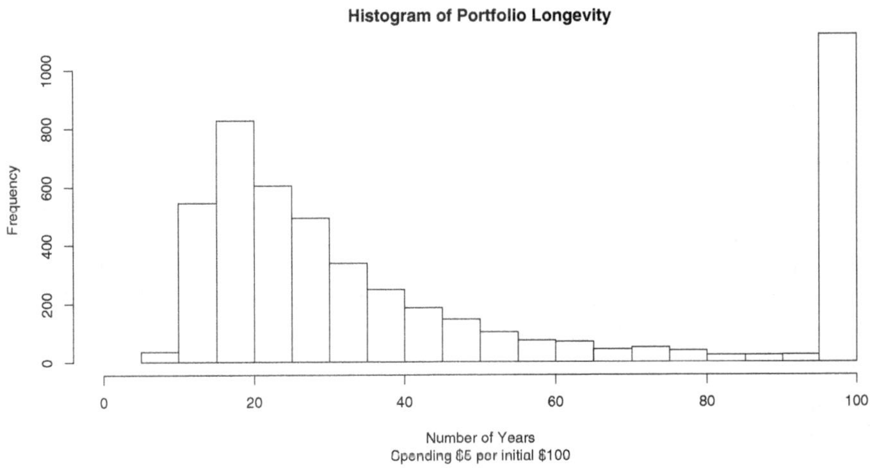

Fig. 5.6 Histogram of portfolio longevity: 5000 paths

analysis and discussion, I now generate a histogram for the *stochastic* portfolio longevity via the following script, and Fig. 5.6 displays the results.

```
hist(sample1,main="Histogram of Portfolio Longevity",
xlab="Number of Years",
sub="Spending $5 per initial $100",
xlim=c(0,100))
```

5.13 Retirement Income Insights

Notice the bi-modal nature of the histogram, that is, the double peak. There are a cluster of numbers in the range of 15–25 years of portfolio longevity, and then the probability density function (pdf) decays very rapidly towards zero. But then, it spikes again at the value of 100. Remember the 100 number was completely artificial because it is when I stopped the run and truncated the scenarios, but the basic intuitive point should be stated as follows. If you start retirement with $F = \$100$, plan to withdraw $c = \$5$ per year in inflation-adjusted terms, and invest the remaining funds in a portfolio that is expected to earn 3% per year with a standard deviation of $\sigma = 20\%$, then one of two things will occur. *You will either run out of money within four decades, or the money will last for a very long time, possible forever.* Notice that there are very few intermediate scenarios or results. The histogram itself is most definitely not uniform, or normally distributed. It would be a grave mistake to report the mean (or median) and assume that it conveys much information about what will happen. Stated even more bluntly, the bad things will happen to your retirement income portfolio in one of two very distinct times: soon or never.

```
L4<-PLSM(100,4,0.035,0.20,5000)
L5<-PLSM(100,5,0.035,0.20,5000)
L6<-PLSM(100,6,0.035,0.20,5000)
L7<-PLSM(100,7,0.035,0.20,5000)
```

To gauge and measure the effect of the withdrawal rate itself on the portfolio longevity, the above script generates similar results for consumption withdrawal rates of $c = 4, 5, 6, 7$, but with $v = 3.5\%$. I label them `L4, L5, L6, L7`, respectively. As you might expect, the greater the consumption withdrawal rate, the lower the portfolio longevity should be, and the following summary confirms that intuition.

```
summary(L4)
   Min. 1st Qu.  Median    Mean 3rd Qu.    Max.
   9.00   26.00   50.00   59.85  100.00  100.00
summary(L5)
   Min. 1st Qu.  Median    Mean 3rd Qu.    Max.
   7.00   21.00   34.00   50.03  100.00  100.00
summary(L6)
   Min. 1st Qu.  Median    Mean 3rd Qu.    Max.
   7.00   17.00   25.00   40.44   53.00  100.00
summary(L7)
   Min. 1st Qu.  Median    Mean 3rd Qu.    Max.
   7.00   15.00   20.00   32.34   34.00  100.00
```

As you can see, when you withdraw $c = \$7$ per original $F = \$100$ of capital, that is, an initial withdrawal rate of 7%, the median portfolio longevity is 20 years. At an IWR of 6% the median portfolio longevity is 25 years. At 5% it's 34 years, and at 4% it's 50 years. In fact, at a 4% IWR, the 3rd quartile value is 100 years, which means that at least 25% of the simulation runs lasted for 100 years.

Finally, the following short script counts the number of simulations—for each of the different consumption withdrawal rates—in which the portfolio longevity was less than 30 years. Three decades of retirement is a common benchmark in the retirement income literature.

```
length(L4[L4<=30])/5000
[1] 0.3214
length(L5[L5<=30])/5000
[1] 0.4562
length(L6[L6<=30])/5000
[1] 0.5962
length(L7[L7<=30])/5000
[1] 0.7118
```

According to my simulated results, which might be slightly different than your simulation results, a consumption withdrawal rate of \$7 per $F = \$100$ results in a *30-year failure* rate of 71%. But, when the IWR is reduced to a mere 4%, a.k.a. \$4 per $F = \$100$, the *30-year failure* rate drops to 32%. Now, to be very clear, I am completely agnostic on whether a 32% failure rate is acceptable, or whether 30 years is the proper horizon against which to measure results. Moreover, at this stage, I will **not** advocate a particular consumption withdrawal rate c as the proper, optimal or suitable number. I'll get to all of that in due time. But I should note that anyone would does pick a favorite number for c is predicating their results on an investment portfolio that is expected to earn a continuously compounded return of $\nu = E[v]$ and a standard deviation of $\sigma = SD[v]$. And, you should be able to ask anyone who advocates or recommends a particular c per F strategy, what those two forward-looking assumptions are. To be clear, in my case they were $E[v] = 3.5\%$ and $SD[v] = 20\%$.

5.14 Final Notes: The Infamous 4% Rule

At this point of the narrative (and chapter) you should be able to simulate a multitude of *portfolio longevity* values, based on the very simple script presented in this chapter. That script can easily be modified to account for different features and caveats. For example, if you so desired, you should be able to modify the simulation to assume that retirees modify their asset allocation (that is, the random properties of $\tilde{v}$) over time. In that case the expected return $E[\tilde{v}]$ might be lower, as well as the standard deviation $SD[\tilde{v}]$, as one progresses through the retirement years. Alternatively, you could modify the consumption withdrawal rate c, so that it too changes (perhaps declining) over time, so that every period has its own c_j value. In fact, you might engineer c_j so that it's a function of F_j, which is something I'll get back to in later chapters. Either way, the recursive nature of the 7-step algorithm (and the script itself) allows for c_j to differ from c_{j-1}, etc. I'll actually ask you to do some of these simple modifications as homework problems and assignments. But, these aren't only textbook matters. Most (rational) retirees are likely to modify their consumption spending as they wind their way through retirement, and especially as returns are realized from the portfolio. After all, if you happen to get unlucky and the first few years of (random) investment returns $\tilde{v}$ were unfavorable, you will probably reduce your spending. Vice versa if you get lucky in the first few years, and using our notation F_j continues to grow over time, there is a good chance you will (feel comfortable and) spend more. Nobody sets a plan in stone at the very start of retirement and leaves it in place forever. That's precisely how financial economists (v.s. many financial planners) think about consumption withdrawals. People adapt. And yet, despite the well-founded criticism, the constant consumption withdrawal-based portfolio longevity numbers I have simulated—and in particular the process of counting the fraction of those numbers that are less than 30 years—has taken on a disproportionate importance among practitioners in the financial planning industry.

Moreover, oddly enough, a consensus has emerged that $c = 4$ is the magic—yes, magic—number. For those who are interested in the history of *why* that number has become so important in the retirement income industry, I refer you to the references listed as [1–8] and more recently and the heavy-hitting [10]. The first few of these were among the first to generate these sorts of simulations, using an algorithm similar to the `PLSM` script. I'll have much more to say about this in the chapters to come. In the meantime, here are a few other related things to note.

- The main simulation script assumed that consumption withdrawals took place at the end of the year. In particular, the key syntax was: `path[i,j-1] *return[j]-c`. Technically, the prior period's portfolio value `path[i,j-1]` was multiplied by `return[j]`, first. Then, the consumption withdrawal `-c` was applied to create the new value `path[i,j]`. In theory, of course, there is no reason why this consumption withdrawal can't take place at the beginning, or even middle, of the year. So, to be clear, I have no preference on when you plan to withdraw money, and you can modify the simulation to account for any cash-flow schedule. Whatever you assume it will have a difference on the simulated results, especially when you consider the very large magnitude of these annual withdrawals. My point is, if you see (use) these sorts of results, make sure you know how they were generated.
- Partially as a result of the above concern—did you withdraw \$100,000 at the beginning or the end of the year?—I would (strongly) recommend modifying the simulation before it's used in *real life* so that consumption withdrawals are taken monthly instead of annually. This modification involves nothing more than creating a large matrix `path` that captures monthly (instead of annual) values. The `return` vector would be simulated with monthly returns, which means using `rnorm(1200,nu/12,sigma/sqrt(12))`, which is the mean and standard deviation for monthly returns. (Note the square root!) The loop for the portfolio trajectory would range over `(j in 2:1200)`. Needless to say, consumption would also be divided by 12 and the output (portfolio longevity) would be reported in months, not years. Of course, this creates a (much) larger simulation matrix, slows down the simulation, and "consumes" a lot of memory. This, of course, is why I focused for the most part on annual returns and consumption.
- Needless to say, although the simulation I described is somewhat slow and a bit clunky, there is nothing special about the normal distribution, as represented by the `rnorm` command in the main script. There is nothing that stops users from implementing a more complex (and realistic) distribution that is calibrated to higher moments. For example, one might include skewness (3rd moment) and kurtosis (4th moment) to account for the non-normality of continuously compounded returns. There is a long list of distributions available within **R** that can be used as possible candidates, some of which I'll get to in later chapters.
- Finally, for those historical purists who believe that one shouldn't make any forward-looking distributional assumptions regarding investment returns, the main simulation script can also be used. But, instead of invoking `rnorm(.)`,

you would use the `sample(.)` command. You can google the exact syntax, but in a nutshell it allows you to specify a historical matrix of investment returns and resample them in every simulation run. I'll use this command in some later chapters as well, but at this point I simply wanted to note that—for those who insist—it can easily be done in **R**.

Questions and Problems

5.1 Create a modified version of the main script (recipe) that generates monthly trajectories, assumes monthly consumption withdrawals of $c/12$, and (obviously) generates monthly investment returns. Call this function the `PLSM.12` to remind you that everything has been converted to monthly values. Now, assume $\nu = 3.5\%, \sigma = 20\%$, which remember are annual values, and compute portfolio longevity for $c = 4, 5, 6, 7$ using a total of $N = 10{,}000$ simulation runs. Compare the median portfolio longevity to the annual values (which appear in the chapter). Finally, compute the probability (or more accurately the frequency for which) portfolio longevity will be less than 30 years, that is, 360 months, for each of these four withdrawal rates. This is the (infamous) *30-year failure* rate. Compare with the results in the chapter and discuss the impact of withdrawal frequency on these probabilities.

5.2 Using your monthly `PLSM.12` simulation script, assume a starting portfolio value of $F = \$100$, and an annual consumption withdrawal rate of $c = 4$. Now, for the (annual) portfolio return values, assume $SD[\tilde{v}] = 15\%$, but for the expected return $E[\tilde{v}]$ assume a range of values (i.e. run five different simulations) ranging from $\nu = 1\%, 2\%, 3\%, 4\%, 5\%$. Then, compute the *30-year failure* rates under these five expected return assumptions and locate the value of $E[\tilde{v}]$ for which the *30-year failure* rate is closest to 90%.

5.3 Modify your basic (monthly) simulation `PLSM.12` so that if-and-when the portfolio value declines by more than three standard deviations in any given month, the consumption withdrawal rate is reduced from $c/12$ to $(0.75) \times c/12$. In words, if the stock market does (very) badly in a particular month, you spend less in that particular month. Note that you will have to implement this with a separate `(IF, ELSE)` branch within the simulation. Now, using the $\sigma = SD[\tilde{v}] = 15\%$, and the relevant $\nu = E[\tilde{v}]$ value from the above problem, please compute the *30-year failure* rate in this case. It should be lower. But by how much?

5.4 Simulate a vector of 100 historical (continuously compounded) inflation-adjusted investment returns, assuming they are normally distributed with a mean value of $\nu = 3\%$ and a standard deviation $\sigma = 15\%$. Export those numbers from **R** into a csv file using the `write.csv` command. (Google the exact syntax.) Then, import this dataset into **R**, and use those numbers with the `sample` command to bootstrap a Monte Carlo simulation for portfolio longevity.

5.5 Instead of the normal distribution with mean ν and standard deviation σ, generate portfolio longevity results, and in particular compute the *30-year failure* rate assuming a uniformly distributed (continuously compounded) return $\tilde{\upsilon}$, using the `runif(.)` command. Google the exact syntax, but assume monthly returns range from $\min[\tilde{\upsilon}] = -2\%$ to $\max[\tilde{\upsilon}] = 2\%$. Discuss and explain the results.

References

1. Bengen, W. P. (1994). Determining withdrawal rates using historical data. *Journal of Financial Planning, 7*(4), 171–180.
2. Cooley, P. L., Hubbard, C. M., & Walz, D. T. (1999). Sustainable withdrawal rates from your retirement portfolio. *Financial Counseling and Planning, 10*(1), 39–47.
3. Ho, K., Milevsky, M., & Robinson, C. (1994). How to avoid outliving your money. *Canadian Investment Review, 7*(3), 35–38.
4. Ho, K., Milevsky, M. A., & Robinson, C. (1994). Asset allocation, life expectancy and shortfall. *Financial Services Review, 3*(2), 109–126
5. Kotlikoff, L. (2008). Economics' approach to financial planning. *Journal of Financial Planning, 21*, 42.
6. Milevsky, M. A. (2006). *The calculus of retirement income: Financial models for life insurance and pension annuities*. Cambridge: Cambridge University Press.
7. Milevsky, M., Moore, K., & Young, V. (2006). Asset allocation and annuity-purchase strategies to minimize the probability of financial ruin. *Mathematical Finance, 16*(4), 647–671.
8. Milevsky, M. A., Ho, K., & Robinson, C. (1997). Asset allocation via the conditional first exit time or how to avoid outliving your money. *Review of Quantitative Finance and Accounting, 9*(1), 53–70.
9. Robert, C. P., & Casella, G. (2010). *Introducing Monte Carlo methods with R*. New York: Springer
10. Scott, J. S., Sharpe, W. F., & Watson, J. G. (2009). The 4% Rt what price? (October 7, 2009). *Journal Of Investment Management (JOIM)*, Third Quarter. Available at SSRN: https://ssrn.com/abstract=1484943

Chapter 6
Modeling the Risk of Sequence-of-Returns

This chapter is focused on a phenomenon known by professionals in the retirement income business, as the *sequence-of-returns* effect. Broadly speaking—and using terminology introduced in the previous chapter—this relates to the disproportionate sensitivity of *portfolio longevity* to realized investment returns in the early stages of retirement withdrawals. More specifically this chapter proposes some formal metrics that measure the extent and magnitude of the risk using statistical correlation and regression methodologies. The chapter concludes by analyzing some derivative-based strategies, using put and call options, that can be used to mitigate the risk of *sequence-of-returns*.

6.1 Functions Used and Defined

6.1.1 Sample of Native R Functions Used

- `lm(.)` generates a linear regression model and reports various statistical summaries including the regression coefficients that will be used to measure the *sequence-of-returns* effect.
- `glm(.)`, generalized linear model used for a logistic regression of retirement income success probabilities on various investment factors.

M. A. Milevsky, *Retirement Income Recipes in R*, Use R!,
https://doi.org/10.1007/978-3-030-51434-1_6

6.1.2 User-Defined R Functions

- PLSM.SR(F,c,nu,sigma,N) simulates and retains portfolio investment returns as well as the portfolio longevity values associated with those returns. This function is a generalized version of the PLSM function introduced in Chap. 5.

6.2 Modifying the Portfolio Longevity Simulation

In the prior chapter I created a basic and rudimentary simulation model to generate N samples of portfolio longevity (PL) values, by randomizing investment returns. In this chapter I dig deeper into the factors that influence the PL values by focusing on the behavior of the random returns during specific periods. To do this I must modify the simulation so that it keeps track and stores the investment return values in a manner that can easily be retrieved and used. I have created a modified version of PLSM, which I'll label PLSM.SR, to remind readers that it's used for the purposes of analyzing the SoR effect, which I will define in a moment. Here is the script.

```
PLSM.SR<-function(F,c,nu,sigma,N){
  path<-matrix(nrow=N,ncol=100)
  PLM<-matrix(nrow=N,ncol=4)
  for (i in 1:N){
    return<-exp(rnorm(100,nu,sigma))
    PLM[i,1]<-prod(return[1:10])^(1/10)-1
    PLM[i,2]<-prod(return[11:20])^(1/10)-1
    PLM[i,3]<-prod(return[21:30])^(1/10)-1
    path[i,1]<-F
    for (j in 2:100){
      path[i,j]<-path[i,j-1]*return[j]-c
      if (path[i,j]<=0) {break}
    }
    PLM[i,4]=j}
  PLM}
```

The structure and syntax should be relatively familiar, given the similarity to PLSM from Chap. 5. The simulation begins by defining and creating N path trajectories, which last for (at most) 100 years. Then, the script creates a matrix PLM with (only) four columns and N rows. The first three of those columns will be used to store information about the investment returns during the simulation process. In particular, each one of the three columns will "remember" the annualized investment return in a given decade. The final column will store the actual portfolio longevity value for that particular investment trajectory. At the very end of this process, the output from the function PLSM.SR is a matrix of values PLM instead of a vector of portfolio longevity numbers PLV. To be clear, I am simulating the familiar PL numbers, but in addition I am keeping track of the investment returns during the first three decades, leading to the portfolio longevity number. Why? Because I want to investigate how PLM[,1], PLM[,2], and PLM[,3], the first three columns in the matrix, affect the PL value. As I have warned many times before, this script might not be the fastest or the most elegant way to code-up the simulation. (I can hear the **R**-gods howling.) But, remember that at this point in the narrative I'm emphasizing pedagogical simplicity and algorithmic intuition over rapid execution and efficiency. This is especially important to those who are new to coding in **R**.

6.3 A First Look at Sequence-of-Returns (SoR)

Once you have coded-up (or modified) and compiled the PLSM.SR script, please run the function with parameter values $F = 100$, $c = 5$, $\nu = 0.025$ (remember, that is a real expected continuously compounded investment return of 2.5% per year) and volatility of $\sigma = 0.15$, also per year. Similarly to the PL or PLSM function, the results scale in (c/F), so what really matters is the initial withdrawal rate. Also, these particular numbers are arbitrary and generated solely for the purpose of playing with the function. Note that I only generated $N = 10$ paths (a.k.a. random portfolio trajectories), and I asked **R** to round the results to three digits. Once again, being a simulation, you will see different results when generating your own paths.

```
round(PLSM.SR(100,5,0.025,0.15,10),digits=3)
        [,1]   [,2]   [,3] [,4]
 [1,] -0.015  0.000  0.019   20
 [2,] -0.036  0.020 -0.025   19
 [3,]  0.060 -0.037  0.077   23
 [4,] -0.008  0.024 -0.084   22
 [5,]  0.099  0.002  0.042  100
 [6,]  0.026 -0.045  0.007   21
 [7,]  0.068 -0.044 -0.022   24
 [8,]  0.012  0.010  0.007   23
 [9,] -0.024  0.084  0.047   23
[10,]  0.026  0.081  0.051   29
```

In the first row of the (new) PLM matrix, you will see PLM[1,1]=-0.015, then PLM[1,2]=-0.000, then PLM[1,3]=0.019 and finally PLM[1,4]=20. Here is how to interpret the numbers. In the first (of 10) simulation trajectories, the random investment return during the *first* decade was a compound annual -1.5%. Notice the minus sign. Negativity should not be surprising given the large 1-year standard deviation of $\sigma = 0.18$, which implies an annualized standard deviation of $0.15/\sqrt{10} = 4.74\%$. So, under an expected (continuously compounded) annualized return of 2.5% and standard deviation of 4.74%, negative returns over the decade are well within the realm of possibility. From a historical perspective, during the

10-year period from January 1st, 2000 to December 31st, 2009, the real value of the SP500 index (with dividends re-invested) declined by 27%. This is an annualized (−3.2%), after inflation. (Another example was March 2020.) Nevertheless, if you don't agree or believe that forward-looking real returns can be negative over a full decade, then use a higher ν and/or lower σ value. (That's precisely the beauty of a book of recipes versus a book of tables. You can modify ingredients and cook your own books!) The point here isn't to argue over whether compound annual returns can be negative over a decade. Rather, what should be indisputable is that **if** returns are lousy in the first decade, and then flat in the second decade and then a bit less than average (at 1.9%) in the third decade, portfolio longevity value is a mere `PL=20` years. The longevity is less than typical life expectancy at retirement. Of course, it isn't catastrophic either.

My general point is as follows. Take a careful look at the remaining 9 values in the matrix, and in particular the first column of the matrix, representing investment returns in the first decade of retirement consumption withdrawals. Notice that when the returns in the first decade are less than anticipated, the portfolio longevity values tend to be lower. And, when the investment returns are better than expected—in the first decade—the longevity values are higher as well. In particular, notice (in my simulation run, which will be different from your results) that when the first decade's compound annual return was 9.9% (the highest number within the first column, which appears in row number 5) the portfolio longevity value was a full century. In contrast, the highest number in the second column—representing the second decade—was 8.4% (in row number 9), but the resulting portfolio longevity value was a mere 23 years. Why was it better to "win the lottery" so to speak, in the first versus the second decade? Answer: Because it's a mathematical fact that *portfolio longevity is most sensitive to investment returns over the first few years of consumption withdrawals.* This is the essence of the so-called *sequence-of-returns* effect which will be demonstrated over (and over) again in this chapter. And, when you think about it long enough it's almost tautological. Realized investment returns during the withdrawal period will obviously affect portfolio longevity. However, the exact order or sequence in which they occur has a larger impact than you might have expected. Here is an abstract way to think about it. Look at the following two expressions, where X and Y represent investment returns in the first and second year, respectively.

$$\texttt{Sequence XY} \rightarrow (F(1+X)-c)(1+Y)-c$$

$$\texttt{Sequence YX} \rightarrow (F(1+Y)-c)(1+X)-c$$

These two expressions represent your wealth at the end of the second year, where F is the initial wealth at retirement, and c is the first year consumption spending. In the first sequence (row) you earned X and then you earned Y. In the second sequence (row) it was reversed. Needless to say, the mathematical product $XY = YX$. But, now assume that $X > Y$, for example $X = 0.07$ and $Y = 0.02$, per year. Now, which ordering would you prefer? It's easy to show that when $X > Y$, the `sequence XY` will be preferred to `sequence YX`. One can solve analytically that the value of the portfolio under the first sequence XY is $c(X - Y)$ greater than the value of the portfolio under the second sequence YX, which is positive given $X > Y$. The next few sections will dig deeper into this affect and will present a standardized way of measuring this phenomenon.

6.4 Correlations as a Measure of SoR Risk

Obviously, $N = 10$ isn't a large enough sample to conclude anything meaningful, so the next step is to generate a (much) larger sample of investment returns and portfolio longevity values, store them in **R**, and conduct some statistical tests. The following script generates $N = 50{,}000$ paths. I'll (arbitrarily) select a (c/F) initial withdrawal rate of 5%, and real continuously compounded investment returns with a mean of $\nu = 2.5\%$ and standard deviation of $\sigma = 15\%$. I can't promise identical values, but to obtain results that are (reasonably) similar to mine, run the following script.

```
sample2<-PLSM.SR(100,5,0.025,0.15,50000)
summary(sample2)
       V1                 V2                 V3                 V4
Min.   :-0.16   Min.   :-0.16   Min.   :-0.14   Min.   :  8.0
1st Qu.:-0.00   1st Qu.:-0.00   1st Qu.:-0.00   1st Qu.: 21.0
Median : 0.02   Median : 0.02   Median : 0.02   Median : 28.0
Mean   : 0.02   Mean   : 0.02   Mean   : 0.02   Mean   : 39.4
3rd Qu.: 0.05   3rd Qu.: 0.05   3rd Qu.: 0.05   3rd Qu.: 46.0
Max.   : 0.24   Max.   : 0.22   Max.   : 0.24   Max.   :100.0
```

The data stored in sample2 is organized in four columns, summarized above. I have truncated some of the digits so that they all fit in the box. The first three columns represent the 10-year **Annualized Real Investment Growth**, which I'll abbreviate by 10-year ARIG. Mathematically this can be defined for any number of years T, via the simple expression:

$$\texttt{T-year ARIG} = \left(\frac{Z_T}{Z_0}\right)^{1/T} - 1, \tag{6.1}$$

where Z_0 is the initial and Z_T is the final investment value. Notice how the numbers displayed in the first column range from approximately -16% (a massive loss) to $+24\%$ (a massive gain). Remember, per Eq. (6.1), that these are annualized values, so (-16%) per annum represents a real decline of $1 - (1 - 0.16)^{10} = 82.5\%$ in the value of the investment portfolio, before any consumption withdrawals are taken into account. This drop might seem extreme to many (bullish) readers. But again, remember that I generated $N = 50{,}000$ portfolio longevity values, and it's not unreasonable to believe that one of those fifty thousand scenarios might be catastrophic. On the flip side, the 10-year ARIG value of $(+24\%)$ translates into a $(1 + 0.24)^{10} = 8.6$ growth multiple. The investment portfolio growth (that is: Z_{10}/Z_0) increases by 860%, which appears only slightly less unlikely. I should remind readers (again) that investment growth and portfolio growth are two different quantities. The former (Z_T) focuses exclusively on the investments portion and the latter (F_T) accounts for consumption withdrawals. Remember, you might experience a positive 10-year ARIG number and still deplete the portfolio if the consumption withdrawals were too large. To this point, notice the range of portfolio longevity values displayed in column four of the box. They range from a minimum of `PL=8` years to maximum of `PL=100` years. That's quite a bit of variation, and yet all of these realizations were under the same investment return (ν, σ) generating process. Welcome to Monte Carlo. Another statistical point worth noting is that the mean (as well as the median) 10-year ARIG value of 2% is lower than the (mean) parameter $\nu = 2.5\%$ used to generate those returns.

Some readers might be wondering why the sample "average" is not equal the theoretical "average." Shouldn't $N = 50{,}000$ simulation paths be enough to get them very close to each other? Why the 0.5% (a.k.a. 50 basis point) gap? Well, the answer is that this is a bit of an apples-to-oranges comparison. The reason for the discrepancy is (rather subtle and) due to the fact $\ln[E[e^{\tilde{v}}]] \neq E[\tilde{v}]$. This discrepancy also relates to the difference between geometric average returns versus arithmetic average returns, which I'll return to (no pun intended) later on in the concluding remarks. For now I'll move on to implementation.

```
DR1<-sample2[,1]; DR2<-sample2[,2]
DR3<-sample2[,3]; PoLo<-sample2[,4]
```

The above script creates individual vectors for the columns in the `sample2` matrix so that they are easier to work with and manipulate. On a side note, in **R** I don't actually have to enter every command on a separate line. I can type them all with a separating semicolon. As a reminder, what the above command does is store the first decade's annualized ARIG in the variable called `DR1`, the second decade's ARIG in `DR2`, the third decade in `DR3`, and the portfolio longevity values corresponding to that particular row's trajectory of returns, in the variable `PoLo`. Now I'll examine correlations.

```
 cor(DR1,DR2)
[1] -0.0001692213
 cor(DR1,DR3)
[1] 0.00194036
```

The correlation between any decade's ARIG return is effectively zero, which shouldn't come as a surprise. After all, this is precisely how they were simulated, as independent and identically distributed (i.i.d.) random variables. The more interesting calculation is to examine correlations between ARIG values and portfolio longevity.

```
 cor(DR1,PoLo)
[1] 0.662725
```

```
 cor(DR2,PoLo)
[1] 0.4230941
 cor(DR3,PoLo)
[1] 0.2186179
```

What can be learned from these numbers? Well, the correlation between the first decade's ARIG and portfolio longevity is (+66%). If the underlying investments did well relatively speaking (think: Z_{10}/Z_0), then realized portfolio longevity tended to be higher than the average `mean(PoLo)=39.4` years. (Remember: I assumed a rather high $\nu = 2.5\%$) But, if the investments performed poorly during the first decade and the ARIG values were lower than average, so were the portfolio longevity values. Once again, this should come as no surprise. But, when the correlation is estimated for the 3rd decade, via the `cor(DR3,PoLo)` command, the output is a lower (+21.8%). The `PoLo` outputs simply aren't as sensitive to investment returns in the third decade. Now, to be very clear, these correlations depend—and were affected by—a number of structural simulation assumptions. First, recall the arbitrary maximum value of `PL=100`, which will impact the correlation coefficients. If I (for example) were to modify the simulation so that portfolio longevity can continue increasing (forever, in theory) those very large values would skew the results. Likewise, the normality assumption `rnorm(.)` and the independence assumption will also impact the statistical correlations. I'll get back to all these "issues" later. Just as importantly, the measured correlations depend on the assumed consumption spending rates, that is the initial withdrawal rate (c/F). For example, look carefully at what happens when I generate another simulation `sample3` in which the initial withdrawal rate is reduced to (only) 2%? In particular, examine the correlations.

```
 sample3<-PLSM.SR(100,2,0.025,0.15,50000)
 DR1<-sample3[,1]; DR2<-sample3[,2]
 DR3<-sample3[,3]; PoLo<-sample3[,4]
 cor(DR1,PoLo)
[1] 0.5066356
 cor(DR2,PoLo)
[1] 0.4377036
 cor(DR3,PoLo)
[1] 0.3143461
```

Notice what happens when consumption spending is reduced (in `sample2`) from $c = \$5$ to $c = \$2$ in `sample3`, per $F = \$100$. First of all, the third decade's correlation coefficient increases to (+31%) from (+21%). On average the portfolio is surviving longer, so the third decade's investment return takes on greater importance. Just as interestingly, the sensitivity to the first decade's return actually declines (as measured by correlation) from (+66%) to approximately (+50%). Yes, the correlation values are all still quite positive and declining by the decade. But, if you are planning on spending less (2 vs. 5) during the retirement income phase, the importance of the first decade's return is lower. Why? Well, as a thought experiment imagine what would happen if the consumption spending c was reduced to (near) zero. To begin with, the portfolio longevity values would all be at their maximum of `PoLo=100`. And secondly, the order of the sequence-of-returns would be almost irrelevant. This is also a good place to remind readers that correlation is a linear measure of association, and if most of the `PoLo` values are 100, regardless of the investment returns, then correlation itself isn't very meaningful either. The consumption spending c amplifies the importance of the sequence-of-returns for the following reason: The difference between $(F(1 + X) - c)(1 + Y) - c$ and $(F(1 + Y) - c)(1 + X) - c$ is exactly $c(X - Y)$. You can think about it like this: assuming you consumed nothing at the end of the first year, then the future value right before the end of the second year (before your next consumption) would be $F(1 + X)(1 + Y)$, however because you consumed c at the end of the first year, you must subtract c times the return of the second year from that future value. If the return in the second year is the smaller value Y, then you are subtracting cY. This is a better future value than if you were subtracting cX. You might have to think about this for a while, but it's as close to a proof as you will get.

Now, as a reminder, the reason I use the phrase *sequence-of-returns* over and over again is (because it's widely used by the industry and) precisely because the same exact return experienced in different decades will lead to different portfolio longevity outcomes. Or, to put it even more bluntly, think again of the following question. When would you rather experience a (lucky) 7% ARIG value? Whould it be in the first decade, the second decade or the third decade of retirement consumption spending. I trust you see (by now) that the answer is: *I want the best one in decade one.*

In contrast, a buy-and-hold investor who starts with F and (never withdraws or adds another dollar) wouldn't care whether he or she got the sequence $(1 + 0.07)^{10}(1 + 0.02)^{10}$ or $(1 + 0.02)^{10}(1 + 0.07)^{10}$. This echoes and reenforces the earlier thought experiment involving X and Y. The investment return order has no impact when you buy and hold, or at least in the classical view where investors and consumers don't panic after a few bad years.

I'll run yet another trajectory simulation, this time with a higher consumption spending of $c = 8$, and store the values in `sample4`. The expected continuously compounded return ν and the standard deviation σ remain the same as before. Notice how the correlation between longevity and the first decade is now 64%, which is lower than the correlation we obtained when consumption spending was a mere $c = 5$. This might be puzzling at first. Why isn't the correlation getting *higher* as we increase the initial withdrawal rate? After all, when the initial withdrawal rate was reduced the correlation declined. Why not the opposite here?

```
 sample4<-PLSM.SR(100,8,0.025,0.15,50000)
 DR1<-sample4[,1]; DR2<-sample4[,2]
 DR3<-sample4[,3]; PoLo<-sample4[,4]
 cor(DR1,PoLo)
[1] 0.6426012
 cor(DR2,PoLo)
```

```
[1] 0.2697221
 cor(DR3,PoLo)
[1] 0.09365656
```

The answer to this is quite subtle and gets to the heart of the portfolio longevity metric and whether or not your investment portfolio (and the nature of your asset allocation) matters. Remember, if your initial withdrawal rate is (very) high, then you are destined to have a portfolio longevity value that is (very) low, regardless of anything else. Think back to the "cone" figures in the prior Chap. 5. The investment return on your portfolio, or what I have called the ARIG values, don't have as great an influence when you are (planning on) spending too much. And, to further this point, look at the correlation between the third decade's ARIG values and the portfolio longevity. At 9%, they are mildly positive at best. To put it bluntly, again, your portfolio isn't likely to "survive" to the third decade if you are spending (too) much, so whatever happens (in the stock market) during that 3rd decade won't have much of a difference. The key takeaway then—in my mind—is the declining value of the correlation by decade, which is regardless of the consumption spending rate c.

Finally, here is one last simulation run with a (ridiculously) high consumption spending rate of $c = 15$, which is an initial withdrawal rate of $(c/F) = 15\%$. Nobody in their right mind would advocate or promote such a withdrawal rate, especially in a portfolio with an expected return of $\nu = 2.5\%$ and risk of $\sigma = 15\%$.

```
 sample5<-PLSM.SR(100,15,0.025,0.15,50000)
 DR1<-sample5[,1]; DR2<-sample5[,2]
 DR3<-sample5[,3]; PoLo<-sample5[,4]
 median(PoLo)
[1] 9
 mean(PoLo)
[1] 9.4378
 cor(DR1,PoLo)
[1] 0.6662201
 cor(DR2,PoLo)
[1] 0.0453003
 cor(DR3,PoLo)
[1] 0.008052151
```

Look carefully at the results. In this box I have also added median and mean `PoLo` values so that you can see how (on average) the longevity of this portfolio is a mere 10 years. The correlation between the first decade's return (i.e. the ARIG values) and portfolio longevity is substantial and positive (+66.6%). Earning positive returns will indeed make the money last longer. But, the second and third decade—although they are declining—will have very little impact on the portfolio's longevity. The sensitivity is basically zero. Why? The portfolio won't survive to those years.

6.5 Visualizing the Correlations

To summarize the discussion of investment returns vs. portfolio longevity correlations, and how they decay over time, here are some visuals (using `plot(DR,PoLo)`). Note that I am using the results from the simulation with consumption spending of $c = \$5$, stored in the `sample2` dataset. Figure 6.1 illustrates the relationship between the first decade's ARIG and portfolio longevity. Figure 6.2 illustrates the relationship for the second decade. And, Fig. 6.3 is for the third decade. The final Fig. 6.4 shows the relationship between portfolio longevity and investment returns during the first decade (blue dots) and the third decade (red rings) on the same chart. For those readers who want to replicate (and cook) this fourth figure using their own parameters and values, I used the following script to generate the results.

```
plot(c(-0.15,0.25),c(5,75),type="n",
xlab="Investment Return During the Decade",
ylab ="Portfolio Longevity")
     for  (i  in  1:5000){
       points(DR1[i],PoLo[i],col="blue",pch=20)
       points(DR3[i],PoLo[i],col="red",pch=21)}
```

In the first Fig. 6.1, there is a clear positive relationship between the x-axis value (returns) and the y-axis (longevity) value. On the left side of zero, the y-axis values are reduced as well. Intuitively, if the compound annual return from the portfolio was a loss of 10% (per year), then portfolio longevity will be well-under 20 years. But, if the x-axis value is to the right, the portfolio longevity value is higher. In fact, there is a large cluster of `PL=100` values at the very top, but they only begin at x-axis values that are near and above zero. It's quite unlikely the portfolio will

Source: Generated by Author in **R**

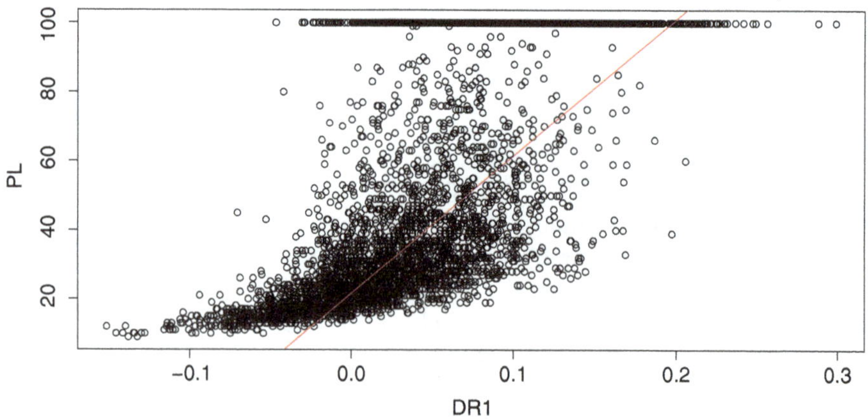

Fig. 6.1 PoLo vs. annualized investment growth in first decade

Source: Generated by Author in **R**

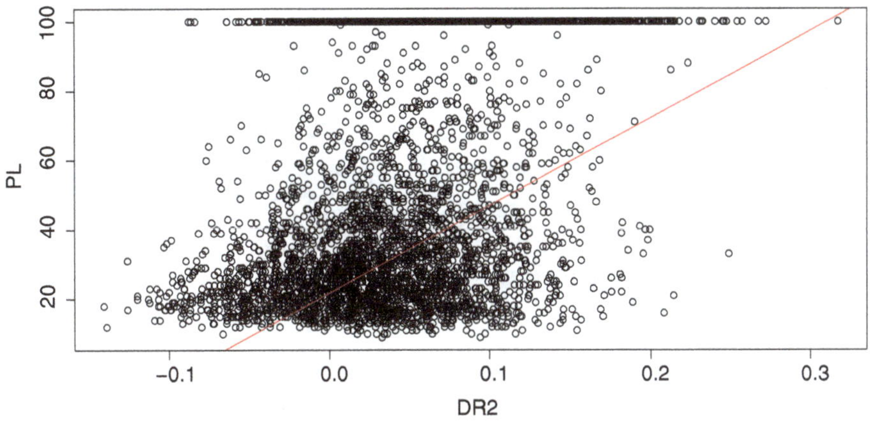

Fig. 6.2 PoLo vs. annualized investment growth in second decade

Source: Generated by Author in **R**

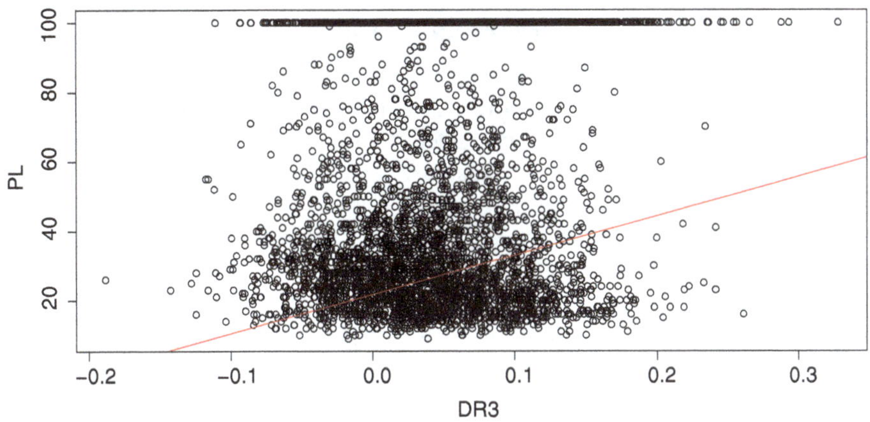

Fig. 6.3 PoLo vs. annualized investment growth in third decade

last for 100 years if the investment return in the first decade was negative. The red line (for those who can see this in color) displays the best-fitting linear relationship between returns and longevity, as per the regression specification described in the next section. In contrast, when you look at Figs. 6.2 and 6.3, the pattern between investment returns and portfolio longevity starts to deteriorate. Yes, larger values on the x-axis are associated with larger values on the y-axis, but the pattern isn't as convincing as it was in Fig. 6.1, for the first decade.

Source: Generated by Author in **R**

Fig. 6.4 Portfolio longevity in years vs. first decade returns (Blue) and third decade returns (Red)

6.6 A (Simple) Linear Regression Model

In this section I'll present another way of examining or quantifying the *sequence-of-returns* effect on portfolio longevity, namely via a (simple) linear regression model applied to a new (clean) simulation dataset stored in `sample6`. The parameters I'll use to generate those data points are $(c/F) = 5\%$, and the familiar $\nu = 2.5\%$ and $\sigma = 15\%$ for the portfolio investment returns. More importantly, I will define the portfolio longevity vector (fourth column in `sample6`) as the dependent variable, and regress it on the three vectors representing the (independent) returns in the three decades. Needless to say I'm assuming here that you have run a regression analysis before and this isn't your "first" rodeo. If you are new to this—or it has been a while—I would urge you to consult a basic textbook on statistics. In brief, think of the $N = 50{,}000$ portfolio longevity data points, in the **R** simulation, as empirical observations from some *black box*, together with the corresponding ARIG values earned during the first three decades.

$$Y_j = \alpha_0 + \alpha_A A_j + \alpha_B B_j + \alpha_C C_j + \epsilon_j \tag{6.2}$$

As you can see from the above equation, the regression approach to *sequence-of-returns* models the portfolio longevity (dependent variable, Y_j) as a linear function of the three ARIG values, A, B, C, plus the usual statistical noise, ϵ_j. Now, to some readers the linear *assumption* might seem odd, given that the relationship between the entire vector of investment returns and portfolio longevity is *by definition* non-linear. In fact, pure mathematicians might wonder why I bother estimating a regression at all when the mapping from the investment return (path) trajectory into the portfolio longevity value is deterministic. It isn't a *black box*. But, in my defense, the point here isn't really to forecast or predict portfolio longevity for any triplet A, B, C. Rather, the objective here is to develop an empirical measure of the *sequence-of-returns* effect and the relative sensitivity of the various decades, via the parameters $\alpha_A, \alpha_B, \alpha_C$. Either way, regardless of your views on the suitability of this regression-based approach, at this point I'll jump right into the statistical results via the following short script.

```
sample6<-PLSM.SR(100,5,0.025,0.15,50000)
DR1<-sample6[,1]; DR2<-sample6[,2];
DR3<-sample6[,3]; PoLo<-sample6[,4]
fit<-lm(PoLo~DR1+DR2+DR3)
summary(fit)
```

The built-in **R** function `lm(.)`, which I have not used before, has a number of additional arguments and specifications that can be added (and should be googled), but at this stage I'll keep it simple. The main command in the above box places the results of the linear regression into a variable called `fit` and the second command displays a `summary` of those results in **R**. I'll remind you of the usual proviso that your randomized results will not be identical to mine, and an abbreviated version of your output should look (something like) this:

```
Call:
lm(formula = PoLo ~ DR1 + DR2 + DR3)

Residuals:
    Min      1Q  Median      3Q     Max
-45.839 -10.775  -3.246   7.485  63.250
Coefficients:
             Estimate Std. Error t value Pr(>|t|)
(Intercept)  20.38136    0.09676  210.65   <2e-16 ***
DR1         368.06129    1.44875  254.05   <2e-16 ***
DR2         232.11449    1.44308  160.85   <2e-16 ***
DR3         119.67219    1.44866   82.61   <2e-16 ***
---
Residual standard error: 15.71 on 49996 degrees of freedom
Multiple R-squared:  0.6609, Adjusted R-squared:  0.6609
F-statistic: 3.248e+04 on 3 and 49996 DF,  p-value: < 2.2e-16
```

Please pause to ensure you (refresh your statistics memory and) understand what every one of these regression (output) metrics represent. First, focus on the estimated coefficients on `DR1`, `DR2`, `DR3`, and the intercept `20.38`. They are the $\alpha_A, \alpha_B, \alpha_C$ and α_0, respectively, in Eq. (6.2). What do they mean? Well, if the 10-year ARIG values in all three decades are zero, the linear model predicts the portfolio longevity will be approximately 20.4 years. On a side note, that's not a bad estimate considering that $(F/c) = 20$, which is the basic formula for portfolio longevity under zero returns. Moving on to the coefficients themselves, here is how to interpret them. If the value of `DR1` increases by 0.01, that is 1% point, then portfolio longevity is (predicted to be) *extended* by $(368)(0.01) = 3.68$ years. However, in contrast to the first decade, if the value of `DR3` increases by the same 0.01, then portfolio longevity is (predicted to be) *extended* by only $(120)(0.01) = 1.20$ years. The additional 1% point increase in 10-year annualized real investment growth (ARIG) rates is much more valuable and impactful when it takes place in the first rather than the third decade. The ratio of the coefficients α_A/α_C, that is between the first and third decade is (coincidentally) 3-to-1, obtained via the syntax:

```
 as.numeric(fit$coefficients[2]/fit$coefficients[4])
[1] 3.075579
```

The script uses the `coefficient` command and extracts the 2nd and 4th regression coefficient, divides them, and expresses the result as numeric. If you are wondering, the 1st regression coefficient is the intercept α_0.

```
 fit$coefficients[1]
(Intercept)
   20.38136
```

For the record, the t-statistic values on each one of these four coefficients are in the hundreds, which is (highly) statistically significant. That's what the three stars (in the output above) represent. Likewise, the R^2 value is a measure of the goodness of fit of the regression. The 66.3% represents the proportion of the variance of the portfolio longevity variable that's explained by the three independent variables (i.e. the individual decade investment returns). Now, at this point you might be wondering, if (only) 66% of the variation in portfolio longevity is explained by the investment returns, what explains the other 33%? After all, nothing else is random (at this point.) The answer of course is that the dependent variables are the 10-year annualized investment returns, and not the year-by-year investment returns. Clearly, earning 3% compounded over 10-years can be achieved along many different investment paths. But some of those paths are more favorable than others. The individual returns (a.k.a. non-linear path dependency) during the 10-year period aren't captured in the linear regression, which explains the unexplained 33%. I hope this is clear.

6.7 Regression Diagnostics

Before I move on to more advanced (logistic) regression approaches to measuring the *sequence-of-returns* effect in the next section, I should remind you that the relationship between portfolio longevity and investment returns is most definitely not linear. In fact, the simple (derivative) calculations I presented in the prior chapter, Sect. 5.6, illustrated this quite clearly. Again, I'm not using my linear regression model to predict or forecast portfolio longevity. I know how to estimate that analytically. Rather, what I am doing is approximating portfolio longevity with a linear relationship solely to illustrate the relative impact of the SoR. With that in mind, I'll now investigate the underlying assumptions in this (linear) model by using four (widely used) model-checking plots via the `plot(fit)` command. Think of them as a visual test of assumptions, and I'll confess the results don't look good.

In the left panel of Fig. 6.5 you will see a picture of the fitted values in the regression (on the x-axis), plotted against the residuals (on the y-axis). Generally speaking, a statistician or econometrician will *not* want to see any structure or patterns in these plots, because they should represent the noise or random error terms ϵ_j in Eq. (6.2). Alas, Fig. 6.5 doesn't look like noise (or random dots along the x-y plane) which tells us that something is wrong—or more specifically that our linear model (indeed) is a flawed assumption. In fact, if you look carefully at the left panel the regularity is quite startling. As the fitted value increased, the residuals decline almost linearly. The right panel in Fig. 6.5 plots the theoretical quantiles (for a normal distribution) against the standardized residuals from the regression. If these were results from a "healthy" linear regression, the standard residuals would appear (randomly scattered) along a straight line. But, as you can see they are not.

For the sake of completeness, the two panels in Fig. 6.6 display the 3rd and 4th diagnostic (a.k.a. model-checking) plots. They are the fitted values displayed against the square root of (the absolute value of) the standardized residuals, on the left panel. The standardized residuals are plotted against the so-called leverage, on the right. In particular, the right panel (leverage) provides a visual indication of which data points (from the 50,000 we generated) have the largest impact on the parameter estimate. It also gives a sense of the outliers, although with that many data points it's hard to grasp which data points are to blame for the poor (linear) fit. The two panels in Fig. 6.6 don't contain as much information as those in Fig. 6.5. Nevertheless, all four plots are generated automatically by the `plot(fit)` command in **R**, and are worth familiarizing yourself with because they are extremely helpful and useful in "checking" your regression assumptions.

In sum, while portfolio longevity most certainly is not a linear function of the returns during the first three decades of retirement, the model does in fact provide us with (1) a very rough rule-of-thumb for predicting longevity, and more importantly it teaches us about (2) the relative importance of investment returns during the first years of consumption withdrawals. Another benefit of thinking in terms of regression coefficients is that if you want to simulate portfolio longevity using a different return generating process (perhaps using historically bootstrapped returns) and by changing the relevant portions of the `PLSM` code, the relative value of your coefficients will provide important information about sensitivity to returns. Similar modifications can also be made to the ARIG values, if you want to keep track of (say) 5 versus 10 years. In the next section I'll describe another regression-based approach, which corrects for some (although not all) of the concerns noted in the last few paragraphs.

Source: Generated by Author in **R**

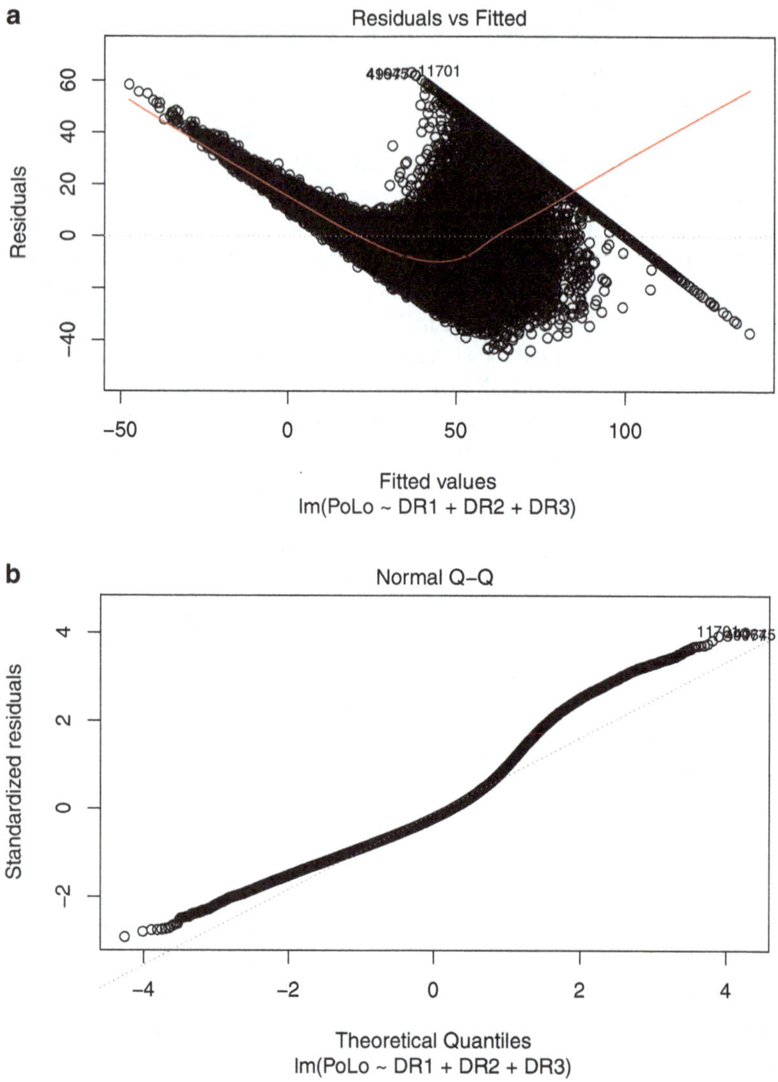

Fig. 6.5 Diagnostics: (**a**) Residuals vs. Fitted and (**b**) Normality

6.8 Logistic Regression: Will the Portfolio Last 30 Years?

Instead of analyzing and modeling the magnitude of the portfolio longevity value, I will restrict my attention to a (much) simpler question. Namely, did the portfolio last for 30 years, or not? In this case the dependent variable in the regression is set to a value of *zero* if the portfolio did not survive for the full 30 years, and set

Source: Generated by Author in **R**

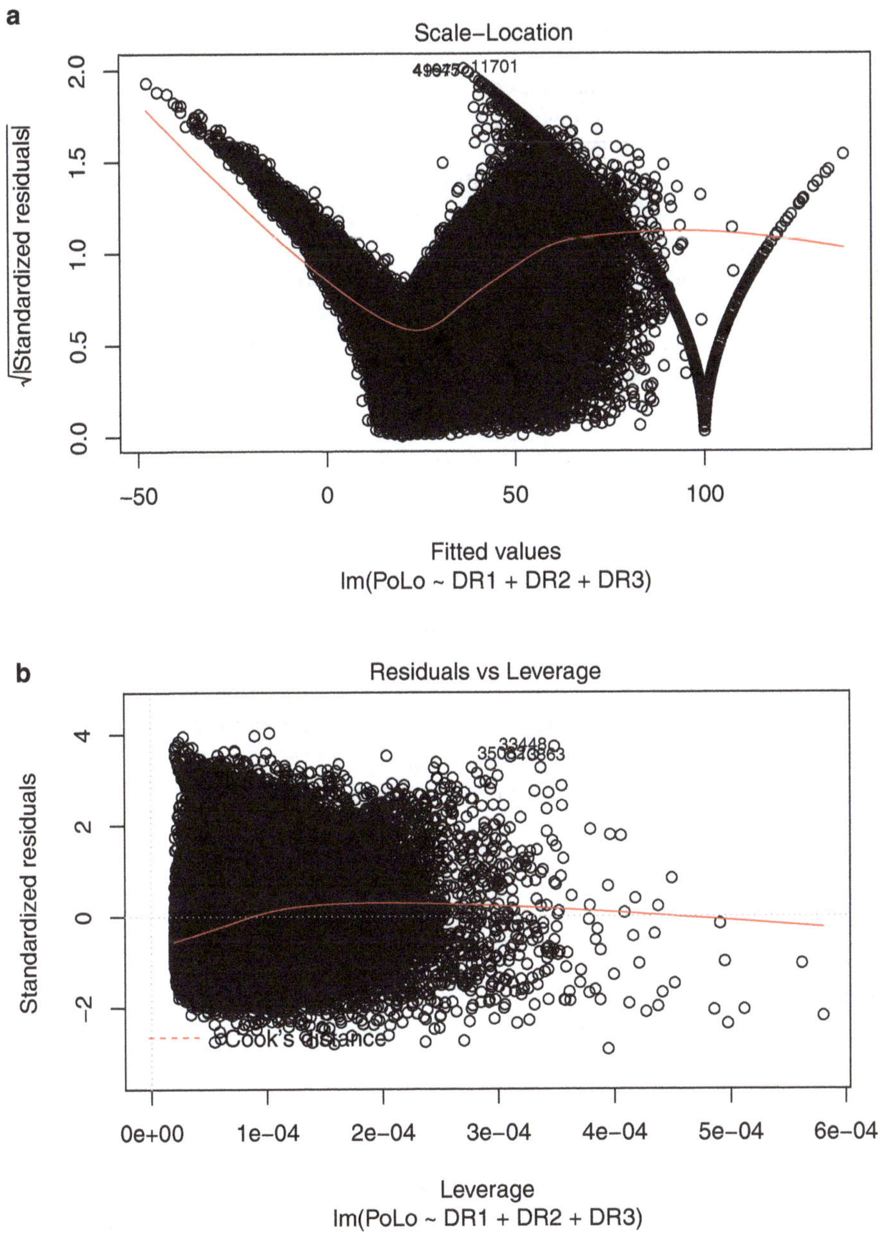

Fig. 6.6 Diagnostics: (**a**) Scale-Location and (**b**) Residuals vs. Leverage

to a value of *one* if the portfolio lasted for 30 years, or more. The justification or origin of the binary 30-year benchmark comes from the previous chapter, and the prior (practitioner) research in this area that has focused on 30 years of retirement income. The simulation data is based on (the same as before) spending rate of $c = 5$ per initial $F = 100$, a continuously compounded (mean) return of $\nu = 2.5\%$ per year, and a standard deviation of $\sigma = 15\%$. But, by construction, the so-called logistic regression formalized here will no longer be skewed by the artificial (and arbitrary) ending of PLSM at year 100. To be very clear, I will implicitly assume that the *logit transformation* of the dependent (a.k.a. outcome) variable, $\ln[P/(1-P)]$, has a linear relationship with the independent (a.k.a. predictor) variables, the ARIG values. This assertion caries the same baggage as the linear model in the previous section, but isn't skewed by the outliers. The model I will be estimating can be expressed mathematically as follows:

$$Y_j := \ln\left[\frac{P}{1-P}\right] = \alpha_0 + \alpha_A A_j + \alpha_B B_j + \alpha_C C_j + \epsilon_j \tag{6.3}$$

Look carefully at the left-hand side of Eq. (6.3) and compare it to Eq. (6.2). Although I am using the same name Y_j, for the dependent variable, the value of Y_j is no longer the number of years the portfolio lasted, but rather the log-odds ratio, where $P/(1-P)$ represents the odds the portfolio will last for 30 years (or more). Now, as far as the syntax is concerned, the following command in **R** will replace the PoLo vector with either a value of 1 or a value of 0, depending on whether (in that particular simulation run) it lasted for 30 years, or more. Once the values have been replaced, I can compute mean(PoLo) which is the average number of simulation runs that last for 30 years or more, which was approximately 47.5%. With these numbers, the success odds are $0.90 = (0.475)/(1-0.475)$, a.k.a. 90%. And, the log-odds ratio is $\ln[0.90] = -0.1$. More precisely, the numbers are as follows:

```
 PoLo[PoLo<30]<-0
 PoLo[PoLo>=30]<-1
 mean(PoLo)
[1] 0.47588
 (0.47588)/(1-0.47588)
[1] 0.90796
 log((0.47588)/(1-0.47588))
[1] -0.09655494
```

Similar to what I did in the simple linear regression, I can also compute the correlation coefficient between the (binary) success or failure of the retirement portfolio and the returns in the three initial decades. Once again, there should be no surprises here. The correlation with the first decade is almost six times higher than the correlation with the third decade.

```
 cor(PoLo,DR1)
[1] 0.6400479
```

```
 cor(PoLo,DR2)
[1] 0.3788107
 cor(PoLo,DR3)
[1] 0.1076461
```

We are ready to run the logistic regression, which in **R** is called using the `glm(.)` command, plus the extra `binomial` added at the very end. Notice that the regression model itself is written using the exact same syntax `PoLo DR1+DR2+DR3`, but the left-hand side `PoLo` variable is now either 0 or 1. I urge you to google the exact syntax of `glm(.)` so you can see the other options and features that can be added to the generalized linear model, which can fill an entire book (which is why I'll return to them later on.)

```
fit<-glm(PoLo~DR1+DR2+DR3, family = "binomial")
summary(fit)
```

The summary results of the logistic regression must be interpreted with caution—and the economic meaning of the coefficients is quite different from the linear model—because the dependent variable Y is a binary vector.

```
Call:
glm(formula = PoLo ~ DR1 + DR2 + DR3, family = "binomial")

Deviance Residuals:
    Min       1Q    Median       3Q      Max
-3.6119  -0.2664  -0.0094   0.2436   3.4605

Coefficients:
            Estimate Std. Error z value Pr(>|z|)
(Intercept)  -4.3668     0.0463  -94.32   <2e-16 ***
DR1          88.9481     0.8960   99.27   <2e-16 ***
DR2          51.7800     0.5921   87.44   <2e-16 ***
DR3          14.7048     0.3654   40.24   <2e-16 ***
---
Null deviance: 69198  on 49999  degrees of freedom
Residual deviance: 23877 on 49996  degrees of freedom
AIC: 23885
Number of Fisher Scoring iterations: 7
```

At the risk of *flogging a dead horse*, the most important takeaway is as follows. All three coefficients are (highly) statistically significant, but notice that the first decade's coefficient contributes six times (89/15) more to the probability of reaching a 30-year longevity, compared to the third decade. But, in contrast to the longevity magnitude problem noted with the linear model, these results do *not* depend on whether the (extreme) longevity value is set at 100 (or 50 or 1000) years. Remember, the dependent variable was either zero or one. That said—and one final time—if you run a `plot(fit)` of this model (not displayed) and examine the regression residuals versus the fitted values, you will encounter the same concerns noted in the linear model. To conclude, don't use this to forecast retirement success rates!

6.9 Extending Portfolio Longevity with Derivatives

Let me summarize where we are at this point. The last few sections should unequivocally establish that poor or bad investment returns early on during the drawdown (retirement income) phase can greatly reduce the longevity (a.k.a. sustainability) of the portfolio. This is known as *sequence-of-returns* risk or phenomenon widely quoted and mentioned by industry practitioners. This **Sequencing Risk** is the main reason practitioners recommend modern annuity products, such as Guaranteed Living Withdrawal Benefits (GLWBs) and Guaranteed Minimum Income Benefits (GMIBs), as well as traditional income annuities, the details of which I'll cover in more advanced chapters. Other practitioners, motivated by the same *sequence-of-returns* challenge, have advocated for a dynamic asset-liability management strategy using real-return bonds (TIPS) and/or potentially using leveraged ETFs to gain limited equity exposure. The universe of suggestions is quite broad. But, what all these different strategic approaches have in common is the recognition that generating a sustainable retirement income is a different problem from conventional accumulation, and requires more than simply tinkering with stock and bond mixes. Portfolio insurance is easier to justify, on the theoretical basis, in the decumulation and income phase.

In this section I will discuss (and cook) a different and slightly more advanced portfolio strategy. More specifically, I would like to discuss and examine whether retirees who are in withdrawal mode can protect against a negative *sequence-of-returns* by using traded equity **Put** and **Call** options. Elsewhere, I have labeled this strategy a *longevity extension overlay* (LEO). For more, see the reference [6] or the Ph.D. thesis written by one of my students at the University, cited as [10]. Here I will (and only) briefly discuss how it can be implemented (and cooked in **R**), since a more lengthy and detailed discussion of this idea is provided in the above-noted references.

I should note though, that creating portfolio insurance using put and call option, a.k.a. *collaring* as it's sometime known, isn't new or novel. The idea has been available to sophisticated investors and used for decades, if not centuries. However, my objective in this section is to demonstrate how it might add a few years to the (expected) portfolio longevity, and how to modify the basic `PLSM` algorithm to measure its efficacy. Of course, nothing is free in life and one by-product of using this protection strategy is that portfolio growth will be curtailed due to the call options, which often expire in the money. Nonetheless, for the most part, the life or longevity of the portfolio can be extended using such techniques. Using the language of stochastic processes one might say the following. The conditional expected *ruin time* of the investment portfolio can be extended by reducing the diffusion (volatility) coefficient, at the expense of a lower drift (investment growth) rate. Note that this longevity extension isn't guaranteed (for all sample paths or eventualities), nor is it expected under all combinations of withdrawal and option parameter values.

The article cited as [6] illustrates a variety of historical scenarios in which the retiree sells a call option with a strike price of K_c and then uses the proceeds to purchase a put option with a lower strike price of K_p. Accordingly, if the market price of the investment asset falls below K_p at maturity, you are guaranteed a minimum return, because of the right to sell at a price of K_p. However, if the asset's value increases above a value of K_c, you have to sell to the holder of the call at a price of K_c, limiting the gains you could have otherwise earned on the portfolio. In [6] my co-author and I examined how this (K_p, K_c) combination would have performed during the great recession in 2007/2008. Those results were real world and historical. Again, in this section I only describe (at a high level) how to simulate forward-looking results using hypothetical put and call option prices.

Using the famous Black–Scholes–Merton formula for option pricing, I can generate sample paths for the entire retirement horizon, the subsequent table displays the results of $N = 100{,}000$ such simulations. The table assumes that nominal investment returns are normally distributed with a nominal $\nu = 4\%$ return and volatility $\sigma = 20\%$. This is before inflation, so I then added an inflation rate of 2% to the investment returns as well as to the quarterly withdrawals, which range from $c = \$4$ to $c = \$6$ per year. In other words (and unlikely the algorithms and scripts presented in the first few sections of this chapter) I now simulate nominal instead of real returns, because most liquid options are priced and expressed with strike prices that are nominal. Note that this involves only a modification to the `PLSM.SR` code, namely increasing the withdrawals every year for the 2% assumed inflation rate. I'll leave the exact mechanics as an end-of-chapter assignment question. Also, given that (most) options are on index (not total) returns, I must add dividends on the stock index of approximately 2%. Finally, the risk-free valuation rate (for option pricing purposes) is 3% nominal, which is approximately 1% real. I simulated 3-month investment returns and 3-month option prices which were settled every 3 months. In practice, longer maturities could be used, to correspond with withdrawal dates.

Since we used the Black–Scholes–Merton formula to price options, and a fixed volatility of 20% (or in some later cases 25%) per year, the relationship between the collar's put and call was implicitly fixed for the entire horizon. The nice thing about building the simulation in **R** is that it allows me to build a perfect zero-cost portfolio. That is, I can find the precise pairs of put/call strikes that have a net cost of zero. Once again, this can only be done in a (theoretical) simulation, since in practice it will be impossible to locate a call and put combination with exactly offsetting prices. I stress (again) that in reality there would have to be some net cash inflow or outflow at the time of the option purchase/sale. Now, I will leave the actual **R** script as a homework problem (yes, I can hear the moaning) and at this point display the simulation results.

Table 6.1 Analysis of a portfolio longevity extension overlay (LEO) strategy

	Volatility $\sigma = 20\%$		Volatility $\sigma = 25\%$	
Consumption Withdrawal	No collar	with collar $K_p = 0.95$	No collar	with collar $K_p = 0.95$
Relatively Low ($c = \$3$)	19.5 years	25.4 years	17.5 years	24.8 years
Medium ($c = \$4$)	17.8 years	22.5 years	15.9 years	22.1 years
Relatively high ($c = \$5$)	16.3 years	19.9 years	14.6 years	19.6 years

Note: average portfolio longevity (`PoLo`) is computed conditional on **not** surviving 30 years

To be very specific, I (again) assumed a rather mechanical and naive strategy in which the portfolio is collared a new every quarter by purchasing out-of-the-money put options (strike price K_p) with funds obtained from selling an out-of-the-money call options (with strike price K_c). The strike price of the call option was dictated by the premium received for the written put, which made the overlay (truly) zero cost. For the most part, though, the implied call option (with identical price) was approximately 4–6% above the market level, which is consistent with actual prices one might observe in practice (Table 6.1).

On to the results. In the case where $c = \$5$ is withdrawn (in addition to the option cash-flow settlements) I extracted 1.25 from the portfolio at the beginning of each quarter in real terms, adjusted nominally for inflation by 0.5%. Again, this is somewhat of a fiction since inflation does not progress in this perfect (deterministic) manner nor does consumption withdrawals take place quarterly. The point here is to test (and cook) the concept and see whether these overlays can extend the life of the portfolio. With that preamble, the results are quite encouraging.

Notice that the expected (a.k.a. weighted) longevity of the portfolio is higher with collars at all withdrawal rates. In other words, the collars work. These values are qualitatively consistent with the results from the historical (real world) empirical work reported in the references [10] and [6]. Relatively speaking, the longevity extension is more effective when the withdrawal rate is higher. Note also the impact or effect of higher (25% versus 20%) volatility assumptions. The more volatile your asset mix, the lower the longevity—all else being equal—but the collar helps.

I conclude this section with a warning. First, this is a pedagogical exercise and there are many different ways to structure a *longevity extension overlay* using traded options. Some of them might not extend the life of the portfolio for a given consumption withdrawal rate c. Second, my simulations indicate that when consumption withdrawal rates are low (i.e. less than $c = 3$ per $F = 100$ of initial nest egg) the *longevity extension overlay* isn't very effective and can sometimes reduce the longevity of the portfolio. In other words, giving up upside in exchange for downside protection isn't a guaranteed proposition for retirees. Third and finally, historically speaking the *longevity extension overlay* was more effective at higher spending rates, especially when the *sequence-of-returns* effect was more pronounced. In sum, despite the complexity of traded options—and the philosophical questions regarding their suitability for elderly and retired investors—

there is a strong case to be made that they can effectively help manage retirement risks. Indeed, the exotic options embedded inside modern variable annuities (VA) with withdrawal benefit guarantees, which I'll discuss later on in this book, are (arguably) no less complicated than using vanilla options. Perhaps buying them directly should be considered no less suitable than buying them as part of a (more expensive) package. In fact, insurance companies with their variable and indexed annuities aren't the only participants in the financial services industry who can create retirement collars, and I (commercially) am involved with similar attempts using Exchange Traded Funds (ETFs).

6.10 Final Notes

- This entire chapter (similar to Chap. 5) was predicated on the (rather unrealistic) concept that retirees will continue to consume the exact same amount every year regardless of the realization of the *sequence-of-returns*. Moreover, I presented the *success probability* of such a strategy as a reasonable number to measure and analyze. However, as any financial economist (such as myself) will argue, people adapt their consumption spending to the current value of their portfolio and wealth. In fact, there are deep economic problems with probability as a measure of retirement success and failure, and have discussed my concerns in the article cited as [5]. See also [4] for the financial economists view. So, I am absolutely not advocating blind adherence to a fixed c, until the money runs out, as a normative strategy. Rather, the point here is to (1) examine the sensitivity of portfolio longevity to investment returns, (2) provide some background to and justification for protection-based strategies, and (3) make sure anyone who does simulate success and failure rates does it properly. See also references [1–3] for more on simulations in the context of retirement ruin probabilities.
- Regardless of whether we focus on the (linear regression) portfolio longevity, or the (logistic regression) success rate, the impact of investment returns is non-linear, but the sensitivity to returns is much higher in the early years of withdrawals. This is the (famous) *sequence-of-returns* effect and the regression coefficients are an intuitive way of displaying those sensitivities. In theory, I could write down an explicit analytic expression for the portfolio longevity (or success rate) as a function of the entire investment return path, and then take derivatives with respect to segments of those paths. That process would also give us the relevant sensitivities and an estimate of the relative magnitudes.
- The *sequence-of-returns* problem, if I can call it that, has led to a number of interesting suggestions around how to manage the retirement portfolio (right) before and (soon) after the withdrawals. Within this context, see the articles referenced as [7], or [8] as well as [9].
- At the very least, from a pedagogical perspective, this chapter has given me the opportunity to introduce the `lm(.)` and `glm(.)` functions in **R**, even if the linear models themselves didn't fit very well.

Questions and Problems

6.1 Assuming the same consumption withdrawal of $c = 5$ per $F = 100$, as well as $\nu = 2.5\%$ and $\sigma = 15\%$ investment values, generate $N = 500$ instead of the (much larger) $N = 50{,}000$ paths. Run the same `lm(.)` and `glm(.)` regressions and discuss the statistical significance of your results. Is 500 enough data points for a Monte Carlo simulation of retirement income?

6.2 Modify the basic `PLSM.SR` simulation so that you keep track of **five** 7 (instead of 10) year ARIG values, which represents investment returns during the first 35 years of consumption withdrawals. Using the same $c = 5$ per $F = 100$, and $\nu = 2.5\%$, $\sigma = 15\%$ values, run a logistic regression (only), where success is defined as surviving for 35 years. Please report and interpret the coefficients in this regression.

6.3 All else being equal (that is assuming the same values of c/F, ν, what happens to the coefficients in the logistic regression when you increase the volatility σ from 15 to 30%. What is the interpretation of the coefficients? Explain intuitively.

6.4 Per discussion in Sect. 6.9, please modify the basic `PLSM.SR` simulation so that year-by-year investment returns are normally distributed but truncated and upper and lower bounds. In other words, if the random continuously compounded return exceeds 1.5σ, either above or below the mean ν, it is capped. And, while this isn't quite the option-based collar described in Sect. 6.9, it's close enough. Please compute the portfolio 30-year success rate using the usual parameters (from the prior questions) and compare with the uncapped (a.k.a. un-collared) portfolio.

6.5 Create a modified `PLSM.SR` simulation in which inflation is uniformly distributed between $[-1\%, 3\%]$ in any given year, investment returns are normally distributed with a nominal ν_n, σ, and consumption withdrawals $c = 4\%$ are adjusted every year by realized inflation. Run a simulation with $\nu_n = 5\%, \sigma = 15\%$ and estimate coefficients using the `lm(.)` command in **R**.

References

1. Abaimova, A., & Milevsky, M. A. (2006). Will the true Monte Carlo number, please stand up? *Journal of Financial Planning*. available from https://www.financialplanningassociation.org/learn/journal
2. Abaimova, A., Cavalieri, B., & Milevsky, M. A. (2009). Retirement income sustainability: How to measure the tail of a black swan. *Journal of Financial Planning, 22*, 56–67.
3. Huang, H., Milevsky, M. A., & Salisbury, T. S. (2009). A different perspective on retirement income sustainability: The blueprint for ruin contingent life annuity. *Journal of Wealth Management, 11*, 1–8.
4. Kotlikoff, L., & Milevsky, M. A. (2012). The two worlds of personal finance: A discussion. *Life-cycle investing: Financial education and consumer protection*. Charlottesville: CFA Research Foundation Publications.

5. Milevsky, M. A. (2016). It's time to retire ruin (probabilities). *Financial Analysts Journal, 72*(2), 8–12.
6. Milevsky, M. A., & Posner, S. E. (2014). Can collars reduce retirement sequencing risk? Analysis of portfolio longevity extension overlays. *Journal of Retirement, 1*(4), 46–56.
7. Pfau, W. D., & Kitces, M. E. (2013). Reducing retirement risk with a rising equity glide-path. http://ssrn.com/abstract=2324930
8. Scott, J. S., & Watson, J. G. (2013). The floor-leverage rule for retirement. *Financial Analysts Journal, 69*(5), 45–60.
9. Sexauer, S. C., Peskin, M. W., & Cassidy, D. (2012). Making retirement income last a lifetime. *Financial Analysts Journal, 68*(1), 74–84.
10. Wang, J. (2006). *Numerical PDE techniques for personal finance and insurance problems*. Ph.D. Thesis on file at York University, Toronto, Canada.

Chapter 7
Modeling Human Longevity and Life Tables

Up to this point in the book, I have assumed a great fiction, namely that human longevity is known and finite. The success or failure of a retirement income plan was monitored and measured until a finite, e.g. 30 year, horizon. This chapter is the first to focus on the uncertainty or randomness in human longevity versus portfolio longevity. It begins with a detailed description and analysis of (historical) cohort life tables from the Human Mortality Database. The cohort life tables are used to extract population survival and death rates, which are then used to reconstruct life tables. The chapter concludes with a high-level discussion of mortality projections and improvements for future birth cohorts. The main emphasis is on gaining familiarity with the basic atomic structure (q_x) of actuarial life-science.

7.1 Functions Used and Defined

7.1.1 Sample of Native R Functions Used

- `diff(.)` creates a vector of differences of adjacent values.
- `which(v == q)` returns the index number for which `v` equals `q`.
- `cumprod(.)` multiplies the vector elements.
- `abline(.)` plots horizontal lines.

7.1.2 User-Defined R Functions

- `SPQR(x,y,qx)` computes the survival rate (a.k.a. probability) to the age of `y`, conditional on living at age `x`, given the 1-year death rate vector `qx`.

M. A. Milevsky, *Retirement Income Recipes in R*, Use R!,
https://doi.org/10.1007/978-3-030-51434-1_7

7.2 Death for Financial Economists: Motivation

Within the context of commerce, measuring life and death used to be the exclusive purview of insurance actuaries, while the serious business of managing capital *between* those two important dates was left to financial practitioners and economists. But today times have changed. In the last few decades the actuarial community has moved (aggressively) into the financial and economic industry as evidenced by curriculum changes for their stringent exams. In contrast, the community of financial economists and practitioners—very broadly defined—has remained somewhat ambivalent towards, and at times even hostile towards actuarial models of longevity and mortality. On an academic note, one is hard-pressed to locate a finance department in a business school, or even a proper economics department, in which life contingencies are taught in any serious way. To many financial economists, death is just a basic (Poisson) arrival process and as far as pricing is concerned, mortality is a diversifiable risk, and the rest is just noise. Yes, the recent COVID-19 crisis has seen an uptick of interest in models of mortality, even among economists and financial specialists, but for the most part it isn't part of the formal canon of knowledge. Graduate and undergraduate students who are interested in something deeper than a toy model of life and death are directed to the mathematicians and statisticians in other faculties. I find that many economists echo Macbeth, who in Shakespeare's famous play declares: *There's nothing serious in mortality, all is but toys, renown and grace is dead.* And yet, how is a financial life-cycle economist (a.k.a. retirement income expert) supposed to have an intelligent conversation about the fair value of a pension annuity, or the role of longevity insurance in the retirement portfolio, without a proper quantitative understanding of life and death? Likewise, to have a meaningful and constructive dialogue with insurance actuaries one must understand their language, framework and world-view. In sum, the plan with for the next three Chaps. 7, 8 and 9 is to offer a practical need-to-know framework on how to approach, think about and construct models involving life and death, using **R** (obviously.)

7.3 Will You Live to Age 100?

The first step in a proper discussion of human longevity is to consider whether *you* personally will reach the age of 100. Do you have a family member, parent or grandparent who reached this age? It's quite rare. In fact, I find it interesting that when audiences (i.e. large groups) are surveyed and asked to estimate how many people are alive (in their own country) above the age of 100, they tend to over-estimate the number (especially in Florida). Likewise, the scholarly research suggests that individuals are overly optimistic about their own survival odds to (very) advanced ages. Of course, the fact is no one *really* knows their true probabilities of reaching 100, or any other age. Such forecasts are **not** like predicting the outcome from spinning a roulette wheel or mixing a deck of cards. Those gaming

Table 7.1 Hitting 100: estimated number of centenarians around the world

Location	Number (in 2015)	Rate per 10,000
Australia	4280	0.3
Canada	8000	2.3
China	48,000	0.3
Japan	61,000	4.8
U.S.	72,000	2.2
World	451,000	0.6

Data source: pew research center (Accessed May 2018), www.pewresearch.org

probabilities are known and immutable. Who can predict the sudden emergence of a virus that changes everyone's survival odds? With that in mind, the following table displays the (most recently available data on the) number of centenarians around the world (Table 7.1).

There are quite a few interesting—and perhaps even surprising—factoids worth noting. First, the country with the most centenarians in the world is the USA (and not Japan) despite the public perception that Japan is the "old country." The USA wins the centenarian gold medal (for now). Of course, Japan does have the highest *fraction* of centenarians, at 4.8 per 10,000 citizens. But their aggregate total is 61,000 versus the 72,000 in the USA. Moving down the list, China has 48,000 centenarians, Canada has 8000, Australia has 4280. Of course, there are many other countries with centenarians, and some regions have an abnormal concentration of 100-year-olds, for example, Okinawa (in Japan), Bulgaria, and the Italian island of Sardinia. Add them all up, and the planet (is estimated to have) slightly less than 0.5 million centenarians out of a total of approximately 7.5 billion people. That is 0.6 per 10,000 earthlings. Needless to say, counting (and verifying the age of) very old people involves many demographic assumptions that I won't get into, which is why you should view these numbers as indicative as opposed to definitive.

From the perspective of retirement income planning, the main objectives in the next few chapters are to (1) *quantify* the uncertainty around human longevity, and learn how to (2) *incorporate* that uncertainty into your consumption, withdrawal and investment plans. To answer the first question I'll begin by tapping into one of the best and most popular sources of historical mortality data.

7.4 The Human Mortality Database (HMD)

The main source of data used in the next few chapters is the Human Mortality Database (HMD), all of which can be downloaded (after you register for a free account) from http://www.mortality.org/. They collect, validate, and "clean" data on all aspects of death (yes, a bit morbid) for many different countries around the world. The numbers I will use for many of the examples are from Canada. The crude data can also be downloaded from http://www.bdlc.umontreal.ca/ without registering (the last time I checked).

For ease of use, I have extracted a (very) small subset of the Canadian data and have made it available as a special `csv` file, together with the other scripts and files. So, I'll start by importing the file using the usual procedure (last described in Chap. 4). Technically speaking this is a synthetic cohort life table (CLT) for all Canadians born in the year 1925. I'll explain exactly what these terms mean in a moment, but for now here is a reminder of the commands required to get the data into **R** and then stored as a local `CLT` variable, which is a shorter name and easier to work with. To be very clear though, the raw data available from the websites of the HMD and/or the Canadian HMD is stored in a slightly different (cumulative) format. I'll return to the HMD formatting of the data at the very end of this chapter, in Sect. 7.13.

```
CLT <- read.csv("./Canada_Cohort_Lifetable_1925.csv")
```

To begin with, notice the emphasis on the word COHORT, which is a group of people born in the exact same year and (technically) on the exact same date, which is why I use the word synthetic. The synthetic cohort life table tracks and monitors the life status of this group over the next 85 years (to the year 2010), and the only way to *leave the table* is to die. It's important to emphasize that these (synthetic) cohort life tables ignore immigration (again, the only way out is to die) or migration, which is why the values never increase.

Now, this particular synthetic cohort life table assumes a group of 100,000 males and 100,000 females, all born on January 1st, 1925. To put that number in perspective, the total population of Canada in the year 1925 was slightly less than ten million, and was increasing by approximately 1.75% per year (albeit including immigration.) So, it's not unreasonable to assume that a total of 200,000 people were born in the year 1925. But they certainly weren't born on January 1st. That's the synthetic part of the cohort. Not to get carried away by minutia, but the number of births expected in Canada during the year 2020 is approximately 400,000, which results in slightly more than 1000 births per day. And, for those readers in the USA, multiply the numbers by a factor of ten, resulting in approximately 10,000 births per day. This really is an astonishing number and places the 72,000 (American) centenarians in perspective.

Back to the synthetic cohort life table, which from here on I'll abbreviate CLT. Some members of the original 1925 cohort are still alive today, but the data (I have used) ends in the year 2010 (at age 85). In fact, the HMD has (incomplete) cohort data going back to the year 1850, which you can (and I will ask you to) access and download for some of the end-of-chapter questions. Once you have downloaded and imported the data, ask **R** to summarize the `CLT` variable, and make sure you obtain these results. (Remember, this isn't simulations. Your numbers should match mine.)

```
summary(CLT)
       AGE              FEMALE              MALE               YEAR
 Min.   : 0.00   Min.   : 42021   Min.   : 24183   Min.   :1925
 1st Qu.:21.25   1st Qu.: 75343   1st Qu.: 64119   1st Qu.:1946
```

```
 Median :42.50   Median : 83754   Median : 78750   Median :1968
 Mean   :42.50   Mean   : 78760   Mean   : 70991   Mean   :1968
 3rd Qu.:63.75   3rd Qu.: 85971   3rd Qu.: 82245   3rd Qu.:1989
 Max.   :85.00   Max.   :100000   Max.   :100000   Max.   :2010
```

Let me review and explain the four columns. The age of individuals represented in the CLT range from 0 to 85, located in the first column. That should be obvious by now. The second and third column contain the number of female and male survivors at every age (and year). The fourth and final column contains the years covered in this cohort life table. So, the last observation is (hypothetically, on January 1st, 2010) when a total of 42,021 females and 24,183 males were still alive at age 85 (which, hypothetically, was their birthday). Assuming your data summary matches mine, you can move on to plots and figures. In particular, I'll graph the 2nd column `CLT$FEMALE` and the 3rd column `CLT$MALE` using the following script.

```
plot(c(0,90),c(0,1),type="n",
     xlab="Age of Cohort (top), Year (bottom)",
     ylab="Fraction Surviving")
title("Cohort Life Table: 1925 Canada")
grid(ny=18,lty=20)
for (i in 1:86){
  points(i-1,CLT$FEMALE[i]/100000,col="red")
  points(i-1,CLT$MALE[i]/100000,col="blue") }
abline(h=0.25,col="black",lty=3,lwd=2)
abline(h=0.50,col="black",lty=3,lwd=2)
abline(h=0.75,col="black",lty=3,lwd=2)
year<-1925+c(0:5)*20; age<-0+(0:5)*20
axis(side=1,line=1,at=age,labels=year,tick=F)
text(81,0.65,"Females",col="red")
text(58,0.65,"Males",col="blue")
```

Figure 7.1 plots the *survival rate* for males and females, which is the fraction of the initial cohort born on January 1st, 1925, still alive on subsequent birthdays. There is quite a bit going on in the script, including a few extra tricks I haven't used before, so make sure you understand the new commands. As in all prior figures, I start with an empty plot `type="n"` and then layer on the data points. Notice the double x-axis covering the observation `year` as well as the chronological `age` of the cohort, via the `axis(.)` command. The `abline(.)` creates horizontal lines at 25%, 50%, and 75% survival, making it easier to discern ages at which those fractions survived. Finally, google the `lty`, `lwd` or `col` arguments to learn how they can be modified.

Notice the patterns in Fig. 7.1, which for the record are observed in every other country as well as Canada. At every age, the female survival curve (in red) is above the male survival curve (in blue). Initially the gap between the two curves is rather small, but it increases over age and time. By the year 2010, only 24% of the (1925 cohort) males have survived, but 42% of the females are still alive. Needless to say,

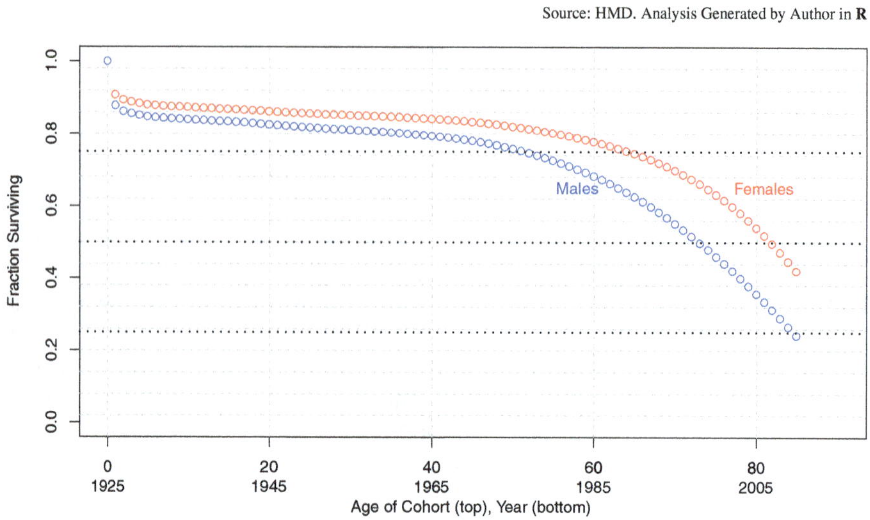

Fig. 7.1 The declining size of the Canadian 1925 birth cohort

quite a lot of history took place during those 85 years, including World War II (in the 1940s) which reduced the size of the male cohort, who enlisted in their late teens and mid-20s. Notice the large precipitous declines in the very first year of life—from age 0 (in 1925) to age 1 (in 1926)—which captures the (very) high infant mortality rates in the first year (and few weeks) of life. That first-year drop plays a large role in the 24% (males) and 42% (females) who survive to age 85. But, if they (males or females) survived those first few years, their chances of reaching age 85 improved quite dramatically. I'll get to that critical *conditional on survival* matter in just a bit. For now I'll note that infant mortality rates (in Canada, 2020) are down to 5-per-1000 births. This number would hardly create a blip in the upper-left corner. So, Fig. 7.1 is a microcosm of the many issues addressed in the next few chapters. For example: What fraction of the (Canadian) 1925 cohort will survive to the year 2025? Needless to say, the full data hasn't materialized yet. Or, what will Fig. 7.1 look like for the 1960s or 1980s cohort? Will you be one of those who survives to age 85 (or even 100?) What will your cohort's full plot look like? Is there a continuous function that can approximate Fig. 7.1? I trust you appreciate that without some (approximate) answers to these questions it's quite hard to build a proper retirement income plan. And, although the randomness of *human longevity* is fundamentally different from the randomness of *portfolio longevity*, the mathematical tools are quite similar.

7.5 Cohort Survival Rates from Life Tables

I'll now examine the data in CLT more closely, and start by answering the following questions. What fraction (male vs. female) of the birth cohort survived their first year of life, to reach the age of $x = 1$? What fraction (male vs. female) survived to the age of $x = 60$? What fraction (male vs. female) survived to the age of $x = 75$? Given that we have data until the year 2010, there is no need to guess, estimate, or forecast these numbers. I count survivors and divide by the initial 100,000. Using the symbol S_x to denote the number of survivors at any age x, I compute S_{75}/S_0, S_{60}/S_0 and S_1/S_0 using the following syntax in **R**:

```
CLT$FEMALE[CLT$AGE==75]/100000
 [1] 0.631155
CLT$FEMALE[CLT$AGE==60]/100000
 [1] 0.777939
CLT$FEMALE[CLT$AGE--1]/100000
 [1] 0.907693
CLT$MALE[CLT$AGE==75]/100000
 [1] 0.460165
CLT$MALE[CLT$AGE==60]/100000
 [1] 0.682913
CLT$MALE[CLT$AGE==1]/100000
 [1] 0.877325
```

So, 77.8% of the females and 68.3% of the males (in the 1925 birth cohort) survived to the age of 60, which you can think of as an *early* retirement date. The other 22.2% of females and 31.7% of males died sometime between birth and (early) retirement. Almost a third of males and a quarter of females never made it to (early) retirement, from the 1925 birth cohort. These numbers aren't unique to Canada. The death rates are in fact higher—that is less people from the 1925 cohort survived to the year 1985—in other developed countries, including the USA and (especially) Europe. The situation (today) is much different, and I'll discuss how and why in a moment. Moving on, the survival rate to age one was 87.7% for males, and implies that 12.3% of males born in 1925 never reached their first birthday. That is a staggering number and the source of the discontinuity in the upper corner of Fig. 7.1. I should note again that in 2020 the 1-year mortality rate at birth is a mere 0.5%, which is an average for males and females. So, that alone is one (very big) difference between the evolution of the 1925 cohort and the (future) 2020 cohort. Fewer people reached age 60 from the 1925 cohort, because many of them died in their first year of life. Naturally, a much larger fraction of the 2020 cohort will survive to the age of 60, because we lose fewer of them to infant mortality. But what fraction of the 2020 birth cohort will reach age 60? They should be (much) higher than the 77.8% (for females) and 68.3% computed in the above box, but how much higher? Keep that question on the back-burner for now.

I would like to focus on a slightly different question, namely, assuming a member of the 1925 cohort survived to the age of 40, what fraction survived to age 60? Please note the subtle conditioning. I am *assuming* or focusing on a subset of the group that actually reached age 40, and asking what fraction from that (smaller) group reached age 60. To answer this I must scale by the appropriate denominator, namely those who are alive at the age of 40. Mathematically, this is S_{60}/S_{40}, and the following script provides the answer.

```
 CLT$FEMALE[CLT$AGE==60]/CLT$FEMALE[CLT$AGE==40]
[1] 0.9248979
CLT$MALE[CLT$AGE==60]/CLT$MALE[CLT$AGE==40]
[1] 0.8604019
```

The 92.5% survival rate for females and 86% survival rate for males, to age 60, are much higher than the 77.8% (for females) and 68.3% computed in the earlier box. Both are associated with reaching the age of 60, but the earlier set of numbers is conditional on age zero, and the current set is conditional on age 40. That's the main difference. This is why you should always get into the habit of asking: *conditional on what?* when given a survival rate. At the extreme, think of the 1-year survival rates contained in the next command.

```
CLT$FEMALE[CLT$AGE==60]/CLT$FEMALE[CLT$AGE==59]
[1] 0.9931369
CLT$MALE[CLT$AGE==60]/CLT$MALE[CLT$AGE==59]
[1] 0.9860349
```

Both number are well over 98%, and by this point in the narrative I hope you understand why. The fraction of 59 year-olds who survive to age 60 is quite high. The closer you get to some target age (60 for example) the higher the odds of getting there. It's tautological, in a sense. Warning, though. It's common to interpret the (backward looking, historical) survival rates as forward-looking survival probabilities, but one should be careful with that extrapolation. At this point all I'm saying is that the survival rates for the 1925 cohort, to any fixed age, increased as they get closer to that age. I'm not making statements about probability (yet.)

7.6 Another Birth Year: Another Cohort

The (Canadian) 1925 CLT tracks the longevity of babies born in 1925. But, as I mentioned a number of times already, cohorts born in other years (either before or after) experience (very) different trajectories of life and death. For example, a non-trivial segment of the 1925 cohort fought (and died) during World War II. The same can't be said of the 1940 cohort, who would have been too young to fight. The 1940

Source: HMD. Figures Generated by Author in **R**

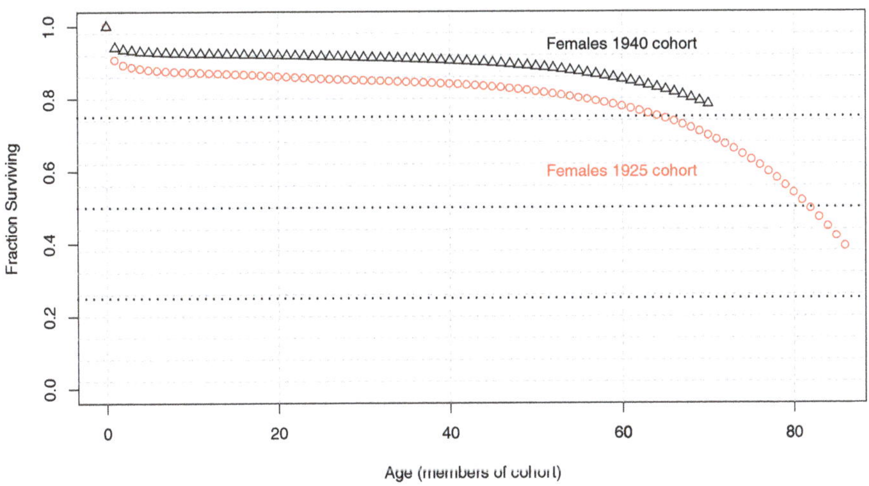

Fig. 7.2 Females: the 1925 versus the 1940 Canadian birth cohort

cohort might have faced other challenges, such as a shortage of food and resources in their early years of life (i.e. during World War II), etc.

To examine the evolution of *survival* for the 1940 cohort versus the 1925 cohort, I have created a corresponding 1940 cohort life table, which you can import (and then plot) using the same procedure I described earlier. Figures 7.2 (females alone) and 7.3 (males alone) display the fraction of survivors at each age for both the 1925 and 1940 cohort, in the same picture. Obviously, the 1940 cohort only has data until age 70, which gets them to the year 2010.

Although both curves trend downward over time (a.k.a. people can die), there are a number of visual differences between the 1925 and 1940 birth cohort. First, the 1940 curve is consistently above the 1925 curve, which means that the survival rate to any given age is higher—and the implied death rate is lower—for the later cohort. This reduction or decline in mortality (a.k.a. improvement) isn't unique to the 1940 versus the 1925 cohort, and is actually observed in (almost) all subsequent birth cohorts around the world. And, while its often difficult to see the change (i.e. the gap between the curves) from 1 year to the next, it's quite evident when examined on a 5-year basis, as you can see from these figures. Now, whether or not this mortality improvement will continue into the future at the same pace, for example, the 2010 birth cohort versus the 2020 birth cohort is a subject of much debate and discussion in the medical, actuarial, and demographic community. Why the debate? Well, for example, look closely at the upper-left corner of both Figs. 7.2 and 7.3. One of the main differences between the 1925 and 1940 curves is the (above noted) first-year infant mortality rate. That creates a large gap between the curves and is a source of the improvements. But, over the last few decades this number (infant mortality) has been reduced quite dramatically (in the developed

Source: HMD. Figures Generated by Author in **R**

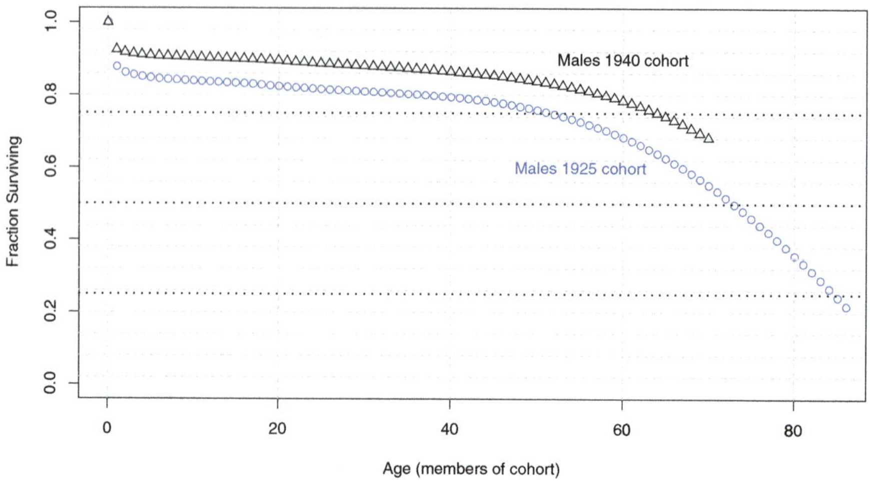

Fig. 7.3 Males: the 1925 versus the 1940 Canadian birth cohorts

world) and is unlikely to be improved much more. This then implies that it's unlikely to have as large an influence on future cohorts and the gap between the two curves will shrink—or possibly even reverse itself. The same argument can be made about other causes of death (declining incidence of large-scale wars?) which might increase survival rates in future cohorts. Alternatively, deaths from opioid and pain medication overdoses (which were negligible until recently) might reduce the survival rate of (for example) the 1980 cohort versus the 1940 cohort.

In sum, I don't want to get entangled or caught up in the demographic minutia, but the important takeaway is as follows. When computing, discussing, or quoting survival and death rates, it's extremely important to be aware of (1) the year of birth of the relevant cohort as well as (2) the conditioning age. Actuaries have been trained to think (and talk) in this manner from quite early in their education, so it's important you keep this in mind as well. The next time you hear someone *predicting* the chances of surviving to age 90, you should inquire about the assumed age (Is it from birth or retirement?) as well as the birth cohort. (Is it 1925 or 1940?) Otherwise, the statement is incomplete and rather meaningless. I'll return to the conditioning point later on when I introduce and discuss tables for **Period Mortality** versus **Cohort Mortality**.

7.7 Extracting Death Rates from Life Tables

Back to the 1925 cohort, I am interested in (more closely) examining the actual number of deaths at any given age to see if I can uncover any patterns that can be exploited from prediction purposes. Remember that my practical objective here is to forecast what fraction (of the 1925 cohort) might live to age 95, 100, or even 105. If there is a predictable pattern to deaths by age, then I might be able to assume that pattern will continue and use that to make an educated forecast. To start this process I calculate the 1-year death decrements via the `diff` command in **R**. Please execute the following command and ensure you get the same numbers.

```
> diff(CLT$FEMALE)
 [1] -9230.7 -1429.4  -586.0  -418.8  -344.5  -209.6  -168.8
 [8]  -126.8    -99.3  -103.1  -108.3   -89.5  -110.0  -102.0
[15]  -105.9  -104.6  -116.3  -130.2  -131.9  -138.9  -138.7
[22]  -142.2  -121.5  -116.6   -94.8  -102.4   -96.8   -86.4
[29]   -88.5   -64.0   -85.9   -63.2   -99.0   -97.2   -86.5
[36]   -95.2  -112.5  -112.1  -112.7  -118.4  -130.4  -149.8
[43]  -152.7  -181.5  -207.0  -220.3  -249.7  -245.5  -273.6
[50]  -327.9  -301.6  -334.1  -360.1  -410.0  -420.6  -363.5
[57]  -468.4  -485.3  -497.3  -537.6  -587.6  -634.4  -680.4
[64]  -731.6  -723.3  -773.4  -884.6  -911.9  -978.3 -1080.2
[71] -1173.0 -1240.8 -1306.1 -1429.3 -1543.5 -1535.5 -1755.1
[78] -1794.0 -2016.7 -2020.4 -2131.2 -2209.1 -2461.7 -2524.8
[85] -2645.9
```

I'll get to the reason for the non-integer numbers in a moment. (How can 0.4 people die?) There are a total of 85 numbers, representing the 85 years until the cohorts 85th birthday. The `diff(.)` function in **R** subtracts any two adjacent numbers, technically $S_{x+1} - S_x$ using the notation I introduced in the prior section, and displays the results. Between the age $x = 0$ and $x = 1$, a total of $S_1 - S_0 = 9230.7$ females died (during the year 1925) from the 1925 birth cohort. Between age $x = 1$ and $x = 2$, a total of $S_2 - S_1 = 1429.4$ females died (during the year 1926) from the 1925 birth cohort, etc. Let's see if there is any discernible pattern. The first year contains the most deaths, and the smallest number of deaths were between the ages of $x = 31$ and $x = 32$, for a total of $S_{32} - S_{31} = 63.2$ deaths. The number of deaths appear to increase from age $x = 32$ onwards, although they jump around and occasionally do decline. Now, I'll get back to 0.4 deaths. The reason you see fractions is because the cohort life tables themselves have fractional lives. Why? Because the cohort life tables started with 100,000 (synthetic) people who were then *killed* based on the 1-year death rates denoted by $q_x \leq 1$ and reported in the Human Mortality Database. Stated formally:

$$
\begin{aligned}
S_0 &= 100{,}000 \\
S_1 &= S_0 \times (1 - q_0) \\
S_2 &= S_1 \times (1 - q_1) \\
S_x &= S_{x-1} \times (1 - q_{x-1}) \\
S_{x+1} - S_x &= -S_x \, q_x
\end{aligned} \tag{7.1}
$$

To be very clear, the S_x values in the csv file you imported were manufactured (by the author) from the q_x values reported and stored in the HMD. So, the diff(.) command subtracts S_{x+1} from S_x and reports the values of $(-S_x \times q_x)$, per Eq. (7.1). Another way to present and think about the cohort life table is as follows:

$$S_x = S_0 + \sum_{i=1}^{x}(-S_{i-1} \times q_{i-1}) \tag{7.2}$$

The number of survivors at some age x is the initial number of individuals in the cohort, $S_0 = 100{,}000$, minus all those who died in between those two ages. So, for example, at the age of $x = 85$, the number of survivors S_{85} is equal to the initial 100,000 minus the sum of deaths during the ages $x = 0$ to $x = 84$. This can be computed and confirmed in **R** as follows:

```
100000+sum(diff(CLT$FEMALE))
[1] 42021.1
CLT$FEMALE[CLT$AGE==85]
[1] 42021.1
```

So, although we know (in the year 2010) that there were $S_{85} = 42{,}021.1$ survivors from the 1925 (synthetic) birth cohort, we will not learn the 1-year death rate q_{85} for this group, until January 1st, 2011, when the survivors reach age 86. Notice that the table CLT contains 86 rows, but the vector created via the diff(.) contains 85 elements. These pesky things (e.g. 85 versus 86 elements) can make the difference between a script that works, versus one that refuses to co-operate.

7.8 The One-Year Death Rate q_x

The symbol q_x plays a very important role in this book and more generally in actuarial life-sciences. Rearranging equation (7.1), the central q_x value can be extracted directly from the cohort life table S_x, via the relationship $q_x = (S_x - S_{x+1})/S_x$. To be precise, in the context of the 1925 cohort, $0 \le q_x \le 1$ represents the *realized* 1-year death rate between age x and age $(x + 1)$. Although it's a number between zero and one, it isn't a probability (yet) and at this point should be interpreted as a decrement or proportional reduction in the number of survivors at a given age x. This q_x vector is (obviously) gender specific and can be computed in **R** using the following syntax for the 1925 cohort.

```
qx_f<-(-diff(CLT$FEMALE))/CLT$FEMALE[-length(CLT$FEMALE)]
qx_m<-(-diff(CLT$MALE))/CLT$MALE[-length(CLT$MALE)]
summary(round(qx_f,digits=6))
    Min.   1st Qu.    Median      Mean   3rd Qu.      Max.
0.000743 0.001330 0.003006 0.010020 0.010390 0.092307
summary(round(qx_m,digits=6))
```

```
    Min.   1st Qu.    Median      Mean   3rd Qu.      Max.
0.001394 0.001964 0.005139 0.016274 0.019497 0.122675
```

Notice how I standardized the death decrements: $(S_x - S_{x+1})$ by the number of survivors: S_x in each year. The denominator of the defining function for `qx` includes the new command `[-length(.)]`, which drops the last (age 85) element in the relevant `CLT` vector so that the numerator and denominator are of the same length. (The negative sign removes an index and `length` returns the length of the vector, which is the last index.) The 1-year death rate vector q_x takes on its highest value of 9.23% (females) and 12.26% (males) in the first year of life (a.k.a. the infant mortality rate.) The lowest value can be located via the command:

```
which(qx_f==min(qx_f))
[1] 32
which(qx_m==min(qx_m))
[1] 12
qx_f[32]
[1] 0.00074346
qx_m[12]
[1] 0.00139421
```

Notice how the `which(.)` command locates the index of the smallest number in the `qx` vector, which is a useful command to know when working in **R**. At the index value of 32, which is between age $x = 31$ and age $x = 32$, the 1-year death rate was 0.07%. For males it's at age $x = 11$, at 0.1%. Note again that in **R** the element `qx[1]` is a death rate between age $x = 0$ and $x = 1$, etc. Finally, here is a script that plots the q_x values from the age of $x = 0$ to the age of $x = 84$. Remember that I don't have q_{85}, and only S_{85} is known.

```
plot(c(0,90),c(0,0.14),type="n",
xlab="Age of Cohort (top), Year (bottom)", ylab="Death Rate")
grid(ny=18,lty=20)
for (i in 1:81){
  points(i-1,qx_f[i],col="red")
  points(i-1,qx_m[i],col="blue") }
year<-1925+c(0:5)*20; age<-0+(0:5)*20
axis(side=1,line=1,at=age,labels=year,tick=F)
text(88,0.05,"Females",col="red")
text(70,0.05,"Males",col="blue")
```

Figure 7.4 displays the 1-year death rates for the 1925 cohort, but is actually a good picture and general indication of 1-year death rates for almost any cohort and in any country. They start out (very) high in the first few years of life, begin to decline and reach a minimum (at age $x = 31$ for females and $x = 11$ for males, in the 1925 cohort) and then begin steadily climbing by age, to reach values of between 8 and 10% around the age of $x = 80$ (again, for the 1925 cohort.) At the risk of stating the obvious, the older you are the more likely it is you will not survive to your next birthday.

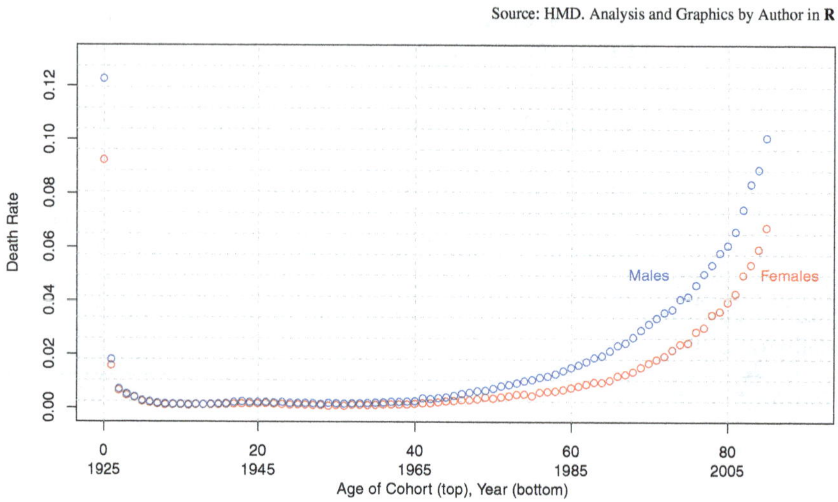

Fig. 7.4 Death rate by age for the 1925 cohort

7.9 Reversing the Process: From Death Rates to Life Tables

Starting with a mortality table (or vector) denoted by q_x, and keeping Eq. (7.1) in mind, I can reconstruct a life table, and the value of S_x at any age x, based on the following algorithm.

$$S_x = S_0 \prod_{i=0}^{x-1} (1 - q_i) \tag{7.3}$$

The intuition here is that I begin with $S_0 = 100{,}000$ and then *kill* members of the cohort at the rate of q_i per year, thus leaving $(1 - q_i)$ survivors. In **R** this can be achieved via:

```
LifeTable<-100000*cumprod(1-qx_f)
LifeTable<-c(100000,LifeTable)
all.equal(LifeTable,CLT$FEMALE)
[1] TRUE
```

The first command `cumprod(.)` multiplies the individual elements of the `qx` vector, and the second command adds the initial 100,000 people to the beginning of the vector. In some sense, the `LifeTable` vector is back where I started: `CLT`, and the final command `all.equal` tests to confirm that indeed they are the same. The benefit of going full circle is that if you have any vector of q_x values, you should be able to compute survival rates, from any age y to any age $z > y$. You would compute those numbers by creating the entire cohort life table S_x, and then dividing S_z/S_y, etc.

7.10 Death Rates and Survival Rates: n-Years

More generally, if the 1-year death rate q_x is defined as one minus the ratio: S_{x+1}/S_x, then the n-year death rate, that is the fraction of people who are alive at age x, who die before age $(x + n)$, can be computed via S_{x+n}/S_x, where n is an integer number of years. I will adhere to the actuarial convention of denoting the n-year death rate by placing a subscript on the lower-left of the q_x symbol. This may seem odd and cumbersome, but carved in stone (by actuaries) over a century ago. The n-year death rate is as follows:

$$({}_{y-x}q_x) = ({}_nq_x) := 1 - \left(\frac{S_{x+n}}{S_x}\right) = 1 - \prod_{i=x}^{x+n-1} (1 - q_i) \tag{7.4}$$

Here is an example of an n-year death rates vector, using the (female) numbers from the 1925 cohort life table. I'll compute 20-year and 30-year values, conditioning of the age of $x = 50$.

```
 1-CLT$FEMALE[CLT$AGE==70]/CLT$FEMALE[CLT$AGE==50]
[1] 0.1483938
 1-CLT$FEMALE[CLT$AGE==80]/CLT$FEMALE[CLT$AGE==50]
[1] 0.3413173
```

The fraction of 50-year-old females (in the year 1975) who died before their 70th birthday (the year 1995) was a mere 14.8%. That is the value of: $({}_{20}q_{50})$, according to the above definition. But, the fraction of 50-year-old females who died before their 80th birthday, before the year 2005, was a heftier $({}_{30}q_{50}) = 34.1\%$. This should be intuitive given the longer (30 year) window. Finally, I conclude this section by defining a function in **R** that computes n-year survival rates for a given vector of 1-year death rates.

```
SPQR<-function(x,y,qx){
  LT<-cumprod(1-qx)
  LT<-c(1,LT)
  LT[y+1]/LT[x+1]}
```

For example, the command `SPQR(50,80,qx)`, where the `qx` vector is the relevant vector for females (q_{x_f}) in the 1925 cohort, should return the value

`0.6586`, which is a 65.85% survival rate to age 80, for those who made it to age 50. This is exactly: (1 − 0.3415), which is one minus the 30-year death rate computed in the prior box. Note, the y value in the `SPQR(x,y,qx)` function is technically $x + n$ in the definition of $_nq_x$, because a person that is x years old must live another n years to reach age y.

7.11 A First Look at Natural Laws Governing Death

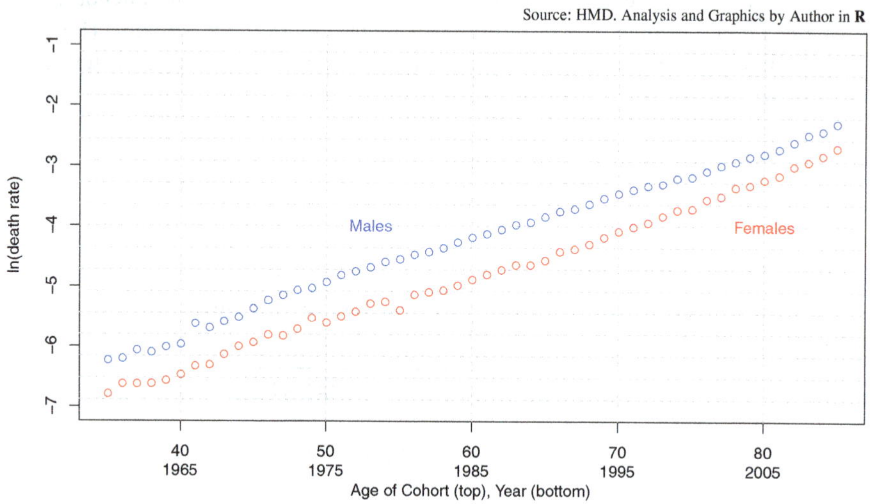

Fig. 7.5 Linear relationship between log of mortality rate and age

At this point I will casually postulate that the q_x values grow exponentially between the age of (approximately) 35 and 85. I use the words *casually postulate* because at this point it's really a conjecture. In the next chapter #8 I'll provide theoretical support for this assertion, but for now I'll examine whether it's a reasonable approximation. Remember that my goal is to predict or forecast the 15 or so missing values of $q_{85}, q_{86} \ldots q_{99}$ so I can predict what fraction of the 1925 cohort will ever get to age 100. From a mathematical point of view (approximate) exponential growth in death rates implies that

$$q_{x+n} = q_x \, e^{gn}, \tag{7.5}$$

where q_x is the death rate at some baseline age x, the index n is measured in years, and g is the growth rate of death rates (notice the double use of the word *rate*). Then, taking natural logarithms of both sides implies that

$$\ln[q_{x+n}] = \ln[q_x] + gn \tag{7.6}$$

which is a *testable hypothesis.* And, although I do plan to do this formally (and rigorously) in the next chapter, for now I'll simply plot the natural logarithm of the 1-year death rates qx, and display them in Fig. 7.5. Alas, we have found a pattern to death: a straight line! Again, the $\ln[q_x]$ values are approximately linear in age, after the age of 35 or so. Moreover, using standard regression (or least square) techniques, I can estimate the slope of the line in Fig. 7.5, using various starting ages for x, for both the 1925 and the 1940 cohort. In fact, the next table displays 95% confidence intervals for the coefficient of the linear regression of the log of the death rate when the regression is conducted from three different starting ages 35, 45, 55, to age 85. The 95% confidence intervals in Table 7.2 are obtained by adding (and subtracting) 1.96 standard errors to the point estimate of the regression coefficient. I realize that I'm being vague and somewhat elusive, for the important takeaway is that the growth rate of the death rate is between 7 and 8%, for the 1925 cohort.

Table 7.2 Estimated growth rates in 1-year death rates (Canada)

	Cohort born in 1925		Cohort born in 1940	
From age	Female	Male	Female	Male
$x = 35$	(0.0773, 0.0802)	(0.0751, 0.0779)	(0.0739, 0.0769)	(0.0697, 0.0738)
$x = 45$	(0.0766, 0.0808)	(0.0717, 0.0734)	(0.0721, 0.0768)	(0.0737, 0.0775)
$x = 55$	(0.0829, 0.0869)	(0.0714, 0.0739)	(0.0687, 0.0761)	(0.0676, 0.0729)

Data source: human mortality database. analysis by author

7.12 Projecting Survival Rates to Age 100

Given the 1-year death rates at age $x = 84$ for males and females, I can project those values forward for the next 15 years to obtain values of $(q_{85}, q_{87} \ldots q_{99})$ and finally forecast survivors to age 100. I will manufacture (forecast) these 15 additional death rate values based on the "theory" that mortality rates (starting at q_{85}) continue to grow at 7.6% for males and 7.8% for females, based on the table. Then, I'll simply use those 15 numbers to create new S_x values, and stitch them together into the life table. Here is the script that does all of that.

```
qx_m.new<-qx_m[85]*exp(c(1:15)*0.076)
qx_m<-append(qx_m,qx_m.new,after=85)
LT<-100000*cumprod(1-qx_m)
LT<-append(LT,100000,after=0)
LT[101]
[1] 1372.044
```

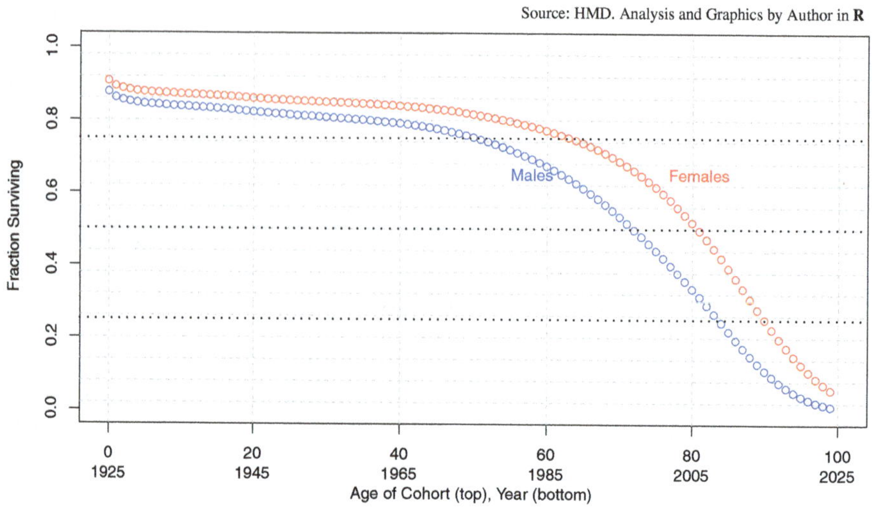

Fig. 7.6 Projecting a cohort life table in the future

What do I get from all this? My prediction is that 1372 males from the 1925 cohort will survive to age 100, to the year 2025. This is a 100-year survival rate (forecast) of 1.37% from age zero. Doing the same for females, but assuming the 1-year death rate q_x will grow at 7.8% per year (instead of the male 7.6%), results in 6410 females who survive to age 100. This is a 100-year survival rate (forecast) of 6.4% for females from the 1925 cohort. Remember one last time, that `LT[101]` is the number of survivors at age $x = 100$, because you can't get **R** to accept an `LT[0]`. The lowest index value is `[1]`, which is age zero.

```
qx_f.new<-qx_f[85]*exp(c(1:15)*0.078)
qx_f<-append(qx_f,qx_f.new,after=85)
LT<-100000*cumprod(1-qx_f)
LT<-append(LT,100000,after=0)
LT[101]
[1] 6410.31
```

Figure 7.6 plots these values and shows the projected fraction of survivors of the 1925 cohort up to age 100. Just to be clear, The first 85 years in Fig. 7.6 are based on realized mortality rates from the Human Mortality Database (HMD). I extrapolated the values from age 86 to age 99 by growing the 1-year death rates by g percent per year, and then appended those values to the cohort life table. So, end this chapter with my first statistical prediction. The fraction of survivors.

7.13 Final Notes

- You might have noticed that the word *probability* didn't appear anywhere in this chapter. Rather, this chapter offers a first stab at *thinking* about death *rates* from a historical population perspective. Forward-looking probabilities—that is thinking about your own human longevity as a random variable T_x, with its own probability density function, will come in the next chapter.
- Note that the Human Mortality Database (HMD)—of which a screenshot appears in Fig. 7.7—stores the cohort mortality tables (the so-called death rate in the column labeled 1x1), in q_x format, instead of S_x format. In other words, you have to create the life tables from the death rates, which is the opposite of how I introduced the topic in this chapter. Be careful when you download the data, to use the *cohort* and not the *period* values. The exact URL is provided in reference [2]. For more on longevity see reference [3, 4], or reference [1] for a classic textbook on actuarial methods.
- Towards the end of this chapter, when I was working with q_x values, I should have been (more) careful to (constantly) remind readers these are 1-year death rates for the 1925 cohort, or occasionally the 1940 cohort. If and when I need to forcefully remind readers that the q_x vector is from a specific cohort birth year, I will use the notation $q_x[1925]$, just to ensure everyone is on the same page.
- See the following Table 7.3 and make sure you understand the difference between $q_{60}[1940]$ versus $q_{40}[1960]$. In particular, the elements that have a question mark, can't be known at the end of the year 2020, because those deaths haven't occurred yet. Stated differently, in any given year (for example 2020), deaths at all ages will complete the diagonal of the table.

Source: HMD. Author's Screenshot of HMD on 8 April 2020

Complete Data Series [Explanatory notes]

	Available dates	Age interval × Year interval			
		1x1	1x5	1x10	5x1
Period data					
Births	1921 - 2016	1-year			
Deaths	1921 - 2016	1x1	1x5	1x10	5x1
Deaths by Lexis triangles	1921 - 2016	Lexis			
Population size	1921 - 2017	1-year			5-year
Exposure-to-risk	1921 - 2016	1x1	1x5	1x10	5x1
Exposure-to-risk by Lexis triangles	1921 - 2016	Lexis			
Death rates	1921 - 2016	1x1	1x5	1x10	5x1
Life tables	1921 - 2016				
Females		1x1	1x5	1x10	5x1
Males		1x1	1x5	1x10	5x1
Total (both sexes)		1x1	1x5	1x10	5x1
Life expectancy at birth	1921 - 2016	1-year	5-year	10-year	
Cohort data					
Exposure-to-risk	1840 - 1986	1x1	1x5	1x10	5x1
Death rates	1840 - 1986	1x1	1x5	1x10	5x1

Fig. 7.7 Human mortality database: Period vs. Cohort

Table 7.3 Cohort vs. Period mortality: which q_x is known by end-of 2020?

Birth year	Age 0	Age 20	Age 40	Age 60	Age 80
1920	$q_0[1920]$	$q_{20}[1920]$	$q_{40}[1920]$	$q_{60}[1920]$	$q_{80}[1920]$
1940	$q_0[1940]$	$q_{20}[1940]$	$q_{40}[1940]$	$q_{60}[1940]$	$q_{80}[1940]$
1960	$q_0[1960]$	$q_{20}[1960]$	$q_{40}[1960]$	$q_{60}[1960]$	?
1980	$q_0[1980]$	$q_{20}[1980]$	$q_{40}[1980]$	?	?
2000	$q_0[2000]$	$q_{20}[2000]$	?	?	?

Questions and Problems

7.1 Referring again to Fig. 7.7, download the 1960 Canadian cohort (not period!) death rate vector, $q_x[1960]$, and compute the fraction of those born in the year 1960, who survived to the age of 50 (in the year 2010.) Using our notation, that is S_{50}/S_0. Compare the values to the corresponding numbers for the 1925 and 1940 cohort.

7.2 Estimate the slope and intercept of $\ln[q_x]$ for the 1940 cohort (both males and females), using data from the age of 35–70. You can either do this using the built-in least squares (a.k.a. linear model) function in **R**, called `lm(.)`, or look up the formula for the slope and intercept (in any textbook on statistics) and compute these values using brute-force. Please discuss some of the methodological concerns with such a (small) set of numbers.

7.3 Forecast or estimate the fraction of the 1960 cohort (who are 50 years-old in the year 2010), who will survive to the age of 100, based on the methodology described in the chapter. How does it compare to the 1925 cohort?

7.4 Please estimate values of S_{90}/S_{60}, which is the 30-year survival rate conditional on being age $x = 60$, for the 1925, 1940, and 1960 cohort.

7.5 Pick one other country (anyone) from the Human Mortality Database (HMD), which should all look quite similar to Fig. 7.7, and download 1-year (cohort) death rates, create a 1940 cohort life table, and compare projected survival rates S_{90}/S_{60}, conditional on age 60.

References

1. Dickson, D. C. M., Hardy, M. R., & Waters, H. R. (2010). *Actuarial mathematics for life contingent risks*. Cambridge: Cambridge University Press.
2. Human Mortality Database (CHMD). http://www.bdlc.umontreal.ca/CHMD/prov/ont/ont.htm
3. Maier H., Gampe J., Jeune B., Robine J.M., & Vaupel J.W. (Eds.) (2010). *Supercentenarians*. Heidelberg: Springer.
4. Olshansky, S. J., & Carnes, B. A. (2001). *The quest for immortality: Science at the Frontiers of aging*. New York: W.W. Norton & Company.

Chapter 8
Life and Death in Continuous Time: Gompertz 101

Continuing from where the prior Chap. 7 left off, this chapter explains how to construct and work with (a.k.a. cook) the remaining lifetime random variable: T_x. The approach to lifetime randomness is based on the underlying mortality hazard rate λ_x, which is the continuous-time (and probabilistic) analog of the 1-year death rate q_x. This chapter models and constructs T_x variables for a variety of given mortality hazard rates λ_x. This then sets the stage for the main intellectual objective, which is to introduce (and justify) the Benjamin Gompertz law of mortality. That important and famous law is *experienced* via a number of simulation exercises and experiments in **R**. The Gompertz model is the computational backbone for many of the subsequent computations (and recipes) in the book.

8.1 Functions Used and Defined

8.1.1 Sample of Native R Functions Used

- `optimize(.)` searches for a minimum or maximum of a function.
- `runif(.)` generates random numbers that are uniformly distributed.
- `sqrt(.)` computes the square root.
- `sort(.)` sorts a vector of numbers.
- `ceiling(.)` returns the smallest integer larger than an argument.
- `integrate(.)`, one-dimensional integration of a given function.

M. A. Milevsky, *Retirement Income Recipes in R*, Use R!,
https://doi.org/10.1007/978-3-030-51434-1_8

8.1.2 User-Defined R Functions

- `TPXG(x,t,m,b)` computes survival probabilities based on the Gompertz law.
- `GRAN(N,x,m,b)` generates N *random* lifetimes based on the Gompertz law.
- `LTLD(z)` creates a cohort life table (CLT) from a dataset of random lifetimes.

8.2 The Calculus: Survival Probabilities from Hazard Rates

Imagine it's the year 1925, and you were just born. Some members of your cohort will survive to age $x = 85$, and others will die before they reach retirement. Only time can (and did) tell. Your remaining lifetime (measured in years) is random. I'll denote that variable by the symbol T_0, where the subscript reminds you that it's conditional on age $x = 0$. The question I address in this chapter is how to *model* the random human lifetime. *What distribution should be used for the uncertainty?* Indeed, there are many candidates, for example, the normal, the exponential, or even the uniform distribution. In theory I could select any mathematical representation for $\Pr[T_0 \geq t]$, which is the probability of surviving t years from birth. However, as per Chap. 7, there is ample data on the fraction of people from prior cohorts who have actually survived t-years, which gives many clues for the structure of $\Pr[T_0 \geq t]$ as a function of t. In particular, recall from Sect. 7.8, that the 1-year death rates q_x could be expressed as:

$$q_x = -\frac{S_{x+1} - S_x}{S_x}. \tag{8.1}$$

Given any vector of 1-year death rates q_x, I showed how to *construct* a unique cohort life table S_x, per the algorithm in Sect. 7.7. But now, instead of a discrete and declining function S_x, counting the number or *fraction of survivors* at age x, think of a (new) continuous function $\theta(t)$, measuring the *survival probability* to any given time t. That function starts off at a value of $\theta(0) = 1$ and declines until $\theta(\omega) = 0$ at some sufficiently large value of ω. With that analogy in mind, look closely at the numerator and denominator of Eq. (8.1). The numerator is the change in the value of a function $(S_{x+1} - S_x)/1$, and the denominator is the value of that function itself, S_x. Motivated by Eq. (8.1), I'll *construct* the new function $\theta(t) = \Pr[T_x \geq t]$, which is the survival probability, in an analogous manner:

$$\lambda_t = -\frac{\theta'(t)}{\theta(t)}. \tag{8.2}$$

Again, notice similarity between the *discrete time* Eqs. (8.1) and (8.2). This is the essence of the recipe for constructing $\theta(t) = \Pr[T_0 \geq t]$ based on any given function λ_t. Basically, it comes down to solving an ordinary differential equation (ODE) for $\theta(t)$, which can also be written as:

$$-\lambda_t = \frac{\partial}{\partial t}\ln[\theta(t)] \tag{8.3}$$

In sum, I "cook" random lifetimes by starting with a λ_t function, and then solving for the survival probability $\theta(t)$, by integrating both sides of Eq. (8.3), which at the very least can be done via numerical integration in **R**:

$$\theta(t) = e^{-\int_0^t \lambda_s ds}. \tag{8.4}$$

8.3 Constant Mortality and Exponential Lifetimes

Here is an example of how to *construct* a random lifetime T_x using the simplest form of mortality hazard rate, a constant, where $\lambda_t = \lambda$, which doesn't depend on either age or time. Obviously, age-invariance doesn't happen in the real world, as evidenced by the fact older people die at higher rates than younger people, but let's investigate where such an assumption might lead. There is no need for *numerical integration* in **R**, because the solution to the ODE in Eq. (8.4) can be obtained analytically as:

$$\theta(t) = \mathrm{e}^{-\int_0^t \lambda_s\, ds} = \mathrm{e}^{-\lambda t}. \tag{8.5}$$

Figure 8.1 plots the $\theta(t)$ function (again, the solution to the ODE) which is one minus the cumulative distribution function of the random variable T_x. I selected values of $\lambda = 1/30$ (which is 3.33% mortality hazard rate) and $\lambda = 1/20$ (a 5.00% rate.) At first glance Fig. 8.1 looks reasonable. For an $x = 65$ year-old (time $t = 0$), it displays the probability of surviving to a continuum of ages, until age $y = 100$

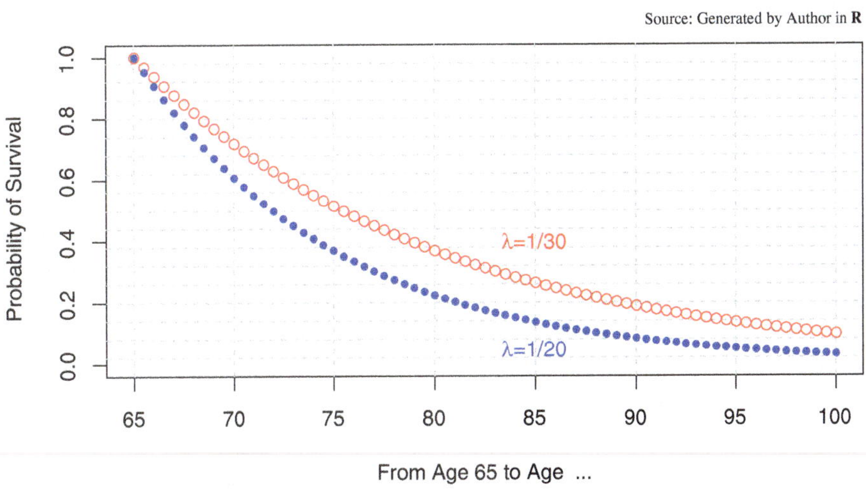

Fig. 8.1 Survival $\theta(t)$ declines exponentially under constant mortality: λ

(time $t = 35$). Indeed, the exponential lifetime assumption, synonymous with a constant mortality hazard rate, is often used in financial and economic models. However, it suffers from a number of *problems*, namely it doesn't reflect how people actually die. Also, the strictly *convex* survival probability curve is at odds with empirical survival frequencies (in Chap. 7), which were mostly *concave.* Bottom line: exponential lifetimes don't fit the data. How's that? Well, remember that (log) 1-year death rates $\ln[q_x]$, which in continuous time is $\ln[\lambda_x]$, should increase with age. So, we need a better mortality rate model.

8.4 The Gompertz Law of Mortality

Although the constant $\lambda_t = \lambda$ assumption is convenient and easy to work with, it's unrealistic for retirement income planning (unless you are advising lobsters, who actually have a constant mortality hazard rate). A more realistic assumption for the λ_x curve, inspired by the final observations in Chap. 7, is that $\ln[\lambda_x]$ is a linear function of chronological age, which implies that the mortality hazard rate curve is an exponential function. In other words, in this section I'll assume that $\lambda_x = h_0 e^{gx}$, or equivalently that $\ln[\lambda_x] = \ln[h_0] + gx$, where h_0 is an (initial) time-zero mortality hazard rate, and g is the mortality growth rate. I'll start by investigating what this particular specification implies for the conditional survival probability $\theta(t) = \Pr[T_x \geq t]$. First, I'll solve the relevant ODE from Eq. (8.4) and then I'll plot some survival probability curves and see how they compare with Fig. 8.1. Now, while the parameterization (h_0, g) for an exponential specification of λ_x seems natural and easy to work, I'll re-parametrize using a slightly different formulation. In particular, assume the following functional form for the mortality hazard rate function, a.k.a. the mortality rate:

$$
\begin{aligned}
\lambda_x &= \frac{1}{b} \mathrm{e}^{(x-m)/b} \\
\ln[\lambda_x] &= \overbrace{-\ln[b] - m/b}^{\ln[h_0]} + \overbrace{(1/b)}^{g}\, x
\end{aligned} \tag{8.6}
$$

At first this might seem overly complicated, relative to a simpler $\lambda_x = h_0 e^{gx}$, specification. But there are good reasons for writing the mortality rate in this manner (reasons I'll get to in a moment), although I will return to the (h_0, g) formulation in later chapters. Regardless of the exact parameter specification, solving the fundamental ODE for the survival probability (with a bit of calculus), combining equations (8.6) and (8.4), leads to the following expression:

$$
\theta(t) = \Pr[T_x \geq t] = \exp\{\mathrm{e}^{(x-m)/b}(1 - \mathrm{e}^{t/b})\} \tag{8.7}
$$

Using this formulation, the parameter m represents the modal value (in years) of the distribution and the b parameter represents the dispersion (in years) coefficient.

For example, I might say that your random lifetime has a modal value of $m = 85$ years and a dispersion coefficient of $b = 10$ years. Note that the modal value isn't the mean (average) value, and that the dispersion coefficient isn't quite the standard deviation either, although both are close. This particular specification of the mortality rate is known as the Gompertz assumption, which will play a very central role in many of the models (and recipes) in the next few chapters. So, the first step is to gain some intuition for this particular model, and I'll create a user-defined function for the Gompertz survival probability. It is a simple implementation of Eq. (8.7).

```
TPXG<-function(x,t,m,b){exp(exp((x-m)/b)*(1-exp(t/b)))}
```

Notice that the function has four arguments (x, t, m, b). The first argument is the current (conditioning) age x, the second argument is time t , and the third and fourth arguments are the Gompertz parameters. Here are some numerical examples.

```
> round(TPXG(0,100,85,10),digits=3)
[1] 0.011
> round(TPXG(85,15,85,10),digits=3)
[1] 0.031
```

The interpretation is as follows. If you are (a.k.a. conditional on) age $x = 0$, the probability of surviving to age $y = 100$, which is $t = 100$ years, is 1.1%, under a Gompertz model with parameters $m = 85$ and $b = 10$. But, if you are already (conditional on) age $x = 85$, the probability of surviving to age $y = 100$, which is $t = 15$ years, is 3.1%. As we saw in the prior chapter, the older you are, the greater the probability of reaching any given age. Now, for the sake of completeness (and an independent verification) I will compute the 15-year survival probability, a.k.a. $\theta(15)$ using the functional notation, by asking **R** to solve the ODE in Eq. (8.4), numerically. To do this properly (and without error messages) I must set all the Gompertz parameter values (first) and then define the mortality rate function in terms of time (only). Then, I can perform the numerical integration, between $t = 0$ and $t = 15$. The result (to 3 digits) is as follows:

```
m<-85; b<-10; x<-85
lambda<-function(t){-(1/b)*exp((x+t-m)/b)}
round(exp(integrate(lambda,0,15)$value), digits=3)
[1] 0.031
```

So, the analytic result is consistent with the brute-force numerical integration. For further insight, the following (very familiar) script plots survival probabilities, $\Pr[T_x \geq t]$, a.k.a. the $\theta(t)$ function, under a Gompertz specification:

```
plot(c(65,100),c(0,1),type="n",
xlab="From Age 65 to Age...", ylab="Probability of Survival")
grid(ny=18,lty=20)
for (i in 0:70){
  points(65+i/2,TPXG(65,i/2,90,10),col="red")
```

```
  points(65+i/2,TPXG(65,i/2,80,10),col="blue",pch=20)}
text(85,0.75,"m=90",col="red")
text(85,0.10,"m=80",col="blue")
```

The survival probabilities decline with age (and time), and they decline faster with smaller m, which should be intuitive. The lower the modal value of the remaining lifetime random variable T_x, the sooner the person is expected to die, so the survival probability to any future age should be lower. To be clear, the modal value of life m is the age at which this person is most likely to die, which is different (and actually higher) than the mean lifetime, denoted by $E[T_x]$, in a Gompertz model. Although there are no exact (analytic) expressions for the mean of the Gompertz random variable, I can use numerical routines in **R**. In particular, I can leverage the extremely useful and fundamental construction of the expectation as the integral of the survival probability function. This is one of the first things taught in a course on probability theory, and in the context of the Gompertz law of mortality it implies that:

$$E[T_x] = \int_0^\infty \Pr[T_x \geq t]dt. \tag{8.8}$$

So, with that relationship in mind, here is a short script in **R** that computes $E[T_x]$, using the numerical integration routine I noted earlier, in conjunction with the user-defined `TPXG(.)` function (Fig. 8.2).

```
m<-88; b<-10; x<-65
theta<-function(t){TPXG(x,t,m,b)}
round((integrate(theta,0,45)$value), digits=2)
[1] 20.13
```

The lower bound of integration is zero (years) and the upper bound is 45 (years), after which the survival probability is assumed to be negligible. (Although I could have continued to infinity as the upper bound and it wouldn't have made much of a difference.) So, at $x = 65$, your expected remaining lifetime is 20.13 years, and your expected age at death is 85.13, whereas your modal age at death is $m = 88$. Note the difference between mean, mode as well as median age at death, which is the $(x + t)$, at which `TPXG(x,t,m,b)=0.5`.

Finally, there is little-known gem of an expression for $E[T_0]$, in terms of Euler's constant $\gamma_e := 0.5772$, as well as an approximation to $SD[T_0]$, in terms of: $\pi = 3.1415$, as follows:

$$\begin{aligned} E[T_0] &= m - b\gamma_e \approx m - (0.5772)b, \\ SD[T_0] &\approx b\frac{\pi}{\sqrt{6}} \approx (1.28255)b, \end{aligned} \tag{8.9}$$

which implies that (at age $x = 0$) the standard deviation of life is greater than the dispersion coefficient b. The source for Eqs. (8.9) is the reference cited as [2]. I'll return to these later on, but for now let's develop some intuition for the Gompertz law of mortality via simulation.

Source: Generated by Author in **R**

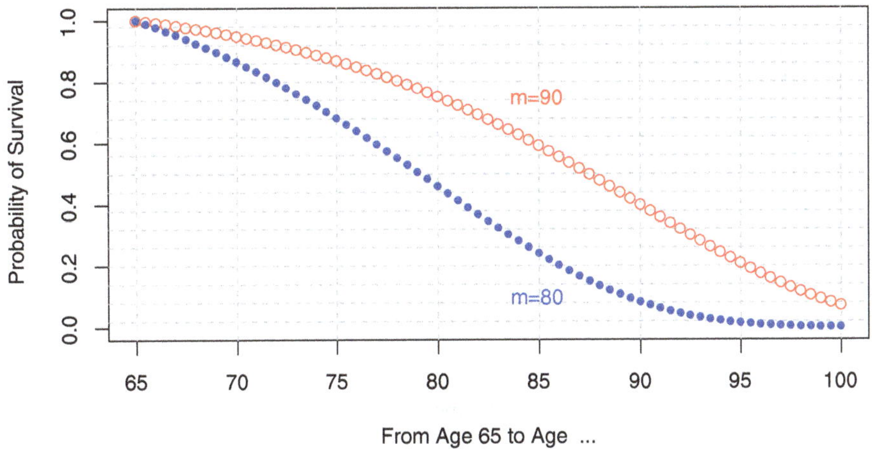

Fig. 8.2 Gompertz: survival $\theta(t)$ declines faster than exponentially

8.5 Simulating Human Lifetimes

Back in Chaps. 5 and 6, I created an **R** script that simulated a large sample of *portfolio longevity* values by randomizing investment returns and recursively iterating the market value of the retirement portfolio under the assumption of a fixed withdrawal level. Similarly, in this section I'll explain how to create a random sample of human longevity lifetimes, based on the previously introduced Gompertz representation. And, unlike the multi-line code for *portfolio longevity*, the simulation of *human longevity* only requires one very short line. In addition to the elegance, the recipe will help you gain a deeper (and different) understanding of the Gompertz law of mortality. It can also be used to test the robustness of a retirement income plan against different longevity scenarios. I'll get to the *robustness testing* later on, and in subsequent chapters, but first I'll explain how to generate random Gompertz lifetimes. Recall from Eq. (8.6) that the *probability* of surviving to time t, which is the `TPXG(.)` function in **R**, is defined and denoted by

$$\Pr[T_x \geq t] = ({}_t p_x) = e^{-\int_0^t \lambda_s ds} = \exp\{e^{(x-m)/b}(1 - e^{t/b})\}, \tag{8.10}$$

where the first expression $\Pr[T_x \geq t]$ represents how a "probabilist" thinks about random lifetimes, the second expression $({}_t p_x)$ is how an "actuary" denotes the survival probabilities, the third expression represents the mathematical construction via the mortality hazard rate λ, and the fourth (and final) item in Eq. (8.10) is the analytic expression for the actual Gompertz survival probability. By taking logarithms and then isolating t, one arrives at the expression:

$$t = b \ln[1 - \ln[{}_t p_x]\, e^{(m-x)/b}]. \tag{8.11}$$

This may seem like an odd way of presenting Eq. (8.10), but it should be interpreted as follows. Under the Gompertz law with parameters (x, m, b), if you know the *tail* probability, you can solve for the *tail* age. For example, under parameters $(x = 65, m = 80, b = 10)$, the *tail* survival probability 0.1% is at *tail* age 99.6. Or, in the other direction, the probability of surviving to the very right (and ripe) tail age of 99.6 is 0.1%. Using our notation $\Pr[T_{65} \geq 34.6] = 0.001$. See the following:

```
x<-65; m<-80; b<-10; p=0.001
t<-b*log(1-log(p)*exp((m-x)/b))
round(x+t,1)
[1] 99.6
```

To be clear, under these Gompertz parameters, one-in-a-thousand 65-year-olds will survive to age 99.6, a.k.a. the tail. In contrast, the (ten times as high) 1% point is at the age of 95.7, per the next script. Stated using our notation: $\Pr[T_{65} \geq 30.7] = 0.01$, and should be intuitive given the higher (1% versus 0.1%) probability.

```
x<-65; m<-80; b<-10; p=0.01
t<-b*log(1-log(p)*exp((m-x)/b))
round(x+t,1)
[1] 95.7
```

This one-to-one mapping between time t (or age $x + t$) and probability p, under the Gompertz specification, makes it (very) easy to simulate random values of t (or ages $x + t$). The idea here is as follows. I generate uniformly [0, 1] distributed random variables, and then replace the $({}_t p_x)$ in Eq. 8.11 with those uniform random numbers. Under a random right-hand side, the transformed variable (on the left-hand side) t will have a Gompertz distribution. This trick (for lack of a better word) is used in many Monte Carlo simulations when the cumulative distribution function (CDF) of the random variable can be inverted and isolated as a function of t. For those who are new to simulations, I would recommend the classic book called *Simulation*, written by Sheldon M. Ross, or the book *Random Number Generation and Monte Carlo Methods*, by James E. Gentle. Both of them will teach you many other ticks. But as far as I'm concerned, the final step here is to put this into a dedicated script.

```
GRAN<-function(N,x,m,b){b*log(1-log(runif(N))*exp((m-x)/b))}
```

The `GRAN` function, which is an abbreviation for Gompertz random number, generates N random conditional remaining lifetimes for an individual who is currently x-years-old. The `runif(N)` generates uniform [0, 1] random numbers, and the rest of the script is an implementation of Eq. (8.11). Here are some examples.

```
round(GRAN(20,65,90,10),1)
round(65+GRAN(20,65,90,10),1)
 [1]  88.8   92.4 102.3 104.3   86.9   81.6   79.7   77.9
 [9]  98.1   84.0   96.8   86.9   89.5   72.6   89.7   88.7
[17]  73.2   91.8   78.7   87.5
```

These are 20 (random) ages to which a 65-year-old might live, under a Gompertz law of mortality. The oldest person (in the simulation) dies at the age of 104.3 (yes, that's possible) and the youngest person dies at the age of 72.6, which is a mere 8 years after age 65. Remember that these simulations are all conditional on reaching age $x = 65$. I could have simulated 20 random lifetimes conditional on reaching age 30, which would look a bit different.

```
round(30+GRAN(20,30,90,10),1)
 [1]  97.5   74.5   81.1   91.1   98.9   96.6 101.3   87.8
 [9]  95.5   36.5 101.9   85.1   82.1   92.7   47.7   87.7
[17]  84.3   92.2 101.9   96.7
```

In the above (albeit very small sample) simulation run, one of the 20 people died at the very young age of 36.5. This might seem very odd, but is mathematically possible when conditioning on age $x = 35$ versus age $x = 65$. Of course, if you simulate 20 random remaining lifetimes T_{30}, there is a high probability that you will not get a death at the age of 30 (technically, plus epsilon), 40, or even 50. Those are the statistical properties of small samples. In fact, just for the fun of it, if you condition on being age $x = 100$, and then simulate 20 random lifetimes T_{100}, they all die within 10 years. Recall that the mortality hazard rate is very high at advanced ages, and survival beyond 110 is extremely unlikely—even if you are already $x = 100$ years-old. Here is that command and the results.

```
round(100+GRAN(20,100,90,10),1)
 [1] 100.3 100.2 100.0 100.8 102.7 103.4 100.5 109.5
 [9] 101.5 105.6 100.5 103.0 102.1 101.0 101.5 100.1
[17] 100.5 100.7 104.1 103.0
```

Reminder: In continuous time, $\Pr[T_x > 1] = \Pr[T_x \geq 1]$. Either way, pay attention to where the current (conditioning) age x appears within the above **R** command. First, it's used within the `GRAN(.)` script, for conditioning the random remaining lifetime, and then age x is added to compute the age at death. By definition, when $x = 0$, the remaining lifetime T_0 is in fact the age at death. But, when $x > 0$, the remaining lifetime must be added to x. To make sure this distinction is clear, the next command will generate a (much) larger sample of remaining lifetimes T_x, both at age $x = 0$ and age $x = 65$, and plot them via the `hist(.)` function. Here is the command for generating two samples of $N = 100000$ random lifetimes, for $m = 85$ and $b = 10$.

Source: Generated by Author in **R**

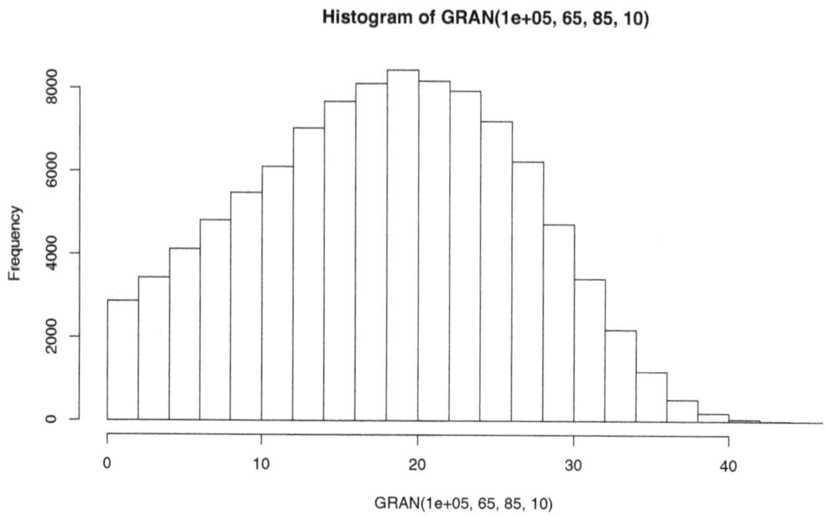

Fig. 8.3 Histogram of 100,000 remaining lifetimes at age $x = 65$

```
hist(GRAN(100000,65,85,10))
hist(GRAN(100000,0,85,10))
```

The first sample is conditional on age $x = 65$, and the second sample is conditional on age $x = 0$, so those numbers also represent ages at death (in addition to remaining lifetimes.) Notice the qualitative as well as quantitative difference between Fig. 8.3, which is associated with T_{65}, and Fig. 8.4, which is for T_0.

The important difference between Figs. 8.3 and 8.4 is the skew in the data (and the figure). They are (obviously) both generated by the underlying Gompertz law, but for T_{65} the distribution is (almost, but not quite) bell-curve like, albeit with a right skew. In contrast, for T_0 the distribution has a noticeable left skew. There is a (small) chance of dying in the first few years of life, but most of the deaths occur between the ages of (roughly) 65 and 95. It's quite interesting how the Gompertz distribution can accommodate a rather wide range of "pictures" for the remaining lifetime. Practically speaking this re-iterates yet again the importance of conditioning when discussing human longevity. The question: *How long will I live?* has a different numerical as well as qualitative (shape of graph) answer, depending on your current age. In later chapters, I will condition and index T_x on more than (only) chronological age x, but I'll keep it clean and simple.

Source: Generated by Author in **R**

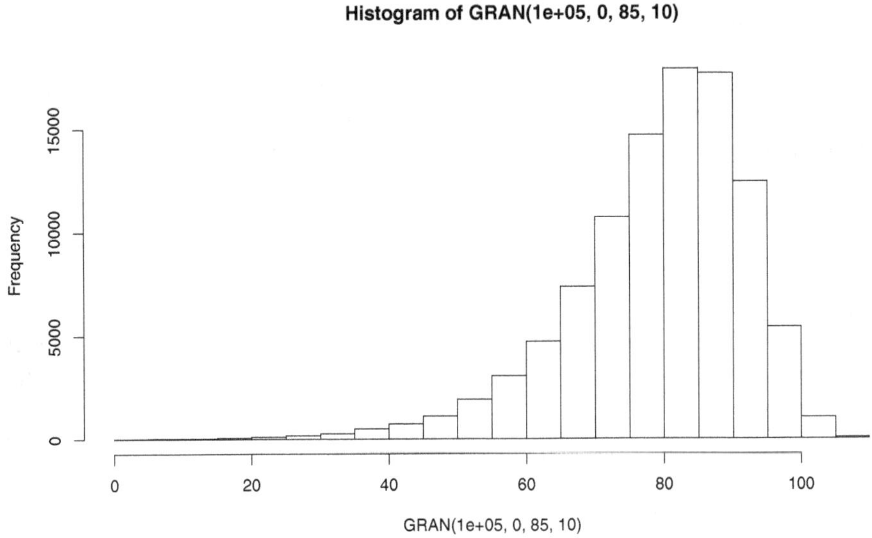

Fig. 8.4 Histogram of 100,000 remaining lifetimes at age $x = 0$

8.6 Gompertz Experimentation via Simulation

I suggest you spend some time playing with the `GRAN(.)` function, to develop a deeper intuition for the Gompertz lifetime assumption. Use a variety of conditioning ages x, as well as the modal value of the age at death m, and the dispersion parameter b. Plot histograms and compute summary statistics. Generate a (large) simulation and *verify* that the approximations for the mean and standard deviation of the Gompertz lifetime, which I presented in Sect. 8.4, are reasonably accurate. For example, here are summary statistics for a sample of one million random lifetimes, generated under a Gompertz law with a modal value of $m = 85$ and dispersion coefficient of $b = 10$, conditional on age $x = 0$.

```
zdat<-GRAN(1000000,0,85,10)
round(summary(zdat),digits=2)
Min. 1st Qu.  Median    Mean 3rd Qu.    Max.
0.03   72.55   81.34   79.23   88.26  110.26
```

The oldest person died at the age of 110, and the youngest person (very sadly) died after 11 days, or 0.03 years. Now, this is a good time to remind readers (yet again) that the Gompertz law does a (very) bad job of describing mortality at younger ages: $x < 30$. In the real world, out of a sample of one million babies, a larger proportion will die earlier in life (versus the above data), and the median, mean, and modal value will all be lower *in real life*. The point here is to develop a deeper understanding of the Gompertz law, which I'll (only be) using for advanced ages. Stated differently, for most of what follows in this book I will be focused on T_x values for which $x >> 0$ (that is *much* greater than zero).

Nevertheless, assuming that the Gompertz law is (theoretically) appropriate at all ages, the sample mean and standard deviation should match the analytic age-zero values. Recall, from Eq. (8.9) that the standard deviation of the Gompertz distribution (conditional on age $x = 0$) can be approximated by $\pi b/\sqrt{6}$, and the mean of the Gompertz distribution is $m - b\gamma_e$, where γ_e is Euler's constant. (Once again, please see the article cited as [2] for details). In what follows I'll investigate how close those formulas match the simulated results. The sample `zdat` mean was $E[T_0] = 79.23$ years, and the (sample) standard deviation is `sd(zdat)=12.78` years.

Now compare with the analytic expression. In **R**, Euler's γ constant is obtained via the command: `-digamma(1)`, which produces the value `0.577`. Note the negative sign, so $(m - b\gamma_e)$ is

```
round(85+10*digamma(1),digits=2)
[1] 79.23
```

That number is bang-on the mean to two digits after the decimal, which is what you would expect (pun intended) from a sample of one million random Gompertz lifetimes. As for the standard deviation, using the `pi` variable, the relevant command in **R** is

```
round(pi*10/sqrt(6),digits=2)
[1] 12.83
```

That number is just slightly higher than the statistical sample value (from one million Gompertz lifetimes) of 12.78 years. The gap—of slightly less than one half of 1%—is to be expected, considering that the analytic expression: $\pi b/\sqrt{6}$ is only an approximation to $SD[T_0]$, and not an exact value. While on the topic of the standard deviation of the remaining lifetime random variable T_x, I'll use the same simulation techniques to estimate $SD[T_x]$, conditional on ages $x = 55, 60, 65, 70$. For the following script, the modal value is $m = 85$ and the dispersion coefficient is $b = 10$.

```
sd(GRAN(100000,55,85,10))
[1] 10.2301
sd(GRAN(100000,60,85,10))
[1] 9.455903
sd(GRAN(100000,65,85,10))
[1] 8.548168
sd(GRAN(100000,70,85,10))
[1] 7.532129
```

Notice how the sample standard deviations start (when $x = 55$) at 10.23 years, and decline to 7.53 years by age $x = 70$. In other words, the dispersion coefficient b, which is one of the two critical parameters in the Gompertz model, is lower than (and underestimates) the true standard deviation of life, early in life. Then, at advanced ages x, the $SD[T_x] < b$. In the above simulation (remember: your results might differ) this happened between age $x = 55$ and $x = 60$, but depends on both (m, b). So, while b and $SD[T_x]$ are both measured in years, relatively close to each other and attempt to capture longevity uncertainty, they aren't quite the same thing.

In one last test of the analytic formulas, let's compare the simulation-based survival frequencies to the `TPXG(.)` function I coded-up from the prior section. For this particular experiment, I will "cook" a million random Gompertz lifetimes, and then count the number who survive beyond age 100. Here is the script.

```
zdat<-65+GRAN(1000000,65,90,10)
zdat[zdat<100]<-0; zdat[zdat>=100]<-1
#Simulation Frequency (your results might differ)
round(sum(zdat)/length(zdat),digits=4)
[1] 0.0718
#Analytic Probability (you should get the same number)
round(TPXG(65,35,90,10),digits=4)
[1] 0.0716
```

The first line creates the `zdat` dataset with a million random Gompertz lifetimes. The second line replaces those one million entries with either a value of `0` or a value of `1`, depending on whether the given simulated life survived to age 100, or not. You will notice (for the first time) the # symbol within the box, which commands **R** to ignore anything after # and is a great way to add comments to a script. (And, I probably should have mentioned this about 100 pages ago.) The line that follows reports the number (or more precisely the frequency) of simulated 65-year-olds who became centenarians, which is 7.18% of the million at $x = 65$.

The final line reports the analytic probability based on the Gompertz law, which is 7.16%. This is slightly lower than the simulated value. So, in this particular simulation run I ended-up with (approximately 200) more centenarians than predicted by theory. Needless to say, the extra number of very old people doesn't mean that the Gompertz assumption was wrong, or that his law of mortality isn't working simply because people are dying at slower rates. Rather, it's all part of random noise (even in a sample of a million retirees). Indeed, if you conduct this simulation experiment again (and again), sometimes the simulated frequencies will exceed the analytic `TPXG(.)` values, and sometimes they will fall short. You should remember this later when I discuss parameter estimation (with smaller sample sizes).

8.7 Cohort Life Tables from Random Lifetimes

In this section I'll return to where I started at the beginning of Chap. 7, with cohort life tables. Recall that a CLT is a list of descending numbers, starting at arbitrary 10,000 lives and declining uniformly to zero, representing the number of survivors at each integer age from $x = 0$ until $x = 120$ (or beyond). The CLT was used to extract 1-year death rates q_x, which inspired the mortality hazard rate λ_t, and the Gompertz representation in continuous time, etc. In this section I'll explain how to move the other way and convert a sample of random lifetimes, such as the values contained within the `zdat` vector, into a proper cohort table. Then, I'll compute the corresponding 1-year death rates q_x. What's the point of all this manipulation? Well, it's all done to increase your understanding of Gompertz, and to help you "cook" the probability your portfolio will last as long as you do. My pedagogical objective is $\Pr[L_x > T_x]$. So, assume you have a dataset (vector) of lifetimes, which might even be real lives. The following user-defined function creates a cohort life table from the given dataset.

```
LTLD<-function(z){
z<-sort(z); N<-length(z); LT<-c();
LT[1]<-N; T<-ceiling(max(z))+1
for (i in 2:T){
LT[i]<-N-length(z[z<=i-1])
}
LT}
```

The first thing the script does is `sort` the vector and measure its `length`. Then, it creates a new (empty) vector `LT`, and proceeds to count the number of people who die before age `i=1` and `i=2`, etc., in a loop, all the way to the oldest person in the dataset. The key command within the script is `N-length(z[z<=i-1])`, which counts the number of people who are above the age of `i-1`, and places that value in the `LT[i]` vector. As the parameter `i` increases, the number of people decline, thus creating a proper cohort life table that begins with `N` and declines to zero survivors. Here is an example with `zdat` containing a million random lifetimes.

```
zdat<-GRAN(1000000,0,90,10); summary(zdat)
     Min.   1st Qu.    Median      Mean   3rd Qu.      Max.
  0.05348  77.54704  86.36598  84.24681  93.27858 116.37412
zdat.clt<-LTLD(zdat); zdat.clt
# Remember. This is a simulation. Your results will differ.
```

Notice that the oldest (simulated) person dies before age 117, which becomes the last entry in the manufactured cohort life table at position `[118]=0`. I now apply the `LTLD` function and convert the dataset of simulated lifetimes `zdat` into a proper cohort life table, denoted by `zdat.clt`. For the sake of completeness, here is (my) entire cohort life table which is created from the Gompertz simulated lifetimes.

```
  [1] 1000000  999983  999974  999962  999945  999922  999903
  [8]  999879  999854  999827  999796  999749  999711  999676
 [15]  999622  999577  999503  999435  999367  999294  999216
 [22]  999108  998987  998873  998743  998598  998420  998225
 [29]  998040  997834  997578  997320  997022  996699  996384
 [36]  995978  995556  995052  994521  993928  993287  992568
 [43]  991808  990942  989978  988921  987760  986402  984938
 [50]  983475  981807  979944  977817  975552  973083  970263
 [57]  967258  963814  959982  955900  951501  946474  941011
 [64]  935094  928433  921091  913198  904538  895017  884578
 [71]  873200  860887  847401  832827  817078  799981  781663
 [78]  761757  740097  717428  692846  666476  638442  609239
 [85]  578388  545997  512610  477627  441999  405440  368523
 [92]  331780  295508  259747  225722  192825  162164  133945
 [99]  108467   85995   66433   49776   36156   25613   17483
[106]   11470    7211    4278    2352    1227     613     286
[113]     114      40      14       3       1       0
# Warning: Simulation. Your maximum age might differ.
```

The table's first entry (at age zero) begins with 100,000 lives and declines to zero, by age $x = 118$, which was the maximum lifetime in **my** random sample. These are more than just a collection of random numbers. We can use them to locate percentiles of the Gompertz distribution (when $m = 90$ and $b = 10$). For example, 95% of the cohort survive to the age of 61–62, likewise 75% survive to 77–78, 50% survive to 86–87, and 25% to 93–94. Moreover, with a proper cohort life table, I can extract 1-year death rates q_x embedded within the table by computing differences in adjacent cells and scaling by the number of people alive at the start of the year. This should be familiar from Sect. 7.8, where I extracted q_x from the 1925 Canadian cohort. Here I do the same for the simulated values.

```
qx<-(-diff(zdat.clt))/zdat.clt[-length(zdat.clt)]
plot(log(qx))
```

To get a visual and intuitive sense of the results, Fig. 8.5 plots the log of the 1-year death rates q_x, extracted from the simulated Gompertz lifetimes. The (almost perfect) linear relationship between chronological age on the x-axis and $\ln[q_x]$ on the y-axis is (obviously) designed by construction and should not be surprising. That is the essence of Gompertz law. Although, once again I will state emphatically that I am not claiming or assuming the first 30 years of life are Gompertz-like in the real world. The q_x for the *young* exhibit a very different and declining pattern, which I noted and discussed in Chap. 7. Now, for one final diagnostic (or verification) test, I regress the (constructed) log 1-year death rate $\ln[q_x]$, on the chronological age x, and estimate the slope. This number should be very close to the value of $1/b$, which is the coefficient multiplying x in the defining relationship of Eq. (8.6). The script syntax is

Source: Generated by Author in **R**

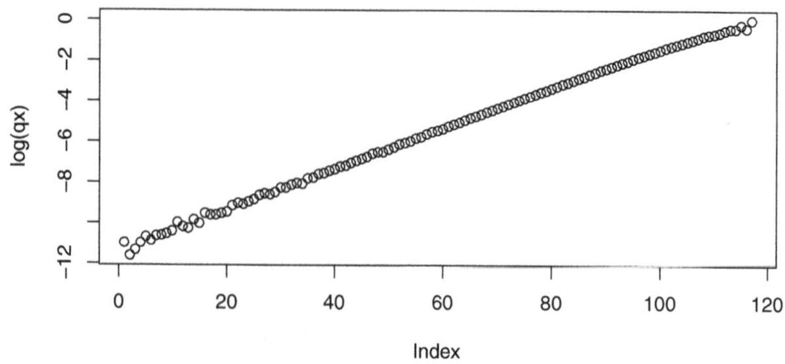

Fig. 8.5 Log mortality rate of the simulated life table

```
y<-log(qx)
omega<-length(y)
# In my simulation the maximum age (omega) was 117.
x<-0:(omega-1)
fit<-lm(y~x)
summary(fit)
```

The x vector starts at the age of $x = 0$, corresponding to q_0, and terminates at $x = 116$, where $q_{116} = 1.000$, and everyone dies by age 117. Now I'll use the `lm(.)` function, which generates a linear regression (least squares model) introduced and explained in Chap. 6. Here I simply summarize the main results.

```
Call:
lm(formula = y ~ x)
Coefficients:
             Estimate Std. Error t value Pr(>|t|)
(Intercept) -1.117e+01  2.216e-02  -504.1   <2e-16 ***
x            9.770e-02  3.302e-04   295.8   <2e-16 s
Residual standard error: 0.1206 on 115 degrees of freedom
Multiple R-squared:  0.9987, Adjusted R-squared:  0.9987
```

The estimated coefficient on the x-variable is (0.0977), which is quite close to (but not exactly) the $g = 1/b = 0.10$ from the Gompertz definition in Eq. (8.6). Likewise, the estimated intercept value of (-11.17) is quite close to (but not exactly) the analytic value $(\ln[1/b] - m/b)$, also from Eq. (8.6). In particular, the analytic intercept for $\ln[\lambda_x]$ is

```
log(1/10)-90/10
[1] -11.30259
```

The reason for the discrepancies between the estimated coefficients and the known analytic result is the usual noise and uncertainty induced by simulated values, as well as the approximation of λ_x by q_x, which I'll return to in later chapters. Recall that the 1-year death rate is not equal to the mortality hazard rate, although they are close to (and often confused with) each other. To understand this, think of *interest rates* and the difference between the effective annual rate $e^r - 1$ versus the continuously compounded rate r. The relationship between q_x (effective annual) and λ_t (continuously compounded) is quite similar. At the very least you should remember that in the context of mortality λ_t can grow to infinity (in theory), while q_x is capped at one.

8.8 Simulating Joint Gompertz Lives

Back to the topic of retirement income planning (which I indeed neglected over the last few pages), many plans involve couples, and the money should last for the life of the longest survivor (of two). In most conventional cases and couples the longer life ends up being the *healthier* or the *younger*, but life can be full of surprises and this section will try to quantify those risks. To analyze the odds, I will simulate sets of couples of random Gompertz lifetimes, one element representing the female and one the male (without prejudice to all the other combinations of couples).

```
zdat.male<-GRAN(10000,70,80,10)
zdat.female<-GRAN(10000,65,90,10)
female.advantage<-zdat.female-zdat.male
```

I have assumed that the male has a modal value of life of $m = 80$ years, and the female has a modal value of life of $m = 90$ years. Furthermore, I assumed that the male is currently $x = 70$ years-old, and the female is 5 years younger, at the age of $x = 65$. So, given the younger age and higher mode, it's to be expected (although not guaranteed) that these (10,000) females will outlive the males. The vector `female.advantage` is defined by subtracting the female number of remaining years from the male. Mathematically it captures $(T_{65}^F - T_{70}^M)$, with the implicit understanding that (1) they have different m values, and that (2) their life (and death) are independent from each other. The former assumption is rather obvious, but the latter is somewhat inconsistent with recent evidence of the so-called *broken heart syndrome*. Regardless, I can now compute the average number of years the female will outlive the male, as well as the probability this event will occur. The syntax in **R** is

```
mean(female.advantage)
[1] 10.75389
median(female.advantage)
[1] 11.19251
range(female.advantage)
[1] -27.55297  47.55333
sum(female.advantage>=0)/10000
[1] 0.8163
```

It shouldn't be surprising that the female is expected, in the sense of `mean(.)`, to outlive the male by approximately 10.75 years. In fact, the `median(.)` value is 11.19 years, and the right-skewed range is from −27.55 years to 47.55 years. In other words, of the 10,000 pairs of couples in the simulation, the largest gap (at death) between female and male was 47.55 years. She spent almost 50 years as a widow. The smallest gap was actually a negative 27.55 years, which means that she predeceased him and he spent those years as a widower. Finally, the frequency (loosely, probability or chance) that she outlived him was 81.6% of the time. In **R** this is computed by counting the number of elements greater than zero, `sum(female.advantage>=0)` and dividing by the 10,000 simulated pairs. (Warning. Please don't confuse this with the command `sum(female.advantage)=107538.9`, which adds-up the 10,000 individual values in the vector.) In fact, we can use the same syntax to estimate the chances she will outlive him by more than 15 years, which is over one third of the cases.

```
sum(female.advantage>=15)/10000
[1] 0.3754
```

On the flip side, the overall 81.6% implies an 18.4% chance that he will actually outlive her, despite his higher age and reduced mortality prospects. (So, there is no guarantee *she* will always be around to care for *him*!) Finally, some readers might be interested in computing the chances (or counting the frequencies with which) either member of the couple lives to the age of 100, for example. In **R** this can easily be counted via the following syntax:

```
sum(zdat.male>=30)/10000
[1] 6e-04
sum(zdat.female>=35)/10000
[1] 0.0676
sum(zdat.male>=30 | zdat.female>=35)/10000
[1] 0.0682
```

Notice the | between the `zdat` values, which is the *either* condition, in **R**. Bottom line, the chances of one (or even both) members of the couple becoming centenarians is 6.8%, which is slightly higher than the 6.76% for the female alone, because there is a (very small) chance the male lives for another 35 years, even if the female doesn't. Note also (for the probability novices) that the 6.8% is not the sum of the two individual numbers. In fact, there is different way in which to arrive at the same numbers, one that doesn't involve simulation at all, but rather a bit of basic probability theory. You see, if p denotes the probability of either them surviving to age 100, then $(1 - p)$ is the probability they are both dead before the age of 100. But that number (i.e. the event both are dead) can be computed *analytically* by multiplying the independent probabilities of dying. Mathematically, that is:

$$\texttt{Survival} = 1 - \left(1 - \Pr[T_x^M \geq (z - x)]\right)\left(1 - \Pr[T_y^F \geq (z - y)]\right), \quad (8.12)$$

where in our case $x = 70$, $y = 65$, $z = 100$. This can be computed in **R** with repeated use of the `TPXG(.)` function, via the following script:

```
1-(1-TPXG(70,30,80,10))*(1-TPXG(65,35,90,10))
[1] 0.07246201
```

Compare this with the simulated value of 6.8%, with the difference (and reason) being simulation versus analytic. In fact, while on the topic of analytic, it's possible to obtain a numerical (although not analytic) expression for the earlier number that I reported, namely the 18.4% chance he will outlive her. This requires the evaluation of a *double integral* involving the Gompertz probability density function, i.e. integrating over the region in which *he* outlives *her*. Although this is certainly doable, especially in **R**, it does take us (unnecessarily) farther into life contingencies and actuarial theory.

8.9 A First Look at Calibration

Up to now I have been rather cavalier with the exact (m, b) parameter specification of the distribution. In some parts of this chapter I used (and assumed) a modal value of $m = 80$ years, in other sections I used $m = 95$ years, although for most of the discussion I adhered to a dispersion coefficient of $b = 10$ years. So, what are the best parameter values that *should* be used in retirement income calculations? Well, the answer (as usual) is that: *it depends*. And, at this point of the narrative I don't want to commit to any specific best-fitting values. The pedagogical objective in this chapter was to introduce, explain, and learn how to cook with the Gompertz distribution. In fact, no different from predicting interest rates of stock market returns, I am somewhat agnostic about the true value of the two critical parameters (m, b). They obviously depend on gender, whether you are modeling the 1925, 1945, or 1965 cohort, country, and many other factors that I'll return to in later chapters. Stated bluntly, there are no universal parameters that can be used for all retirement income calculations. Indeed, you have to be extremely careful with mortality assumptions, no different from expected stock and bond portfolio return assumptions. This concern will resurface in some of the later chapters, when I get to pricing life annuities and the concept of biological age.

Nevertheless, in this section I'll offer a crude and simple recipe for selecting reasonable (m, b) Gompertz parameters, by fitting them to given cohort life table, or vector of 1-year death rates, such as the tables I discussed in Chap. 7. To test the recipe—before it *goes live*—I'll simulate a new dataset with 10,000 random Gompertz lifetimes, labeled `zdat2`, assuming (and knowing) that $(m = 85, b = 10)$. I then create a cohort life table `zdat2.clt` from those values and finally construct the relevant `qx` vector, which is the 1-year death rate.

```
zdat2<-GRAN(10000,0,85,10)
zdat2.clt<-LTLD(zdat2)
qx<-(-diff(zdat2.clt))/zdat2.clt[-length(zdat2.clt)]
```

My plan is to build (and test) a very simple procedure that estimates the Gompertz modal value from the `qx` vector, which should recover the original $(m = 85)$ value I used to generate the random lifetimes. Then, once I have confirmed the recipe works, I'll use it on a real-world 1-year death rate vector q_x to estimate its best fitting (m). The estimation (a.k.a. calibration) procedure is as follows. First, I create a user-defined function that measures the distance between the known analytic Gompertz survival probabilities, via the `TPXG(.)` function, and the survival rates from a given 1-year death rate vector, via the `SPQR` function. See the following script:

```
#Remember to set x,b and qx values.
gap<-function(m){
  gap<-c()
  for (i in 1:45){
  gap[i]<-abs(TPXG(x,i,m,b)-SPQR(x,x+i,qx))}
  sum(gap)
  }
```

Notice how this `gap(.)` function (which could be called anything, really) takes as its only argument the (m) value, from the Gompertz model, while the age (x) and dispersion (b) value are global parameters, which for the most part I will set to `b=10` and `x=55`. The `gap` function then computes the (1) sum of the (2) absolute value of the (3) differences between the analytic `TPXG(.)` and the survival rate `SPQR`. The bigger the gap between the two functions, the worse the fit. For example, the `gap(78)` and the `gap(82)` values are

```
gap(78)
[1] 5.890722
gap(82)
[1] 2.608833
# Warning. Based on my simulated values.
```

Why do these numbers mean? Well, assuming that ($m = 82$) is slightly better than assuming ($m = 78$), because the gap between the two curves is lower. Of course, I know the true answer is ($m = 80$), because I simulated the lifetimes using that precise value. So, the next step is to get **R** to figure that out. In particular, I ask **R** to iterate around possible m parameters and locate the unique value that minimizes this gap. The following script invokes the built-in **R** function `optimize`, which conducts a one-dimensional search for an implicit parameter value that minimizes a given function. The script is one line:

```
optimize(gap,c(70,100))$minimum
[1] 85.0507
optimize(gap,c(70,100))$objective
[1] 0.06858828
# Warning: Based on my simulated values.
```

Technically, I force **R** to search between the values of ($m = 70$) and ($m = 100$), which is the `c(70,100)` segment in the `optimize` command, and the answer is `85.0507`. This number is very slightly higher than the true value of ($m = 85$), but not bad considering all the noise. And, for the record, the `$objective`, which is the value of the `gap` function when it's minimized is a mere `0.0685` units, which is a far cry from either the `gap(78)=5.89` and `gap(82)=2.60` when the wrong number is used for m. Now obviously the perfect fit (and very small gap between the function) is due to the fact that I cooked-up the 1-year death rate vector q_x using a Gompertz simulation. The important question is: What happens when I use real-world (including noise, perhaps non-Gompertzian) data, such as the 1925 cohort life table from the prior chapter, to estimate parameters? Let's do that now.

```
b<-10; x<-55
# Female, Canadian, 1925 cohort
qx<-qx_f
optimize(gap,c(70,100))$minimum
[1] 88.93776
optimize(gap,c(70,100))$objective
[1] 0.7019272
```

In my first run, the best-fitting value of m is close to 89 years, but the lowest function value is `$objective=0.70`, which is much higher than `$objective=0.068` when I tested the procedure on the simulated data. Now, it could simply be that Gompertz is a worse fit, or perhaps the (forced) value of b wasn't quite right. So, let me try to increase the dispersion coefficient, and run the exact same script with `b=11`.

```
b<-11; x<-55
#Female, Canadian, 1925 cohort
qx<-qx_f
optimize(gap,c(70,100))$minimum
[1] 89.08737
optimize(gap,c(70,100))$objective
[1] 0.1886543
```

The best-fitting value of m remains in the vicinity of 89 years, but the gap or error is reduced from `$objective=0.70` to a much smaller `$objective=0.188`, which is much better. So, the "true" value of the Gompertz b coefficient capturing the 1925 cohort is higher than 10 years, which will do for now. But, for the sake of completeness, let's do the same for males. I'll start with the same $b = 10$ assumption.

```
b<-10; x<-55
#Male, Canadian, 1925 cohort
qx<-qx_m
optimize(gap,c(70,100))$minimum
[1] 83.02773
optimize(gap,c(70,100))$objective
[1] 1.374666
```

Notice that the gap-minimizing value modal value is $m = 83$, which is almost 6 years less than the gap-minimizing value for females in the 1925 cohort. However, the gap itself, per the `$objective=1.374` command is very large, relative to the female "gap" and certainly relative to the simulated values. I can do better. So, as before, if I increase the assumed dispersion coefficient (background) variable to `b=13.5`, and then run the exact same script, **R** locates an even better estimate.

```
b<-13.5; x<-55
#Male, Canadian, 1925 cohort
qx<-qx_m
optimize(gap,c(70,100))$minimum
[1] 82.04717
optimize(gap,c(70,100))$objective
[1] 0.1637622
```

Notice that the best-fitting value for males is now `m=82.05`, but the magnitude of the gap, or the `$objective`, is greatly reduced. The lesson here? First, regardless of gender, $b = 10$ isn't a very good estimate or assumption for the Canadian 1925 cohort. Or, another way to report this is that the log 1-year death rate grows at a lower rate than $1/b = 10\%$. Although, as you will see in later chapters, for recent cohorts an assumption of $b = 10$ is more reasonable (and certainly much

Data Source: HMD. Original Figure Source: [10]

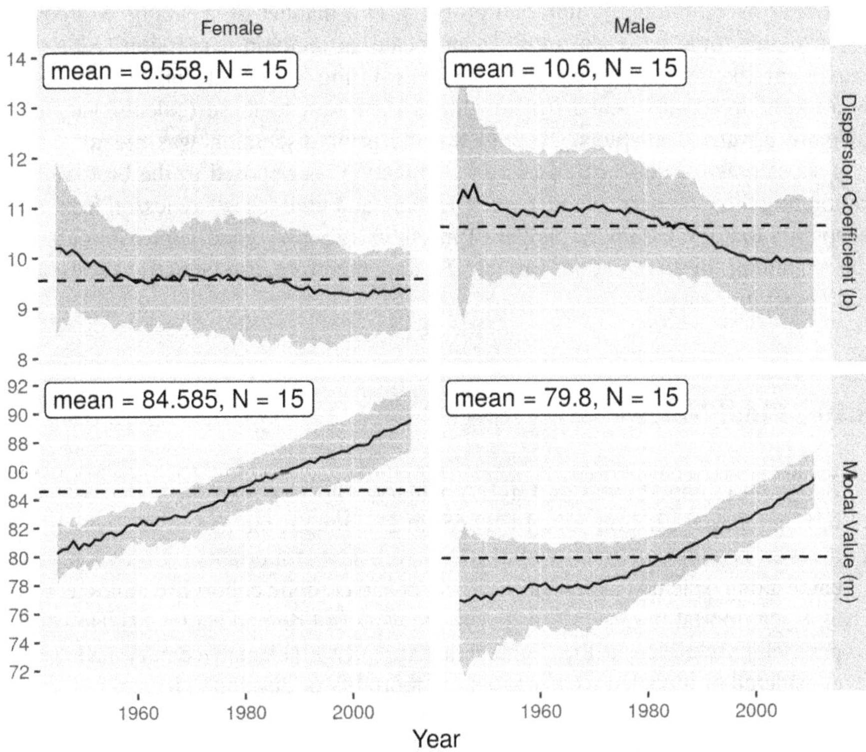

Fig. 8.6 History of Gompertz (m, b) parameters: 15 countries, 70 years

easier to remember.) More importantly, the takeaway here is that for males the error-minimizing value of b appears to be higher than it is for females, which is a universal factoid and actually holds for all cohorts. The dispersion of the remaining lifetime random variable—and hence the standard deviation—is greater for males than for females, by at least 2 years, per the above (very crude) estimates. So, life is riskier for males! I'll return to the *why* in later chapters, but as a preview I offer Fig. 8.6 which reports the best-fitting (m, b) parameters for a sample of 15 countries, from (period) 1-year death rates in the Human Mortality Database (HMD), over the last 70 years. The shaded region represents $+/-$ two standard errors (from the 15 data points for each year.) Notice the clearly increasing trend (thick middle line) in the modal value of life, (m), as well as the gradual decline in (b). I'll return to a discussion of how (m, b) have changed over time and differ across countries, in Chap. 13.

Now, to be clear, the proper and mathematically rigorous way to estimate (m, b) is by optimizing over both the modal lifetime and dispersion of lifetime at the same time, as opposed to randomly guessing one (b) and then searching over the other (m). After all, there might actually be a combined value of (m, b) that reduces the gap even further than what you see in the boxes. Figure 8.6 was generated by estimating jointly and properly, in a manner of speaking. Moreover, by invoking some basic calculus, I can locate an analytic expression (a.k.a. the maximum likelihood estimator) for the best-fitting values of (m, b), and there is no need to blindly search for anything. I'll return to these (calculus) matters in more advanced chapters. To sum up, the prior discussion was meant to get you accustomed to the `optimize(.)` function, as opposed to the best way of calibrating the Gompertz parameters. The main and final takeaway lesson from this chapter is that the Gompertz model of mortality is a very good approximation for the remaining lifetime random variable T_x, and, therefore, can be used to stress test retirement income plans.

8.10 Final Notes

- Benjamin Gompertz was an English actuary, who was born on March 5, 1779, in London and died on July 14, 1865, in London, at the age of 86 (which, by the way, is quite consistent with the Gompertz law of mortality). Until Gompertz came along, scientists knew how to collect and compile cohort life tables as well as 1-year mortality rates, starting with the work of Edmond Halley [7]. However, practicing actuaries in the eighteenth and early nineteenth century had never considered or modeled forward-looking mortality or developed formal laws.
- The main "contribution" of Benjamin Gompertz to the actuarial and demographic literature was the recognition that mortality rates increased exponentially with age, which meant that survival probabilities could be obtained by integration. Although, Gompertz himself never actually wrote down the survival probability function bearing his name. In fact, the 70-page paper, cited as [6], which he presented to the Royal Society of London in 1825, is a rather obtuse and hard-to-read document, from the perspective of the twenty-first century. In fact, it took a while for his groundbreaking idea to catch on (perhaps for these reasons). Nevertheless, he was quite a modest and un-assuming scholar who would have been surprised to learn how famous he became (after his own death, ironically). It was a fellow actuary by the name of William Makeham, a younger contemporary of Gompertz, who helped formalize the Gompertz law of mortality, in the paper cited as [9]. Today the law of mortality is often expressed as:

$$\lambda_x = \lambda + \frac{1}{b} e^{(x-m)/b},$$

  and is called the Gompertz–Makeham law, where λ is the so-called Makeham term, and the remainder is the familiar Gompertz part. Here is a brief explanation.
- Any law of mortality that claims your probability of death increases by $g\%$ per year obviously ignores freak accidents and other unnatural causes of death. This is something that is quite evident in North America around the age of 18 to 25

when youngsters first learn how to drive, or with the recent opioid epidemic. The AIDS epidemic also distorted mortality probabilities, as do wars and plagues and freak viruses. So, besides natural biological aging—captured by λ_t, and what this entire chapter has been focused on—there are other (random) causes of death that may not be related to age or aging, which is the constant λ in the above equation. Even Benjamin Gompertz himself realized this. In 1825 he wrote (in his famous paper): *"It is possible that death may be the consequence of two generally co-existing causes. The one [is] chance, without previous disposition to death or deterioration. The other [is] a deterioration, or an increased inability to withstand destruction?"* But Makeham formalized this by adding the constant. I'll return to this specification in Chap. 13.

- Gompertz was no ivory tower academic. He worked as the chief actuary at one of the largest insurance companies in England, the Alliance Assurance Company, where he served for almost three decades. He also became a full member of the London Stock Exchange (LSE) at 30 while retaining active involvement in the (nascent) actuarial community in England, as well as the Astronomical Society.
- As I noted many times in this chapter, the Gompertz law doesn't work (and goes in the wrong direction) at younger ages. But even at (very) old ages Gompertz is problematic. Demographers and actuaries have recently collected enough data to claim the following. If you are 90, 95, or 100 and trying to compute the probability of living to 105, 110, or beyond, the Gompertz probability `TPXG(.)` underestimates the chances you'll actually reach these higher ages. Gompertz is too pessimistic when applied to retirees who are already centenarians. In fact, when mortality tables are compiled for people who died at age 100 and beyond, the 1-year death rate no longer increases by 9%, 5%, or even 1% per year. It stops increasing altogether, the 1-year death rate mortality flattens somewhere around 104. Furthermore, the odds of dying in the next year plateau at about 50%. See the article cited as [1], as well as [13], and the classic book [4], for more on this rather intriguing behavior, which I'll return to (and reference again) in later chapters.
- While on the subject of surprising or intriguing mortality and longevity facts, the `female.advantage` vector, which had a positive mean and median in the simulation, wasn't always that way metaphorically. Up until the sixteenth and seventeenth century, women didn't live as long, *even* if they did survive childbirth. In the language of Gompertz, their m was lower than males. See the work cited as [5] for more on the (recent) emergence of the female advantage in longevity.
- For readers who are interested in a bit more of the history of Gompertz and how his law has faired over the last two centuries, see the article cited as [8], and [11]. For those who want to delve (more) deeply into the actuarial science and other laws of mortality, see the (classic) textbooks cited as [12] as well as [3].

Questions and Problems

8.1 Simulate $N = 10{,}000$ random lives using the Gompertz model conditional on age $x = 40$, with parameters $(m = 85, b = 10)$ and compute the fraction of this group who die between the ages of $y = 75$ and $y = 95$, with plus/minus one dispersion coefficient (not standard deviation). Please repeat this experiment five (5) times to obtain five (5) different estimates of this number. Finally, compare those numbers to the analytic result using the `TPXG(.)` function. Discuss.

8.2 Use the simulation "trick" (inverting the survival probability p, and extracting t) that I described in section #8.5 of this chapter, to create a script that simulates exponential (i.e. not Gompertz) remaining lifetimes, with parameter λ. Now use that script to simulate $N = 10{,}000$, with $\lambda = 1/50$, which is a mortality hazard rate of 2%. Compute the fraction of random lives that died between time $T = 35$ and time $T = 55$, and compare with the analytic expression. Discuss.

8.3 Jack is 50, Jill is 45 and they have a daughter Joanne, who is 25. What is the probability that Joanne will outlive both Jack and Jill? Assume they all "die" according to the Gompertz law, with $m = 80$ for Jack, $m = 90$ for Jill, and $m = 95$ for Joanne, and assume that $b = 10$ for all three of them. Please use simulation-based techniques if you can't figure out and solve the relevant three-dimensional integral.

8.4 Simulate two samples of $N = 10{,}000$ random Gompertz lifetimes, conditional on age $x = 40$, but one with $(m = 75, b = 13)$ and the other will $(m = 95, b = 7)$, and combine them into one (larger) vector of 20,000 numbers. Now, create one cohort life table (yes, for this combined mixture), extract the one q_x vector, from the age of $x = 40$ to the age of $x = 100$. Plot the log 1-year death rate (similar to Fig. 8.5), and run a simple linear regression model, recall the `fit<-lm(.)` command, to estimate the slope of log 1-year death rate. How good is the fit over the range $(40, 100)$? How good is the fit over the range $(70, 100)$? Discuss your results, and compare with Fig. 8.5.

8.5 Finally, some finance and economics. Imagine that you are $x = 40$ years-old and offered a *retirement income* "product" that pays you \$100,000 (in real, inflation-adjusted dollars) if-and-when you reach that age of $y = 80$. And, if you never reach that age, you get nothing. Assume that long-term (continuously compounded) interest rate is 1.25%, so the present value (for 40 years) of this \$100,000 is approximately \$60,000. Of course, there is a chance you will not survive to age 80, so you shouldn't be charged \$60,000. So, please use the `TPXG(.)` function to estimate the survival probability, and use that information to "value" this product. As far as parameter estimates are concerned, solve this problem assuming two cases. The (what I would call) *sick male* one, with $(m = 75, b = 13)$ and the *healthy female* one with $(m = 95, b = 7)$.

References

1. Barbi, E., Lagona, F., Marsili, M., Vaupel, J. W., & Wachter, K. W. (2018). The plateau of human mortality: Demography of longevity pioneers. *Science, 360*(6396), 1459–1461.
2. Carriere, J. F. (1994). An investigation of the Gompertz law of mortality. *Actuarial Research Clearing House, 2*, 161–177.
3. Dickson, D. C., Hardy, M., Hardy, M. R., & Waters, H. R. (2013). *Actuarial mathematics for life contingent risks*. Cambridge: Cambridge University Press.
4. Gavrilov, L. A., & Gavrilova, N. S. (1991). *The biology of life span: a quantitative approach*. Chur: Harwood Academic Publishers.
5. Goldin, C., & Lleras-Muney, A. (2019). XX> XY?: The changing female advantage in life expectancy. *Journal of Health Economics, 67*, 102–224.
6. Gompertz, B. (1825). XXIV. On the nature of the function expressive of the law of human mortality, and on a new mode of determining the value of life contingencies. In a letter to Francis Baily, Esq. FRS &c. *Philosophical Transactions of the Royal Society of London, 115*, 513–583.
7. Halley, E. (1693). An estimate of the degrees of the mortality of mankind, drawn from the curious tables of the births and funerals at the city of Breslaw. *Philosophical Transactions of the Royal Society of London, 17*, 596–610.
8. Hooker, P. F. (1965). Obituary: Benjamin Gompertz (5 March 1779–14 July 1865). *Journal of the Institute of Actuaries, 91*(2), 203–212.
9. Makeham, W. (1860). On the law of mortality and the construction of annuity tables. *The Assurance Magazine and Journal of the Institute of Actuaries, 8*(6), 301–310.
10. Milevsky, M. A., (2019). Calibrating Gompertz in reverse. Available at SSRN: https://ssrn.com/abstract=3481182 or http://dx.doi.org/10.2139/ssrn.3481182
11. Olshansky, S. J., & Carnes, B. A. (1997). Ever since Gompertz. *Demography, 34*(1), 1–15.
12. Promislow, S. D. (2006). *Fundamentals of actuarial mathematics*. Toronto: Wiley.
13. Thatcher, A. R., Kannisto, V., & Vaupel, J. W. (1998). *The force of mortality at ages 80–120 monographs on population aging*. Odense: Odense University Press.

Chapter 9
The Lifetime Ruin Probability (LRP)

This chapter returns to the realm of portfolio longevity and focuses on computational algorithms for success and failure rates associated with various retirement income strategies, but accounting for longevity risk. The chapter begins by defining the so-called lifetime ruin probability (LRP), which is the simplest retirement risk metric, widely used by practitioners. After reviewing the underlying probability concepts, the chapter provides a number of analytic expressions and simulation-based recipes for computing, interpreting, and understanding the limitations of the LRP.

9.1 Functions Used and Defined

9.1.1 Sample of Native R Functions Used

- `par(mfrow(n,m))` builds a window for figures, with n rows and m columns.
- `cumsum(.)` cumulatively sums up the elements in a vector.
- `pgamma(.), gamma()` generates values of the gamma distribution and function.

9.1.2 User-Defined R Functions

- `G(a,c)` computes the incomplete Gamma function.
- `a(nu,x,m,b)` computes a Gompertz random lifetime present value.
- `LRPG(v,xi,x,m,b)` computes the lifetime ruin probability (LRP) at age x, under a valuation rate v, initial withdrawal rate ξ (`xi`), and Gompertz (m, b) lifetime.

M. A. Milevsky, *Retirement Income Recipes in R*, Use R!,
https://doi.org/10.1007/978-3-030-51434-1_9

- `VARPHI.SM(N,x,m,b,xi,nu,sigma)`, using simulation, approximates the lifetime ruin probability when investment returns are random with parameters (ν, σ), under a Gompertz (m, b) model.
- `VARPHI.MM(x,m,b,xi,nu,sigma)`, same as `VARPHI.SM`, using moment-matching techniques.

9.2 Exponential Living to When the Money Runs Out

Recall from the discussion in Chap. 5, that if you have an investment portfolio (i.e. financial capital) worth F, earning a fixed interest rate v, and are withdrawing a constant c per year, the longevity of your portfolio satisfies the following equation:

$$L_{\xi} = \frac{1}{v} \ln \left[\frac{\xi}{\xi - v} \right], \quad \text{as long as: } v < \xi, \tag{9.1}$$

where ln[.] denotes the natural logarithm, the (new) symbol $\xi = c/F$ is the (previously introduced) initial withdrawal rate, and: $L_{\xi} := \infty$, when $v \geq \xi$. This familiar equation was coded-up and stored in **R** as the: `PL(v,c,F)` function. So, for example, if the initial withdrawal rate is (the famous) $\xi = 4\%$, and the real rate of interest is $v = 1\%$, the portfolio longevity is `PL(0.01,0.04,1)=28.77` years. Notice that I used $F = 1$ and $c = 0.04$, because portfolio longevity scales in c/F. So, is 28.77 years *enough* time? In Chap. 5 I alluded to a convention of 30 years, but didn't provide much justification, which was rather *ad hoc* and arbitrary. By this point, though, after spending (pun intended) two chapters discussing models of human longevity, we are in a better position to address lifetimes head-on. The pertinent question is: If indeed the longevity of your portfolio is 28.77 years, will you still be alive at that age? The answer obviously depends on the exact age at which you begin those withdrawals. If you start depleting your nest egg at the age of $x = 70$, then 28.77 years of longevity is likely enough. But if you "retire" early, at the age of $x = 55$, for example, it's unlikely the money will last for the rest of your life. This is because there is a high probability you will live to age $y = 83.8$, which is when the money runs out. This is the question motivating the entire chapter.

Will you be alive when the money runs out?

The answer isn't a binary yes or no. Rather, a proper response should be expressed as a *probability* of living to the longevity of your portfolio. So, if the portfolio's longevity is 28.77 years, I can compute the probability of living to that point, using explicit expressions for $\Pr[T_x \geq t]$, which was the focus of the prior chapter. I'll start with a (very) simple example and then move on to more general statements and formal definitions. Assume for the moment that your remaining lifetime random variable T_x is exponentially distributed with a constant mortality hazard rate $\lambda = 1/20 = 5\%$. And, although I dismissed constant mortality rates as being inconsistent with real-world data (unless you are a lobster), I'll leverage the analytic simplicity of this assumption to extract some financial insights. In a later section I'll return to more realistic models of human longevity, such as the Gompertz assumption. Anyway, assuming exponential lifetimes, the probability of surviving to any given t can be written explicitly as $\Pr[T_x \geq t] = e^{-\lambda t}$, where the subscript x is redundant but retained for consistency. Combining the survival probability with Eq. (9.1), we arrive at the formal definition of the *lifetime ruin probability*, for exponential lifetimes, denoted by the Greek letter varphi:

$$\varphi := \Pr[T_x \geq L_\xi] = e^{-\lambda L_\xi} = \left(\frac{\xi}{\xi - v}\right)^{-\lambda/v}, \tag{9.2}$$

with the same restrictions imposed on portfolio longevity in Eq. (9.1), namely that $v < \xi$. Of course, in the event $v \geq \xi$, which means that L_ξ is defined to be $L_\xi = \infty$, then (obviously) $\varphi = 0$. You can never die before the money runs out. When $L_\xi = \infty$, you have nothing to worry about. Here are some numerical examples assuming that ($\xi = 0.04$, $v = 0.01$), but varying the mortality rate λ from low values of $\lambda = 1\%$ to high values of $\lambda = 10\%$. I would like to investigate how an increase (a.k.a. parallel shift) in the (constant) mortality rate affects φ.

```
xi<-0.04; v<-0.01
lam<-0.01; round((xi/(xi-v))^(-lam/v),digits=3)
[1] 0.75
lam<-0.05; round((xi/(xi-v))^(-lam/v),digits=3)
[1] 0.237
lam<-0.10; round((xi/(xi-v))^(-lam/v),digits=3)
[1] 0.056
```

Here is the interpretation. When the mortality rate $\lambda = 1\%$, which is quite low (and means you will live longer), the probability of reaching 28.7 years (the longevity of the portfolio) is $e^{-0.2877}$, which works out to 75%. This is (very) high and probably unacceptable to most retirees. But, when the mortality rate is increased (in the script) to $\lambda = 5\%$ and then $\lambda = 10\%$, the probability of living to the end of the life of the portfolio drops to 23.7% and a mere 5.6%, which is much lower (and better) than 75%. Now, few people control their mortality rate (at least to that extent) so this obviously isn't a strategy for reducing failure rates. Rather, this illustrates how mortality rates—and the associated human *life expectancy*—affect the sustainability of the retirement income plan. How's that? Well, when lifetimes T_x are exponentially distributed with a mortality rate parameter of λ, the value of $E[T_x] = 1/\lambda$, which is the mean (human) lifetime, and $SD[T_x] = 1/\lambda$ as well. So, another way to interpret the number in the above script box is as follows: If you are at an age with a human life expectancy of $100 = 1/(0.01)$ years, there is a 75% probability you will outlive your money. But, if your life expectancy is a mere $10 = 1/(0.1)$ years, with a standard deviation of 10 years, there is only a 5.6% probability of that (undesirable) event occurring. Of course, all of the above (simple) math and formulas assume that lifetimes are exponentially distributed (they are not) and that your financial capital is allocated to an asset earning a constant risk-free rate of v (it rarely is). Thus, to increase the level of realism (in the next section) I'll graduate to a Gompertz law of mortality and show how it affects results. Then, (in the section after that) I'll move on to random portfolio returns, per the methodology that was described in Chap. 5.

9.3 Gompertz Living to When the Money Runs Out

The lifetime ruin probability, φ, is defined in the same way as before, namely $\varphi = \Pr[T_x \geq L_\xi]$. However, under the Gompertz law the survival probability involves both parameters (m, b), which are the mode and dispersion coefficients. An explicit expression for $\Pr[T_x \geq t]$ was derived in Sect. 8.4, and was coded-up in **R** as the `TPXG(.)` function. So, applying the exact same logic that led to Eq. (9.2), namely to compute the probability of living to the time at which the portfolio is exhausted L_ξ, we arrive at the equivalent expression:

$$\varphi := \Pr[T_x \geq L_\xi] = \exp\{e^{(x-m)/b}(1 - (\xi/(\xi - v))^{1/bv})\}, \tag{9.3}$$

which is a bit *messier* than Eq. (9.2), but does share similarities in structure. Recall that the Gompertz survival probability to any time t, can be expressed as: $\exp\{e^{(x-m)/b}(1 - e^{t/b})\}$. The extra step in Eq. (9.3) is to replace e^t with the exponential of portfolio longevity e^{L_ξ}. Replacing the L_ξ with $\frac{1}{v}\ln\left[\frac{\xi}{\xi - v}\right]$ per Eq. (9.1) leads to $(\xi/(\xi - v))^{1/v}$. Bear in mind that the same warnings about $\xi > v$ apply with this version of φ as well. If $t = L_\xi := \infty$, then $e^t \to \infty$, then $(1 - e^t) \to -\infty$, and the lifetime ruin probability equation (9.3) goes to zero. This is exactly what you would expect (and want) from a risk metric when the portfolio lasts forever. Now, on a technical note, the probability *purest* might wonder why the lifetime ruin probability φ also includes the (yes, measure zero) event in which $T_x = L_\xi$. After all, if you go broke the same instant in which you die, isn't that good enough? The answer here is (1) it doesn't make any numerical difference, and more importantly (2) a successful retirement plan is usually defined as dying with positive wealth. Either way this is semantics. For the Gompertz case I'll create a user-defined function for Eq. (9.3).

```
LRPG<-function(v,xi,x,m,b){
  if (xi <= v){ruin<-0}
  else{ruin<-exp( exp((x-m)/b) * (1 - (xi/(xi-v))^(1/(v*b))))}
  ruin}
```

Note that I forced `LRPG(.)` $= 0$ when $\xi \leq v$, because the portfolio is never depleted. In fact, this function is relatively simple, so I could have used **R** to evaluate φ for a variety of parameter values (by plugging in the portfolio longevity function `PL(.)`

as the t value in the Gompertz survival probability`TPXG(.)`) and stopped there. But, the lifetime ruin probability "concept," as well as its converse the *retirement success rate*, is quite central to many of the recipes in this book, which is why it garners a stand-alone formula. Here are examples, where I fix ($\xi = 0.04, x = 65, m = 88, b = 10$), and vary the real rate v.

```
LRPG(0.010,0.04,65,88,10)
[1] 0.1863534
LRPG(0.015,0.04,65,88,10)
[1] 0.1107176
LRPG(0.020,0.04,65,88,10)
[1] 0.04468917
```

When the portfolio earns a fixed $v = 1\%$ per year, the lifetime ruin probability is $\varphi = 18.6\%$, but when that rate is increased by a mere 100 basis points, which is 1% point, to 2% per year, the LRP values plummets to 4.47%, which is a 95.53% retirement success rate. Now, you already knew (from Chap. 5) that portfolio longevity was (extremely) sensitive to investment returns. But, once you factor in stochastic lifetimes and the steep decline in survival probabilities after the modal value of life, the difference 100 basis points can make is quite stark. Now let's change the retirement age x and see how it affects the LRP. In particular, I'll retain $v = 2\%$, as well as $\xi = 4\%$, but vary x around the age of 65.

```
round(LRPG(0.02,0.04,55,88,10),digits=2)
[1] 0.32
round(LRPG(0.02,0.04,60,88,10),digits=2)
[1] 0.15
round(LRPG(0.02,0.04,65,88,10),digits=2)
[1] 0.04
round(LRPG(0.02,0.04,70,88,10),digits=2)
[1] 0.01
```

Notice how the early retiree (at age $x = 55$) is subjecting himself (or herself) to a lifetime ruin probability of $\varphi = 32\%$, whereas the late retiree (at age $x = 70$) is faced with a $\varphi = 1\%$ probability, which is a 99% retirement success rate. Ponder this question again. Is the 4% rule safe or is it risky? Well, first of all it depends on the age at which you begin those withdrawals. Start at the age of $x = 55$ and it looks extremely risky (to me), but delay until age $x = 70$ and it seems "safer," with the proviso the safety is in the eye (and tail) of the beholder. More on that in a later section. Now, you might have noticed that in the above script I forced **R** to only report two significant decimals, which might appear like excessive rounding to some readers. I did this quite deliberately to remind everyone about all of the assumptions that have gone into this simple formula (a.k.a. how I made the sausage). Not only did I assume constant withdrawals, which I critiqued in Chap. 5 (and will do so again), I also made assumptions about Gompertz (m, b) parameters, which one never really knows with certainty. And, while most academic studies (and commercial software) that measure retirement success rates do disclose these assumptions, it's hard to over-emphasize the importance of these implicit parameters in the final results. In fact, to further illustrate how mortality (table) assumptions can change the results, notice what happens when the $x = 65$ year-old withdrawing $\xi = 4\%$ assumes a higher (and perhaps more conservative) modal value of the remaining lifetime random variable.

```
round(LRPG(0.020,0.04,65,88,10),digits=2)
[1] 0.04
round(LRPG(0.020,0.04,65,92,10),digits=2)
[1] 0.12
round(LRPG(0.020,0.04,65,96,10),digits=2)
[1] 0.25
```

The lifetime ruin probability, increases from a comforting $\varphi = 4\%$ to a rather scary $\varphi = 25\%$, which is a one-in-four chance of living longer than your money. And remember that all I have changed in the above script is the modal value m, from 88 to 96 years. I have not changed the initial withdrawal rate ξ, nor have I changed the assumed (real) interest rate (a.k.a. investment return), v. You can iterate and change those numbers yourself, just to get a sense of how they impact the results. Finally, for the sake of completeness, let's see how the Gompertz dispersion parameter b affects the lifetime ruin probability φ, without changing anything else.

```
round(LRPG(0.020,0.04,65,88,8),digits=2)
[1] 0.01
round(LRPG(0.020,0.04,65,88,10),digits=2)
[1] 0.04
round(LRPG(0.020,0.04,65,88,12),digits=2)
[1] 0.08
```

Increasing the dispersion coefficient b, all else being equal, increases the value of φ. This should make intuitive sense, since we are increasing the uncertainty (think standard deviation) associated with your remaining lifetime, so it's no surprise that greater uncertainty makes things worse. Of course, to prove this rigorously (for all values of ξ, v, x, m), one would have to take partial derivative of φ, with respect to b, in Eq. (9.3), and show that all "signs" are positive. I leave this (calculus) problem as a technical exercise for ambitious students.

To extract some final insights from the topic of lifetime ruin probabilities under deterministic returns, I offer a summary plot in Fig. 9.1. For the sake of space and brevity, I haven't displayed the usual **R** commands that generated this particular plot, but the syntax should be (more than) familiar by now. In fact, going forward I will refrain from displaying any more `plot(.)` scripts unless there is something new and important within the **R** code itself. Now, as far as Fig. 9.1 is concerned, I have assumed that $(m = 88, b = 10)$, as well as $v = 2\%$, which is deterministic interest, and have varied the initial withdrawal rate ξ, as well as the retirement (withdrawals begin at) age x. Once again there should be no surprises, or any counter-intuitive

Source: Generated by Author in **R**

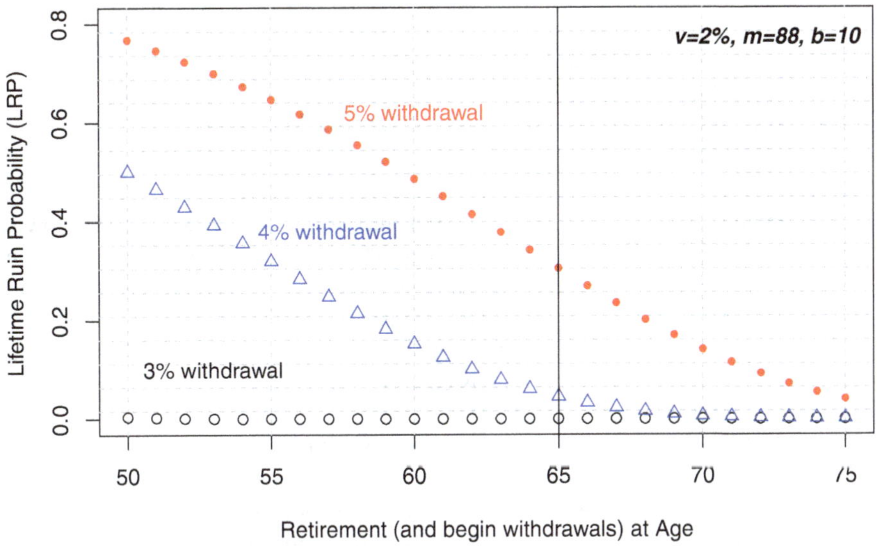

Fig. 9.1 LRP: deterministic returns under Gompertz longevity

results. At higher values of ξ, the lifetime ruin probability is higher. Likewise, if you start the withdrawals at more advanced (later) ages, the LRP values drop, and quite dramatically. The main takeaway is the sheer difference a few extra years of work, or withdrawal percentage points, can make on the lifetime ruin probabilities—even without varying the asset allocation or changing the investment returns. Now, I will certainly get to (what I called) stochastic $\tilde{v} \sim N(v, \sigma)$, in a few pages, but the objective here is develop full intuition for the deterministic case, first.

9.4 Analytic vs. Simulation: How Many?

I can replicate (closely) the above analytic results via simulation by actually randomizing human longevity and then counting the number of people (i.e. lives) who exceeded portfolio longevity. Of course, there is no need to estimate probabilities via simulation when you have access to a closed-form analytic expression. However, since I plan to eventually migrate to simulations when analytic expressions aren't available, this gives us an opportunity to measure some errors, but when the "truth" is known. So, let's go back to the case when (the interest rate) $v = 1\%$ and (the withdrawal rate) $\xi = 4\%$, starting at the age of $x = 70$. We already know that portfolio longevity is `PL(0.01,0.04,1)=28.77` years, and the Gompertz survival probability to age $y = 98.76$ is `TPXG(70,28.76,88,10)=0.06281`, which is also the value of `LRPG(0.01,0.04,70,88,10)=0.0626`. But now,

I'll simulate $N = 1000$ random Gompertz lifetimes, conditional on age $x = 70$, and count the number of those people who actually lived beyond age $98.76 = (70 + L_{0.04})$. The script is simply:

```
zdat<-GRAN(1000,70,88,10)
sum(zdat>=PL(0.01,0.04,1))/length(zdat)
[1] 0.051
```

The estimated value (in this one simulation run) of $\varphi = 5.1\%$ is obviously lower than the "true" (analytic) value of $\varphi = 6.26\%$. This is to be expected in a simulation with only $N = 1000$ lifetimes. Indeed, if you take the time to execute this small script, your numbers might be closer to (or farther from) the 6.26%, which is why it's always preferable to use an analytic expression if you have (or know) one. But, what I would like to investigate now is exactly *how many* random lifetimes I have to simulate before the estimated LRP values are "close enough" to the true value of φ. I'm driven by more than simple curiosity. This is a rather vexing issue in practice, when researchers and practitioners report simulated (a.k.a. Monte Carlo) values for retirement success and failure rates. Obviously the bigger the N, the better, but simulations take time and slow down the algorithms. *So, how many runs are enough?*

Well, Fig. 9.2 offers some perspective on this question, in the context of our (simple) φ. It displays the results of a repeated experiment which simulated samples of N random lifetimes, from $N = 100$ all the way to $N = 10{,}000$. In each experiment (that is for each tested value of N), I computed all the estimated φ

Source: Generated by Author in **R**

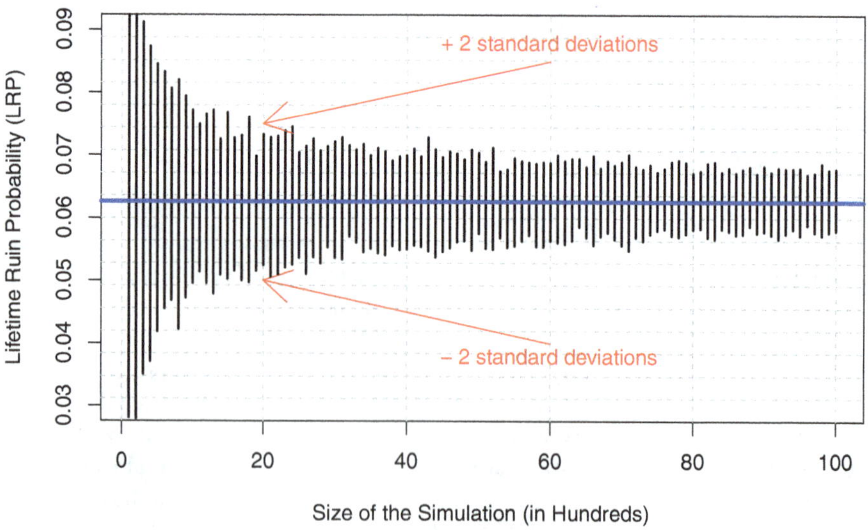

Fig. 9.2 Lifetime ruin probability: Simulation vs. Analytic

values, and then plotted the sample mean *plus/minus* two standard deviations. In Fig. 9.2, I also traced out the horizontal line corresponding to the (true) value of $\varphi = 6.26\%$. And, for the sake of replication, here is the core portion (recipe) of the **R** script generating Fig. 9.2.

```
for (i in 1:100){
  for (j in 1:50){
  zdat<-GRAN(100*i,70,88,10)
  y[j]<-sum(zdat>=PL(0.01,0.04,1))/length(zdat)
  }
  y.max<-mean(y)+2*sd(y); y.min<-mean(y)-2*sd(y)
  segments(i,y.min,i,y.max,col="black",lwd=2)
  }
```

If you want to reproduce (a similar graph), don't forget to add the usual `plot(.)` commands at the beginning. For now, look carefully at the two loops within the script. The inner one: `for (j in 1:50)`, generates 50 simulations of $N = i \times 100$ random lifetimes, and the outer loop is: `for (i in 1:100)`. In each run of the outer loop (that is for each value of N) the script computes the `mean(.)` and `sd(.)` of the 50 samples, and then plots the relevant segment from `mean(.)+2*sd(.)` to `mean(.)-2*sd`. Notice that when $N < 2000$, the upper and lower bounds are well above and below the true value of 6.26%, by quite a large margin. But, as N increases the variation dissipates, although never reaches zero for the range of N displayed. There are a number of practical takeaways here, some obvious and some less so. First, simulation-based estimates should always be displayed with ranges (obviously). Second, and perhaps more controversially, if we accept the fact that retirement income simulation *probability values* are rather meaningless after the 2nd or 3rd digit, it might not be necessary to generate more than a few thousand lifetimes to get a reasonable estimate (plus/minus ranges) for the value of φ. Thus, while I concede that Monte Carlo simulations (in statistics, physics, engineering, etc.) should be conducted with values of N in the hundreds of thousands, and possibly millions, it's overkill when it comes to retirement income lifetimes, and will create a false sense of precision. After all, how much do you really trust your inputs?

9.5 Stochastic Portfolio Returns

Up to this point I have made a number of assumptions worth repeating. First, in addition to the constant withdrawal rate ξ, I assumed a known, fixed real investment return v. In practice, retirees own pensions and annuities, which guarantee an income for life—a topic I'll return to in Chaps. 10 and 11. But even in the absence of these unique longevity-hedging products, they also hold diversified portfolios which are subject to unknown rates of return. Indeed, that was the focus of Chaps. 5, and 6.

So, I will now combine the technology (scripts) for simulating *human lifetimes* with *portfolio lifetimes* to compute more realistic values of $\varphi = \Pr[T_x \geq L_\xi]$. You will see that the algorithm is quite similar to what I did in Sect. 8.8, when I simulated pairs (couples) of joint lifetimes. In this case I'll simulate pairs of lifetimes, but one of them is human and the other is financial. See the following script:

```
#Portfolio Longevity (PL)
zdat.pl<-PLSM(1,0.04,0.025,0.15,5000)
summary(round(zdat.pl,digits=2))
Min.   1st Qu.   Median   Mean    3rd Qu.    Max.
11.00    26.00    39.00    51.52   83.00   100.00
#Human Longevity (HL)
zdat.hl<-GRAN(5000,65,88,10)
summary(round(zdat.hl,digits=2))
Min.   1st Qu.   Median   Mean    3rd Qu.    Max.
0.02    13.29    20.74    20.10   26.96    45.34
```

The variable zdat.pl contains $N = 5000$ simulated values of *portfolio longevity*, assuming an initial withdrawal rate of $c/F = \xi = 4\%$, and $\nu = 2.5\%$ (which, recall, is the expected value of the log return) with a standard deviation of $\sigma = 15\%$. The summary statistics for *portfolio longevity* displays the usual spread between very low values (11 years) and the (artificial, forced) maximum of 100 years. In parallel, the variable zdat.hl contains $N = 5000$ simulated values of *human longevity*, conditional on age $x = 65$ under a Gompertz law of mortality, with $m = 88$ years and $b = 10$ years. A summary of these 5000 numbers offers no surprises. The earliest death occurred in 1 week, and the longest (of the 5000) survivors made it to 45.34 years, which is a few months after age 110. Think of two large urns from which pieces of paper are drawn at retirement. The first urn informs you how long you will live and the second urn informs you how long your money will last. Bottom line: If the former number is greater than the later number, you are *ruined*.

Figure 9.3 displays (a sample of) those 5000 pairs of values, with a diagonal line representing the (rare) cases when the two numbers (in the two urns) match exactly. The first thing to notice is all the dots clustered at the portfolio longevity value of 100, which remember implies that the money lasted for *at least* 100 years of retirement; more than enough. The dots under the (red) diagonal line represent "urn pairs" for which the human longevity (x-axis) was greater than portfolio longevity (y-axis). Falling under the diagonal is obviously not a desired outcome, but there aren't that many pairs in that region. The majority of dots are above the diagonal, which means that the money lasted longer than your retirement, and in many cases far longer. Zoom in and look at the number of dots (a.k.a. pairs) that are clustered just above the diagonal (*phew, that was a close call!*) and those clustered under the diagonal (*ugh, if only the money had lasted another year or two!*). Indeed, those dots that are just under the diagonal make a strong case for portfolio insurance (a.k.a. collars, options, and derivatives), topics which were discussed towards the end of Chap. 6. Finally, I count the number of dots within the triangle under the diagonal,

Source: Generated by Author in **R**

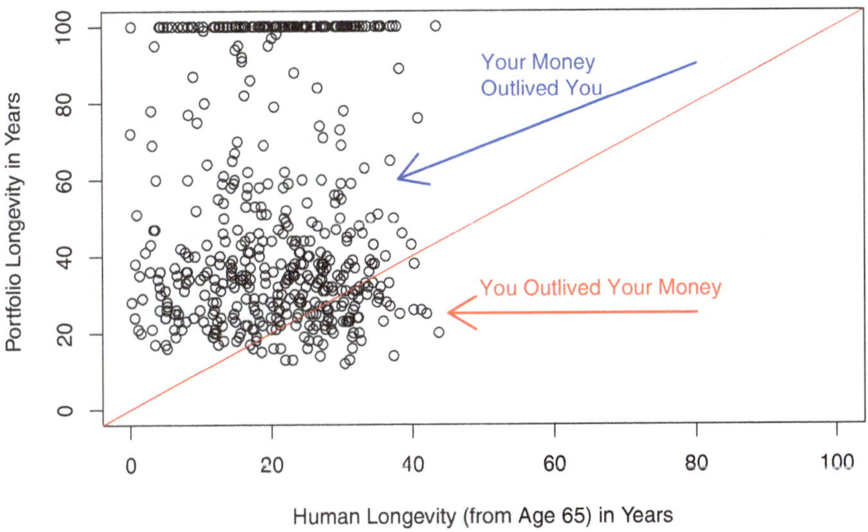

Fig. 9.3 Who lived longer, you or your money?

or more precisely the overall *fraction* for which portfolio longevity L_ξ was lower than human longevity T_x. This is computed as:

```
# Crude Simulation-based Estimate of Varphi.
> sum(zdat.hl>=zdat.pl)/length(zdat.hl)
[1] 0.1542
```

In this simulation run, the value of $\varphi = 15.4\%$, under the above-noted parameter values. Or, more optimistically, the retirement success rate was $(1 - \varphi) = 84.6\%$. Notice that I am quite cautious about declaring whether this (15.4%) is a good or a bad result, nor am I opining on whether a proper and safe φ metric should be higher or lower. I'll get to that (thorny, controversial) topic at the very end of this chapter. For now, I'm just "cooking" numbers.

To conclude this particular discussion, Fig. 9.4 combines 9 individual figures into one, using the `par(mfrow=c(3,3))` command in **R**. After you type that, the next 9 figures created will be stacked into 3×3 boxes, similar to Fig. 9.4. It might not be easy to read the labels or axis, but at least you get all the pictures into one figure. After you are done generating the (nice) 3×3, make sure to run `par(mfrow=c(1,1))`, returning to normal settings for your next figure. Figure 9.4 varies the initial withdrawal rate ξ, from a low value of 1% to a (very high) value of $\xi = 9\%$. Obviously I'm not suggesting (or even hinting) that 9% would ever be suitable, but rather I'm interested in the pattern of the resulting φ estimates. Notice how a larger fraction of the dots fall under the diagonal, as ξ increases. In fact, the cluster of dots at the horizontal value of 100 years declines

Source: Generated by Author in **R**

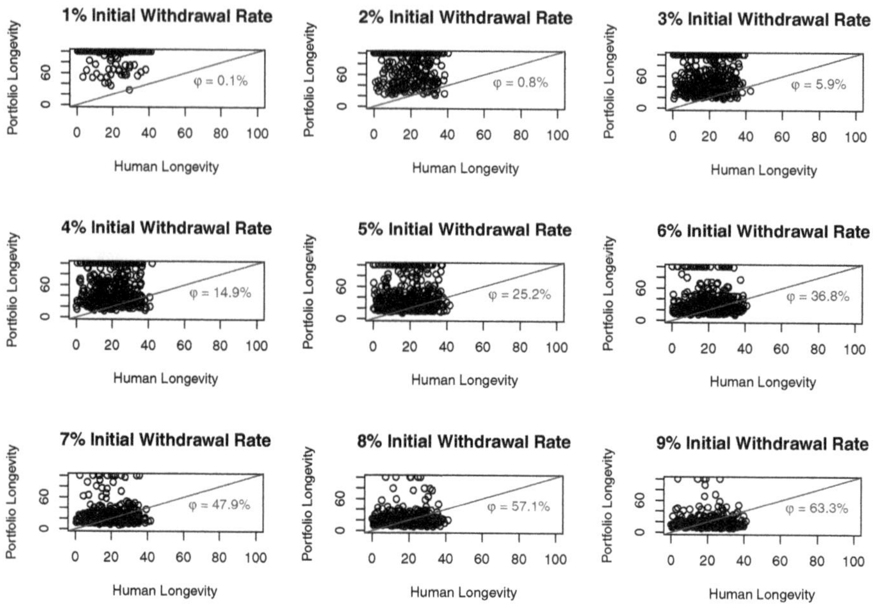

Fig. 9.4 Visualizing LRP: initial withdrawals from $\xi = 1\%$ to $\xi = 9\%$

(i.e. drops from the ceiling) as the initial withdrawal rate increases. Likewise, the lifetime ruin probability ranges from $\varphi \approx 0\%$, all the way to $\varphi = 63\%$, when $\xi = 9\%$. Remember, this represents an $x = 65$ year-old, subject to Gompertz parameters $m = 88$ years and $b = 10$ years, withdrawing ξ from a portfolio earning $\nu = 2.5\%$ (real) with a standard deviation of $\sigma = 15\%$. If you don't like any of these assumptions (a.k.a. ingredients), you have the algorithm (a.k.a. recipe) to generate (a.k.a. cook) your own results and figures.

9.6 LRP by Simulating Stochastic Present Values

Although there aren't any known closed-form expressions for φ, when investments (and L_ξ) are stochastic, there are a number of decent approximations that have been developed over the years (some that are quite elegant). One of those approximations, based on the concept of **Statistical Moment Matching**, is the focus of the next two sections. In fact, φ can also be expressed as the solution to a partial differential equation (PDE), which takes us far beyond the scope of this (recipe) book. See the reference cited as [3]. So, for those readers who might not relish the stochastic calculus, and for whom simulation estimates are more than sufficient, I suggest skipping to the final section (9.8) of this chapter, where I take an axe to φ. But for those who are brave enough, I move on to some definitions and formalities.

Recall from Chap. 6, that the vector or stochastic process Z_t, $t \geq 0$ denoted the real (inflation adjusted) investment process driving portfolio longevity. For any given path of Z_t, I defined the annualized real investment growth (ARIG) as: $(Z_T/Z_0)^{1/T} - 1$, for any period T. In this section I'll begin by delving (more) deeply into the randomness of Z_t. I'll start by defining the investment process in continuous time, via the following stochastic process:

$$Z_t = e^{(\nu t + \sigma B_t)}. \tag{9.4}$$

The two parameters in Eq. (9.4) are the familiar ν, σ, which are the (continuously compounded) expected rate of return and the volatility. The new (foreign) B_t is the continuous-time analog of the normal distribution which generates the investment returns, which is called a **Brownian Motion.** And, while I am casually introducing this symbol (and process), one could fill an entire book on the proper definition, construction, and properties of Brownian Motion. I refer you to the reference [8] and [4] for (much) more information about B_t, which is famous in its own right. If you have never heard of B_t before, you will have to take it on faith that the process Z_t can be written and expressed in differential form as:

$$dZ_t = (\nu + \sigma^2/2)Z_t\,dt + \sigma Z_t dB_t, \tag{9.5}$$

where $(\nu + \frac{1}{2}\sigma^2)$ is known as the *drift coefficient*, which in the mathematical finance literature is often denoted by the letter μ, and σ is known as the *diffusion coefficient* of the stochastic process. So, for example, if the expected continuously compounded rate of return is $\nu = 2\%$ (for example) and the volatility (a.k.a. standard deviation of the continuously compounded return) is $\sigma = 20\%$, then the *drift coefficient* in Eq. (9.5) is 4%. This might seem odd at first (Does Z_t grow by 2% or by 4%?), but relates to the difference between the geometric (2%) and arithmetic mean (4%), and on a more deeper level (something called) **Ito calculus.** Nevertheless, bearing in mind that my goal here is recipes and algorithms, versus theory, if the return generating process is governed by Eq. (9.5), then the trajectory of the retirement portfolio will satisfy the following stochastic differential equation (SDE):

$$d\tilde{F}_t = \Big((\nu + \sigma^2/2)\tilde{F}_t - c\Big)\,dt + \sigma \tilde{F}_t dB_t, \quad \tilde{F}_0 = F_0, \tag{9.6}$$

where F_0 is the initial portfolio value at retirement and c is the constant consumption rate (a.k.a. ξF_0). Compare equation (9.6), which is the *stochastic* trajectory of wealth, to the deterministic trajectory $dF_t = (\upsilon F_t - c)dt$, derived in Sect. 5.7, and coded-up as `DTRJ(.)` in **R**. Notice the similarities between the two and the fact they match when $\sigma = 0$. Now, for the final bit of stochastic calculus, the solution to the **Stochastic Differential Equation** (SDE) in Eq. (9.6) can be written explicitly as:

$$\tilde{F}_t = Z_t\left[F_0 - c\int_0^t Z_s^{-1}\,ds\right]. \tag{9.7}$$

In words: The value of the retirement portfolio at any future time t, is equal to the value of the investment process $Z_t > 0$ multiplied by the difference between the original portfolio value F_0, minus the consumption c, times the integral of the inverse of the investment return process Z_s, until time t. What this means, among other things, is that you can simulate portfolio values of $\tilde{F}_\tau$, at any time $\tau > 0$, by simulating a single path for $Z_s; 0 \leq s \leq \tau$, then integrating (i.e. adding up) the reciprocal of Z_s from $s = 0$ to $s = \tau$, and plugging them all into Eq. (9.7). Without any loss of generality, τ can also be the random lifetime based on a Gompertz model, and $\tilde{F}_{T_x}$ becomes the value of the portfolio at the time of death. So, if $\tilde{F}_{T_x} \leq 0$, this retiree was ruined. But here is the main "trick" in this section. Look closely (again) at Eq. (9.7). The only condition under which $\tilde{F}_{T_x} \leq 0$ is if the item in the brackets is negative, because $Z_t > 0$. So, φ can be expressed as the probability that the (yes, random) integral expression in Eq. (9.7) is greater than F_0/c, which is also $1/\xi$ (and measured in units of initial retirement wealth). Voila! Simulate many (many) values of the random integral, by simulating many paths for Z_s, and you have (yet another) estimate of φ. Formally, here is yet another expression for the lifetime ruin probability:

$$\varphi = \Pr\left[\frac{1}{\xi} \leq \int_0^{T_x} Z_s^{-1}\, ds\right] = \Pr\left[\frac{1}{\xi} \leq \int_0^{\infty} Z_s^{-1}\, 1_{\{T_x > s\}} ds\right] \tag{9.8}$$

Now, strictly speaking you can't really define an integral with an upper bound of integration that is random, which is the time of death. So, the first expression to the right of the equal sign in the above equation isn't a proper integral (to a proper mathematician), which is why I added the second and final expression integrated to infinity, but with an indicator function $1_{\{T_x > s\}}$, to denote the person is still alive. To bring some clarity to the integral in Eq. (9.8) , here is an implementation in **R**.

```
VARPHI.SM<-function(N,x,m,b,xi,nu,sigma){
V<-c()
wks<-round(GRAN(N,x,m,b)*52,0)+1
for (i in 1:N){
sB<-sigma*sqrt(1/52)*cumsum(rnorm(wks[i]))
Z<-exp((nu/52)*c(1:(wks[i]))+sB)
V[i]<-sum((1/Z)/52)}
sum(V>=1/xi)/length(V)
}
```

This function takes as arguments the number of simulations `N`, the Gompertz parameters `(x,m,b)`, the initial withdrawal rate ξ, and the portfolio investment parameters ν, σ. It generates an estimate for φ based on Eq. (9.8). More specifically, it simulates values of the integral of the inverse of the exponential Brownian motion, discretized over $\Delta t = 1/52$, which is weekly. The algorithm begins by simulating `N` values of the number of *weeks* the person lived (I added one to eliminate any problems with zero). Notice that `sB` is the analog to the σB_t in Eq. (9.4). The cumsum adds-up the normally distributed values, and then scales them by $\sigma\sqrt{\Delta t}$, where $\Delta t = 1/52$ weeks per year. Then, for each one of those random lifetimes T_x, the algorithm computes the value of Z_s, and then Z_s^{-1} and finally $\int Z_s^{-1}\,ds$ to arrive at one possible portfolio path. Then, at the end of N such paths, it counts the number greater than $1/\xi$, which denotes an event of lifetime ruin. To make sense of this all, here are some numerical examples.

```
VARPHI.SM(10000,65,88,10,0.05,0.02,0.20)
[1] 0.3525
VARPHI.SM(10000,65,88,10,0.04,0.02,0.20)
[1] 0.2419
VARPHI.SM(10000,65,88,10,0.04,0.02,0.15)
[1] 0.2079
```

In the first run (which you will notice, is a bit slower than our prior simulations), the retiree spends $\xi = 5\%$, but only earns an expected continuously compounded real return of 2% with a standard deviation of $\sigma = 20\%$. In that scenario the lifetime ruin probability is $\varphi = 35.25\%$, which is quite high. In the second simulation the withdrawal rate is reduced to $\xi = 4\%$, resulting in a (better) $\varphi = 24.19\%$. Finally, if the volatility can be reduced from 20% to $\sigma = 15\%$ (somehow), without affecting the expected (continuously compounded) return ν, the lifetime ruin probability can be reduced to 20.79%.

9.7 LRP by Moment Matching

The approach I just described, simulating the integral in Eq. (9.8), suggests a third and final way of approximating the lifetime ruin probability φ, when lifetimes are Gompertz distributed and (the logarithm) of investment returns are normally distributed. Without getting lost in the details, there are some good (theoretical) reasons for why the reciprocal of the integral, that is $Y = 1/\int Z_s^{-1}\,ds$ can be approximated by a Gamma distribution. The cumulative distribution function (CDF) can be expressed as:

$$\Pr[Y \leq y] = \int_0^y \frac{s^{\alpha-1}e^{-s/\beta}}{\beta^\alpha \Gamma(\alpha)} ds, \tag{9.9}$$

where $\alpha > 0$ is known as the *shape* parameter and $\beta > 0$ is known as the *scale* parameter. The mean of the Gamma distribution is $\alpha\beta$, and the variance is $\alpha\beta^2$ So, *if* I make the (bold, and to this point completely unjustified) assumption that $1/\int Z_s^{-1}\,ds$ has a Gamma distribution, then the probability $\Pr[\int Z_s^{-1}\,ds \geq 1/\xi]$, per Eq. (9.8) can be expressed as $\Pr[1/\int Z_s^{-1}\,ds \leq \xi]$, which is the expression in Eq. (9.9). To get the parameters (α, β), I will match the moments of $\int Z_s^{-1}\,ds$ to the Reciprocal Gamma distribution, which is explained in (much) more detail in a technical research paper cited as [5] as well as [3]. Once again, my interest here isn't proofs and theorems, but recipes. To implement this in **R**, there are a number of functions I have to create first, before I can define a new `VARPHI.MM`. First, I need a robust function `G(a,c)` for the incomplete Gamma function.

```
G<-function(a,c){
#Avoid c=0, when a=0.
  integrand<-function(t){(t^(a-1)*exp(-t))}
  integrate(integrand,c,Inf)$value
}
```

Check to ensure your numbers match the above ones for `G(2,3)=0.19914` and `G(3,2)=1.3533` and that you haven't reversed the values. Also, ensure the function works for values of `a<=0`, which can wreak havoc on some numerical approximations to the Incomplete Gamma functions. For example, make sure you obtain `G(-0.5,1)=0.1781477`, versus a `warning message`. Also note that `G(1,0)=1`, `G(2,0)=1` and `G(3,0)=2`, and `G(N,0)=(N-1)!`, for any integer, per the definition of the Gamma function. Anyway, with that digression out of the way I can define the second (intermediate) function needed:

```
a<-function(v,x,m,b){
b*exp(exp((x-m)/b)+(x-m)*v)*G(-b*v,exp((x-m)/b))
}
```

To confirm this is working properly, here are two values: `a(0.01,65,88,10)` which should yield a value of `17.888` as well as the value for a higher discount rate, `a(0.03,65,88,10)` leading to `14.408`, both of which should confirm your code is working properly. I will actually have (much) more to say about this little `a(.)` function in the next Chap. 10, but for now it's introduced as a stepping stone for the moment-matching approximation. Finally, the user-defined function that computes that approximation can be constructed as follows:

```
VARPHI.MM<-function(x,m,b,xi,nu,sigma){
mu<-nu+(0.5)*sigma^2
M1<-a(mu-sigma^2,x,m,b)
M2<-(a(mu-sigma^2,x,m,b)
     -a(2*mu-3*sigma^2,x,m,b))/(mu/2-sigma^2)
alpha<-(2*M2-M1^2)/(M2-M1^2)
beta<-(M2-M1^2)/(M2*M1)
#Shape is Alpha, Scale is Beta
pgamma(xi,shape=alpha,scale=beta,lower.tail=TRUE)
}
```

The source, proof, and overall justification for these expressions are in the article cited as [5], and in particular equations (18), (20), and (21) in that article. Practically speaking, here are numerical examples of the `VARPHI.MM` function. I will use the same parameters used for the simulated results. Let ($x = 65, m = 88, b = 10$), and assume a portfolio with an expected continuously compounded real return of $\nu = 2\%$ with a standard deviation of $\sigma = 20\%$. This, by the way, implies that the drift coefficient in Eq. (9.5) is $\mu = 4\%$. Again, think of this as the real arithmetic mean ($\mu = 4\%$) versus the real geometric mean ($\nu = 2\%$).

```
VARPHI.MM(65,88,10,0.05,0.02,0.20)
[1] 0.3362243
# Simulation = 0.3525
VARPHI.MM(65,88,10,0.04,0.02,0.20)
[1] 0.2216641
# Simulation = 0.2419
VARPHI.MM(65,88,10,0.04,0.02,0.15)
[1] 0.1744054
# Simulation = 0.2079
```

The *moment-matching* estimates for φ are slightly lower (by 2–3% points) compared to the simulation-based results. Note that VARPHI.SM>VARPHI.MM isn't always the case, and is actually reversed at higher withdrawal rates ξ. For example, when $\xi = 10\%$, $\nu = 5\%$, and $\sigma = 25\%$, the LRP under the MM technique is higher by a few percentage points compared to SM. I report results and conclude the section.

```
VARPHI.SM(10000,65,88,10,0.10,0.05,0.25)
[1] 0.6073
VARPHI.MM(65,88,10,0.10,0.05,0.25)
[1] 0.6269
```

9.8 Final Notes: Concerns with Ruin

Starting with the Swedish mathematicians Filip Lundberg (b. 1876, d. 1965) and Harald Cramer (b. 1893, d. 1985), insurance actuaries have used *ruin probabilities* to measure liabilities and insurance company's risk for over a century. In the insurance context it represents the probability a stochastic process subjected to random additions (i.e. premiums) and subtractions (i.e. claims) hits zero (bankruptcy) before some terminal date. Bottom line, the credit for using φ in a business context (as opposed to gambling problems) goes to actuaries. But, in the last 2–3 decades these ruin probabilities (and their converse, success rates) have transitioned from the insurance world to quite popular metrics in personal finance, wealth management, and retirement income planning. Indeed, in addition to my own work cited as reference [6], the first articles in this area were [1] and [2] as well as [9] in the portfolio management literature. Although many didn't use the phrase ruin, nor did they account for mortality risk, the motivation was similar. So, while this entire chapter (and most of this book) has focused on the benefits of thinking about retirement income plans thru the lens of probabilities, I do have some concerns about how φ might be abused if taken too far. I have expressed these concerns elsewhere, for example, the article cited as [7], but in this concluding section I will only highlight caveats about this (fickle, temperamental) metric.

To start, the underlying *fix-ξ-until-you-die* assumption, namely that people will adhere to a deterministic spending schedule and then wake up one morning, check their account online, and find the money has reached zero, i.e. the portfolio has failed, is silly and naive. Nobody waits until that point to take restorative action to repair their finances. I mentioned this earlier, in Chap. 5, when I introduced portfolio longevity, and emphasize it here again. It's a big assumption, but most commercial software packages and algorithms in the retirement income business suffer from the same weakness. They assume *static and pre-determined* consumption behavior that is at odds with economic theory. I'll return to the *economics* in later chapters.

But, here are some additional things to keep in mind, especially now that you understand all the assumptions that go into producing (simulating) φ. To be blunt, nobody has any idea what lifetime ruin probability is acceptable in the context of retirement income planning. Is $\varphi = 10\%$ too high? Is a healthy $\varphi = 1\%$, or is the one-in-four $\varphi = 25\%$ acceptable? I have actually heard practitioners argue that a 51% chance of success (which is a 49% LRP) is good enough for a retirement plan. But, then think about it this way. Would you get on an airplane with a 0.1% probability of crashing? Why should a retirement income plan be any different?

Another issue arises when two different retirement income "strategies" are compared side by side. Assume that Plan A is estimated to have a $\varphi = 5\%$, but for Plan B the number is $\varphi = 4\%$. Ergo, the reader concludes that Plan B is preferred to Plan A. But is a 1% reduction in a lifetime ruin probability really that much better? Think back to the scattered dots in Fig. 9.3. The 1% reduction in φ only implies that a few dots have moved from under diagonal to over the diagonal. Will this make a real difference?

In fact, even if the industry (or the financial engineers) could agree on acceptable thresholds and bounds for φ, there are many different statistical distributions or financial plans that can generate the same failure rate. Should a retiree be indifferent between all plans of equal success or failure rate? To echo George Orwell, all 10% shortfall probabilities are equal, but some are more equal than others. Or, in less Orwellian but slightly more technical terms, different statistical distributions can share the same tail probability but have distinct risk and return profiles. Figure 9.5 illustrates three such curves. It models the distribution of financial legacy in discounted or present value terms, representing (very abstractly) the amount of money left at death (think: $\tilde{F}_{T_x}$) if you adhere to a fixed ξ forever. All three curves are Gaussian and very well behaved. For Case A the legacy has an average of \$100,000 and a standard deviation of \$78,000. For Case B, the legacy curve has an average of \$200,000 and a standard deviation of \$156,000 and for Case C, the average is \$300,000 with a standard deviation of \$234,000. If you want something more concrete to imagine, think of a very conservative retirement portfolio (Case A); a more balanced asset allocation mix (Case B) and a very aggressive asset allocation (Case C). All three portfolios are subjected to the same withdrawal rate ξ. The bulk

Source: Generated by Author in **R**

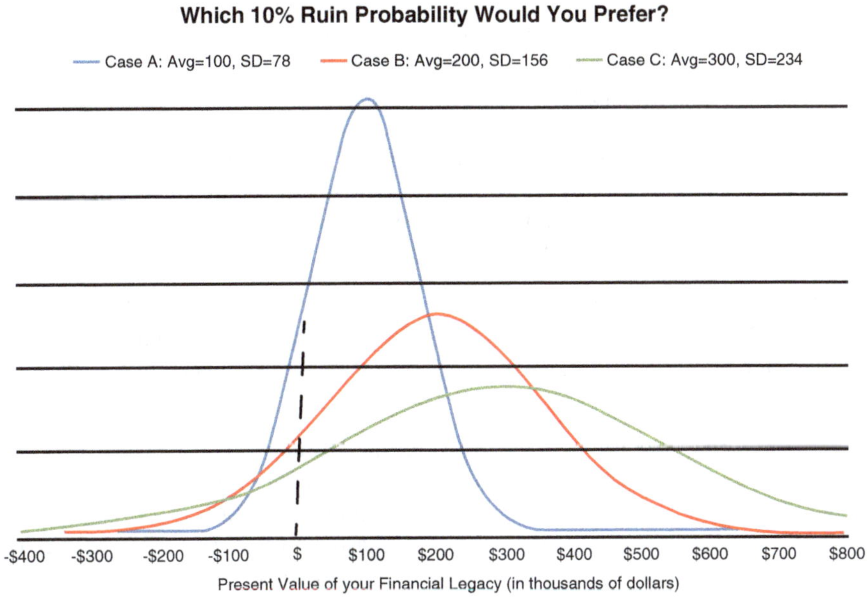

Fig. 9.5 Know your tail magnitudes

of the probability distribution is to the right of zero, which means that you can expect to leave a positive financial legacy. Notice that all three curves have the same area to the left of zero (i.e. the dashed line). The lifetime ruin probability is the same 10% under all three, but the severity of the potential rescue operation is quite different. Would retirees be indifferent between the plans? Indeed, it is not uncommon to read simulation-based studies in which counter-intuitive Strategy A is shown to have a higher success rate than more intuitively reasonable Strategy B, because the authors assume a 9% lifetime ruin probability (the area to the left of zero) is better than an 11% LRP, when in fact the entire distribution of outcomes is quite different. In particular, riskier stocks have a nasty habit of reducing lifetime ruin probabilities but wreaking havoc on higher statistical moments. Oddly enough, lower φ values are not necessarily better. In plain English, the lifetime ruin probability doesn't seem to care about what happens to all the dots *above the diagonal* in Fig. 9.4, but most humans do.

In sum, whether your Monte Carlo is using log-normal returns, bootstrapping historical data, or using a forward-looking equilibrium model for investment returns, you are implicitly making assumptions about the world in the very distant future. Effectively, your *black box* is forecasting how interest rates, stock prices, inflation as well as mortality will evolve over the next 50 years and how they will co-vary with each other. If all these assumptions were questionable before COVID-19, they are quite dubious afterwards. Please use ruin with caution!

Questions and Problems

9.1 Simulate $N = 10{,}000$ random Gompertz lifetimes, with a modal value of $(m = 88)$ and dispersion value of $(b = 10)$, as well as random portfolio longevity values with $\nu = 2.5\%$ and $\sigma = 15\%$. Call these vectors `zdat.hl` and `zdat.pl`. Compute the lifetime ruin probability φ for initial withdrawal rates of $\xi = 4\%$ using the method explained in the chapter. Very simple. But in addition, please compute the *expected number of shortfall years*, in the event you are alive when the money runs out. How? Think very carefully about the dots under the diagonal in Fig. 9.4, and then measure the magnitude by which L_ξ falls short of T_x.

9.2 Going back to the `LRPG(.)` function, locate the spending rate ξ that leads to *at most* a 3% lifetime ruin probability at retirement ages $x = 55, 65, 75$, under a $\nu = 2.5\%$ real rate of return assumption, $\sigma = 15\%$, and Gompertz $(m = 88, b = 10)$.

9.3 I introduced three different estimates for the lifetime ruin probability, denoted by $\varphi := \Pr[T_x \geq L_\xi]$. The first revolved around simulating `zdat.pl` for portfolio longevity and `zdat.hl` for human longevity and comparing vectors. The second method revolved around simulating the stochastic present value of the wealth trajectory until the time of death, and counting the number of negative values via the `VARPHI.SM` function. The third and final method was based on the moment-matching approximation to the stochastic present value, which (although rushed) was captured in the `VARPHI.MM` function. Compare the accuracy (and speed) of these methods by creating a table of φ values for initial withdrawal rates: $\xi = 2\%$, 4%, 6%, assuming two pairs: $(\nu = 2.5\%, \sigma = 10\%)$ and $(\nu = 4\%, \sigma = 25\%)$. Discuss results.

9.4 Advanced: Modify the `VARPHI.SM` from $(\Delta t = 1/52)$ to $(\Delta t = 1/12)$, and compare numerical results for standard (x, m, b) and (ξ, ν, σ) values.

9.5 Advanced: Modify the `PLSM` simulation from yearly to monthly and compare results with the answers to question 9.4.

References

1. Bengen, W. P. (1994). Determining withdrawal rates using historical data. *Journal of Financial Planning, 7*(4), 171–180.
2. Cooley, P. L., Hubbard, C. M., & Walz, D. T. (1999). Sustainable withdrawal rates from your retirement portfolio. *Financial Counseling and Planning, 10*(1), 39–47.
3. Huang, H., Milevsky, M. A., & Wang, J. (2004). Ruined moments in your life: How good are the approximations?. *Insurance: Mathematics and Economics, 34*, 421–447.
4. Kloeden, P. E., Platen, E., & Schurz, H. (1994). *Numerical solutions of SDE through computer experiments*. Berlin: Springer.
5. Milevsky, M. A., & Robinson, C. (2000). Self-annuitization and ruin in retirement. *North American Actuarial Journal, 4*(4), 112–124.

6. Milevsky, M. A., & Robinson, C. (2005). A sustainable spending rate without simulation. *Financial Analysts Journal, 61*(6), 89–100.
7. Milevsky, M. A. (2016). It's time to retire ruin (probabilities). *Financial Analysts Journal, 72*(2), 8–12.
8. Oksendal, B. (1998). *Stochastic differential equations: An introduction with applications*. Berlin: Springer.
9. Pye, G. B. (2000). Sustainable investment withdrawals. *The Journal of Portfolio Management, 26*(4), 73–83.

Chapter 10
Life Annuities: From Immediate to Deferred

This chapter develops a methodology for valuing **simple** cash-flow streams that last a lifetime, which are part of most Defined Benefit (DB) pensions. The focus is on the longevity-contingent building blocks of: (1) immediate, (2) temporary, and (3) deferred income annuities. The chapter begins with a discussion of the value of a longevity-contingent claim and how it differs from the *market price* versus the *manufacturing cost* of the product. The algorithms and user-defined **R** functions are mostly based on the Gompertz law of mortality, although a number of alternative continuous and discrete mortality models are discussed as well. The chapter concludes with a mathematical derivation and implementation of a closed-form expression for the Gompertz Annuity Valuation Model.

10.1 Functions Used and Defined

10.1.1 Sample of Native R Functions Used

- `legend(.)` adds legends to plots.
- `rect(.)` adds text rectangles to plots.
- `uniroot(.)` numerically solves for root of univariate equation.

10.1.2 User-Defined R Functions

- `IRR(v)` computes Internal Rate of Return.
- `GILA(x,v,m,b)`, Gompertz *immediate* life annuity.
- `GTLA(x,tau,v,m,b)`, Gompertz *temporary* life annuity.
- `GDLA(x,y,v,m,b)`, Gompertz *deferred* life annuity (a.k.a. ALDA, DIA, QLAC)

M. A. Milevsky, *Retirement Income Recipes in R*, Use R!,
https://doi.org/10.1007/978-3-030-51434-1_10

10.2 Actuarial Present Value (APV)

It should be obvious from the discussion and analysis in the last few chapters, that if you insist on spending a fixed amount of money (or fraction ξ of your initial wealth), there is a possibility you will still be alive when the funds run out. Indeed, live long enough and you will exhaust your nest egg if your spending is too high. Now, I have stated repeatedly that consuming a fixed amount regardless of economic and financial circumstances is *not* a good idea, and I'll discuss rational drawdown strategies in Chap. 11. Rather, I remind you of *longevity risk* here in Chap. 10, solely to introduce and motivate a possible alternative approach: *annuities.*

Annuities are similar to Social Security (in the USA), or the Canadian Pension Plan (CPP), and other corporate retirement systems. Classical (Defined Benefit) pensions entitle you to an income for the rest of your life, possibly inflation adjusted, regardless of how long you live. The provider assumes the longevity risk and you can retire assured that the longevity of that pot of money is effectively infinite. You can never live longer than a true pension. Well, annuities are pensions that are purchased from an insurance company. So, if you already have a retirement pension that entitles you to $1000 per month for the rest of your life—and you in fact like your pension—then, *in theory* you can buy even more lifetime income from an insurance company. How do they do this? How can they assume the risk you will live longer? Well, the insurance company (like a pension plan) has the ability to *pool* a large number of annuitants, thus reducing their longevity risk. And, by using proprietary pricing algorithms they can fix a price that balances fairness (to you) and safety (to them.)

Now, there are many (many) types of annuities and pension-like "products" that you can purchase from an insurance company. In fact, some products with the word annuity in their label have very little to do with pension income, but are nevertheless classified as annuities for legal and regulatory reasons. Indeed, I have written elsewhere (extensively) about the different types of annuities, see, for example, the references cited as [6] and [7], and I have no interest in repeating myself. Rather, the objective in this chapter is to (1) focus on basic life annuities, and provide a flavor of the (2) basic *valuation* algorithms and recipes.

I should note that insurance companies are subject to a myriad of government regulations, financial frictions, and strategic considerations, many of which can't be "modeled" with a simple script in **R**. So, the market price you see quoted for any insurance product, including annuities, is determined by very complex algorithms and considerations. It would also be incorrect (or extremely simplistic) to take a purely economic point of view and declare that market prices of annuities are determined by classic *supply and demand* considerations, especially when you consider capital constraints. What I can say with confidence is that you can get a reasonable estimate of the *actuarial present value* of any insurance product using the familiar concepts of (1) time value of money, (2) survival probabilities and perhaps a bit of (3) option pricing theory.

To understand how this approach differs from the (old) present value, I'll begin by computing the *actuarial present value* (APV) of the most basic *longevity-contingent* claim, which is fancy name for annuity. Assume that you know with *certainty* the value of q_x, which recall is the 1-year mortality rate, at some given age x. Then, the APV of a 1-year annuity that pays \$1 to survivors and \$0 to the (estate of the) deceased at the end of the year, is defined and equal to:

$$\texttt{APV Temporary Life Annuity} = \frac{1 - q_x}{1 + v}, \tag{10.1}$$

where v is the familiar valuation rate. To wrap your head around the issue of *why* this is a proper valuation methodology, think of a large insurance company selling many of these \$1-if-you-are-alive lottery tickets to a very large number of policyholders or retirees. On a per policy basis, the numerator represents a fraction of people who are alive at the end of the year, instead of the usual \$1. For example: if $q_x = 58\%$, and the survival probability is 42%, then under $v = 5\%$ the value of this annuity is $\texttt{APV} = 0.42/1.05 = \$0.4$, per \$1. Now, to be clear, this artificial type of insurance policy (a.k.a. pure endowment, a.k.a. 1-year temporary life annuity) doesn't really exist in practice, and if it did I'm not quite sure how the insurance company would price it (or if regulators would allow it). Rather, what I have presented here is a basic valuation methodology, which can be used to value multi-period insurance and annuity structures that *do* exist in practice. To understand how the concept can be applied more generally, please generate the following simulation in **R**.

```
zdat<-GRAN(10000,65,88,10)
summary(zdat)
    Min.  1st Qu.   Median     Mean  3rd Qu.     Max.
 0.01303 13.51822 20.74380 20.11040 26.87627 46.64789
apv<-RGOA(0,0.04,zdat)
summary(apv)
    Min.  1st Qu.   Median     Mean  3rd Qu.     Max.
 0.01277 10.28773 13.91837 12.88813 16.28741 20.98791
```

The `zdat` set of numbers generates $N = 10{,}000$ Gompertz lifetimes, and the second `apv` variable contains the $N = 10{,}000$ present values of an annuity that pays \$1 per year until the time of death. The (oldest) person who lived for 46.6 years ended-up costing the insurance company \$20.99 in present value terms. But, for the median person who lived 20.74 years, the cost (at time zero) to the company of providing that income is \$13.92. (Note: Given the concavity of the `RGOA` function, the (hypothetical) average person who lived 20.11 years, the time-zero cost to the company of providing their income would actually be higher than average (higher than \$12.89) (you can test this yourself). Google Jensen's inequality for more information on why this is true.) The mean (average) value of `apv` would be defined as the *actuarial present value*, which—if you think about it carefully—is an extension of Eq. (10.1). Again, it's an average of all the different possible present values, where the average is taken across all the possible times of death. The valuation methodology relies on the *law of large numbers*, which implicitly assumes the insurance company is issuing many identical policies and diversifying their longevity risk. Voila! I have just priced a life annuity via simulation, but in the next section I'll do it properly and formally.

10.3 Single Premium Income Annuity (SPIA)

I'll create the first user-defined **R** function in this chapter. This one computes the *value* of an immediate—which starts paying income *immediately* after purchase—life annuity under a Gompertz law of mortality. Once again, as I have noted many times before, the following script might not be the most efficient (i.e. fastest) way to code-up the formula or algorithm, but it's straightforward and logical. To be clear—and to differentiate this from the prior sections—this isn't a simulation, but rather a (crude) numerical integration scheme.

```
GILA<-function(x,v,m,b){
  omega<-x+b*log(1+10*log(10)*exp((m-x)/b));
  dt<-1/52; grid<-ceiling((omega-x)/dt); t<-(1:grid)*dt
  pgrid<-exp(exp((x-m)/b)*(1-exp(t/b)))
  rgrid<-exp(-v*t)
  sum(pgrid*rgrid)*dt}
```

The function has four arguments; the current valuation age `x`, the valuation rate `v`, as well as the standard Gompertz parameters `(m,b)`, which are the modal value and dispersion coefficients in years. The first line of the function script—which does require some explanation—defines a new variable ω, the assumed maximum lifetime. The rationale for introducing this number, and its odd form, is as follows. Recall from Chap. 8, Sect. 8.5, that the Gompertz survival probability can be re-arranged and expressed as:

$$t^* = b\ \ln[1 - \ln[p^*]e^{(m-x)/b}], \tag{10.2}$$

where p^* is the survival probability to age $(x + t^*)$, conditional on current age x. This equation was the "secret sauce" in the recipe used to simulate random lifetimes. Recall that I uniformly randomized: $p \in U[0, 1]$, which led to a random value of t that was Gompertz distributed. In the context of this chapter I use the same expression to fix the maximum age to which the annuitant can live. More precisely, it will be the age at which the probability of survival is $p^* = 10^{-10}$, which is one in ten billion, (slightly more than the earth's inhabitants), or $\ln[p] = -10 \times \ln[10]$. Under that probability the maximum age is

$$\omega := x + t^* = x + b\ \ln[1 + 10\ln[10]e^{(m-x)/b}]. \tag{10.3}$$

This might seem somewhat convoluted, so here is a numerical example (before I get back to annuity valuation.) Assume the current age `x=65`, and Gompertz parameters `m=88,b=10`. The (maximum assumed) age to which there is a one-in-ten-billion probability of survival, per Eq. (10.3), is

```
x<-65; m<-88; b<-10
omega<-x+b*log(1+10*log(10)*exp((m-x)/b))
round(omega,digits=2)
119.41
```

Again, assuming the Gompertz law of mortality is correct, one person (on planet earth with 10^{10} inhabitants) would reach the age of 119.4. That age is fixed as the point I stop adding cash-flows and assume everyone is (and all annuitants are) dead. Now, the point here isn't to predict by when our annuitant will be dead with 100% certainty, but rather to set an upper bound for the integration required to value the life annuity. Anything after that time would be ignored. In the above case it would be approximately 55 years after the annuity begins.

Moving on, the next step in the script is to partition the integration grid into units of $\Delta t = 1/52$, that is weeks, and set the upper bound (ω) in units of weeks as well. Finally, the script multiplies the survival probability vector `pgrid` by the discount factor vector `rgrid` and adds-up the pieces via the `sum` function in **R**. Here are some values, which are per $1 of lifetime income, starting at age $x = 65$.

```
GILA(65,0.025,88,10)
[1] 15.16471
GILA(65,0.015,88,10)
[1] 16.89727
GILA(65,0.005,88,10)
[1] 18.94856
```

Notice that as I reduce the valuation rate from $v = 2.5\%$ down to $v = 0.5\%$ (which is 200 basis points), the actuarial present value (APV) of the $1 of lifetime income increases from $15.16 to $18.95, which should be intuitive and no different from the relationship between bond values and bond yields. As a comparison to the APV, the (regular) present value (PV) of an ordinary annuity, using the (old) `RGOA` function, for a period of $N = 20$ years (roughly the life expectancy of a 65-year-old) is

```
RGOA(0,0.025,20)
[1] 15.58916
RGOA(0,0.015,20)
[1] 17.16864
RGOA(0,0.005,20)
[1] 18.98742
```

Source: Generated by Author in **R**

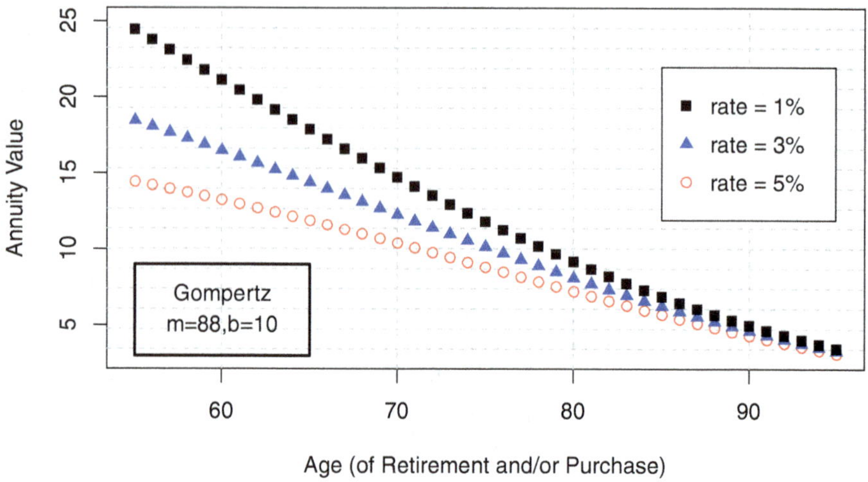

Fig. 10.1 The value of a (Gompertz) life Annuity: At 1%, 3%, and 5%

Notice how these numbers are extremely close, but yet slightly higher than the `GILA(.)` values. I'll get back to the formal mathematical relationship between these two quantities, in a later chapter. For now I'll state that the similarity between the two is the reason it's quite common (although not very accurate) to approximate the APV of a *life annuity* with the present value of a *simple annuity*, in which the number of periods is set equal to the expected number of years until death.

Similarities and differences aside, to obtain a more refined understanding of the `GILA` valuation function, Fig. 10.1 plots the value of Gompertz life annuity, from age $x = 55$ to age $x = 95$, assuming discount rates of 1%, 3%, and 5%.

The **R** script that generates Fig. 10.1 consists of the usual `plot(.)` sequence from prior chapters, but I have added two new **R** commands. The first creates a legend for the three curves, using the `legend(.)` command, and the second creates a rectangular box around the text of the Gompertz parameters. The displayed section of the script elaborates on how to use these two commands, and the exact syntax that should be included in your plot. For example, both the `legend(.)` and the `text(.)` command begin with the coordinates where the boxes should be placed, and then include parameters that dictate color, the type of symbol, etc. Note that (in the printed script) I have suppressed the `%` sign, which you might want to include when you generate the figures in **R**.

```
legend(85,22,legend=c("rate=1p","rate=3p","rate=5p"),
       col=c("black","blue","red"),pch=c(15,17,1))
text(60,5,"m=88,b=10")
```

```
text(60,7,"Gompertz")
rect(55,3,65,9,lwd=2)
```

Moving on to the substance of the figure, notice how the three curves begin (at age $x = 55$) at relatively large values, and reasonably far from each other, and then slowly decline and decay towards zero. The older you are when you value the life annuity, the less it's worth—after all, you are closer to death, so to speak. And, at advanced ages the valuation rate makes less of a difference. For example, at the age of $x = 60$, the annuity factor at $v = 1\%$ is `GILA(60,0.01,88,10)=21.13895`, but under the $v = 5\%$ valuation rate, `GILA(60,0.05,88,10)=13.234`. To put this in perspective, the annuity value (for a 60-year-old) is 60% higher, (a.k.a. more expensive) when interest rates are at 1% versus 5%. If you do the same at the age of $x = 80$, and compare `GILA(80,0.01,88,10)` to `GILA(80,0.05,88,10)`, the relative difference is (only) 27%. Moreover, to convert these annuity factors into more relevant units, a lifetime income of $100,000 starting at the age of $x = 60$ (e.g. a pension) is worth $2.1 million, at a 1% valuation rate, versus a mere $1.3 million at a 5% rate. Indeed, the choice of valuation rate (which can be rather subjective in practice) can make an enormous difference to the sum of money you would be entitled to, if you (can) cash-in your lifetime pension. The topic of cash-value, and whether it is worth-it to surrender your annuity, is something I'll return to later on. For now, I should also remind readers that the Gompertz (m, b) assumptions themselves make a difference to the discounted economic *value* of the annuity factor. For example, adding 5 years to the modal value of life, that is increasing from $m = 88$ to $m = 93$ will add about 14% to the value of the annuity at the age of $x = 65$, under a $v = 3\%$, per the following script.

```
GILA(65,0.03,93,10)/GILA(65,0.03,88,10)
[1] 1.14415
GILA(65,0.03,88,15)/GILA(65,0.03,88,10)
[1] 1.031991
```

Likewise, adding 5 years to the dispersion coefficient, so that $b = 15$ years instead of $b = 10$, adds a mere 3% to the value of the annuity. Although, I caution (and warn) that this assumes one can arbitrarily change either m or b without affecting the other parameter. Indeed, no different from the economic relationship between risk and return, nature places restrictions on how much we can tinker with b without affecting m, and vice versa. I'll return to these (advanced) mortality matters in Chap. 12.

While on the topic of mortality here is another useful trick. Go back to Chap. 8, Sect. 8.4, where I introduced Gompertz. I mentioned that $E[T_x]$ (of any random lifetime) can be computed by integrating the survival probability $\Pr[T_x \geq t]$, from zero to the end of life. In particular, see Eq. (8.8) and the script that follows. This implies that `GILA(x,0,m,b)`, which is the annuity value under a valuation rate of zero, also happens to be the expected remaining lifetime. So, instead of using the brute-force integration methodology, I can use the `GILA(.)` function. For example:

```
GILA(60,0,88,10)
[1] 24.24838
GILA(65,0,88,10)
[1] 20.11617
GILA(70,0,88,10)
[1] 16.28852
```

What this means is that the expected remaining lifetimes at ages: $x = 60, x = 65, x = 70$ are $T_{60} = 24.25$ years, $T_{65} = 20.12$ years, and $T_{70} = 16.29$ years, respectively. Note that expected remaining lifetimes (a.k.a. annuity factors when $v = 0$) are always greater than annuity factors, when $v > 0$. Stated differently, the value of the \$1 for life (in dollars) is always less than your remaining life (in years.) A quick and easy way to remember this is: Don't pay more than your life expectancy! To conclude, and for comparison purposes, the simulated (with one million lives) expected values are, to within three digits, identical to the `GILA(x,0,m,b)` values.

```
mean(GRAN(1000000,60,88,10))
[1] 24.25704
mean(GRAN(1000000,65,88,10))
[1] 20.1271
mean(GRAN(1000000,70,88,10))
[1] 16.27491
```

10.4 Alternative Paths to GILA

As I alluded to earlier, there are other ways in which I could have coded-up the annuity valuation script for `GILA(.)` in **R**, using built-in functions. For example, instead of the crude integration (which is just summation over weeks) I can leverage the `integrate` function in **R**, and use that to compute the annuity value. See the following script, which starts with the Gompertz survival probability multiplied by the discount factor `exp(-r*t)`, and then integrates from ($t = 0$) to ∞, the upper bound.

```
x<-65; m<-88; b<-10; v<-0.015
integrand<-function(t){exp(-v*t+exp((x-m)/b)*(1-exp(t/b)))}
integrate(integrand,0,Inf)$value
[1] 16.90688
```

Using this recipe, the annuity value is slightly higher than the prior value of `GILA(65,0.015,88,10)=16.897`, due to the finer grid embedded inside the `integrate(.)` function, and (possibly) the upper bound of infinity, versus $(\omega - x)$. These differences are minor and can be dismissed as rounding errors—at least from a pedagogical point of view—unless you are valuing very large annuities, in which case you would probably use a discrete mortality table anyway. Nevertheless, the above script does open-up a number of possibilities (and generalizations) for valuing life annuities under *any* discount rate function. Recall that v is assumed constant over the entire *term structure* in the `GILA(.)` function, but in reality the valuation rate might depend on the time. For example, imagine a world in which valuation (interest) rates can be modeled by the function $r(t) = 0.03/(t^{1/4} + 1)$, which is a (completely *ad hoc*) downward sloping term structure over time. This can be coded-up and then evaluated in **R** as:

```
v<-function(t){0.03/(t^(1/4)+1)}
v(0); v(5); v(10); v(30)
[1] 0.03000
[1] 0.01202
[1] 0.01079
[1] 0.00898
```

Now, using that specific built-in function for `v(t)`, I can value the Gompertz annuity by substituting the constant `v` with the time-dependent function `v(t)`, which is then multiplied by `t` in the integrand. Everything else in the script remains the same, and in this case the value of the annuity factor is as follows:

```
x<-65; m<-88; b<-10;
integrand<-function(t){exp(-v(t)*t+exp((x-m)/b)*(1-exp(t/b)))}
integrate(integrand,0,Inf)$value
[1] 17.86035
```

Notice the higher \$17.86 versus the lower \$16.89, for the constant $v = 1.5\%$ case. The higher annuity factor is due to the fact that (overall) I am discounting by a lower rate (curve), even though the initial (time zero) valuation rate was $3 > 1.5\%$. The point here isn't to suggest that you should use this particular curve `v(t)` rather than a constant, but rather to illustrate how time-varying discount rates can easily be incorporated into the valuation algorithms. Likewise, I can use more complex survival probability functions, instead of the simple `TPXG` in the integrand. For example, joint life annuities which I'll introduce at the end of this chapter, will be valued this way. Finally, in Chap. 12 I will discuss general (non-Gompertz) models for mortality, in which the (logarithm of the) force of mortality is not linear in (chronological) age. Those too can be easily incorporated into a valuation framework by modifying the integrand. Enough about modifications, and for now I'll move on to valuing other types of life annuities.

10.5 Temporary Life Annuity (TLA)

Not all life annuities (1) start immediately and (2) continue paying income for the rest of your life. Some, called *temporary* life annuities begin paying \$1 per year (for example) but terminate in 10, 20, or 30 years, even if you are still alive. So, if you happen to survive 10, 20, or 30 years, you will no longer receive any more income from the annuity. And, while this may seem like a bad idea (Note: I didn't say it was a popular product), it's cheaper than a true life annuity. As far as notation is concerned, I'll use the Greek letter tau τ to denote the number of (temporary) years and the usual `(x,v,m,b)` parameters. Remember, this annuity "dies" once you reach age $(x + \tau)$, even if you are still "alive." Here is the script that values the *temporary* life annuity.

```
GTLA<-function(x,tau,v,m,b){
  if (tau==0){0}
  else {
  dt<-1/52; grid<-ceiling(tau/dt); t<-(1:grid)*dt
  pgrid<-exp(exp((x-m)/b)*(1-exp(t/b)))
  rgrid<-exp(-v*t)
  sum(pgrid*rgrid)*dt}
  }
```

Practically speaking the only difference between the above `GTLA(.)` script and the main (original) script for `GILA(.)` is that instead of stopping the integration (a.k.a. summation) at the very end of the lifespan $(\omega - x)$ years, the upper bound is at τ. I also forced the value of `GTLA=0` if `tau=0`. The remainder of the algorithm is identical, and in fact copied verbatim, from `GILA`. Here are some numerical values:

```
GTLA(55,30,0.03,88,10)/GILA(55,0.03,88,10)
[1] 0.931956
GTLA(70,30,0.03,88,10)/GILA(70,0.03,88,10)
[1] 0.9968028
```

In the first row I computed the value of a temporary life annuity, at age $x = 55$, paying for (only) $\tau = 30$ years, or until death, whichever comes first. I then divided the `GTLA(.)` value by the immediate life annuity value `GILA(.)` to illustrate the discount for *not* being protected beyond age $85 = 55 + 30$. The TLA is about 7% cheaper than the ILA, because the TLA doesn't "protect" you beyond age 85. In contrast, in the second row of the above script, the annuity is valued (e.g. purchased) at the age of $x = 70$. The temporary annuity for $\tau = 30$ years implies that the income will continue until age $100 = 70 + 30$, at which point it will terminate (even if this person is alive.) Now, the probability of an $(x = 70)$ Gompertz life surviving to age 100 is: `TPXG(70,30,88,10)=0.043`, which is less than 5%. Add to that (low) probability, the fact that \$1 in 30 years is worth approximately `exp(-0.03*30)=0.41` today, and you can see why the TLA is 99.6% of the ILA value. They provide very similar levels of protection or insurance. I'll return to this sort of analysis in Chap. 13, when I discuss the topic of **heterogenous mortality** and the fact that separate demographic groups (and countries) should be modeled with different values of (m, b). Finally, to wrap up this section, here is a small script that replicates the TLA value, via integration.

```
x<-65; m<-88; b<-10; v<-0.03; tau<-25
GTLA(x,tau,v,m,b)
[1] 13.6876
integrand<-function(t){exp(-v*t+exp((x-m)/b)*(1-exp(t/b)))}
integrate(integrand,0,tau)$value
[1] 13.69574
```

The slightly higher value, using the `integrate()` command, is due to its finer grid relative to the weekly increments in the `GTLA(.)` function. And, if you go back and modify the `GTLA` script so `dt<-1/1000` instead of `dt<-1/52`, and re-run the numbers, they match to 5 digits. Try it, and make sure you understand why.

10.6 Deferred Life Annuity (DLA)

Due to the "risk" that you outlive your annuity income, I wouldn't recommend including `GTLA(.)` as part of your retirement portfolio. And, the truth is, they aren't very popular either. Don't confuse the `GTLA(.)` with a life annuity that pays a lifetime of income, guaranteed for `RT` years. That's another variation I'll discuss in a later section. Rather, the `GTLA(.)` is more of an artificial structure used to analyze and value other (more popular) structures, and in particular the *deferred* life annuity, which is the focus of this section. Let me begin by referring to Fig. 10.2, which represent the three basic types of life annuity.

Source: Generated by Author

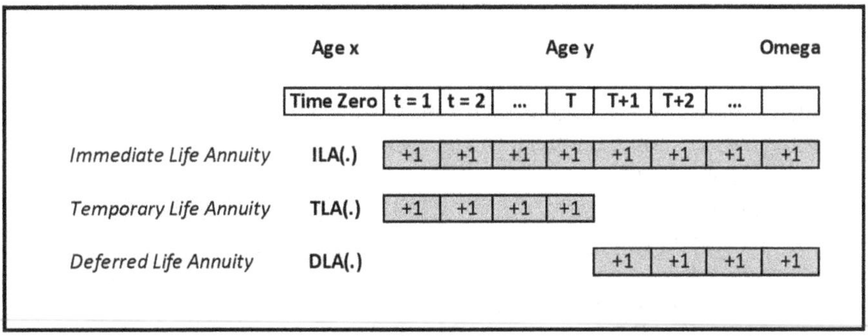

Fig. 10.2 Life Annuity algebra: Immediate = Temporary + Deferred

As you can see visually, the deferred life (which is often called delayed, or advanced life) annuity begins paying at age $y > x$, and continues to pay until age ω, which is the very end of the lifetime. It is the symmetric opposite of the *temporary* life annuity, and the two combined form an *immediate* life annuity. Notice how the *temporary* LA makes its last payment at time T, whereas the (focus of this section, the) *deferred* LA makes its first payment at time $T+1$. So, although I will refer to the *deferred* as being delayed to time T, you should think of it as an ordinary annuity, paying-out at the end of the period. Of course, when operating in continuous time these distinctions are irrelevant. Mathematically, I can express the relationship as:

$$ILA = TLA + DLA. \quad (10.4)$$

This relationship, which should be intuitive, becomes the defining equation for the value of *deferred* life annuity. Notice that I didn't include the (Gompertz) G in front of the expressions, because the relationship holds true regardless of the underlying law of mortality. Nevertheless, I will use the pre-existing Gompertz-based functions: `GILA(.)` and `GTLA(.)` to build the new function `GDLA(.)`, per the following script.

```
GDLA<-function(x,y,v,m,b){GILA(x,v,m,b)-GTLA(x,(y-x),v,m,b)}
```

The `GDLA(.)` function inherits the restrictions, baggage and speed of the other two functions from which it is constructed. I won't dwell too much on the alternative (integration-based) approaches that can be used instead other than to mention that the following script would compute a very similar value, as well.

```
x<-55; m<-88; b<-10; v<-0.03; tau<-20
integrand<-function(t){exp(-v*t+exp((x-m)/b)*(1-exp(t/b)))}
integrate(integrand,tau,Inf)$value
[1] 4.398772
GDLA(x,x+tau,v,m,b)
[1] 4.394604
```

The interpretation is as follows. At the age of $x = 55$, and under a $v = 3\%$ valuation rate, the value of a deferred life annuity, which begins paying at age $y = 55 + 20 = 75$, is worth approximately \$4.39, per \$1 of lifetime income. This assumes the (usual) Gompertz law of mortality with parameters $m = 88$ and $b = 10$. For the sake of diagnostics, the probability of dying before the income ever starts is `1-TPXG(55,20,88,10)=0.21`. That is obviously a risk, and something I'll return to in the next Chap. 11, when I discuss the economic rationale for buying such an annuity.

Some readers might justifiably wonder why I bother creating three separate `GILA(.)`, `GTLA(.)`, and `GDLA(.)` functions, using coarse grids and weekly cash-flow summations, when I could just as easily run the `integrate` command to price any-and-all variations of life annuity, and under any survival probability functions. Truth be told it's unclear whether weekly cash-flows themselves are *too refined*, considering that most annuities pay out monthly or even yearly. In practice, if that is the case, the function scripts should be modified so that `dt<-1/12`. Nevertheless, at this point I leave both recipes—*continuous* and *discrete*—on the table and let the user decide which is appropriate given the circumstances. Either way, now that I have the basic valuation expressions, I can move on to the interesting and relevant work, that is some real-world case studies.

10.7 Annuity Formula Applications

10.7.1 DB Pension Buyout

You are $x = 65$ years-old, and are about to "retire" from a company that offers you a defined benefit (DB) pension, promising an income of \$45,000 for the rest of your life. The pension plan gives you the option to "cash-in" your entitlements and take a lump sum (today) instead. The lump sum they are offering you (a.k.a. the bribe to give up your life annuity) is \$500,000. The issue I address in this section is whether the money they are offering is a fair deal relative to the pension annuity. Now, obviously, there are many issues to consider in the decision of whether to take the pension annuity or the lump-sum cash. In fact, the broader question of whether pension annuities add "utility" will be addressed in the next Chap. 11. However, in this section (and chapter) I'll focus on relatively simple valuation exercises using the `GILA(.)` function, as well as `PL`, `PLSM`, as well as `LRPG` and `VARHPI` functions from prior chapters. For the most part I'll assume that your (human lifetime) longevity prospects can be described by a Gompertz law with ($m = 88, b = 10$), which (depends on your health status and) is a critical assumption and yet another issue I'll revisit in Chap. 12. So, let's get started. I'll compute the actuarial present value (APV) of the pension annuity, using the `GILA(.)` function, assuming the pension annuity begins immediately (and technically is paid weekly) the value under $v = 1, 3$, and 5% is as follows:

```
pension<-45000; lumpsum<-500000
x<-65; m<-88; b<-10;
GILA(x,0.01,m,b)*pension
[1] 804548
GILA(x,0.03,m,b)*pension
[1] 647961
GILA(x,0.05,m,b)*pension
[1] 534225
```

Notice the values range from a low of \$534,225 to a high of \$804,548, which is higher than the half a million dollars offered as a lump-sum substitute. What this tells us is that unless you can earn a (much) higher inflation-adjusted return, you are getting more "value" from the pension annuity than the lump sum. In fact, I can use the built-in `uniroot(.)` function in **R** to compute the exact break-even valuation rate that equates the pension annuity to the lump sum. The syntax for that command, and the resulting number is

```
IRR<-function(v){pension*GILA(x,v,m,b)-lumpsum}
# The values of x,m,b were fixed in the prior script.
round(uniroot(IRR,c(0:1))$root,digits=3)
[1] 0.057
```

The (user-defined) `IRR` computes the difference between the value of the pension annuity and the lump sum, as a function of the valuation rate v. When the value is positive, the pension annuity is worth more. And, when the value is negative the lump sum is worth more. The `uniroot` then locates the value of v which sets the value of the `IRR` function to zero, thus equating the `pension` to the `lumpsum`. That number, under the assumed parameters, is 5.7%. Here is another way to think about (and express) these results. If real interest rates in the marketplace are higher (better) than 5.7%, then you are better off taking the `lumpsum` of half a million dollars. But, if rates are lower than 5.7%, then you get more value from the pension annuity of $45 thousand per year. Now, I must warn you (yet again) that this sort of analysis addressed only one dimension of the matter, which is market value. Indeed, in the current (year 2020) environment it's almost impossible to guarantee a 5.7% real return from any investment, but that doesn't mean you should decline the lump sum and accept the pension annuity. This is just one aspect of the decision, and there are other ways to analyze the tradeoff. For example, returning to the concept of portfolio longevity, if you decide to take the lump sum of $500 thousand and try to replicate the pension annuity yourself (a.k.a. self-annuitization) the money may not last for the rest of your life. Let's examine the longevity of the portfolio assuming three different valuation a.k.a. (a.k.a. investment) rates. See the following script:

```
PL(0.01,pension,lumpsum)
[1] 11.7783
PL(0.03,pension,lumpsum)
[1] 13.5155
PL(0.05,pension,lumpsum)
[1] 16.2186
```

So, at a $v = 1\%$ investment rate, the longevity of the portfolio would be (only) 11.77 years, and under a (much higher) 5% rate it would be a mere 16.2 years. If you live beyond that time horizon, the nest egg (a.k.a. lump sum) would be depleted. Along the same lines, recognizing that $\xi = 45/500 = 9\%$, the lifetime ruin probability (LRP), which was introduced in the prior Chap. 9, would be

```
x<-65; m<-88; b<-10; xi<-pension/lumpsum
LRPG(0.01,xi,x,m,b)
[1] 0.7982657
LRPG(0.03,xi,x,m,b)
```

```
[1] 0.75045
LRPG(0.05,xi,x,m,b)
[1] 0.6654435
```

The values of φ (under fixed investment returns) range from 66.5 to 79.8%, which are extremely high. These numbers all tell a similar story, namely that a \$45,000 pension annuity is "worth" more than a \$500,000 lump sum. Of course, one can envision a (very unscrupulous) financial advisor recommending the lump sum after running Monte Carlo simulations, using my `VARPHI.SM` function, claiming to have a low risk (σ) and high return (ν), resulting in:

```
# Do You Believe in Low Risk & High Return?
nu<-0.10; sigma<-0.08
VARPHI.SM(100000,x,m,b,xi,nu,sigma)
[1] 0.08967
```

This is a lifetime ruin probability $\varphi \approx 9\%$, and a success rate of over 90%. Note that can only be "cooked" with the (very dubious) assumption the portfolio earns a geometric mean of 10% after-inflation, with volatility risk of only $\sigma = 8\%$. Needless to say, you can generate almost any result you want with the right assumptions. So, the lesson is to question your parameters as much as your model. *Bottom line:* In this particular situation it's very hard to beat the pension annuity. But, I'll return to the tradeoff again in Chaps. 11, 12, and 13, there are a number of other factors to consider (such as health) in the choice between the two.

10.7.2 DB Pension Reserves

Let's take a look at this from a different perspective, namely from the point of view of the (pension, insurance) company promising to pay the pension annuity. Now assume that you are (only) $x = 45$ years-old, which is two decades before your planned retirement date, and that you have worked at the company for the last 10 years. You earn $w =$ \$75,000 per year and the company promises you an inflation-adjusted DB pension consisting of 2% per year of service, multiplied by the number of years you have worked at the company multiplied by your final year's salary. (Note. That is a product of three distinct items.) So, *assuming* you continue to earn \$75,000 for the next 20 years, you will have accrued a full 30 years of service and your pension would be: $(0.02) \times (30) \times 75{,}000$, which is (the above-mentioned) \$45,000 per year. Of course, right now, you are 20 years short of that benefit, and you have only accrued 10 years of credited service.

Question: What is the *value* of your pension entitlement, today? More specifically, how much money should the company have set-aside in reserves (a.k.a. pension fund) to pay those delayed benefits? To be clear, few (if any) employers will allow you to cash-out of a delayed DB pension this way. Rather, I am looking at this from the perspective of the company and its *solvency* or its *funded status.* Well, in this case the appropriate life annuity formula to use is the GDLA(.) factor, because the benefit (lifetime income) you promised doesn't begin for another 20 years. Furthermore, since you have only accrued 10 years of working credits (and not the full 30), your salary multiplier is (0.02) × 10, which is 20% of the \$75,000, and only \$15,000 per year, starting at age 65. Using the same valuation rates of $v = 1\%$, $v = 3\%$, $v = 5\%$, the resulting numbers are

```
x<-45; y<-65; m<-88; b<-10;
future_pension<-15000
GDLA(x,y,0.01,m,b)*future_pension
[1] 201336
GDLA(x,y,0.03,m,b)*future_pension
[1] 108693
GDLA(x,y,0.05,m,b)*future_pension
[1] 60070
```

Depending on the valuation (a.k.a. discount) rate, the company should have between \$60,070 and as much as \$201,336 set-aside, in your name, to pay your accrued benefits—even though they aren't due (to you) for another 20 years. Now, let me ask this question. Do you think the company would rather set-aside the low number of \$60,070, or the high number of \$201,336? Well, the answer is obviously the low number (because they can obviously use the money for other things.) This then creates a huge (and very problematic) incentive for the pension fund (trustees, managers, actuaries) to use very high ($v = 5\%$) valuation rates instead of (more reasonable, and) lower ($v = 1\%$) rates. Now, I certainly don't want to get into the controversy around proper discount rates for DB pensions. My sole intention was to illustrate the use of GDLA versus GILA.

10.7.3 DB Pension Funding

The third and final application or use for the *life annuity* pricing formulas relates to pension contributions, instead of benefits. This gives me an opportunity to use the final GTLA(.) function for valuing the *temporary* life annuity. Assume for the sake of argument that you are $x = 45$ years-old and contribute (that is pay-in) \$5000 per year towards your pension, which is then paid out to you at retirement. What is the discounted value of these \$5000 payments for the next 20 years? Remember that if you happen to pass away and die before reaching the age of 65, you will (obviously) stop making those payments. So, you can't multiply the periodic cash-flows by RGOA(.), and then call it a day. Well, this is precisely where the GTLA(.) function can be used.

```
x<-45; tau<-20; m<-88; b<-10;
contributions<-5000
```

```
GTLA(x,tau,0.01,m,b)*contributions
[1] 88107
GTLA(x,tau,0.03,m,b)*contributions
[1] 73277
GTLA(x,tau,0.05,m,b)*contributions
[1] 61738
```

The discounted value of your contributions is between \$61,738 and \$88,107, depending on the valuation rate, as usual. Finally, and for the sake of comparison, notice that if I use the `RGOA(.)` formula and assume this person will survive for the entire 20 years, the present value is

```
RGOA(0,0.01,tau)*contributions
[1] 90227
RGOA(0,0.03,tau)*contributions
[1] 74387
RGOA(0,0.05,tau)*contributions
[1] 62311
```

Notice that the difference between using the `RGOA(.)` formula versus the `GTLA(.)` to discount cash-flows is only one or two thousand dollars. Stated differently, the discount for mortality doesn't make a very big difference when the individual is $x = 45$ years-old. The chances of dying (under a Gompertz law) between the ages of $x = 45$ and $y = 65$, which is when the cash-flows terminate, is quite small. In fact, they can be easily computed in **R** via the function: `1-TPXG(45,20,88,10)=0.083`. In other words, the 8.3% probability of dying during the next 20 years reduces the present value of the \$5,000 cash-flows by less a few thousand dollars (only.) Of course, at advanced ages—where death is more likely and prevalent—discounting for mortality will have a much larger effect. For example—and this is something I'll get back to in the next chapter—let's compare the following two financial products, purchased at the age of $x = 70$. The first product provides an income \$10,000 per year for life. We can value that using the standard `GILA(.)` function. The second product pays you \$10,000 per year, for the next 35 years, which gets you to the age of 105. How much more expensive is the term-certain annuity (the second product) versus the life annuity? Well, here is the answer:

```
GILA(70,0.01,m,b)/RGOA(0,0.01,35)
[1] 0.501436
GILA(70,0.03,m,b)/RGOA(0,0.03,35)
[1] 0.5706936
GILA(70,0.05,m,b)/RGOA(0,0.05,35)
[1] 0.633827
```

The immediate life annuity is worth between 50 and 64% of the value of the term-certain annuity, that is much cheaper, because of the discounting for mortality. This is another way of stating (or proving) that life annuities are a much cheaper way of financing a stream of income payments at retirement, although at the expense of legacy and bequest. After all, when you die, there is nothing left for your heirs with the (standard, conventional) life annuity. Whereas the term-certain annuity would pay out for 35 years regardless of the status of your life.

10.7.4 DLA with COLA

To this point in the chapter I have been rather *lazy* with the topic of inflation. The formulas and algorithms I presented for `GILA`, `GTLA`, and `GDLA` assumed that the valuation rate (v) was measured in the same units as the \$1 of lifetime income. So, if the pension promise was in nominal dollars (very common) the valuation rate would be in nominal dollars. And, if the pension promise was provided in real inflation-adjusted dollars (somewhat rare), the discount rate would have to be real as well, which at the time of writing this, is close to zero. However, in some cases the pension (or annuity) promise mixes-and-matches the real with the nominal, and in this subsection I'll provide a brief example and describe how to value (a.k.a. cook) these hybrid cases.

To make this more concrete I'll consider the following annuity "product," which a number of insurance companies (in the USA) have been promoting quite aggressively in the last few years as pension replacements—for those who aren't fortunate to have a DB pension. In essence it's a *deferred* income annuity, in which the payments are delayed to some advanced age, but once they begin (say at the age of 80 or 85) the payments will increase every year by a pre-determined cost of living adjustment (COLA). So, for example, the company might promise \$10,000 per year for life, starting in 30 years, and the payments would increase every year by (say) 2%. So, in year #30 you would receive your first \$10,000, assuming you were alive, and in year #31 you would receive \$10,000(1.02) = \$10,200, and in year #32 you would receive \$10,000$(1.02)^2$, etc. The 2% is meant to protect against (or keep up with) inflation, but it may under (or over) shoot depending on the actual realized inflation rate, as measured by the (random) consumer price index (CPI). Note also that the COLA adjustments begin—and the payments increase—once the buyer reaches the payout age. There is nothing to adjust until then. So, how would you value such a modified delayed life annuity? Using the (very general) symbol a to denote a generic annuity factor, the relevant one in this case is

$$a = \int_{\tau}^{\infty} \mathrm{e}^{-vt}\mathrm{e}^{\rho(t-\tau)}\,({}_tp_x)dt = \mathrm{e}^{-\rho\tau}\int_{\tau}^{\infty} \mathrm{e}^{-(v-\rho)t}\,({}_tp_x)dt. \tag{10.5}$$

In the above equation $\tau = (y - x)$ is the usual difference in ages, which is the time in years until payments begin. The ρ parameter (in this chapter) denotes the cost of living adjustment (COLA), expressed using continuous compounding, and $({}_tp_x)$ is the (by now familiar) notation for the conditional survival probability: $\Pr[T_x \geq t]$.

As explained earlier, the underlying \$1 of lifetime income begins at time τ and then starts growing at a rate of ρ, which is the reason for: $e^{\rho(t-\tau)}$ in the integrand of the first part of Eq. (10.5). The second integral in Eq. (10.5) is a regular GDLA in which the valuation rate is reduced by the COLA, $(v - \rho)$, and in fact might be negative. Here is an implementation in **R**, using the integration methodology. I have assumed an $x = 53$ year-old, delayed to age $y = 80$, which is $\tau = 27$ years, with a $\rho = 1\%$ cost of living adjustment and a valuation rate of $v = 2\%$, which was (approximately) the long-term 30 years U.S. Treasury Bond yield at the time I generated these numbers. The final number displayed represents the *monthly* lifetime income generated by a \$1000 premium (paid today). So, while $1000/a$ would represent the annual income entitlement (since $\$1000 = a \times$ annual income), the number $(1000/a)/12$ would be the monthly income.

```
# Valuing the Deferred Income Annuity (DIA) with a COLA
x<-53; y<-80; m<-88; b<-10; rho<-0.01; tau<-(y-x); v<-0.02
ING<-function(t){exp(-(v-rho)*t+exp((x-m)/b)*(1-exp(t/b)))}
afa<-exp(-rho*tau)*integrate(ING,tau,Inf)$value
#Monthly income (with COLA) per $1,000 Purchase Today.
round((1000/afa)/12,digits=2)
[1] 23.67
```

So, the \$1000 premium (paid at age $x = 53$) will entitle me to \$23.67 at the age of $y = 80$, assuming the $(m = 88, b = 10)$ mortality assumptions are appropriate for the buyer, and the valuation rate is indeed $v = 2\%$. For comparison purposes, when I re-run the exact same script but with $x = 52$ (which is 1 year younger) and a slightly higher valuation rate of $v = 2.9\%$, the monthly income is \$32.99 per \$1000 of premium, or \$16.5 per month per \$500 of premium. Where did the \$500 come from? Well, I actually purchased (and now own) one of these deferred annuities, see Fig. 10.3, and that is the price I paid when I was $x = 52$, and long-term (U.S. government) interest rates were $v = 2.9\%$. So, this isn't theoretical, and I refer those interested in my rationale to the article cited as [4].

Source: Photographed by Author

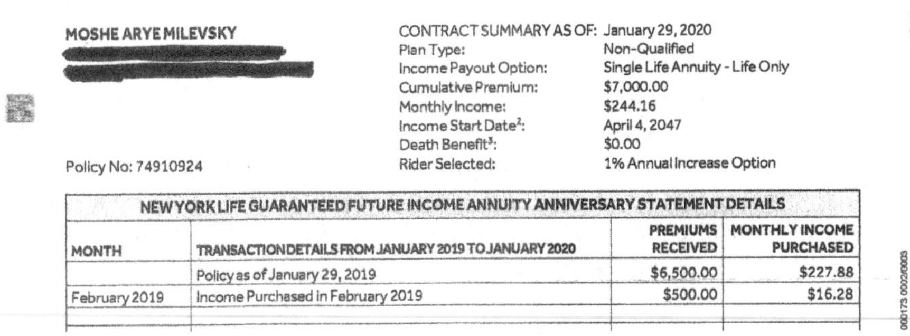

MOSHE ARYE MILEVSKY

Policy No: 74910924

CONTRACT SUMMARY AS OF: January 29, 2020
Plan Type: Non-Qualified
Income Payout Option: Single Life Annuity - Life Only
Cumulative Premium: \$7,000.00
Monthly Income: \$244.16
Income Start Date[2]: April 4, 2047
Death Benefit[3]: \$0.00
Rider Selected: 1% Annual Increase Option

NEW YORK LIFE GUARANTEED FUTURE INCOME ANNUITY ANNIVERSARY STATEMENT DETAILS

MONTH	TRANSACTION DETAILS FROM JANUARY 2019 TO JANUARY 2020	PREMIUMS RECEIVED	MONTHLY INCOME PURCHASED
	Policy as of January 29, 2019	\$6,500.00	\$227.88
February 2019	Income Purchased in February 2019	\$500.00	\$16.28

000173 0002/0003

Fig. 10.3 My deferred income Annuity: Will I get to 80?

Table 10.1 Deferred: monthly income at 80 per $1000 premiums at 50

Gompertz mode	$m = 84$ years	$m = 88$ years	$m = 92$ years	$m = 96$ years
$E[T_{50}] + 50$	Age 79.5	Age 83.2	Age 86.9	Age 90.7
$v = 1\%$	$27.50	$17.56	$12.28	$9.17
$v = 2\%$	$39.20	$25.33	$17.93	$13.57
$v = 3\%$	$55.78	$36.44	$26.10	$20.00
$v = 4\%$	$79.23	$52.29	$37.87	$29.36

Assumes: 1% COLA from age 80, no death benefit and Gompertz dispersion: $b = 10$ years

While I have your attention there are a few other issues I should point out in Fig. 10.3. First, it's a non-qualified annuity which means that it is not part of a tax-sheltered retirement plan (such as a 401(k) or IRA in the USA.) So, if-and-when I get to age $y = 80$ and receive my $244 per month, a fraction of that payment will be taxable income and the rest will be return-of-principal. The exact portions are computed by the company. Also, and more importantly, this is a pure *deferred* income annuity, which means that if I don't survive, my family, heirs, and spouse receive absolutely nothing. This is a single (my) life annuity and there is no death benefit. (I had to get my wife's permission to purchase this!) Now, I could have purchased a deferred annuity in which there are some guarantees attached—and I'll discuss those in the next section—but they would have reduced the amount of income I receive at the age of 80.

The following is a summary table, using the same **R** script, of the monthly income I would be entitled to based on the **valuation** formula under different rates v. The purchase age is $x = 50$, the income age is $y = 80$, and cash-flows and rates are in continuous time. To be clear, the numbers in the table aren't market payouts (a.k.a. prices), but rather my estimate of what those would be, assuming the valuation in Eq. (10.5). I'm reasonably confident my "model" approximates the insurance company's pricing mechanism (Table 10.1) contains the numerical analysis.

Notice that if I assume a higher $m = 96$, which leads to an expected age at death of $E[T_{50}] + 50 = 90.7$ under the Gompertz law, the monthly income is much lower compared to the $m = 88$ assumption. For example, using the $v = 2\%$ valuation rate, if I assume that (the 50-year-old's) life expectancy is age 79.5, the monthly payout should be $39.20 per $1000 premium. But, if add 10 years to life expectancy the monthly payout plummets to $13.57, because the person is more likely to survive to age 80 and receive income for (much) longer. In fact, if you look carefully at the diagonal numbers from top-left to bottom-right you will notice they are all close to $26–$29 per month. So, back to the real world, if that happens to be the payout they are offering you at age 50—and you don't know the valuation rate they are using—it could be they are discounting at $v = 4\%$ and assuming you will live to age 90. Or, they may be more pessimistic and assuming a life expectancy of 80 years, but are discounting cash-flows at lower rates. The only way to tell for certain—and infer the embedded (m, v) values—is to obtain a variety of quotes and then solve for the values. Alas, that takes me far beyond my objectives for this chapter, and refer readers to the article cited as [10], in which this technique is discussed further.

10.8 Life Annuity with Period Certain

Few people are willing to purchase a life annuity that is as risky as the one I just described. Most buyers want assurances that if they "die early," their heirs continue to receive payments for a fixed and predictable number of years. So, in this section I'll review how to value an annuity that includes a guarantee known as a *period certain.* Namely, payments continue to someone, even if you aren't around to receive them. The period certain can be 5, 10, or even 20 years, and is really up to the buyer. Of course, the longer the *period certain* the more expensive the annuity (or the lower the periodic income) and vice versa. Now, the annuity factor with a PC is relatively easy to value in a Gompertz framework, and is a slight modification of the algorithm you have already seen before. It's best to think of the immediate life annuity with a T-year period certain as the sum of two different components. The first component is a basic term-certain annuity (think `RGOA`) and the second component is a *deferred* life annuity, valued via `GDLA(.)` in a Gompertz framework. I'll let that sink in for a moment.

I'll value the *period certain* portion using the analytic expression derived and explained (many pages ago) in Chap. 2, Sect. 2.8, which was the expression `RGOA.CT`. And, the *deferred* life annuity is computed by integration. Here is a numerical example assuming an $x = 65$ year-old buys an immediate life annuity, but with 20 years period certain. Remember, even if this person dies tomorrow, the beneficiary (who is specified in advance) will continue to receive the payment of $1 until the end of the 20-year period.

```
x<-65; m<-88; b<-10; PC<-20; v<-0.03
integrand<-function(t){exp(-v*t+exp((x-m)/b)*(1-exp(t/b)))}
# Value of Life Annuity Factor (with no period certain)
integrate(integrand,0,Inf)$value
[1] 14.40875
# Value of Life Annuity Factor with 20 years Period Certain
(1/v)*(1-exp(-v*PC))+integrate(integrand,PC,Inf)$value
[1] 16.84663
```

Notice that the *pure life* annuity factor is $14.40875 per dollar of lifetime income, but the factor for the life annuity with 20-year period certain is $16.84663, which is approximately 17% more. Stated differently, the guarantee of 20 years of payments, to an heir or survivor, will obviously reduce the payout from the life annuity. Starting with $100,000, for example, the lifetime income under the life plus 20-year period certain would be $5936 per year (again, divide the lump sum by the annuity factor), whereas the *life only* would generate $6940. This claim, that the guarantee will cost you 17% more, assumes a $v = 3\%$ valuation rate, and (just as importantly) that market prices are identical to the valuation expressions. Of course this again gets back to the earlier discussion of valuation models versus market prices which I don't want to repeat. My only point is that PC costs money.

10.9 Joint Life Annuity with 100% Survivor Benefit

While some people are willing to pay for a guarantee period on their life annuity, other buyers (are part of a couple and) want to ensure the income will continue for the life of a spouse. In other words, the $1 must continue for as long as *one* member of the couple is still alive. In terms of valuation, this can easily be implemented by modifying the survival probability (${}_tp_x$) so it accounts for either of them being alive. And, the key (or trick) is to realize that the probability that either member of the couple is alive at any time t, is *one minus* the probability they are both dead. So, formally, the probability that at least one of them is alive is

$$P(t) = \texttt{Probability Either Alive} = 1 - [(1 - p_1(t))(1 - p_2(t))], \tag{10.6}$$

where $p_1(t)$ is the survival probability for one member of the couple (e.g. male), and $p_2(t)$ is the survival probability for the other member (e.g. female.) Now, with the (bigger) value of $P(t)$ in hand, we can use that to integrate the discounted cash-flow. So, the only complication in the following script is the more elaborate (and longer) expression for the survival probability $P(t)$. The rest of the algorithm should be familiar by now, although I do urge you to be careful when typing the function(t), which is the above-referenced probability multiplied by the discount function: $e^{-vt}P(t)$. Ideally, don't have any spaces between the lines and type the entire expression on one line.

```
x1<-65; m1<-88; b1<-10;
x2<-70; m2<-85; b2<-10;
v<-0.03
ING<-function(t){
exp(-v*t)*
(exp(exp((x1-m1)/b1)*(1-exp(t/b1)))+
exp(exp((x2-m2)/b2)*(1-exp(t/b2)))-
exp(exp((x1-m1)/b1)*(1-exp(t/b1)))*
exp(exp((x2-m2)/b2)*(1-exp(t/b2))))
}
integrate(ING,0,Inf)$value
[1] 15.96476
GILA(x1,v,m1,b1)
[1] 14.39913
GILA(x2,v,m2,b2)
[1] 10.98004
```

So, the immediate annuity factor for the joint life with 100% survivor benefit is \$15.96 per \$1 of lifetime income, whereas the immediate annuity factor for the individuals (at age $x = 65$ and age $x = 70$, respectively) are \$14.40 and \$10.98, assuming the relevant Gompertz $m1$, $b1$ and $m2$, $b2$ values noted in the script.

10.10 Analytic Expression for Gompertz Annuity

This final section might seem a bit more mathematical than the rest of the chapter (and book), but it sets the stage for the material in the next Chap. 11, which is Calculus-heavy. In particular, the objective in this section is to derive a closed-form analytic expression for the Gompertz annuity factor, which I'll denote using the function `a()`, which you might recognize from the prior Chap. 9. Before I get to that, I'll augment and modify the standard Gompertz representation by adding a constant to the force of mortality.

$$\lambda_x = \lambda + \frac{1}{b} e^{(x-m)/b}. \tag{10.7}$$

The $\lambda \geq 0$ constant is often called the Makeham term, named after the nineteenth century actuary William Makeham who I already mentioned in Chap. 8 as being a student (and promoter) of Benjamin Gompertz. So, from this point onward I'll refer to the more general equation (10.7) as the Gompertz–Makeham (GM) law of mortality. This additional constant λ, which wasn't emphasized or even mentioned in Chap. 8, Sect. 8.4, captures accidental (i.e. non-age related) deaths, while the familiar $m > 0$ is the usual modal value of life and $b > 0$ is the dispersion coefficient. Notice that at the modal age the force of mortality is now: $\lambda_m = \lambda + 1/b$. And, while on the topic of notation and parameterization, there are other ways to express the GM force of mortality. For example, another popular representation used by actuaries is $\lambda_x = A + BC^x$, where A is the accidental death rate, $B = \exp\{-m/b\}$, and $C = \exp\{1/b\}$. This parameterization is common in some economics articles, as well as (old) actuarial textbooks and was even used by Benjamin Gompertz [7] himself. Another possible way to write the GM law is $\lambda_x = \lambda + h_0 e^{gx}$, which is a notation scheme I'll return to in Chap. 12, when I discuss mortality heterogeneity.

The (expanded) GM law implies that the conditional survival probability, which actuaries denote by $({}_t p_x)$ and mathematically is $\Pr[T_x \geq t]$, can be expressed as:

$$p(x, t, m, b) = e^{-\int_x^{x+t} \lambda_y \, dy} = \exp\{-\lambda t + \eta (1 - e^{t/b})\}, \tag{10.8}$$

where the new variable $\eta := \exp\{(x - m)/b\}$ is a *standardized* age x, introduced to simplify the derivations. For example, under a GM law with $m = 85$ years and $b = 10$ years, your standardized age at $x = 85$ is $\eta = e^0 = 1$. At age $x = 95$, which is one dispersion unit (b) above the modal lifetime, the standardized age is $\eta = e$.

And, when age $x = 105$ which exceeds the modal lifetime by two dispersion units, the standardized age is $\eta = e^2$. In fact, it might be suitable to label η your Euler age. But, regardless of the exact name a reasonable range for this new variable is $0.03 \leq \eta \leq 4.48$, when age x is in the (retirement) range $50 \leq x \leq 100$. This is a numerical factoid relevant for some of the examples to come later.

On to annuity valuation. Let $T_1 \geq 0$ denote the time at which a *deferred* life annuity begins paying \$1 per year and let $T_2 \leq \infty$ denote the contractual time at which payment is terminated *even* if the annuitant is still alive. (Think of a temporary annuity.) To be clear, the current chronological age is x and the life annuity begins payment at chronological age $(x + T_1)$ and continues until the *earlier* of death or age $(x + T_2)$, whichever comes first. I will augment the actuarial annuity factor: $a(x, m, b, r)$ to include three extra parameters, by writing: $a(x, m, b; T_1, T_2, \lambda)$. Note that: $a(x, m, b, r; 0, \infty, 0)$ is effectively: $a(x, m, b, r)$. Also, by definition of a *temporary and deferred* life annuity, the following relationship will always hold:

$$a(x, m, b, r; T_1, T_2, \lambda) = a(x, m, b, r; T_1, \infty, \lambda) - a(x, m, b, r; T_2, \infty, \lambda), \tag{10.9}$$

which is the difference in value between two (pure) deferred annuity contracts, one starting at age $(x + T_1)$ and continuing until death and then subtracting the value of a (very) deferred annuity starting at age $(x + T_2)$. The point of all of this is that by having a neat and compact expression for $a(x, m, b, r; u, \infty, \lambda)$, under any value of u, I can value any type of annuity. Moving on, recall that any life annuity factor can be expressed as:

$$\begin{aligned} a(x, m, b, r; u, \infty, \lambda) &= \int_u^\infty e^{-rt}\, p(x, t, m, b)\, dt \\ &= \int_u^\infty e^{-rt} \exp\{-\lambda t + \eta\,(1 - e^{t/b})\} dt \\ &= e^\eta \int_u^\infty e^{-(r+\lambda)t} \exp\{-\eta e^{t/b}\} dt \end{aligned} \tag{10.10}$$

I can simplify (or solve) the integral using change of variable techniques. In particular, define a new variable $s := \eta e^{t/b}$. Recall that as far as future time t is concerned, the standardized Euler age η is a constant and therefore:

$$(s/\eta)^b = e^t \quad \rightarrow \quad s = \eta e^{t/b} \quad \rightarrow \quad ds = \frac{1}{b}(\eta e^{t/b}) dt \quad \rightarrow \quad b s^{-1}\, ds = dt$$

Using the new variable s (instead of t) and realizing that:

$$e^{-(r+\lambda)t} = \eta^{(r+\lambda)b}\, s^{-(r+\lambda)b}, \tag{10.11}$$

the *deferred* life annuity factor can now be rewritten, after extracting all the constants from within the integrand, as:

$$a(x, m, b, r; u, \infty, \lambda) = \eta^{(r+\lambda)b} e^\eta\, b \int_{\eta\, e^{u/b}}^\infty e^{-s}\, s^{-(r+\lambda)b-1}\, ds. \tag{10.12}$$

For example when $u = 0, x = 75, m = 85, b = 10$ the value of (standardized Euler age) $\eta = 1/e$. So, if $(r + \lambda) = 0.05$ whatever their individual values, the constant in front of the integral in Eq. (10.12) becomes $10\,e^{(1/e-0.5)} \approx 8.76235$ and the integral portion itself is $\int_{1/e}^{\infty}(e^{-s})(s^{-1.5})ds = 0.89635$, using numerical integration techniques. Ergo, the *immediate* annuity factor $\mathtt{a}(75) = (8.76235)(0.89635) = 7.85415$, to five significant digits.

Now, from the messy looking Eq. (10.12) it might not *appear* as if I have improved matters, but the underlying integral can actually be identified as the Incomplete Gamma (IG) function:

$$\Gamma(\alpha, \beta) = \int_{\beta}^{\infty} e^{-s}\, s^{\alpha-1} ds. \tag{10.13}$$

When the lower bound of integration $\beta = 0$ the IG function collapses to the basic Gamma function and when α is an integer then $\Gamma(\alpha, 0) = (\alpha - 1)(\alpha - 2)\ldots$ etc., a.k.a. $(\alpha - 1)$ factorial, with the understanding that both $\Gamma(1, 0) = 1$ and $\Gamma(2, 0) = 1$. For general values of α and β the $\Gamma(a, c)$ function is readily available in **R**, using the `G` command I coded-up in Chap. 9, and repeat here for completeness:

```
G<-function(alpha,beta){
integrand<-function(t){(t^(alpha-1)*exp(-t))}
integrate(integrand,beta,Inf)$value}
```

For example, the value of `G(-0.5,1)=0.178148` to five digits and the value of `G(-0.5,0.3678)=0.89659`. I do caution that for non-positive values of α there are some numerical stability issues. Merging equation (10.13) and (10.12) I can write annuity factor using a closed-form expression:

$$\mathtt{a}(x, m, b, r; u, \infty, \lambda) = \frac{b\,\Gamma(-(r+\lambda)b, \eta e^{u/b})}{\eta^{-(r+\lambda)b}\, e^{-\eta}}, \tag{10.14}$$

For calibration and testing purposes, note that $\mathtt{a}(x, m, b, r; u, \infty, \lambda)$ collapses to: $b\,e\,\Gamma(0, 1) \approx (0.596)b$, when $u = 0$ (immediate annuity), at $x = m$ (modal age) and $r = 0$ as well as $\lambda = 0$, and there are no accidental deaths in life. For now, replacing the standardized Euler age $\eta = \exp\{(x - m)/b\}$ with actual age x, I re-write the general *deferred* annuity factor in Eq. (10.14) as follows:

$$\mathtt{a}(x, m, b, r; u, \infty, \lambda) = \frac{b\Gamma(-(r+\lambda)b, \exp\{\frac{x-m+u}{b}\})}{\exp\{(m-x)(r+\lambda) - \exp\{\frac{x-m}{b}\}\}}. \tag{10.15}$$

Finally, the full explicit expression for the *deferred and temporary* annuity factor based on the identity in Eq. (10.9) is

$$a(x, m, b, r; T_1, T_2, \lambda) = \frac{b\Gamma(-(r+\lambda)b, \exp\{\frac{x-m+T_1}{b}\}) - b\Gamma(-(r+\lambda)b, \exp\{\frac{x-m+T_2}{b}\})}{\exp\{(m-x)(r+\lambda) - \exp\{\frac{x-m}{b}\}\}}, \tag{10.16}$$

with the convention that $\Gamma(., \infty) = 0$. For example: $a(65, 85, 10, 0.03; 0, \infty, 0) =$ \$13.13 and $a(75)$=\$3.77537, which is much lower due to the higher valuation rate 5 vs. 3% and later starting date 75 vs. 65. See reference [5] for more on the Calculus.

10.11 Final Notes: More Risks

- Private insurance companies are subject to a certain amount of default risk, or even financial distress that might delay annuity payments, which should manifest itself in (market) annuity prices. And, although there are a number of national and state guarantee associations that (partially) cover these risks, its important to understand the annuities are not risk-free instruments.
- The actual market pricing of annuities—that is what you actually pay when you buy one of them—versus their valuation, which was the focus of this chapter, is covered in the article cited as [1]. In particular I should note that there is a lag of a few weeks and possibly some months between changes in (market) interest rates and (changes) in annuity prices. Also, the response to changes in interest rates is asymmetric and depend on the entire term structure of interest rates. This fact is especially relevant when interest rates are volatile and/or have recently changed. Once again, the valuation expressions in this chapter are *models*, which are intuitive and helpful *approximations to reality*. Don't expect to see these exact numbers in your local (annuity) supermarket.
- The *deferred* life annuity, which I described and actually purchased, raises the interesting question of (1) when it should be purchased, and (2) in what increments. I refer interested readers to the articles cited as [3] as well as [8] for more on the subject of optimal purchasing strategies.
- For more information about the rationale for the *actuarial present value*, and the role of the law of large numbers in eliminating idiosyncratic risk, see the classic actuarial textbooks cited as [11] as well as [2]. And, for a discussion of the conditions under which the law of large numbers isn't as effective in diversifying away longevity risk—for example, when survival probabilities themselves are uncertain—see the article cited as [9].

Questions and Problems

10.1 Please use integration techniques described in this chapter to value of an *immediate* life annuity (factor) at the age of $x = 50$, that pays \$1 of income for life until age $y = 85$, but then if-and-when you reach the age of $y = 85$, the payment is reduced by 50% to only \$0.50, from that point onward. Assume the usual ($m = 88, b = 10$) Gompertz parameters, and valuation rates of $v = 1\%$ as well as $v = 5\%$. How does the value (or annuity factor) compare to a basic, simple *immediate* annuity that pays \$1 for life?

10.2 At the very start of this chapter, I simulated Gompertz lifetimes and effectively valued an *immediate* life annuity by computing the average `RGOA(.)` value for each of those $N = 10{,}000$ random lifetimes. That was another way of computing the actuarial present value (APV). Using the same idea, please use simulation techniques to compute the APV of a *deferred* annuity, issued at age $x = 50$, which begins paying at age $y = 80$, and assuming a $\rho = 1\%$ cost of living adjustment. In other words, I would like you to replicate the payout numbers displayed in Table 10.1, assuming the same Gompertz parameters.

10.3 The derivation in Sect. 10.10 provides an explicit expression for the value of an *immediate* life annuity under an (expanded) Gompertz–Makeham law. Assuming ($m = 88, b = 10$), please value an immediate annuity at age $x = 65$, under $v = 1\%$ and $v = 3\%$, assuming that Makeham constant $\lambda = 3/1000$. This means that every year *three-out-of-a-thousand* people die accidentally. So, how much of a difference does accidental deaths have on annuity valuations at advanced ages?

10.4 Value a 100% joint life annuity, under a $v = 3\%$ valuation rate, when $x_1 = 65$, $x_2 = 60$, but assuming that $m = 88$ and $b = 10$ for both lives. (i.e. they are homogenous lives.) Can you simplify the expression for the annuity value?

10.5 In the above "problem," assume the couple request a 15-year period certain on their life annuity. What is the annuity factor in that case?

References

1. Charupat, N., Kamstra, M., & Milevsky, M. A. (2016). The sluggish and asymmetric reaction of life annuity prices to changes in interest rates, *Journal of Risk and Insurance, 83*(3), 519–555. https://doi.org/10.1111/jori.12061
2. Dickson, D. C., Hardy, M., Hardy, M. R., & Waters, H. R. (2013). *Actuarial mathematics for life contingent risks*. Cambridge: Cambridge University Press.
3. Huang, H., Milevsky, M. A., & Young, V. (2017). Optimal purchasing of deferred income annuities when payout yields are mean-reverting. *Review of Finance, 21*(1), 327–361.
4. Milevsky, M. A. (2005). Advanced life delayed annuities: Introduction to real longevity insurance with deductibles. *North American Actuarial Journal, 9*(4), 109–122.
5. Milevsky, M. A. (2006). *The calculus of retirement income: Financial models for pension annuities and life insurance*. New York: Cambridge University Press.
6. Milevsky, M. A. (2013). *Life annuities: An optimal product for retirement* (120 p.). Charlottesville, VA: CFA Institute.
7. Milevsky, M. A. (2018). Annuity Fables: Some observations from the Ivory Tower, Available at as quoted in the New York Times, 14 December 2018, and available here https://www.nytimes.com/2018/12/14/your-money/annuity-explainer.html.

8. Milevsky, M. A., Huang, H., & Young, V. (2015). A glide path for target date annuitization. *Journal of Retirement, 3*(1), 27–37.
9. Milevsky, M. A., Promislow, S. D., & Young, V. (2006), Killing the law of large numbers: Mortality risk premiums and the Sharpe ratio. *Journal of Risk and Insurance, 73*(4), 673–686.
10. Milevsky, M. A., Salisbury, T. S., & Chigodaev, A. (2016), How long does the market think you will live? Implying longevity from annuity prices. *Journal of Investment Consulting, 17*(1), 11–21.
11. Promislow, S. D. (2006). *Fundamentals of actuarial mathematics*. Toronto, Canada: Wiley.

Chapter 11
Intelligent Drawdown Rates

This chapter, which could have been called rational decumulation, introduces **dynamic** risk-adjusted approaches to spending during retirement. The *intelligent drawdown* philosophy is contrasted with **static** approaches, such as the 4% rule and its variants, the focus of prior chapters. The material begins with a light-hearted game that develops an intuition for how longevity uncertainty should affect retirement spending as well as a discussion of the benefits from risk pooling. Moving on to the technical content, after a brief crash course on utility theory, the chapter develops algorithms for (1) computing optimal withdrawal rates based on *risk aversion* preferences and (2) adjusting ongoing spending based on realized financial and longevity variables. One of the surprising aspects of an *intelligent* approach to retirement spending is that planning to deplete one's liquid wealth at some advanced age is "rationale" if you have ample pension annuity income.

11.1 Functions Used and Defined

11.1.1 Sample of Native R Functions Used

- No new **R** functions were used in this chapter.

11.1.2 User-Defined R Functions

- `IDDR(Fx,pi,x,m,b,r,rho,gam)` computes a "rational" amount of consumption (a.k.a. drawdown or portfolio spending), as a function of current age x, financial capital F_x, assumed return r, the Gompertz parameters (m, b), as well as the amount of pre-existing pension income π, longevity risk aversion γ, and a subjective discount rate ρ.

M. A. Milevsky, *Retirement Income Recipes in R*, Use R!,
https://doi.org/10.1007/978-3-030-51434-1_11

11.2 Preferences for Retirement Spending

For the most part—over the course of the first ten chapters in this book—I have explicitly (or implicitly) assumed a generic retiree who is solely interested in maintaining a **constant real** standard of living for the rest of their natural life. The constant withdrawal and/or spending assumption was at the heart of the lifetime ruin probability (LRP) recipes in Chap. 9, it was the working-horse life annuity valued in Chap. 10 and the foundation of the *portfolio longevity* material in Chaps. 5 and 6. Of course, the justification for desiring a "smooth" constant real standard of living is intuitive and can be traced to the financial life-cycle model introduced in Chap. 3. In other words targeting a fixed $x\%$ of your initial nest egg over the course of your life does have a basis in economic theory, notwithstanding the criticism leveled at LRP at the end of Chap. 9. However, the problem with what I call the **static** approach to retirement income planning is that it doesn't give much guidance on how to adjust behavior to unexpected changes in portfolio values and economic realities. Ponder this question. What if the stock market and your portfolio (unexpectedly) drop by 10%, 20%, or 30% when you are in your 60s and 70s? You know from the discussion and analysis of *sequence-of-returns* in Chap. 6 that your revised *portfolio longevity* might be reduced by a decade or even more. Should you continue withdrawing at the same rate ($x\%$ of your initial nest egg) which you were doing before the drop? Risk materialized, so how do you adjust? Just as importantly as you get older and closer to the end of the life-cycle, longevity risk takes on greater visibility. How should mortality risk impact those withdrawal adjustments? After all, everyone has their own unique attitude to the "risk" they live to 100. So, this chapter is really about planning for expected events as well as recipes for adjusting to unexpected scenarios. Allow me to explain with a story.

One of the courses I teach at our university's business school is an advanced finance elective (in our executive MBA program) on the topic of retirement income planning; for which the material in this book is intended to serve as a supplementary text. Early on during the semester—to help motivate the challenges of the subject—I like to play the following game or exercise. Here's how it works. After the students arrive at the lecture hall at the start of class, I hand every one of them 60 poker chips, similar to the ones you might find in a casino. These chips are the same color, size, and denomination, identical in all regards. When the students sit down at their tables, they also find a small cardboard box in front of them, similar to a large matchbox. The box is separated into six compartments, and each one of them has a label. The first compartment on the very left-hand side of the box is labeled *70-to-75*, the second compartment next to it is labeled *75-to-80*, all the way to the final compartment on the right-most side that reads *95-to-100*. I inform the students that they should consider each of these compartments or slots as representing a total of 5 years of their retirement and all six of them together as the entire 30 years. It starts at the age of 70 and ends at the age of 100. I tell them to ignore anything after the age of 100.

The main point of the exercise is for them to imagine chips as representing their nest egg (i.e. retirement savings, pension pot, etc.). I ask them to allocate these 60 chips across the six slots in a manner that best represents how they would personally like to spend and spread them over their retirement years. Before the students allocate their precious chips into the slots, I reassure them that these are real spending chips. They are meant to be used for expenses that give them pleasure, not anxiety. I ask them to imagine that stressful spending like medical care has been insured (e.g. nationalized healthcare) and those expenses will be covered without chips. Again, these chips are for enjoyment. How would you like to spend them? I give them a few minutes, so they might debate and consult with people at their small classroom tables. (I should remind everyone that these chips don't earn any interest and you can't invest chips hoping to get more later. It's my game, so I can make the rules!)

I then ask to see what they've done and have them describe their chip allocations. Interestingly enough, very few students in the class divide the chips evenly across the three decades and allocate 10 chips to each of the identical 6 slots. The boring answer of 60/6 is quite rare. And yet, splitting the 60 chips evenly across the retirement slots is sort of the so-called 4% rule, which I discussed in earlier chapters. Technically, allocating 10 chips per 5-year bucket works out to 2 chips per year, which is about 3.33% of your initial 60 chip nest egg. Again, nobody does that, at least when I ask them how they would like to actually spend their chips. Rather, what tends to happen in this game is quite different, and I suspect the reason is that **human longevity** isn't a certainty. The probability of living to the furthest boxes (i.e. advanced ages) declines over time, which I discussed at length in Chaps. 7 and 8.

For a typical or average 40-year-old executive, the chances they reach the first slot in the box is quite high, perhaps even greater than 95%. But, the odds or probability of reaching that final box—the one that says *95-to-100*—are quite small. Recall the discussion about the Gompertz law of mortality and the exponentially increasing force of mortality. Now, I can't say for certain what their probabilities of hitting 100 are without knowing more about them (their cohort, health, etc.), but I would say that generally speaking the probability is less than 5%. With those slim odds, how many chips will they allocate to that last slot?

My careful reminder of longevity risk made the uncertain horizon salient for them, at least for a few minutes, which led to average chip allocations similar to the one you see in Fig. 11.1. The last box only has three (on average), and the numbers increase as you move backwards and to the left. Now, to be clear, the numbers I'm displaying are sample averages across the many classes I have taught, and there is a lot of variation across participants. But, on average, the last slot receives 3 chips. The slot next to it, representing ages *90-to-95*, and associated with a slightly higher probability, receives an average of 7 and so on and so forth until the left-most slot has an allocation of 16 chips. Remember, they all must add up to 60 chips. You can't leave any chips on the table (outside the box) or overspend your chips.

Now, to one of the main points underpinning this chapter, not everyone in the class allocates their chips in the 16-14-11-9-7-3 pattern displayed in Fig. 11.1. Some

Source: Generated by Author

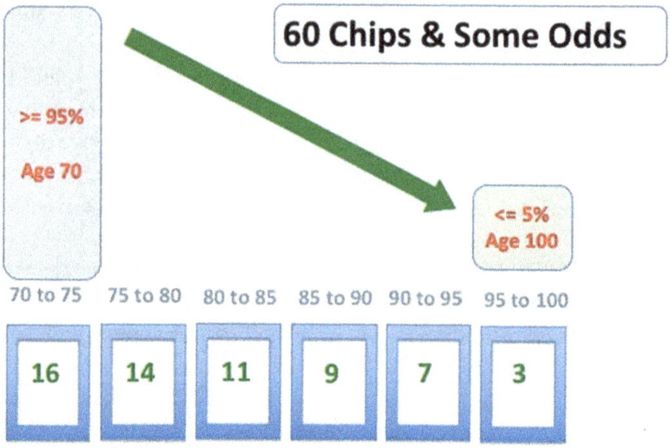

Fig. 11.1 How would you like to spend your retirement chips?

students allocate more chips in the latter years—perhaps they can't imagine living on only three chips—while others front-load more of them to the early years, when they are more likely to be alive and can enjoy them. A few participants implemented a U-shaped pattern, which is quite different from the (average) declining pattern exhibited in the figure. The U people spend more in the first few years (travel, live-it-up in the go–go years) as well as the last few years (to die with dignity is expensive). But, in the middle years they expect to slow down. Hence, the middle slots are allocated the least chips. I interpret these variations or the heterogeneity across participants as reflecting two fundamentally different and perhaps even opposing preferences. In the language of economics, one represents their **Subjective Discount Rate** (a number I'll later define as ρ) that is their preference for consuming more today versus less tomorrow. The second preference has to do with **Longevity Risk Aversion** (a number I'll later define as γ). Some retirees worry a great deal about living to very advanced age and provision more to that scenario (slot) regardless of how small those probabilities might be. Other participants are longevity-risk tolerant, perhaps synonymous with investment-risk tolerance when it comes to financial markets. They are willing to take their chances and "live" with the consequences. Indeed, one size doesn't fit all, and there are hundreds of thousands of different ways to allocate these chips. The *intelligent drawdown* algorithm I will introduce in the next section will provide withdrawal guidance based on these two preferences. At the risk of putting the cart before the horse, I use the Greek letter rho ρ to measure subjective discount rates and gamma γ to measure longevity risk aversion. For now I refrain from elaborating about these two parameters until the next section.

Returning to the game and the chips, once a student took their entire 60 chips and instead of spreading them across the six boxes, placed all 60 of them on the first slot, representing ages 70–75. Going from right to left his allocation was zero, zero, zero, zero, zero, 60. He was going to spend it all on the first day of retirement. Now, when the class noticed this chip allocation, everyone laughed heartily, and perhaps that was his intention. *"Blow it all on a boat, eh?"*, one class member yelled. But, when I asked this (boater?) what he expected to live on for a possible 25 years of retirement, if he lived that long, his response was dead serious: *"Hey, I have a Defined Benefit pension at work, which guarantees me an income annuity for the rest of my life. I don't really care so much about these chips."* Others in the group, mostly mid-level executives, were jealous of this exceedingly rare employment benefit and had to provision some of their chips in the event they did reach an advanced age. They could not ignore the longevity risk entirely. Either way, I noted how interesting it was that a guaranteed pension changed spending habits and allowed for spending more with less guilt, early on in retirement. This isn't just observed in a game. Those fortunate enough to have a true (DB) pension annuity seem to worry less about drawing down their precious nest egg too quickly, versus others whose sole source of income are the chips. So, from this I take away that another important ingredient in the retirement income drawdown recipe is pension income, which I'll denote by the Greek letter, π.

However, the main reason I started this chapter with stories and games is because of what happened one semester, when I ran this routine exercise with yet another group. In that particular term the game was upstaged by a clever few. As most students were quietly pondering and reflecting how they might allocate their chips, I noticed a small group of four sitting at one table and visibly arguing with each other. It sounded like they were negotiating a deal or business agreement. It got quite loud and when I asked them what was going on, they responded with a very interesting question.

They pointed to that last slot on the right, the one that said *95-to-100*. They wanted to know: *"Can we allocate our chip as a table, as opposed to as an individual?"* They explained that their strategy was to collect 3 chips from all four participants at the table and place the 12 chips collectively into that *95-to-100* slot. Their long-term plan was as follows. If they all survived and reached the final slot—an outcome which is quite unlikely I should add—the 12 chips they had allocated collectively would be divided among the 4 survivors and they would get back their 3 chips. That is exactly what they had contributed. No loss there. But, here comes the brilliant idea. If only one person survived and reached the final slot, that person would get all 12 chips. If only two participants survived, they would each get 6 chips, which is 12 divided by the 2 survivors. And, if 3 people survived, which is also quite rare, the survivors would get 4 chips, which is still better than the 3 they had invested. So, best-case scenario, the lucky one gets 12 chips, worst-case scenario, they all get 3 chips. They would never get back less than 3. Their question to me was: *"Can we play the game this way? Can we allocate collectively instead of individually?"*

I was impressed with their ingenuity and replied that they had discovered longevity *risk pooling* and the economic rationale for buying the life annuities I described in Chap. 10. In fact, I told them, the extra chips they would receive—above and beyond the three allocated—are called mortality credits (by actuaries). And, since they would all be quite frail in those far boxes, perhaps cared for by their kids and grandkids, I'm sure their next of kin would appreciate those extra chips to help out. This gave me the opportunity to raise a bigger issue. I asked them and the class: Why did you create this pool for the last slot or box? Why not do the same with the one to the left, the one that provides for ages 90-to-95. How about the earlier boxes? Moreover, why allocate in an all or nothing manner? Perhaps contribute some chips collectively, as a table via pooling, and some individually. To press the point, I emphasized that if they were willing to pool, I could make their 60 chips behave like 100 chips. It gets a bit technical and I didn't delve into the math, which follows in the next section, but they could see the intuition. They start retirement with 60 chips, but by pooling them they can spend—if they survive—as if they had 100 chips. That's the benefit of pooling longevity risk. It expands the original budget by 40 chips. It's as if you have 40 more chips, per initial 60, on day one.

Now, not everyone—in the class or in real life—was enamored by this collective pooling arrangement. One class member stood up and asked for clarification. *"So, if I die, then my table mates inherit my chips?"* When I nodded, she then said: *"But I hate my table mates! I don't want them to get my chips when I die."* I made it clear to this student that whatever she decided—collectively or individually—was perfectly fine with me. There was no right or wrong allocation and nobody would coerce her to pool any chips, but she better be able to live within the original budget of 60. If that nest egg wasn't too constraining, there was no need to pool. But if she wanted to spend more early on or couldn't survive on the 60 chips, she might have no choice but to pool. Despite the questions raised and dilemmas identified, by the very end of that game the class consensus was that it was good practice for everyone to allocate at least a few chips to a longevity pool, because it allowed them to spend more. The objective of the next section then is to convert this informal game into more formal mathematics, so that it can eventually be coded-up in **R**.

11.3 A Crash Course on Utility

Seeing how every person has their own way of quantifying the subjective benefit of future cash-flows, I now introduce the variable ρ (measured as a rate per year, like interest), to quantify this subjective and personal value. Remember that the letter r stands for a financial, economic, or market interest rate. It discounts future cash-flows (dollars and cents) to the present day and can project current money into a later date. You can see r and easily measure r. In contrast, ρ is a psychological or biological (subjective) interest rate. It's the rate at which you discount your personal *happiness* (a.k.a utility) from the future into the present.

This ρ is measured using the same units (rates) as r, and the two are often confused. Indeed, your subjective ρ could be higher than the market interest rate r, making you relatively impatient. Or, it could be lower than the market, making you relatively patient compared to the market. Of course, you could have a neutral ρ, where your inner psychic discount rate matches the market. Also, your ρ can change over time, getting more patient as you get older, and could even depend on your mood, gender, or nationality (or whether you had coffee in the morning. My ρ is quite high before my first). You might have heard about this famous study, which is really about attempting to measure ρ. Give a young child a juicy marshmallow, let them hold it for a few seconds, and then ask them to give it back to you (right now) in exchange for two marshmallows tomorrow. Most will refuse. Using my language, their subjective discount rate ρ is greater than 100% per day or 2^{365} per year (for marshmallows). They don't care that the Federal Reserve has lowered the risk-free r to near zero. They are impatient and that drives their optimal strategy (for marshmallows or chips or money.)

Yes, ρ is tough to measure and a bit of an economic fiction to be honest, but the assumption in this chapter is that (1) such a number exists and (2) you know yours by the time you retire and (3) it's in the vicinity or range of r. Furthermore, (most, classical) economists believe that the market interest rate r, observable in practice, is an amalgamation or aggregation of individual values of ρ across the entire economy. So, while I mostly assume that you know your ρ and it might differ from the market r, in many (although not all) cases over the next few pages I'll take them to be the same thing. You will continue to see ρ and r and often $\rho = r$, when I want to simplify the problem.

Now back to the chip game and how that ties into subjective utility. Every player in the game allocated their retirement income chips in a manner that maximized their total personal *happiness function*, very broadly defined. I will call this their **Discounted Lifetime Utility** and denote it by the (new) symbol $U_x^*(F, \pi)$, where x is age, F denotes wealth (e.g. starting with 60 chips), and $\pi \geq 0$ denotes pension income. So, for example, F could be a million dollars in investable wealth and π is \$60,000 per year in defined benefit (DB) pension income. I will also let $u(c)$, which a small letter u, denote a utility (a.k.a. felicity) function parameterized by longevity risk aversion γ. Very loosely speaking the big U (i.e. total happiness) is an amalgamation of a bunch of small u (i.e. local happiness). Formally, this little-u function is written as: $u(c) = c^{1-\gamma}/(1-\gamma)$, where γ denotes longevity risk aversion. The idea here is that if you have a higher level of longevity risk aversion, you get less *marginal* utility from higher consumption. Finally, the maximal utility (adding up all the small u's) can be written as:

$$U_x^*(F, \pi) = \max_{c_t} \int_0^\infty e^{-\rho t} \, ({}_t p_x) \, u(c_t) \, dt. \tag{11.1}$$

This adds up the *local* happiness to arrive at a *total* happiness (and hopefully my 2nd year economics professor doesn't read this explanation and become very unhappy).

Now, moving on, in economics every optimization problem has some associated constraint, and in this case the dynamic budget constraint is

$$dF_t = (rF_t + \pi - c_t)\,dt, \quad F_0 = F. \tag{11.2}$$

The objective function in Eq. (11.1) and the constraint in Eq. (11.2) might seem like it appeared out-of-the-blue, but I should remind you that there were traces of it in Chap. 5, Sect. 7, and is actually a formal representation of the financial life-cycle model, discussed in Chap. 3. In the objective function (that I plan to maximize), I am effectively computing the sum of utility you get from instantaneous consumption $u(c_t)$, multiplying it by the probability you will survive to consume it: $({}_tp_x)$ and then *subjectively discounting* that utility by your own ρ value: $e^{-\rho t}$.

Looking at the budget constraint, intuitively, the pension income π flows into the (one) account that is earning an investment return of r, and then consumption c_t is extracted from the same account. The optimal total consumption function is denoted by c_t^*. The difference: $(c_t^* - \pi)$, between annual consumption and pension income, is the net spending rate from liquid wealth, In comparison, $(c_t^* - \pi)/F_t$ is the spending rate as a fraction of current wealth F_t, which I will call (and eventually provide a recipe for) the *intelligent drawdown rate.* On a technical note, saving (that is $c_t^* < \pi$) might continue into retirement and wealth might continue to grow temporarily, for someone with a sufficiently low discount rate ρ (remember a higher ρ compels you to spend money sooner). But the model does not allow any borrowing (against future pension income) so that wealth $F_t \geq 0$ at all times.

Ok, let's get back to cooking. Remember that my goal with all of this is to create an **R**-script that computes c^*, at any age x, for any level of wealth F and pension π. To do that, I need an analytic expression for the left-hand side of Eq. (11.1), that is to solve the problem. So, the next step is to decompose the integral in Eq. (11.1) into two arbitrary parts as follows:

$$U_x^*(F,\pi) = \max_{c_t} \left[\int_0^{\tau} e^{-\rho t}\,({}_tp_x)\,u(c_t)dt + \int_{\tau}^{\infty} e^{-\rho t}\,({}_tp_x)\,u(c_t)dt \right], \tag{11.3}$$

where the break takes place at time τ. It might seem odd to split up the objective function in this manner, but in fact when $\pi > 0$, there is a qualitative change in optimal consumption at some point during the horizon $t \in [0, \infty)$. That is, liquid wealth F is actually depleted and the optimal consumption rate $c_t^* = \pi; t \geq \tau$, from that point onward. That is the τ value we select to break up the integral. Until that **Wealth Depletion Time** consumption is sourced from both pension income and investable wealth. But after $t \geq \tau$ consumption is exactly equal to the pension, the individual has run out of liquid (non-annuitized) funds and $F_t = 0$, for $t \geq \tau$. The previous paragraph, which might sound odd at first passing, is at the core of the *intelligent drawdown* algorithm.

If I can back up a bit here, the maximization of utility of consumption is really a (complicated) problem from a branch of mathematics known as the **Calculus of Variations.** It involves searching for an entire function (the consumption function

c_t) that maximizes another function (discounted lifetime utility U). That branch of mathematics generalizes the usual calculus that (only) searches for a number or a vector of numbers that maximizes a multidimensional function. By chance, happenstance, and luck, the mathematical problem I have to solve here collapses to solving two equations and two unknowns, which is a much easier (and older) branch of mathematics. Those two equations will be derived in a moment, and the two unknowns are c_0^*, the initial consumption rate and τ. Get those and you can describe the entire (optimal) consumption function.

Back to the mechanics, in the algorithm itself I set τ to be the lowest value of t at which the optimal consumption rate $c_t^* = \pi$. So, at the very beginning you are consuming c_0^* which is more than π, but your optimal consumption c_t^* declines until it is equal to π (and then it stays at π). The time at which this happens is called τ. And, to be crystal clear I am not imposing this wealth depletion time (WDT) on the problem. It actually *is* the optimal drawdown policy, as elaborated in the references cited as [13] and [11] and carefully explained in the textbook I co-authored, cited as [5]. I can't emphasize enough how critical this (seemingly minor) point is to the calibration of life-cycle models in general and the computation of *intelligent drawdown* rates.

I'll return to this again in Chap. 12, when I discuss the utility value of annuities. So, at the risk of flogging a dead horse, if one assumes all pension income is capitalized and discounted to time zero, or if the pension income is added to optimal consumption as a scaling afterthought, the *wealth depletion time* will be lost in any backward induction algorithm. Meaning, the wealth depletion time depends on the optimal consumption c_t^* and π, and we need to know both values in order to find τ.

Technically, the value of $c_t^* = \pi$ for $t \geq \tau$ and therefore $u(c_t^*)$ from the point of $t = \tau$ onward is constant. This is also (sometimes) called **Smooth Pasting.** Namely, I need to paste the consumption function so it exactly matches π when the money runs out at the wealth depletion time. This enables me to express the objective function (yet again) and optimal utility as:

$$U_x^*(F, \pi) = \max_{\tau, c_t} \left[\int_0^{\tau} e^{-\rho t} \, ({}_t p_x) \, u(c_t) dt \right] + u(\pi) \, a_x(\tau, \rho), \tag{11.4}$$

where $a_x(\tau, \rho)$ is the (deferred) annuity factor at age x, using a valuation rate of ρ (and not r), starting income at time τ. I use ρ and not r over here, because I am discounting your utility. You will recognize $a_x(\tau, \rho)$ as `GDLA(x,x+tau,rho,m,b)` within **R**. As far as notation is concerned, when the deferral period is $\tau = 0$ (this happens when $F_0 = 0$), that expression collapses to the simpler $a_x(\rho)$ instead of the cumbersome $a_x(0, \rho)$. Technically this expression represents the present value of an immediate life annuity, but where cash-flows are discounted using ρ instead of r.

More importantly, when $F = 0$ this all collapses to:

$$U_x^*(0, \pi) = u(\pi) \, a_x(\rho), \tag{11.5}$$

If-and-when the retiree has no investable funds ($F = 0$) and they are living off pension π income only, then discounted (optimal) lifetime utility is simply: $u(\pi)\, a_x(\rho)$ and the wealth depletion time $\tau = 0$, by definition.

To characterize and discuss the optimal consumption function before your nest egg runs out at time τ, I will introduce another summary parameter k. Now that you have a better intuition for ρ (I hope), remember that it can be on either side of r. This is relative patience versus relative impatience. So, I would like to define a summary measure $k = (r - \rho)/\gamma$ which describes what side of r your own ρ sits. A positive number means you are *more* patient, which is quite rate. Vice versa, negative values imply you are *less* patient. Think marshmallows and kids. Finally, when $k = 0$ you have a neutral attitude relative to market rates, which an economist might call the representative investor who determines market rate r.

Now, the reason I scale or divide by γ is twofold. First, the expression $(r - \rho)/\gamma$ appears a number of times in the derivations, so I might as well give it its own symbol. Second, and more importantly, it scales or adjusts your relative time preference ρ by your longevity risk aversion γ. The greater your longevity risk aversion, the less economically impactful is the gap between objective and subjective interest rate. Remember that longevity risk aversion is a measure of how much you fear, worry, or are concerned about living a long time and not having enough money. So, the students of mine who allocated 5 chips to that last (95–100) box might be tagged as $\gamma = 10$ people (for example), and students who only put 1 chip in that last box might be tagged as $\gamma = 1$ people, because they simply don't care or worry about events that have such small probabilities. Or perhaps they are impatient? Think about that. Why did they put a few chips in the last box? So, to be very clear, there are two reasons why someone might not many place chips in that last box, using our language. They might have very small γ values or very large ρ values. I want a summary measure that collapses and combines those two reasons into one, hence the k parameter.

Finally, the optimal consumption before the wealth depletion time τ, when consumption is not yet equal to the pension π, is

$$c_t^* = c_0^* e^{kt} ({}_tp_x)^{1/\gamma}, \tag{11.6}$$

where $k = (r - \rho)/\gamma$ and the optimal initial consumption rate c_0^* is related to (terminal) consumption π, via the relationship $c_0^* = e^{k\tau}\pi/({}_\tau p_x)^{1/\gamma}$, as long as there actually is some pension income $\pi > 0$. But in the absence of pension income, that is when $\pi = 0$, the nest egg must provide income until the very end of the mortality table (and life). That implies: $F = c_0^* \int_0^{(\omega-x)} e^{-rt} ({}_tp_x)^{1/\gamma} dt$, which leads to the corresponding:

$$c_0^* = \frac{(F + \pi/r)e^{r\tau} - \pi/r}{e^{r\tau} \int_0^{\tau} e^{-(r-k)t} ({}_tp_x)^{1/\gamma} dt}. \tag{11.7}$$

At this point I'll note that the integral in the denominator of Eq. (11.7) is a so-called *temporary* annuity factor, but one in which the survival probability $({}_tp_x)$ is shifted or distorted by $1/\gamma$. For example, when $\gamma = 1$ and utility is logarithmic, the optimal consumption function c_t^* from Eq. (11.7) and (11.6) collapses to the hypothetical annuity consumption F/a_x times the survival probability $({}_tp_x)$, which is clearly less than what a true annuity would have provided. The individual who converts all liquid wealth F into the annuity would consume $c_t^* = F/a_x$ forever, but the non-annuitizer must continue to reduce consumption in proportion to their survival probability as a precautionary measure. Once again, although it might seem as if Eq. (11.6) or Eq. (11.7) was plucked out of thin air, neither of these are novel, and all of these are cited in the last section of this chapter. My objective here was to provide the minimum necessary information to code up equation 11.7.

11.4 The Algorithm for Retirement Spending

The algorithm or recipe that I am about to present for (what I am calling) the *intelligent drawdown* rate is based on Eq. (11.7). The user-defined function `IDDR(.)` takes as arguments the usual (F_x, x, m, b, r) which should be familiar from prior chapters, the pension income π, as well as the "new" economic preference variables (ρ, γ). What is noticeably absent from the arguments in this *intelligent drawdown* function is an exogenously fixed consumption rate c, or an initial withdrawal rate ξ. As explained earlier, those variables are solved for by the optimization algorithm. Please review the following script and be careful not to leave any extra spaces between mathematical operators, which **R** might misinterpret.

```
IDDR<-function(Fx,pi,x,m,b,r,rho,gam){
# Positive Pension (pi>0) Only.
k<-(r-rho)/gam
WDT<-function(tau){
  K1<-((Fx/pi+1/r)*exp(r*tau)-1/r)/
     (GTLA(x-b*log(gam),tau,r-k,m,b)*exp(r*tau))
  K2<-exp(k*tau)
  K3<-TPXG(x,tau,m,b)^(1/gam)
  K1*K2*K3-1
  }
tau<-uniroot(WDT,lower=0,upper=100)$root
Cx<-((Fx+pi/r)*exp(r*tau)-pi/r)/
   (GTLA(x-b*log(gam),tau,r-k,m,b)*exp(r*tau))
(Cx-pi)/Fx}
```

The first part of the function `IDDR(.)` creates a new (internal) function `WDT(.)`, which is an abbreviation for wealth depletion time, explained in the prior section. This function takes in a single variable t (called `tau` in the script for reasons that will become clear) and returns $(C_t^*/\pi) - 1$. You can see the value of t that makes `WDT(t)=0` is the value of t that will make $c_t^* = \pi$. This value of t is obviously τ. The subsequent `uniroot(.)` function solves for the value of `tau` that sets the `WDT(.)` function to zero, as per the discussion around Eq. (11.3). Finally, the `IDDR(.)` function "plugs" the wealth depletion time (tau) into the optimal consumption function, per Eq. (11.7), and reports the net consumption from liquid wealth: $(c_0 - \pi)/F_x$. That is the so-called *intelligent drawdown* rate. Now, as you can see, there are quite a number of implicit variables that can affect the *intelligent drawdown* rate, and I will analyze the impact of each one of them separately over the next few pages. I will begin by changing the variable π, which represents the amount of (real, inflation-adjusted) annuity income the retiree is receiving from other sources, such as government benefits or corporate pensions. This income is guaranteed for the life of the retiree. I will also assume an $x = 65$-year-old retiree, subject to Gompertz mortality with parameters ($m = 88, b = 10$). In addition, for the financial (investment return) parameter I'll assume $r = 2\%$, and for the economic preference parameters I'll assume a subjective discount rate $\rho = 2\%$ and $\gamma = 4$, which is a medium level of risk aversion. By changing (and playing with) the values of (ρ, γ), you should be able to develop some intuition for its impact on `IDDR(.)`.

```
IDDR(100,5,65,88,10,0.02,0.02,4)
[1] 0.05421814
IDDR(100,50,65,88,10,0.02,0.02,4)
[1] 0.0890493
IDDR(100,100,65,88,10,0.02,0.02,4)
[1] 0.11033
```

Here is how to interpret the numbers. If you are entitled to a pension of $\pi = \$5$ per year, per $F = \$100$ of liquid wealth (which is a relatively small pension), then your *intelligent drawdown* rate at age $x = 65$ is 5.42% of your liquid wealth. To be clear, your total consumption (i.e. spending) will be the \$5.42 from your liquid wealth **plus** the $\pi = \$5$ of your pension, for a total $c_x = \$10.42$ at the age of $x = 65$. Remember, the focus is on the *drawdown rate* from the investment portfolio, which you can control—and is the topic of much debate in the field of retirement income planning. Again, the main qualitative point I am trying to make (in this chapter) is that the portfolio spending rate should depend on the pension income π. According to the algorithm it certainly does, based on the above numbers. Remember that these numbers "scale" in F_x/π. So, if you are entitled to a government pension of $\pi = \$50{,}000$ per year, and you already have \$1,000,000 in investable assets, the ratio is the same 100-to-5 and the *intelligent drawdown* rate from the portfolio is the 5.42% from the million-dollar portfolio or \$54,200 per year.

Notice that if you have a larger pension of (for example) $\pi = \$50$ per $F_x = \$100$, the results are different. The *intelligent drawdown* rate increases to 8.9% at the age of 65, from the 5.4% in the prior case, when the pension income was a mere

Source: Generated by Author in **R**

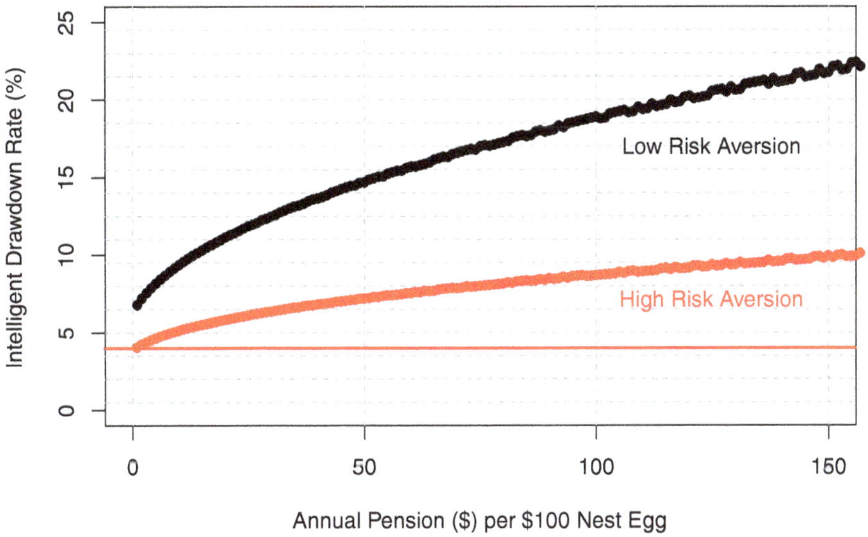

Fig. 11.2 Intelligent drawdown: risk aversion: $\gamma = 1$ (low) and $\gamma = 8$ (high)

$\pi = \$5$. This, again, implies a total consumption (pension income plus portfolio withdrawals) of $c_{65} = \$50 + \$8.9 = \$58.9$ per year. And, the intuition for why the *intelligent drawdown* rate is higher is that you have a pension annuity with "longevity insurance" in case you reach advanced ages (and boxes). Remember, even if you live to $\omega = 122$, you are still entitled to your annual pension income of π, which perhaps can embolden you to withdraw more from the investment portfolio. In fact, if you increase the annual pension income to $\pi = \$100$ per \$100 of initial wealth, the *intelligent drawdown* rate increases to 11% at the age of 65. Bottom line: Some pension annuity income allows you to extract more from the nest egg.

Now, these numbers assumed a medium level of longevity risk aversion γ, which needless to say do impact the *intelligent drawdown* rates. The higher the γ, all else being equal, the lower is the optimal drawdown rate. Figure 11.2 plots the values of `IDDR(.)`, for levels of pension income from $\pi = 1$ to $\pi = 150$, assuming two different levels of longevity risk aversion. In the top curve $\gamma = 1$ and in the bottom curve $\gamma = 8$. Notice how the *intelligent drawdown* rate increases in π, but is higher and increases faster when $\gamma = 1$ versus $\gamma = 8$. Intuitively, a higher γ parameter (say 8 versus 1) means you are more longevity risk averse and aren't willing to take a chance that you live to a very advanced age and might have to reduce spending.

Next I'll examine the impact of (chronological) age x on *intelligent drawdown* rates, and how that interacts with pre-existing pension income π. Figure 11.3 displays numerical results for the `IDDR(.)` function, plotted from age $x = 55$ to age $x = 95$, under a (high) longevity risk-aversion parameter of $\gamma = 8$, as well as pension income values $\pi = 1, 25, 50$, all assuming wealth levels of $F_x = \$100$.

Source: Generated by Author in **R**

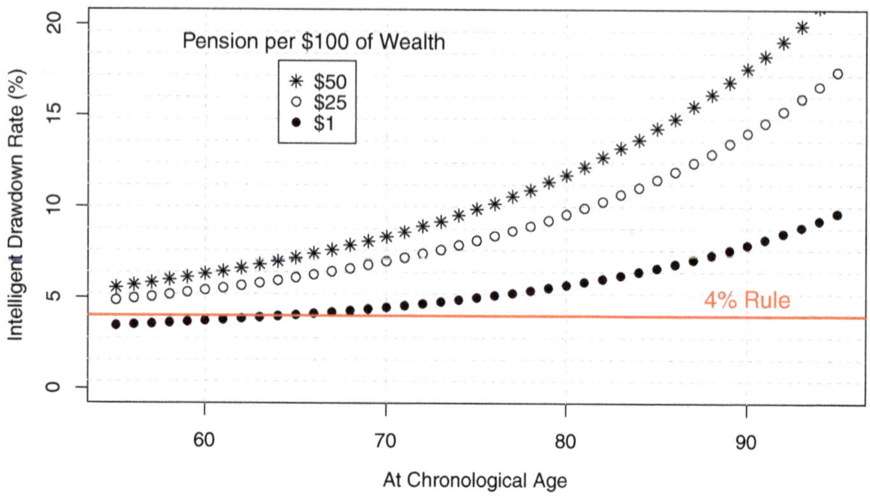

Fig. 11.3 Intelligent drawdown rate with pre-existing pension income

The Gompertz parameters, economic preference parameters, and financial rates are the same as before, namely ($m = 88, b = 10$) and $\rho = r = 2\%$. Here are some sample values, under a mere $1 of pension income (which is the lowest curve in Fig. 11.3), to ensure you can replicate my numbers.

```
IDDR(100,1,55,88,10,0.02,0.02,8)
[1] 0.03469439
IDDR(100,1,60,88,10,0.02,0.02,8)
[1] 0.03730085
IDDR(100,1,65,88,10,0.02,0.02,8)
[1] 0.04055608
```

Notice how (with negligible pension income), the *intelligent drawdown* rate at the early age of $x = 55$ is 3.47%, which is well under the famous 4% rule. At the age of $x = 60$, the function value is 3.73%, and only at the age of $x = 65$ does it pierce the 4% rate. Again, this assumes virtually no pension income and that $\pi = \$1$.

But, notice that as the pension level is increased, to $\pi = \$25$ and then $\pi = \$50$, the curves in Fig. 11.3 move up and well above the 4% line, even at earlier retirement ages. Moreover, all of these curves increase with (chronological) age. What this means is that if you are $x = 75$ with a $100 and a fixed pension, you can afford to withdraw or spend much more, relative to an individual in the same financial circumstances at the age of $x = 65$. And, while this should be qualitatively intuitive because the older you are the lower your life expectancy and the more you can afford to spend, the `IDDR(.)` algorithm makes this precise.

Source: Generated by Author in **R**

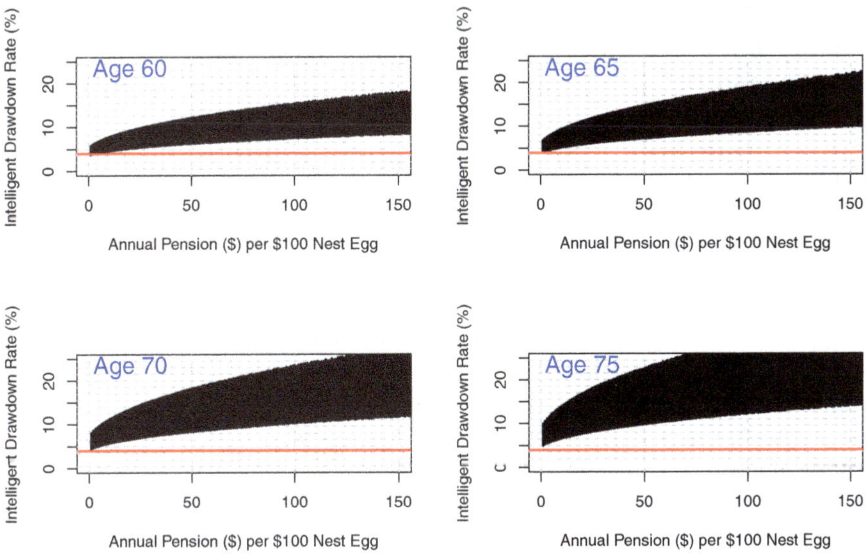

Fig. 11.4 Intelligent drawdown rates by age, pension, and risk aversion

Finally, the four panels in Fig. 11.4 combine the three elements or variables into one concise figure, using the `par(mfrow=c(2,2))` command, which stacks the four subsequent graphs into one figure. The four panels should provide a sense of the wide range of *intelligent drawdown* rates, based on age. The dark shaded regions represent reasonable *intelligent drawdown* rates at the four ages of $x = 60$, $x = 65$, $x = 70$, and $x = 75$. They assume various levels of pension income π (on the x-axis), and the shaded regions depending on your level of longevity risk aversion γ. The top of the shaded region (high drawdowns) represents *low* levels of longevity risk aversion γ and vice versa for bottom of the shaded region. These are visually no different from Fig. 11.2 and use the same range of values $\gamma = 1..8$. Notice again how high the optimal drawdown rates can get, as long as you have sufficient pension annuity income π to protect against longevity risk. But, on the left-hand side of these four panels, which depicts individuals at those ages with little pre-existing pension income, the *intelligent drawdown* rates are much lower, and in some cases even lower than the 4% line.

There are other variables in the `IDDR(.)` function that affect results, other than pension income: π, longevity risk aversion: γ, and (chronological) age: x. I'll investigate those in greater detail. Assume that $x = 65$, $F_{65} = \$100$, a modest level of pension (a.k.a. life annuity) income $\pi = \$10$ per year, and a generic retiree with an average level of longevity risk aversion $\gamma = 4$. I will vary the investment return assumption r to see how it impacts the *intelligent drawdown* rate, assuming the subjective discount rate $\rho = 0\%$, which keeps preferences neutral in time. I'll get back to ρ in a moment, but for now please ensure your algorithm can replicate these numbers.

```
IDDR(100,10,65,88,10,0.01,0.0,4)
[1] 0.05059754
IDDR(100,10,65,88,10,0.02,0.0,4)
[1] 0.05057158
IDDR(100,10,65,88,10,0.03,0.0,4)
[1] 0.051108
IDDR(100,10,65,88,10,0.04,0.0,4)
[1] 0.05223388
```

Ss you raise the investment return r, the *intelligent drawdown* rate increases, because you are earning more on the money that you aren't spending. This is no different than the impact of interest rates or investment returns on portfolio longevity (in chapter #5) or lifetime ruin probabilities (in Chap. 9). Overall, higher investment returns improve sustainability. However, what is interesting is the non-linear way in which r impacts `IDDR(.)`. At the age of 65, under \$10 in pension income per \$100 of wealth, an increase of $\Delta r = 1\%$ doesn't translate into an increase of 1% in *intelligent drawdown* rates. For example, moving to $r = 4\%$ (from 3%) only adds (0.0522 – 0.0511), a mere 11 basis points to affordable spending.

Moving on to other variables (arguments, parameters) inside the `IDDR(.)` function, I now focus on the subjective discount rate (SDR) denoted by ρ. As I explained earlier in the chapter, it captures the extent to which you (or at least an economist) would rather consume *now* versus *later.* If your personal value of ρ is higher, you placed your "chips" in the earlier "boxes" (remember the game) which corresponds to a higher *intelligent drawdown* rate. The following numbers confirm that intuition. I have assumed the investment return is $r = 2\%$, but have varied the subjective discount rate from 0 to 4%.

```
IDDR(100,10,65,88,10,0.02,0.00,4)
[1] 0.05057158
IDDR(100,10,65,88,10,0.02,0.01,4)
[1] 0.0556232
IDDR(100,10,65,88,10,0.02,0.02,4)
[1] 0.06068773
IDDR(100,10,65,88,10,0.02,0.03,4)
[1] 0.0656978
```

In the final set of numerical experiments, I'll vary the Gompertz parameters (m, b) to investigate how they impact the *intelligent drawdown* rate. As you will see from the numbers in a moment, modifying the mortality hazard rate values is akin to changing (shifting) your chronological age. If you increase the modal value, from $(m = 88)$ to $(m = 93)$, which adds another 5 years to your modal lifetime, it's identical (in the Gompertz model) to making you 5 years younger. See the following values to confirm this:

```
# Modal Value 88, Current Age 65
IDDR(100,10,65,88,10,0.02,0.02,4)
[1] 0.06068773
# Modal Value 93, Current Age 65
IDDR(100,10,65,93,10,0.02,0.02,4)
[1] 0.05357512
# Modal Value 88, Current Age 60
IDDR(100,10,60,88,10,0.02,0.02,4)
[1] 0.05357512
```

Notice that when the modal value is increased from ($m = 88$) to ($m = 93$), the *intelligent drawdown* rate drops (at the age of 65), from 6.07 to 5.36%, which should make sense. After all, you are likely to live longer, 4.13 more years, to be precise. You should be able to confirm this by computing the life expectancy at age 65 under both values of m and then subtracting the difference. However, when I set back the age of the retiree from $x = 65$ to $x = 60$, the result is identical to having $x = 65$ and $m = 93$. The number on the third line is identical to the number on the second line in the above **R** script. Why? Because if you look carefully at Eqs. (11.6) and (11.7), the values of x always appear together with the value of m. The `IDDR(.)` output depends on the difference $(m - x)$, thru the `GILA(.)` and `GTLA(.)` functions. Think about this for a bit and make sure it's intuitively clear before you move on.

In fact, while focusing on age x, notice that increasing the value of (longevity risk aversion): γ effectively reduces the age argument within the `GTLA(.)` function. So, being more longevity risk averse makes you act as if you are younger. And finally, with regard to the underlying mortality model, increasing the dispersion coefficient b in the Gompertz model—but holding the modal value constant—will reduce the *intelligent drawdown* rate for relatively low pension values, but will actually have the opposite effect when pension income levels are higher. See the following two sets of parameter examples. One has a relatively low pension income level of $\pi =$ \$10 per $F =$ \$100 of wealth, and the other has a much higher $\pi =$\$50.

```
IDDR(100,10,65,88,8,0.02,0.02,4)
[1] 0.06078812
IDDR(100,10,65,88,10,0.02,0.02,4)
[1] 0.06068773
IDDR(100,10,65,88,12,0.02,0.02,4)
[1] 0.06004833
IDDR(100,10,65,88,14,0.02,0.02,4)
[1] 0.05916218
```

The exact level of π at which this reversal occurs, that is the point at which the partial derivative of the *intelligent drawdown* rate with respect to b switches from negative to positive is tightly related to the wealth depletion time `WDT(.)` in the presence of pension income. The details would take me far beyond the cookbook elements of this chapter and will leave that exploration as an end-of-chapter question.

```
IDDR(100,50,65,88,8,0.02,0.02,4)
[1] 0.0856995
IDDR(100,50,65,88,10,0.02,0.02,4)
[1] 0.0890493
IDDR(100,50,65,88,12,0.02,0.02,4)
[1] 0.09034665
IDDR(100,50,65,88,14,0.02,0.02,4)
[1] 0.09134145
```

11.5 Intelligent Reactions to Sudden Portfolio Declines

The `IDDR(.)` algorithm can also be used to examine how someone should (or might) react to sudden changes in portfolio values. Assume that you formulated and implemented a retirement income plan based on current values of (F, π) and assumptions about r, and soon after the plan was implemented the value of F declined precipitously, to a new value of $F(1 - \Delta)$, where Δ is a percentage decline. Should you reduce your spending and portfolio withdrawals by a full Δ percent? The `IDDR(.)` algorithm and the underlying *intelligent drawdown* approach can be used to obtain the exact adjustment that must be made to the plan. See the following numbers:

```
# Initial Withdrawal Plan
IDDR(1000000,60000,70,88,10,0.02,0.02,4)*1000000
[1] 63600.54
# Portfolio Drops 20 Percent. New Plan
IDDR(800000,60000,70,88,10,0.02,0.02,4)*800000
[1] 52874.41
# Change in Withdrawal Plan
(52874-63600)/63600
[1] -0.1686478
```

Initially the plan was to spend \$63,600 from the portfolio, which is the *intelligent drawdown* rate multiplied by the value of the portfolio at that time. But then, the market (or portfolio) declined by $\Delta = 0.20$ or 20%. The new and revised plan calls withdrawing or drawing down \$52,874 from the portfolio, which is a reduction of only 16.86% and not the full 20%. Stated differently, the pension of \$60,000 per year acts as a buffer, reducing the need to absorb the entire 20% decline in the portfolio value. Note that in the absence of the pension income π, the entire $\Delta = 20\%$ loss would immediately manifest itself in a 20% decline in consumption, per the constant relative risk aversion (CRRA) utility function that underpins the algorithm. If this sounds confusing, look back at the discussion in Sect. 11.3, and in particular what happens in Eq. (11.7) when the pension variable $\pi = 0$. On a related note, at higher ages, for example, $x = 80$ versus $x = 70$, the downward adjustment in portfolio spending is lower. See the following script for an example:

```
# Initial Withdrawal Plan
IDDR(1000000,60000,80,88,10,0.02,0.02,4)*1000000
[1] 87811.33
# Portfolio Drops 20 Percent. New Plan
IDDR(800000,60000,80,88,10,0.02,0.02,4)*800000
[1] 73328.07
# Change in Withdrawal Plan
(73328-87811)/87811
[1] -0.1649338
```

The older retiree, with the exact same portfolio circumstances, would reduce the amount they are withdrawing from the investment portfolio from \$87,811 per year to \$73,328 per year, which is a reduction of approximately 16.5% in spending from the portfolio, versus the 20% decline in the portfolio. Remember, this retiree still receives the pension income of $\pi = \$60{,}000$ regardless of the decline in the market and portfolio value.

```
# Initial Withdrawal Plan, for r=2 percent.
IDDR(1000000,60000,70,88,10,0.02,0,4)*1000000
[1] 56321.83
# Portfolio Drops 25 Percent.
# Create new plan assuming r=5 percent.
IDDR(750000,60000,70,88,10,0.05,0,4)*750000
[1] 47923.11
# Change in Withdrawal Plan
(47923-56322)/56322
[1] -0.1491247
```

Now, on a deeper level, some investors might believe that after a sharp decline in the market (and the value of the portfolio) future investment returns will be higher. For example, if you constructed your *intelligent drawdown* strategy based on an assumption that real investment returns from your portfolio will be $r = 2\%$, then after a sudden decline in the value of your portfolio you might revise those forward-looking estimates to $r = 5\%$. I'm not agreeing with this or debating whether this is a reasonable assumption for capital markets (and the equity risk premium), but the `IDDR(.)` can provide guidance on how to incorporate those sorts of beliefs as well. The above example does exactly that, moving from an assumed $r = 2\%$ to an assumed $r = 5\%$, after the market declines by $\Delta = 25\%$. The end result is that spending from the portfolio should (only) be reduced by approximately 15%.

Table 11.1 Adjusting withdrawals after a sharp decline in portfolio value

Investment return	10% drop	15% drop	20% drop	25% drop
$r = 2\%$	−8.8%	−13.2%	−17.6%	−22.1%
$r = 5\%$	+1.8%	−3.71%	−9.3%	−14.9%

Parameter assumptions: $r = 2\%$, $F_{70} = \$100$, $x = 70$, $\pi = \$6$, $\rho = 0$, $\gamma = 4$, $m = 88$, $b = 10$

Finally, the Table 11.1 provides summary values for how to "adjust" your drawdown strategy after a large and unexpected decline in your portfolio (at the age of $x = 70$). I have assumed an initial drawdown rate based on an $r = 2\%$ investment return and (a neutral) $\rho = 0\%$, a longevity risk-aversion coefficient of $\gamma = 4$, and the usual Gompertz parameters. While most of the numbers should be intuitive and the reduction in withdrawals is less than the reduction in portfolio value, notice the one positive number in the table. Namely, if your revised investment return jumps from $r = 2\%$ to $r = 5\%$ after a 10% drop in the market, you can actually afford to spend more than you did before! Of course, one issue I haven't addressed is how *frequently* to revise and update your retirement income plan, which I'll have to leave for another time (or revision). It obviously depends on **Transaction Costs** as well as your (very subjective) perception of whether or not *markets* have calmed down. After all, adjusting your retirement income plan on a daily basis (or in continuous time, heaven forbid) can be a very costly, time-consuming, and futile exercise!

11.6 Intelligent Drawdown When You Don't Have a Pension

To wrap up the topic of *intelligent drawdown rates*, the following piece of **R** code should be used when the pension income variable $\pi = 0$, and the wealth depletion time (technically) can be at $\tau = \infty$. In this case, the rational consumer must always have some small amount of liquid wealth in reserve, just in case they reach a very (very) advanced age. They will never take the risk of completely running out of money because they have no pension to fall-back on. In that case the `IDDR(.)` should be modified to be:

```
IDDR0<-function(Fx,x,m,b,r,rho,gam){
  k<-(r-rho)/gam
  Cx<-Fx/GILA(x-b*log(gam),r-k,m,b)
  Cx/Fx}
```

The rationale and reason for this much simpler expression can be gleaned directly from the discussion around Eqs. (11.7) and (11.6), and the fact that when $\pi = 0$ the $e^{r\tau}$ terms cancel in the numerator and denominator. Here is a test of numbers, compared against `IDDR(.)` with π very close to zero.

```
round(IDDR0(100,65,88,10,0.02,0.02,4),digits=5)
[1] 0.04344
round(IDDR(100,0.001,65,88,10,0.02,0.02,4),digits=5)
[1] 0.04344
```

I alluded to this in the earlier section #11.5, on the topic of adapting to market losses, when $\pi = 0$, the adjustment is exactly proportional to the drop in market values. So, for example, compare the following two *intelligent drawdown* rates. In the first box the function produces the exact same spending rate, namely 4.34% of the value of F_{65}.

```
IDDR0(100,65,88,10,0.02,0.02,4)
[1] 0.04343609
IDDR0(80,65,88,10,0.02,0.02,4)
[1] 0.04343609
```

Of course, the actual dollar value withdrawals from the investment portfolio will be reduced from \$4.34 per original $F = \$100$, down to \$3.47, which is a reduction of exactly 20%, per the attached script.

```
w.old<-IDDR0(100,65,88,10,0.02,0.02,4)*100; w.old
[1] 4.343609
w.new<-IDDR0(80,65,88,10,0.02,0.02,4)*80; w.new
[1] 3.474888
> (w.new-w.old)/w.old
[1] -0.2
```

11.7 Final Notes: What Ingredients Have I Missed?

- The `IDDR(.)` algorithm or recipe at the core of this chapter is meant as antidote to the (in)famous 4% rule of retirement income planning. There is one rather obvious ingredient missing from the `IDDR` algorithm, and that is volatility or the uncertainty associated with investment returns. This can be incorporated as yet another variable in the function using (something called) the Merton model and is discussed in the article cited as [10]. The good news is that as long as you update your inputs to `IDDR(.)` on a regular basis, it provides results that are quite similar to a (modified) model that includes the σ introduced back in Chap. 5. Nevertheless, a version 2.0 of `IDDR.2(.)` should account for market volatility.
- While on the topic of advanced versions of `IDDR`, and as I have mentioned a number of times in this book, most retirement income planning is done for

couples and not individuals. This has a number of implications for *intelligent drawdown* strategies. First, pension income π might be reduced by some predetermined fraction upon the death of the first member of a couple. Second the overall utility from consumption spending might be reduced as well, so a version 3.0 of `IDDR.3(.)` should include these additional aspects of retirement planning. And, while on the topic of advanced version `IDDR.4(.)` should account for differentially taxed accounts.

- The `IDDR(.)` function—or any of the above-noted extensions—assumes that the user would like to deplete their financial assets over their entire life, the only question is at what rate and how it is impacted by risk aversion preferences. But that assumption might not hold true for (many) retirees with children, grandchildren, and other loved ones to whom they would like to leave some leftovers. This rather obvious desire is called the "bequest motive" in the economics literature and would certainly modify the intelligent or optimal drawdown rates. Now, remember that if you die (relatively young), before the wealth depletion date, you will leave bequests for the next generation. But some retiree would like this transfer to be more than an accident or leftovers. How exactly one goes about *quantifying* the bequest motive takes me well beyond the objectives of this book, but the *intelligent drawdown* level—for any of the parameter values—would have to be lower, to account for this desire. In some sense, the `IDDR(.)` provides an upper bound for how much you can afford to withdraw and spend, assuming you have no bequest motives.
- The theory behind *intelligent drawdown*, which was briefly presented in section #3 of this chapter, is discussed and justified in much greater detail in the appendix of the article cited as [15] the references cited as [1, 3, 4, 14] and textbook [5]. In particular, those readers who are interested in a deeper understanding of life-cycle models with mortality risk, see the original articles [8] as well as [11] and in particular [13], who was actually first to realize that the (famous) Yaari [19] had to be modified to account for pre-existing (fixed) pension income. Also, in the name and spirit of full disclosure, I have a commercial interest in developing "better" and more *intelligent drawdown* algorithms, building on earlier work I have done and some earlier patents I filed in this area, per [6] as well as [16].
- Finally, recall that this book is meant as a collection of (personal) recipes, and other "cooks" (i.e. authors, scholars, and practitioners) have different philosophies and approaches to baking drawdown algorithm. For those who are interested in other (related) approaches, see the articles cited as [2, 7, 9, 12], and in particular [18]. Finally, see [17] for a widely cited article on how real retirees actually drawdown (or don't) their wealth towards the end of the life-cycle.

Questions and Problems

11.1 How would you modify the `IDDR(.)` algorithm to account for a (married) couple for which the Gompertz parameters are (m_1, b_1) and (m_2, b_2), respectively.

Assume that their time and risk preferences (ρ, γ) are identical, and they desire an *intelligent drawdown* strategy that continues until the second member of the couple dies. To be clear, the pension continues at full 100% of π until the second person dies.

11.2 Assuming that $F_{65} = \$100$ at the age of $x = 65$, with Gompertz parameter ($m = 88$ and $r = 2\%$), please investigate the relationship between the dispersion coefficient b, the pre-existing pension π, and the *intelligent drawdown* rate `IDDR(.)`.

11.3 The wealth depletion time is a function that is embedded inside the `IDDR(.)` function. Assuming that $F = \$100$, that $x = 65$, $(m = 88, b = 10)$ and $r = \rho = 2\%, \gamma = 4$, please plot WDT as a function of $\pi = \$1$ to $\pi = \$200$. Describe how the wealth depletion time is impacted by the pre-existing pension income. Explain.

11.4 Assume that you are at age $x = 65$, that you have $F_x = \$100$, that $r = \rho = 2\%, \gamma = 4$, and $(m = 88, b = 10)$. Plot the relationship between π and the *intelligent drawdown* rate, within the range of $\pi = \$1$ to $\pi = \$200$.

11.5 Assuming that $F = \$100$, that $x = 65$, $(m = 88, b = 10)$ and $r = \rho = 2\%, \pi = 10$, please plot WDT as a function of $\gamma = 1$ to $\gamma = 10$. Describe how the wealth depletion time is impacted by longevity risk aversion. Explain.

References

1. Andersen, S. , Harrison, G. W., Lau, M. I., & Rutstrom, E. E. (2008). Eliciting risk and time preferences. *Econometrica, 76*, 583–618.
2. Blanchett, D. M. (2013). Simple formulas to implement complex withdrawal strategies. *Journal of Financial Planning, 26*(9), 40–48.
3. Bommier, A. (2006). Uncertain lifetime and inter-temporal choice: Risk aversion as a rationale for time discounting. *International Economic Review, 47*, 1223–1246.
4. Butler, M. (2001). Neoclassical Life-cycle consumption: A textbook example. *Economic Theory, 17*, 209–221.
5. Charupat, N., Huang, H., & Milevsky, M. A. (2012). *Strategic financial planning over the lifecycle: A conceptual approach to personal risk management.* New York: Cambridge University Press.
6. Chen, P., & Milevsky, M. A. (2006). Inventors; Ibbotson Assoc Inc, assignee. Optimal asset allocation during retirement in the presence of fixed and variable immediate life annuities (payout annuities). United States patent US 7,120,601.
7. Dang, D. M., Forsyth, P. A., & Vetzal, K. R. (2017). The 4% strategy revisited: A pre-commitment mean-variance optimal approach to wealth management. *Quantitative Finance, 17*(3), 335–351.
8. Davies, J. B. (1981). Uncertain lifetime, consumption and dissaving in retirement. *Journal of Political Economy, 89*, 561–577.
9. Finke, M., Pfau, W. D., & Blanchett, D. M. (2013). The 4 percent rule is not safe in a low-yield world. *Journal of Financial Planning, 26*(6), 46–55.
10. Habib, F., Huaxiong, H., & Milevsky, M. A. (2017). *Approximate solutions to retirement spending problems and the optimality of ruin.* Available at SSRN, https://ssrn.com/abstract=2944125 or http://dx.doi.org/10.2139/ssrn.2944125

11. Lachance, M. (2012). Optimal onset and exhaustion of retirement savings in a life-cycle model. *Journal of Pension Economics and Finance, 11*(1), 21–52.
12. Laster, D., Suri, A., & Vrdoljak, N. (2012). Systematic withdrawal strategies for retirees. *The Journal of Wealth Management, 15*(3), 36–49.
13. Leung, S. F. (2007). The existence, uniqueness and optimality of the terminal wealth depletion time in life-cycle models of saving under uncertain lifetime and borrowing constraint. *Journal of Economic Theory, 134*, 470–493.
14. Levhari, D., & Mirman, L. J. (1977). Savings and consumption with an uncertain horizon. *Journal of Political Economy, 85*(2), 265–281.
15. Milevsky, M. A., & Huang, H. (2011). Spending retirement on planet Vulcan: The impact of longevity risk aversion on optimal withdrawal rates. *Financial Analysts Journal, 67*(2), 45–58.
16. Milevsky, M. A., & Huang, H. (2014). Inventors; Qwema Group Inc, assignee, Optimal portfolio withdrawal during retirement in the presence of longevity risk, United States patent US 8,781,937
17. Poterba, J. M., Venti, S., & Wise, D. (2011). The composition and drawdown of wealth in retirement. *Journal of Economic Perspectives, 25*(4), 95–118.
18. Waring, M. B., & Siegel, L. B. (2015). The only spending rule you will ever need. *Financial Analysts Journal, 71*(1), 91–107.
19. Yaari, M. E. (1965). Uncertain lifetime, life insurance and the theory of the consumer. *The Review of Economic Studies, 32*(2), 137–150.

Chapter 12
Pensionization: From Benefits to Utility

This chapter discusses the *economic rationale* for defined benefit (DB) pension plans, such as government social security programs and corporate retirement plans, which are schemes that implicitly provide longevity insurance by pooling participants. The chapter begins by contrasting such collective plans with *do-it-yourself* programs and then goes on to discuss the underlying concept of *pensionization* in greater detail, including the implicit wealth depletion time (WDT). The optimal amount of pension annuity income is linked to the WDT and illustrated with a detailed case study. The chapter concludes by presenting a simple metric for measuring the utility-based benefits of annuitization.

12.1 Functions Used and Defined

12.1.1 Sample of Native R Functions Used

- No new **R** functions are introduced in this chapter.

12.1.2 User-Defined R Functions

- `WDT.PSI(psi,x,m,b,r,rho,gam)` computes the wealth depletion time (WDT).
- `PSI.OPT(tau,x,m,b,r,rho,gam)`, optimal *pensionization* based on WDT.
- `DLTA(x,m,b,v,gam)` computes the utility-based value of a pension annuity.
- `UDHG(x,h0,g,v,gam)`, the same, but using the (h_0, g) formulation.

M. A. Milevsky, *Retirement Income Recipes in R*, Use R!,
https://doi.org/10.1007/978-3-030-51434-1_12

12.2 The ABCs of Gold-Plated Pensions

In this section I'll provide a self-contained overview of the rationale and risk management benefits of a generic defined benefit (from here on, again, DB) pension plan using the language and terminology of the financial life-cycle model from Chap. 3. Once the details are clear, especially as they relate to the underlying mortality and investment assumptions, I'll return to the framework introduced in Chap. 11, to analyze (what I call) *pensionization* from a variety of perspectives.

Let's return to the basic assumption that was introduced very early on in this book, namely that most (rational) people want a smooth (and arguably) constant standard of living, especially **if** they know exactly how long they will live. Now, even if you don't agree with the strict implications of this assumption, if you don't save *anything* during your working and earning years, you will starve during your retirement years. See the left panel in Fig. 12.1, which is the rationale for setting aside some fraction of your disposable income during the working years, so you can finance consumption later on. The `SMCR(.)` function computes the highest standard of living you can achieve, for a given (wage, or) amount of human capital.

Here is a simple example. You are $x = 25$-years-old with no financial capital (yet), a job paying $w = \$100{,}000$ per year, a plan to retire at age $R = 65$ and live to $D = 95$. Assuming an $r = 3\%$ (real) investment return, the flat consumption rate, represented by the constant (blue) line in the right panel of Fig. 12.1, is

```
# SMCR(age,wealth,wage,growth,valuation,Retire,Die)
SMCR(25,0,100000,0,0.03,65,95)
[1] 79368
```

This is achieved by saving \$20,632 per year. Look again at the flat consumption line in the right panel of Fig. 12.1. There's no break or discontinuity in your standard of living in the transition to retirement. I call this a gold-plated retirement pension plan (from here on, a GPP).

Another way to solve for the optimal contribution rate required to create your personal GPP is by graphically equating discounted cash-flows, per Fig. 12.2. The

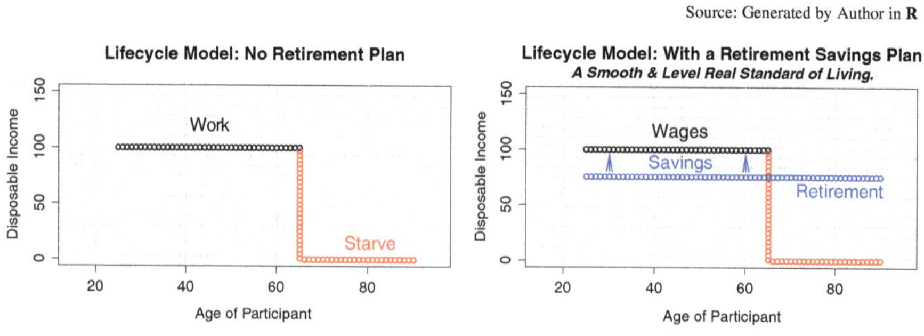

Fig. 12.1 The human life-cycle with and without proper retirement savings

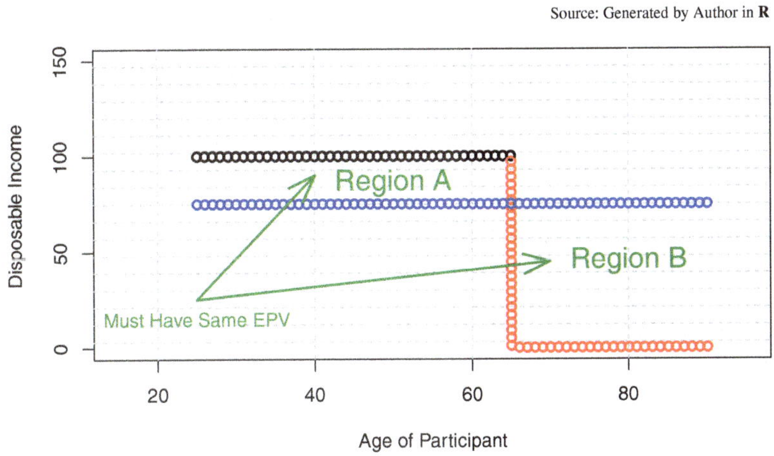

Fig. 12.2 How much should you save? Equate the EPV

economic present value (EPV) of savings in Region A must equal the EPV of consumption spending in Region B. This can be expressed, on a per dollar basis, as:

$$s^* \times \texttt{RGOA(0, r, N1)} = (1 - s^*) \times \frac{\texttt{RGOA(0, r, N2)}}{(1 + r)^{\texttt{N1}}}, \tag{12.1}$$

where `N1` represents the number of *working* years, `N2` represents the number of *retirement* years, and s^* is the contribution rate forcing them to balance. If you contribute s^* of your annual income towards your retirement, then you will consume $1 - s^*$ of your income while you are still working (that is the left side of the equation). Now to keep your consumption smooth, you must continue to consume $1 - s^*$ after you retire (that is the right side of the equation). Isolating the s^* variable in Eq. (12.1) leads to the following expression to fully finance a personal GPP:

$$s^* = \frac{\texttt{RGOA(0, r, N2)}}{\texttt{RGOA(0, r, N1)} \times (1 + r)^{\texttt{N1}} + \texttt{RGOA(0, r, N2)}} \tag{12.2}$$

So, for example, if your working life is `N1=40` years (from $x = 25$ to $R = 65$), and your retirement is `N2=30` years (from $R = 65$ to $D = 95$), then under an assumed (real) investment return of $r = 3\%$, a contribution rate of 20.6% of your salary will create a GPP.

```
N1<-40; N2<-30; r<-0.03
RGOA(0,r,N2)/(RGOA(0,r,N1)*(1+r)^N1+RGOA(0,r,N2))
[1] 0.2063167
```

To be clear, I use the term gold-plated (which is often used to describe these sorts of plans) because the s^* contribution rate replaces 100% of your *consumable* income during your (final) working years. Obviously it will not replace 100% of your *disposable* income—defined as gross income after all government taxes—since a fraction of that money was contributed to the pension plan before retirement. To be precise, the GPP will replace $(1 - s^*)$ of your disposable (working years) income, which in the above example is approximately 80%. Think about it. If the GPP replaced 100% of your *disposable* income, then your standard of living and total consumption would be higher during retirement compared to your working years! (That would be a palladium-plated pension plan, or PPP.)

At the risk of appearing to travel in circles, recall that another way to obtain the same answer to the fundamental question: *How much should I contribute to a gold-plated pension plan?* is by computing the flat consumption rate via the `SMCR(.)` function and then subtracting from $100,000.

```
SAVE<-100000-SMCR(25,0,100000,0,0.03,65,95); SAVE
[1] 20631.67
CONSUME<-SMCR(25,0,100000,0,0.03,65,95); CONSUME
[1] 79368.33
```

The end result is the exact same. The formula to use is a matter of convenience. Either way, the economic present value of both regions A and B can be computed and then compared to each other based on the expression presented in Eq. (12.1).

```
RGOA(0,0.03,40)*SAVE
[1] 476896.4
RGOA(0,0.03,30)*CONSUME/(1.03)^40
[1] 476896.4
```

From the (discounted) perspective of someone at the age of $x = 25$, the total amount you will be saving during your working years as well as the total amount you will be spending during your retirement years is exactly $476,896. And, if for whatever reason the EPV of your savings happens to be less than $476,896—and you short change your pension plan—then you won't have enough to finance the constant standard of living, until death at age $D = 95$. These short and simple scripts allow anyone to generate the relevant GPP contribution rate s^*, for any value of D. Table 12.1, which follows, displays some additional values based on Eq. (12.2).

If you are 20-years-old, planning to age 100 and assume an investment return of $r = 2\%$ on your money, then contributing 25.8% of your salary (every year, until age 65) will create the GPP depicted in Fig. 12.1. But, if instead of $D = 100$ you assume that $D = 85$ years, then the amount you have to contribute to the GPP is only 18.5%, which can amount to a difference of thousands of dollars per year. I mentioned this many times in earlier chapters, knowing D makes a big difference to: *How much should I contribute?*

We now arrive at the rationale for *collective* pension plans, versus the (*do-it-yourself*) plans described in the last few pages. Namely: *How are you supposed to select your date of death?* How do you know D, possibly 50 years in advance? Most people will *play-it-safe* and pick a large value just in case. But that is quite costly

Table 12.1 DIY gold-plated pension: fraction of salary required

Retirement at age $R = 65$, and assumed age at death of;	Investment return assumption $r = 1\%$	$r = 2\%$	$r = 3\%$	$r = 4\%$
$D = 80$	19.7%	15.2%	11.4%	8.41%
$D = 85$	24.2%	18.5%	13.8%	10.1%
$D = 90$	28.1%	21.4%	15.8%	11.4%
$D = 95$	31.4%	23.8%	17.5%	12.5%
$D = 100$	34.2%	25.8%	18.8%	13.4%

Assume $g = 0$, annual discounting, consumption at year-end starting at age $x = 20$

and perhaps even unnecessary. Maybe you pondered this dilemma in Chap. 3 and didn't consider it material. But, after the mortality models introduced in Chap. 8, you know (that I know) better.

The main *actuarial economic* benefit of a large *collective* DB pension plan is that it leverages the *Law of Large Numbers.* It removes the need to guess D, by pooling mortality and longevity risk. Now yes, I'll admit that an additional benefit of large collective retirement plans, compared to smaller accounts, is reduced costs. But, the key insight is that (expensive) term-certain annuities can be replaced with (relatively cheaper) life annuities. In fact, not only does the collective plan absolve you from picking a value of D in Table 12.1, it actually reduces the cost of retirement. Gold-plated pensions (or even the non-gold-plated ones) are less expensive if participants are willing to pool resources. And, in a world of ultra-low interest and investment rates, these extra few percentage points can make a big difference.

Well, now what happens if you pool your resources together and save them as a group? Remember the story I told at the beginning of Chap. 11. Instead of chips, tables, and boxes, imagine everyone pools their investments into a collective pension plan. This allows the plan administrator or trustee to select a value of D, for the purposes of setting contribution rates, based on *population average* longevity patterns. Graphically, in Fig. 12.2, the *actuarial* present value of Region A must equal the *actuarial* present value of Region B on average, but not necessarily for everyone individually. This implies that retirees who live a long time (longer than average) will be subsidized by those who don't. The contribution rate details are as follows. Moving from individual to group contributions (a.k.a. pension pooling) allows me to replace the `RGOA(.)` function, which requires a known number of periods in Eq. (12.2), with the `GTLA(.)` and `GDLA(.)` function.

Look again at Fig. 12.2 and specifically the life-contingent assumption embedded in both regions. The actuarial present value (APV) of Region B is precisely the definition of a *deferred* life annuity, and the APV of Region A is a *temporary* life annuity. It's temporary in the sense that you only contribute to the plan as long as you are alive. The balancing rate s^*, which is the fraction of salary that must be contributed while working to create the GPP, will now satisfy the (cheaper) equation.

$$s^* \times \texttt{GTLA}(.) = (1 - s^*) \times \texttt{GDLA}(.) \tag{12.3}$$

Look at Eq. (12.3) and compare with (12.1). The key is that the term-certain annuity is replaced with the life-contingent equivalent. Rearranging Eq. (12.3), the **collective** GPP funding rate is

$$s^* = \frac{\texttt{GDLA(.)}}{\texttt{GDLA(.)} + \texttt{GTLA(.)}}, \tag{12.4}$$

where the full set of parameters GTLA(x,R-x,v,m,b) and GDLA(x,R,v,m,b) are suppressed to save space, and R is the retirement age.

Table 12.2 displays numerical values of the (collective) pension contribution rate, the above-noted s^*, under a variety of investment return assumptions r. In this table, the left-most column is no longer an actual age of death D (as it was in Table 12.1), but instead an expected age at death: $x + E[T_x]$ for the entire pension pool. The main takeaway here is that when you are pooling resources (chips) with other pension plan participants, you don't have to contribute as much (chips) to create a GPP. Carefully compare the values in Table 12.2 with the values in Table 12.1, for any given investment rate r. Let me repeat again because this is such an important point. The benefit of collective pooling is that you (1) avoid having to pick a safe value of D that is high enough and (2) still safely contribute less to the pension plan.

The following **R** script is a spot-check for values in the table, using the relevant GTLA(.) and GDLA(.) function. The contribution rate s^* to the collective GPP, from Eq. (12.4) is compared to the contribution rate under the individual GPP from Eq. (12.2). The former uses life annuity factors with the relevant Gompertz parameters, and the latter picks a fixed age at death D, with the term-certain factors.

```
x<-20; y<-65; m<-90.75; b<-10; r<-0.04
#Expected Age at Death. A Shortcut from Chapter 8.
GILA(x,0,m,b)+x
[1] 85.03169
#Collective GPP Contribution Rate
GDLA(x,y,r,m,b)/(GTLA(x,y-x,r,m,b)+GDLA(x,y,r,m,b))
[1] 0.09386472
```

The $x = 20$-year-old with an expected age at death of $E[T_{20}] + 20 = 85.03$ can contribute 9.39% to the collective pension plan during his/her working years and guarantee a constant (flat) standard of living over his/her entire life. In contrast to

Table 12.2 Collective pensions: contributions in a longevity risk pool

$20 + E[T_{20}]$	Investment return assumption			
Expected age at death	$r = 1\%$	$r = 2\%$	$r = 3\%$	$r = 4\%$
80	20.6%	15.4%	11.2%	7.9%
85	24.5%	18.3%	13.3%	9.4%
90	28.0%	20.9%	15.1%	10.6%

Assume $g = 0$, Gompertz dispersion $b = 10$ years, start at $x = 20$, retire at $R = 65$

the collective scheme, if this person decides to save and invest themselves and plans to age $D = 85$, they would require 10.1% contribution rate. If they wanted to be safe and planned to age $D = 90$, the required contribution rate would be 11.43%, and for coverage until age $D = 95$, the contribution rate would be 12.5%. (See Table 12.1, again.) So, the collective plan not only eliminates the longevity risk, via the *Law of Large Numbers*, it actually reduces contribution costs.

```
# Do-It-Yourself GPP assuming D=85
N1<-(65-20); N2<-(85-65); r<-0.04
RGOA(0,r,N2)/(RGOA(0,r,N1)*(1+r)^N1+RGOA(0,r,N2))
[1] 0.1009535
# Do-It-Yourself GPP assuming D=90, to be safe
N1<-(65-20); N2<-(90-65); r<-0.04
RGOA(0,r,N2)/(RGOA(0,r,N1)*(1+r)^N1+RGOA(0,r,N2))
[1] 0.1143206
# Do-It-Yourself GPP assuming D=95, to be very safe
N1<-(65-20); N2<-(95-65); r<-0.04
RGOA(0,r,N2)/(RGOA(0,r,N1)*(1+r)^N1+RGOA(0,r,N2))
[1] 0.1250134
```

12.3 Who (Gets and) Pays for Gold-Plated Pensions?

Here are some warnings and caveats, before concluding that *collective* plans are better than *individual* plans. First, replacing term-certain annuities with life-contingent annuities, which is what happens in the transition from Eqs. (12.2)–(12.4), implies that upon death heirs get absolutely nothing from the pot. You can be 1 year away from retirement, after having contributed s^* for the last 44 years, and dying will leave you (a.k.a. your family) with zilch in a *pure* collective plan. Ergo, most participants demand a death benefit in the event of early death. Technically this is easy and achieved by adding certainty periods to the annuity factors, but contribution rates will be higher.

Regardless of the micro-mechanics of your particular DB pension plan, and whether it's gold-plated or not, remember that you have to be part of a (large) group for the pooling, that is the *Law of Large Numbers* to reduce the mortality and longevity risk. These pools can be created by countries (nationally) such as with government social security plans, by large corporate employers or unionized employees across sectors. Either way, the administrators of these (large) plans have to decide (and negotiate) over who actually pays and contributes to the pension plan. So, all of the above numbers and formulas for the fully funded GPP assume that you (the participant) is shouldering the entire burden of s^*. But if you can (somehow) coerce, force, or impose part of the GPP's expense on an employer, the amount that you must contribute and the fraction of your consumable income it replaces might differ from 100%. Of course, the details behind *who-pays-what* and how to determine the appropriate s^*, in those cases, take us far beyond the mandate of this recipe book. In fact, another (very important) consideration is how to invest and allocate the rather large sum of money from the group's contributions, while the pension pot is growing. The assumption embedded inside Table 12.2, for example, is that funds are invested at a conservative and safe rate of interest r. But, in practice that never happens. Sponsors and trustees can't "live" with the implications of low rates of r, namely the very high contribution rates s^*. Instead, they invest the funds in a diversified portfolio of stocks, bonds, real-estate, and other asset classes, which "allows" them to assume a higher r value and lower corresponding s^*. Of course, nothing is free in life—including risk premiums—and this strategy of assuming an aggressive r, instead of being safe creates its own unique set of problems, such as when stock markets decline sharply and for extended periods of time. Alas, these topical matters most definitely take us beyond a simple cookbook.

12.4 What Fraction of Your Balance Sheet is Pensionized?

One thing should be quite clear from the extensive discussion in the prior section. A gold-plated or even a silver-plated or a copper-plated pension plan is a lovely asset to have on your personal balance sheet as you approach and enter retirement. Someone with F in liquid wealth, together with an entitlement to a pension annuity of π per year for life, is obviously much better off than someone who (only) has the F_x. They are in a very different financial situation. Using notation that I introduced in Chap. 11, at the age of x, the *discounted utility* denoted by $U_x(F, \pi)$ is obviously greater than $U_x(F, 0)$, that is someone without any pension income. More importantly:

$$U_x(F, \pi) \; > \; U_x(F + a_1\pi, 0), \tag{12.5}$$

where a_1 is the (fair) actuarial present value of the annuity, `GILA(x,v,m,b)`, and the F suppresses the x subscript, since it appears in U_x. I will return to this utility-based relationship later on in the chapter.

Here is a simple numerical example that illustrates (and should remind you) that someone with (F, π) can afford to withdraw a higher percentage of their nest egg and actually consume more. Assume you have $F = \$200{,}000$ in liquid investable wealth and are entitled to a pension annuity of $\pi = \$50{,}000$ per year. Now, imagine the pension plan allows you to take an equivalent *lump sum*, computed (per section #10.7) via the product: $\pi \times$ `GILA(.)`. With that in mind, this script computes total consumption via the *intelligent drawdown* function, for rather arbitrary values of: $\rho = r = 2\%$ and $\gamma = 2$.

```
# APV of your 50,000 pension annuity
apva<-GILA(65,0.02,88,10)*50; apva
[1] 799.7565
# Consumption in 1st year of retirement, including pension.
IDDR(200,50,65,88,10,0.02,0.02,2)*200+50
[1] 68.4452
# Consumption if you take lump-sum value of pension instead.
IDDR0(1000,65,88,10,0.02,0.02,2)*(200+apva)
[1] 51.08089
```

If you take the *lump-sum* value and then drawdown optimally, the best you can achieve (considering your risk aversion γ and subjective discount rate ρ) in the first year of retirement is \$51,081. But, if you keep the pension annuity income of π = \$50,000 and augment via the *intelligent drawdown* algorithm, you can consume a total of \$68,445, which is over 17 thousand dollars more in the first year, and yet another perspective on the benefit from having the pension annuity. You can be more aggressive with your spending. Now, to be very clear (and I have said this before) the higher drawdown **rate**, which in the above case works out to 9.2% versus 5.1%, implies that you might deplete the nest egg (and still be alive). Look carefully at the following script for the two numbers.

```
IDDR(200,50,65,88,10,0.02,0.02,2)
[1] 0.092226
IDDR0(1000,65,88,10,0.02,0.02,2)
[1] 0.05108089
```

The pension annuity will continue to provide income as long as you are alive, which is a luxury you can't assume from your nest egg F, with a finite portfolio longevity. In sum, having a fraction of your retirement resources (a.k.a. personal balance sheet) in the form of pension annuities, a.k.a. *pensionized* will increase the overall utility of your retirement years.

Mathematically, the fraction of your personal balance sheet that is *pensionized* is defined as:

$$\psi = \frac{\texttt{GILA(x, v, m, b)} \times \pi}{F_x + \texttt{GILA(x, v, m, b)} \times \pi} = \frac{\texttt{GILA(x, v, m, b)}}{F_x/\pi + \texttt{GILA(x, v, m, b)}}. \tag{12.6}$$

The numerator (of the middle expression) is the *actuarial present value* (APV) of the pension annuity. The denominator adds that number to your liquid wealth F_x (making the denominator your total balance sheet). The value of ψ ranges from zero (you have no guaranteed lifetime income) to 100% (all of your wealth is in the form of pension annuities). The value of ψ is a function of the annuity factor `GILA(x,v,m,b)` and the ratio of liquid wealth F_x to pension income π, only. It isn't subjective and doesn't depend on (ρ, γ). For example, assume that you are x = 65-years-old, with F_{65} = \$400 thousand in investable wealth plus a pension annuity entitlement of π = \$37.5 thousand per year for life. To be clear—and apologies for not emphasizing this earlier—assume the pension provides inflation-adjusted income and that the relevant real valuation rate is $v = 2\%$. Based on Eq. (12.6) the value of $\psi \approx 60\%$, per the script, is

```
x<-65; v<-0.02; b<-10; m<-88; Fx<-400; pi<-37.5
# Actuarial Present Value (APV) of Pension Annuity
GILA(x,v,m,b)*pi
[1] 599.8174
#Fraction of Balance Sheet that is Pensionized
psi<-GILA(x,v,m,b)/(Fx/pi+GILA(x,v,m,b)); psi
[1] 0.5999269
```

The APV of your pension entitlement is approximately \$600,000 thousand, which combined with the \$400,000 of investable wealth results in a total balance sheet of \$1 million, of which approximately 60% is *pensionized*. Later on I'll discuss and analyze whether 60% is too high (or too low) relative to the "average" retiree, but at this point I want to ensure the computational process is very clear. Here is another numerical example to build some deeper intuition and appreciation for ψ. Assume this person has the same (F_x, π) of \$400,000 and $\pi = 37{,}500$, but they are in poor health. In the language of Gompertz, their value of $m = 81.2$, instead of $m = 88$, which results in a remaining life expectancy of: `GILA(65,0,81.2,10)=15` years. The expected age at death is now 80. In this case, the fraction of the balance sheet *pensionized* at the age of $x = 65$ is

```
x<-65; v<-0.02; b<-10; m<-81.2; Fx<-400; pi<-37.5;
# Actuarial Present Value (APV) of Pension Annuity
GILA(x,v,m,b)*pi
[1] 468.9499
#Fraction of Balance Sheet that is Pensionized
psi<-GILA(x,v,m,b)/(Fx/pi+GILA(x,v,m,b)); psi
[1] 0.5396743
```

The value of $\psi = 54\%$ instead of 60%, because the actuarial present value of the pension annuity is lower (note the \$469 thousand versus the \$600 thousand), which is a smaller fraction of the overall balance sheet. To be very clear, not only is the dollar value of the entire balance sheet lower, the fraction *pensionized* is lower as well. The situation would be reversed if I increased m, which is a model value and associated with a longer expected life. In that situation the `GILA(.)` factor is higher, the actuarial present value of the pension is higher and therefore ψ is higher, all else being equal. Younger retirees with longer expected lives, assuming the same (F_x, π) values, would also be associated with higher values of ψ, for the same reasons.

The relationship between any of the three inputs: (x, F_x, π) on one side and ψ on the other should be intuitive, and I'll return to the relationship between wealth and health (or income and longevity) in Chap. 13. But at this point I should state (somewhat controversially) if wealthier people do indeed live longer, then *all else being equal* a larger fraction of wealthier people's balance sheet is *pensionized.* That is *ceteris paribus.* Of course, wealth and health are a perfect example of all else *not* being equal. Individuals with lower longevity prospects are likely to have lower wealth as well. In other words, whether or not x-year-olds who are in poor relative health have a higher or lower ψ is an empirical question. Bottom line: ψ offers an alternative perspective on your personal balance sheet. In fact, Eq. (12.6) can be expressed as:

$$\frac{F_x}{\pi} = \left(\frac{1-\psi}{\psi}\right) \times \texttt{GILA(x, v, m, b)}, \tag{12.7}$$

as long as $\psi > 0$. So, knowing ψ and the value of the `GILA(.)` tells me how much pension annuity income you are actually receiving, per dollar of liquid investable wealth (or in Eq. (12.7) how may dollars of liquid investable wealth you have per dollar of your annual pension). In some sense, the knowledge of your unique value of ψ is more important than the individual levels (and dollar values) of either F_x or π.

12.5 Deep Dive into the Wealth Depletion Time (WDT)

The value of ψ provides a summary measure of the resilience of your retirement income plan, influences the rate at which you (intelligently) drawdown your wealth, and dictates the time (or age) at which you should target to deplete your wealth. As I explained in Sect. 11.3, the *wealth depletion time* (WDT) is rather obscure and unknown to non-academic life-cycle economists, but at the heart of the *intelligent drawdown* algorithm `IDDR(.)`. Recall from the game at the start of Chap. 11, most people—when asked properly—would prefer to allocate and place their retirement income "chips in boxes" where they are most likely to be alive. What this also means is that if retirees have ample pension annuity income, then boxes that are sufficiently far and distant (with low survival probabilities) might receive no chips at all. Ergo, they deplete their liquid wealth (and live off their pension) if they live long enough. I'm not arguing that people *should* do this—and some retirees recoil at the thought—all I'm saying is that it's rational. Indeed, if you abhor the idea of (only) living off your pension at some advanced age, then you are deemed to have high levels of longevity risk-aversion γ. Conversely, if you read the above paragraph and say to yourself *Yes, I can live on my pension annuity, only, if I get to some advanced age*, then you are characterized as having lower γ.

So, the objective in this next section is to compute this wealth depletion time as a function of both γ and the fraction ψ of your balance sheet that is *pensionized.* Recall from Chap. 11, and the inner-mechanics of the `IDDR(.)` function, that the WDT satisfies the following equation:

```
WDT.PSI<-function(psi,x,m,b,r,rho,gam){
f<-function(tau){
  k<-(r-rho)/gam
  K1<-(((1-psi)*GILA(x,r,m,b)/psi+1/r)*exp(r*tau)-1/r)/
    (GTLA(x-b*log(gam),tau,r-k,m,b)*exp(r*tau))
  K2<-exp(k*tau)
  K3<-TPXG(x,tau,m,b)^(1/gam)
  K1*K2*K3-1}
uniroot(f,lower=0,upper=100)$root}
```

Now, while a simple and humble cookbook shouldn't try too hard to compete with a proper chemistry text, the intuition behind the `WDT.PSI` function (and algorithm) is that it locates the value of τ, a.k.a. the wealth depletion time, at which the total consumption function c^*_τ is equal to the value of the pension π. That is the definition of depleting wealth. Now, there are many ways to construct a declining function c_t whose value equals π at $t = \tau$, but there is another relationship that must also be satisfied. Namely, the discounted value of the optimal $(c^*_t - \pi)$, from time $t = 0$ until τ, must be equal to the initial liquid wealth F_x, and it must maximize discounted utility, which then pins down the value of τ. If this sounds more like chemistry than cooking, the following numerical example provides concrete values:

```
# 60 Percent of Balance Sheet is Pensionized
# High Level of Longevity Risk Aversion (gamma=1)
WDT.PSI(0.60,65,88,10,0.02,0.02,1)
[1] 20.57696
# Low Level of Longevity Risk Aversion (gamma=8)
WDT.PSI(0.60,65,88,10,0.02,0.02,8)
[1] 35.69232
```

The above **R** script computes the time τ, starting from age $x = 65$, at which liquid wealth is depleted under the *intelligent drawdown* algorithm, assuming that $\psi = 60\%$ of your balance sheet is *pensionized* and that you are characterized by a longevity risk aversion parameter of either $\gamma = 1$ (very low) or $\gamma = 8$, which is rather high. Using these values the wealth depletion time ranges from age $85.58 = x + \tau$ to age 100.7, which is just as you become a centenarian. These results can be interpreted and viewed in two directions. You can start with (estimate, survey, measure) the longevity risk-aversion γ value first and then solve for the corresponding τ. Or, you can ask retirees to **pre-select** an age at which—if they are still alive—they are willing to survive on their pension annuity alone and then back out the relevant γ. I'll return to this latter (from τ to γ) approach later in the chapter. For now, here is another numerical example in which γ is fixed, as is the amount of the pension π, and therefore ψ. The next script focuses on the impact of ψ, the fraction *pensionized.* I picked a high level of $\gamma = 8$, which pushes out (extends) the wealth depletion time.

```
# Remember. The first argument is PSI.
 WDT.PSI(0.05,65,88,10,0.02,0.02,8)
[1] 53.22425
 WDT.PSI(0.25,65,88,10,0.02,0.02,8)
[1] 44.96233
 WDT.PSI(0.50,65,88,10,0.02,0.02,8)
[1] 38.3462
 WDT.PSI(0.95,65,88,10,0.02,0.02,8)
[1] 19.36544
```

Notice how someone with very little pension annuity income π relative to total wealth F_x at retirement will plan to deplete wealth (only) at the age of $65 + 53.23 \approx 118$. Few retirees (if any) survive to that point, so effectively, this person will never "agree" to deplete wealth while still alive. In contrast, when $\psi = 95\%$, the rational (again: utility maximizing) policy is to deplete wealth by age 84. So, oddly enough—and in contrast to the philosophy underlying the first few chapters of this book—planning to *ruin* is optimal. This indeed is a very important point and juncture in this book, so I'll state it again. There is a strong case to be made that if you have a (substantial) pension, *outliving your money* shouldn't be feared. Rather, the question you should be asking yourself is: by what age am I willing to live *only* on my pension? I'll get back to this.

To get a visual sense of wealth depletion times (and ages), Fig. 12.3 plots the `WDT.PSI` function for high ($\gamma = 8$) and low ($\gamma = 1$) levels of longevity risk aversion, over the entire range of possible *pensionized* values: $\psi \in [0, 1]$ (that's the 0–100% in the figure). The starting age is $x = 65$, the subjective discount rate is set

Source: Generated by Author in **R**

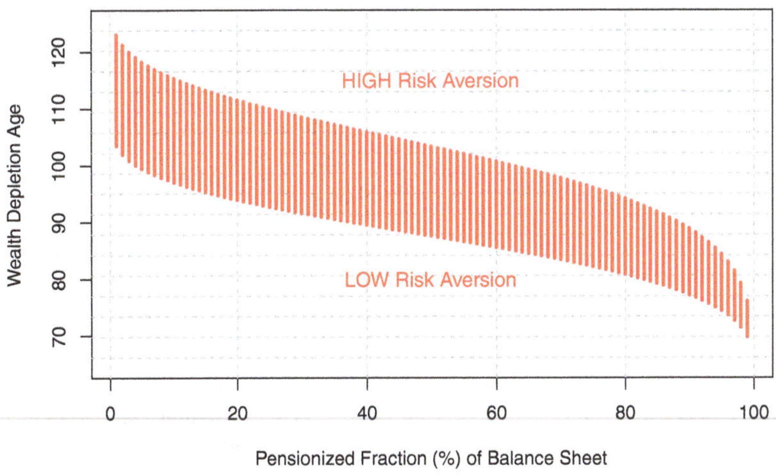

Fig. 12.3 Wealth depletion time (WDT) as a function of ψ and γ

equal to the interest rate $\rho = r = 2\%$, and the Gompertz parameters are the usual ($m = 88, b = 10$). Besides the intrinsic beauty of the figure, it tells an interesting qualitative story. Notice that as ψ increases, which means that you are receiving more pension annuity income relative to your wealth, the depletion age $(x + \tau)$ gets very close to the current age x, and γ doesn't make much of a difference. You can reproduce the lovely figure with the following script:

```
plot(c(1,99),c(65,125),type="n",
     xlab="Pensionized Fraction of Balance Sheet",
     ylab="Wealth Depletion Age")
grid(ny=18,lty=20)
for (i in 1:99){
  y0<-WDT.PSI(i/100,65,88,10,0.02,0.02,1)+65
  y1<-WDT.PSI(i/100,65,88,10,0.02,0.02,8)+65
  segments(i,y0,i,y1,col="red",lwd=3)
}
```

12.6 What Fraction Should be Pensionized?

The above section and **R** script solved the equation for the wealth depletion time (WDT), which is the age by which you should *only* be living on your pension annuity income, assuming a fraction ψ of your balance sheet is *pensionized* and that your longevity risk aversion coefficient is γ. As I explained, the WDT isn't imposed or forced as some exogenous constraints. Rather the value of the WDT is a by-product of the *intelligent drawdown*, which attempts to smooth consumption while accounting for the (very) small probabilities of living to a (very) advanced age. It's consistent with how people *played* the game of chips introduced in Chap. 11.

Nevertheless, some (if not many) readers might find it disconcerting to be told an age at which they should essentially force themselves to deplete their investable wealth. Moreover, naive users of the *intelligent drawdown* methodology (or its variants and refinements) might not be aware of the fact that baked-into the recipe is a formal date at which their account will be ruined. This is yet another reason why I have placed the WDT front and center in the prior section. I certainly don't want to hide it.

For these reasons (and a few others) in this section I will turn the WDT concept on its head, and instead of solving for the WDT, or leaving the WDT quietly in the background of the *intelligent drawdown* calculations, in this section I will actually use it as a formal input. In particular, I will reverse the `WDT.PSI(.)` algorithm based on the age at which retirees *might* be willing to deplete their wealth. Once the WDT becomes an input (instead of an output) I will use that value to determine both (1) the fraction ψ^* of the retiree's balance sheet that should be pensioned and (2) the *intelligent drawdown* rate itself, which follows from ψ^*.

An additional benefit of approaching the problem in this manner is that it addresses a rather fundamental (and rather pesky) question I have yet to answer, namely: *How much pension annuity income* ***should*** *someone have in retirement?* In this section the answer is replaced with another question: *At what age are you willing to live* ***entirely*** *on pension annuity income?* Some people might answer *never!* So, using our language, their wealth depletion time tolerance is $\tau = \infty$. Others might reply in a more nuanced (and intelligent) manner by thinking that if they get to age 105, which odds are they won't, then they would be fine with only consuming the pension annuity income. Yet others might respond with: $(x + \tau = 95)$, or perhaps even $(x + \tau = 85)$, and so on and so forth. It's a preference, it's personal and it varies across retirees.

I'm arguing here that your *acceptable ruin age* is no different from risk aversion (questionnaires) designed to calibrate the value of γ, something which drives so much of (modern) retirement planning. In my view, questions around wealth depletion times τ could help guide optimal *pensionization*, drawdown rates, and asset allocation (although I haven't really addressed that yet). The bottom line is as follows. The following **R** script maps your personal (τ, γ) into the appropriate value of ψ^*. Note that I use an asterisk on top of the psi symbol, to remind readers of the fact it's being solved for, as opposed to an input to the *intelligent drawdown* algorithm.

```
PSI.OPT<-function(tau,x,m,b,r,rho,gam){
  k<-(r-rho)/gam
  a1<-GILA(x,r,m,b)
  a2<-GTLA(x-b*log(gam),tau,r-k,m,b)
  K1<-(a2/a1)*exp(-k*tau)*TPXG(x,tau,m,b)^(-1/gam)
  K2<-(1/r)*(1/a1)*(exp(-r*tau)-1)
  1/(K1+K2+1)
}
```

Here is a simple numerical example to get a sense of what this new `PSI.OPT` function does, after which I'll explain the mathematical logic and provide a brief derivation. Assume you are $x = 65$-years-old, subject to Gompertz parameters $(m = 88, b = 10)$, with an assumed investment return of: $r = \rho = 3\%$ and a longevity risk aversion coefficient of $\gamma = 4$. Based on `PSI.OPT(.)`, the optimal fraction of your balance sheet that should be *pensionized* depends on—here it comes—the age at which you are willing to deplete liquid wealth, *assuming you are still alive.* Here are the values of ψ^* for $\tau = 25, 30, 35$, that is someone who is willing to live (only) on their pension income if they reach the age of 90, 95, and 100.

```
# Willing to Deplete at Age 90
PSI.OPT(25,65,88,10,0.025,0.025,4)
[1] 0.7788439
# Willing to Deplete at Age 95
```

```
PSI.OPT(30,65,88,10,0.025,0.025,4)
[1] 0.6119756
# Willing to Deplete at Age 100
PSI.OPT(35,65,88,10,0.025,0.025,4)
[1] 0.4088285
```

What this implies is that—depending on the stated tolerance for τ—between 40 and 80% of the retirement balance sheet should be *pensionized* by age $x = 65$, which is the start of retirement. Intuitively, the older the age $(x + \tau)$ to which you want liquid assets to survive—*Hey, I want money in the bank even if I reach age 120!*—the lower the fraction of the personal balance sheet that should be *pensionized.* To be very clear, the above script is *not* about the maximum age to which you are planning or the age to which you expect to live. As I stated a number of times before, the *intelligent drawdown* methodology (from Chap. 11) attempts to generate a smooth consumption profile to the very end of your (random) life regardless of how long you actually live.

The above script, and in particular your personally selected τ value, captures the time (and age) after which you are willing to live entirely on pension annuity income—*if you are still alive.* To sum up here, there are two ways to approach (and think about) the role of pension annuity income within the context of the wealth depletion time τ. You can pre-specify the amount of liquid wealth and annuity income (F_x, π) you already have, in which case τ follows. Or, you can stipulate your time horizon for τ, which remember is measured in years and for most reasonable situations will be in the late 90s and then solve for ψ^* which leads to an optimal amount of pension income.

I'll present a very detailed example (and case study) in the next section, but first, those who are interested in the underlying chemistry, the `PSI.OPT(.)` script is based on the following set of equations:

$$\frac{\left(\alpha_1(\frac{1-\psi}{\psi}) + \frac{1}{r}\right) e^{r\tau} - \frac{1}{r}}{\alpha_2 e^{r\tau}} e^{k\tau} \left({}_\tau p_x\right)^{1/\gamma} - 1 = 0, \tag{12.8}$$

where ψ denotes the fraction of your balance sheet that is *pensionized* (which I solve for), and the other (x, m, b) as well as (r) and (ρ, γ, τ) have all been explained and used many times before. The α_1 and α_2 are just annuity factors defined by

$$\alpha_1 = \int_0^\infty e^{-rs}({}_s p_x)ds, \quad \alpha_2 = \int_0^\tau e^{-(r-k)s}({}_s p_{\tilde{x}})ds, \tag{12.9}$$

where $\tilde{x} = x - b\ln[\gamma]$, which is effectively your (chronological) age set back by $b\ln[\gamma]$ years. The first annuity factor in Eq. (12.9) is `GILA(x,r,m,b)` and the second annuity factor in Eq. (12.9) is a temporary `GTLA(x.tilde,tau,r,m,b)`, to time τ, but one in which the input (retirement) age is: $(x - b\ln[\gamma])$. Finally, the

Table 12.3 What fraction of your balance sheet (ψ^*) should be *Pensionized*?

Retirement at age $R = 65$	Target wealth depletion age: $R + \tau$			
Longevity risk aversion	Age 85	Age 90	Age 95	Age 100
$\gamma = 1$	62.3%	37.4%	15.9%	4.1%
$\gamma = 4$	89.1%	77.9%	61.2%	40.1%
$\gamma = 8$	94.1%	88.2%	77.9%	62.7%

Assume: Gompertz parameters $m = 88$, $b = 10$, with real return $r = \rho = 2.5\%$

formula underlying the script for `PSI.OPT(.)` is obtained by isolating ψ, in Eq. (12.8) as follows:

$$\frac{1}{\psi} = \overbrace{\left(\frac{\alpha_2}{\alpha_1}\right) e^{-k\tau} ({}_\tau p_x)^{-1/\gamma}}^{K1} + \overbrace{\left(\frac{1}{r\alpha_1}\right) (e^{-r\tau} - 1)}^{K2} + 1. \tag{12.10}$$

The constants $K1$ and $K2$ are defined for convenience and correspond to (exactly) how the script for `PSI.OPT` was built and constructed on the prior page. To be clear, Eq. (12.10) maps or converts the demographic parameters (x, m, b), together with the investment parameter (r), plus the preference parameters (ρ, γ, τ) into the optimal fraction of the balance sheet that should be *pensionized.* Table 12.3 displays value of the `OPT.PSI(.)` function output for a variety of risk aversion coefficients γ and (acceptable) ruin time τ. Notice that higher values of longevity risk-aversion γ lead to more (that is optimal) pension income, which should come as a big surprise when you think about it. After all, you are *more* worried about longevity. But longevity risk aversion alone isn't enough to determine (a.k.a. pin down) the value of ψ^*. You need a second ingredient. And, as the table shows, optimal *pensionization* declines with τ.

Before moving on to some actual cases, readers might wonder *why* the adjusted age: $(x - b\ln[\gamma])$, a quantity I defined to be $\tilde{x}$, makes repeated appearances in these pages. In fact, some readers might find it especially odd to be taking the natural logarithm $\ln[.]$ of a longevity risk aversion coefficient γ. So, in the next few paragraphs I'll explain where this comes from. Recall from Eq. (8.7) in Chap. 8, that in a Gompertz model the conditional survival probability $\Pr[T_x \geq t]$, for any value of (x, t), can be written and expressed as:

$$({}_t p_x) = \exp\{e^{\frac{x-m}{b}}(1 - e^{t/b})\},$$

where (m, b) are the usual mode and dispersion parameters. Now, look carefully at Eq. (12.8) in this chapter, and in particular the appearance of the expression $({}_t p_x)^{1/\gamma}$, which is the survival probability to the power of one over the longevity risk aversion coefficient γ. By simple algebra and the rule of exponents that can be expressed as:

$$({}_t p_x)^{1/\gamma} = \exp\{\frac{1}{\gamma} e^{\frac{x-m}{b}}(1-e^{t/b})\} = \exp\{e^{\frac{x-b\ln[\gamma]-m}{b}}(1-e^{t/b})\}.$$

Notice how the age variable x only appears once in the above expression, and that it is reduced by $b\ln[\gamma]$. Ergo, I can define a new variable $\tilde{x} = x - b\ln[\gamma]$ and arrive at the relationship:

$$({}_t p_x)^{1/\gamma} = ({}_t p_{\tilde{x}}).$$

In sum, if-and-when I ever have to compute the conditional survival probability (say 10 years) to the power of one over the risk aversion coefficient, I can *instead* compute the conditional survival probability (for 10 years) from a reduced age $x - b\ln[\gamma]$. Here is an example. `TPXG(65,10,88,10)=0.8417`, and raising that to the power of (1/3) is `0.9441`. But, I can modify the age and compute `TPXG(65-10*log(3),10,88,10)=0.9441` instead. This is more of a mathematical *trick* than an economic insight *per se*, but it seems to indicate that longevity risk-aversion γ makes you behave as if the survival probabilities have increased, which makes you behave as if you are (really) younger. Or, at least that's a way to remember this odd factoid.

12.7 A Detailed Client Case Study

You are a financial advisor and a client of yours is $x = 70$-years-old, with $F_{70} = \$1{,}000{,}000$ in investable wealth, earning $r = 2\%$ real returns every year, plus, they are entitled to $\pi = \$30{,}000$ of annual pension annuity income. Their Gompertz parameters (i.e. longevity prospects) are modeled by $(m = 88, b = 10)$, which are also the parameters used to value life annuities. Finally, their risk aversion coefficient (based on observed asset allocation) is $\gamma = 3$, and their subjective discount rate is (assumed to be) $\rho = r = 2\%$, which is a neutral (baseline) preference.

I will not shy away from the fact that both (γ, ρ) are critical inputs to the *intelligent drawdown* methodology and must be calibrated with caution. Nevertheless, I'll assume they are known. Most critically, the client has stated that they *refuse* to deplete their liquid wealth before the age of 95. After that age (assuming they are still alive) they would be willing to live entirely on pension annuity income. This particular client wants to know if they should acquire additional annuities beyond the $\pi = \$30{,}000$ per year. They would also like guidance on how much to withdraw from their retirement account.

Let's start by computing the existing value of ψ for this client, which is the fraction of the balance sheet that is currently *pensionized* and then compare it with what should be *pensionized*. That can easily be done by multiplying the pension annuity of 30,000 per year by the relevant `GILA(.)` factor and then adding that to the million dollars of liquid wealth and finally computing the ratio. So, to begin:

```
# The Actuarial Present Value (APV) of the Pension
30000*GILA(70,0.02,88,10)
[1] 402482.8
```

The APV is slightly more than \$400,000, and the initial value of $\psi = 28.7\%$, which is computed via the `GILA(.)` function:

```
# Current Fraction (psi) Pensionized
30000*GILA(70,0.02,88,10)/(1000000+30000*GILA(70,0.02,
88,10))
[1] 0.2869788
```

The first question I address is whether $\psi = 28.7\%$ is optimal. Does the current balance sheet provide enough pension annuity income relative to the stated $\gamma = 3$ and $\tau = 25$ preferences? I will use the `PSI.OPT(.)` function to compare the current value of ψ with the optimal value of ψ^*, which is

```
# Optimal Fraction (psi) Pensionized
PSI.OPT(25,70,88,10,0.02,0.02,4)
[1] 0.6254613
```

Ergo, this person is under-*pensionized* and should allocate more of their liquid investable wealth to pension annuity income. In particular, they should increase the fraction from 28.7 to 62.5% by converting some F (cash) into more π (annuities). Thinking abstractly, they should go from the current existing pair (F, π) to a modified pair: $(F - \Delta F, \pi + \Delta F/a_1)$, where ΔF is the additional dollar amount of liquid wealth that should be *pensionized*, and $a := \alpha_1$ is the (shorthand, with less subscripts) life annuity factor defined in Eq. (12.9). It represents the cost of every additional dollar of pension annuity income. So, *pensionizing* the amount ΔF will generate an additional $\Delta F/a$ of lifetime income. Mathematically, we are looking for Δ that satisfies

$$\psi^* = \frac{\pi a + \Delta F}{F + a\pi} = \psi + \frac{\Delta F}{F + a\pi}. \tag{12.11}$$

The numerator (of the first expression to the right of the equal sign) is the actuarial present value of the revised amount of pension annuity income, and the denominator is the total balance sheet value, which I'll denote by `BSV` in the subsequent **R** script. The ratio of these two quantities must be equal to the optimal *pensionized* fraction ψ^*. So, after rearranging equation (12.11), the additional amount of liquid wealth ΔF that must be spent on buying annuities is: $\Delta F = (\psi^* - \psi)(F + a\pi)$. The following script provides the relevant numbers in one place:

```
aa<-GILA(70,0.02,88,10)
# Balance Sheet Value
BSV<-1000000+30000*aa
```

```
# Current Fraction Pensionized (psi)
PSI.old<-30000*aa/BSV
# Optimal Fraction Pensionized (psi star)
PSI.new<-PSI.OPT(25,70,88,10,0.02,0.02,4)
# Amount (Delta) to be Pensionized
(PSI.new-PSI.old)*BSV
[1] 474715.9
```

So, a total of \$474,716 should be spent on purchasing (more) pension annuity income—although not necessarily all at once—which will generate an additional \$35,384 of pension annuity income per year. The exact computation is as follows:

```
# Amount of Additional Pension Income
pi.more<-(PSI.new-PSI.old)*BSV/aa; pi.more
[1] 35384.07
```

This then results in a revised value of initial wealth, computed as:

```
 # Revised Current Wealth
 Fx.new<-1000000-(PSI.new-PSI.old)*BSV; Fx.new
[1] 525284.1
```

You can see that the script above is the same thing as Fx.new=1000000+(PSI.old *BSV) -(PSI.new*BSV). If the client sells their old pension plan, they will receive PSI.old*BSV, which would be added to their 1,000,000 in investable wealth. They would then buy the new pension and pay PSI.new*BSV, resulting in the Fx.new in the script above. Finally, the intelligent drawdown rate, dollar amount withdrawn, and the total consumption in the first year (age 70) are computed via:

```
# Revised Intelligent Drawdown Rate
xi<-IDDR(Fx.new,30000+pi.more,70,88,10,0.02,0.02,4); xi
[1] 0.07311902
# Amount Withdrawn from Portfolio
xi*Fx.new
[1] 38408.26
# Total Consumption in First Year
xi*Fx.new+30000+pi.more
[1] 103792.3
```

This is a 7.3% withdrawal rate, \$38,408 withdrawal amount, and total consumption of \$103,792, of which \$30,000 comes from the original pension, and \$35,384 is from the newly acquired pension annuity.

12.8 The Utility of a Pension Annuity

Finally, combining the ideas from the last few sections, in this section I introduce a framework to quantify the benefits of having pension annuity income by measuring the increase in *utility* from converting ΔF into lifetime income $\Delta F/a_1$. While such a "conversion" obviously increases the fraction *pensionized* and allows for higher (intelligent) drawdowns, it also creates a more robust financial plan that can be quantified in dollars and sense. Using the notation I reintroduced earlier in this chapter, the term $U_x(F, \pi)$ captures the (albeit subjective) "happiness" from a personal balance sheet consisting of both F_x in liquid wealth and π in pension annuity income, assuming you are currently at age x.

Now, there is an infinite combination of consumption spending policies you could implement with your balance sheet while enjoying and deriving happiness from (F_x, π), so the absolute maximal value of *utility* is denoted by: $U_x^*(F, \pi)$. The extra asterisk on top of the utility function is meant to remind readers that the consumption spending process c_t^* is optimized as well. Regardless of the notation, my plan in this brief section is to create a user-defined function in **R** that translates utility benefits into units that can be (more) easily understood. I'll jump right in and present the script. Define a new function, which I call the added *wealth delta percentage* of the annuity.

```
af<-function(v,x,m,b){
b*exp(exp((x-m)/b)+(x-m)*v)*G(-b*v,exp((x-m)/b))}
# Converts Utility Benefit of Pension Annuity into Dollars.
DLTA<-function(x,m,b,v,gam){(af(v,x,m,b)/
af(v,x-b*log(gam),m,b))^(gam/(1-gam))-1}
```

As you can see, the `DLTA(.)` function is the ratio of two annuity factors, where instead of the `GILA(.)` functions, I am using the short-form `a1` function, based on the definition in Eq. (12.9), and the Gamma representations that were explained in Sect. 10.10. I could have used the `GILA(.)` function as well, which (if you recall) computes a similar value via crude numerical integration. The results are quite similar, if not identical. The point here is to derive some values.

```
DLTA(65,88,10,0.025,4)
[1] 0.577347
DLTA(65,88,10,0.025,8)
[1] 0.6939839
```

What do these numbers mean? Well, if you are $x = 65$-years-old with a longevity risk aversion of $\gamma = 4$, then you would require $\delta = 57.7\%$ additional wealth, that is $(1.577) \times F_{65}$ to create the same level of utility as someone who converts their entire liquid wealth into pension annuities. In contrast, if the level of longevity risk aversion is increased to $\gamma = 8$, the equivalent level of utility is created by

$\delta = 69.4\%$. Finally, the formula underlying the above script can be expressed mathematically as:

$$U_x(F(1+\delta), 0) = U_x(0, F/a_1), \tag{12.12}$$

which after a bit mathematics leads to the following equation for δ:

$$\delta = \left(\frac{a_x}{a_{\tilde{x}}}\right)^{\gamma/(1-\gamma)} - 1, \tag{12.13}$$

where (once again) $\tilde{x} = x - b\ln[\gamma]$, which is an age setback. To wrap this up, I am also including a script that computes δ, which is also called the annuity equivalent wealth in the economic literature, using the h_0, g formulation. Recall that the Gompertz law can also be expressed as $\lambda_x = h_0 e^{gx}$, which is often preferred by demographers and biologists, and I'll actually return to this at the start of the next chapter. The following script uses the (h_0, g) formulation:

```
ANHG<-function(x,v,h0,g){
# The Gompertz Annuity Valuation Model (GAVM)
# Using equation (A.33) from Milevsky (JPEF, 2020)
  hx<-h0*exp(g*x)
  G(-v/g,hx/g)/(g*exp((-1/g)*(hx+v*log(hx/g)))) }
UDHG<-function(x,h0,g,v,gam){
  # The Delta from Annuitization
  # This is based on equation (12.13)
  (ANHG(x,v,h0,g)/ANHG(x-log(gam)/g,v,h0,g))^(gam/(1-gam))-1 }
```

And, here are some numerical examples, applicable to age $x = 65$, with a coefficient of longevity risk aversion of $\gamma = 4$, and assuming the (hypothetical) age-zero log mortality hazard rate $\ln[h_0]$ is: -12, -11, -10. Recall that this means that the λ_0 mortality hazard rates are e^{-12}, e^{-11}, and e^{-10}, respectively. Changing h_0 like this is called a parallel shift in the term structure of mortality because the (log) Gompertz curve is increased at all ages by a constant amount. The bottom line is that the shifts or shocks to mortality (perhaps during a virus) will increase the utility-based value of annuitization, per the following numbers:

```
UDHG(65,exp(-12),0.10,0.03,4)
[1] 0.3626672
UDHG(65,exp(-11),0.10,0.03,4)
[1] 0.5590619
UDHG(65,exp(-10),0.10,0.03,4)
[1] 0.8795001
```

What do they mean exactly? Well once again, the interpretation is as before. You would require between 36 and 88% more wealth to create the same level of utility (happiness) as the life annuity. These numbers are on the same order of magnitude as the prior page using the ($m = 88, b = 10$) formulation, except that I'm using the (h_0, g) parameters for Gompertz instead of (m, b). It's really six of one versus half-a-dozen of the other. The point is to be able to converse fluently in (and convert from) the language of (m, b) and (h_0, g).

12.9 Final Notes

- As I mentioned in the prior chapter, the idea of an *intelligent drawdown* algorithm, and in particular how it is improved by having pension income, can be traced to the work cited as [13]. But, for more information on how (exactly) and where (exactly) the δ values come from, please see the articles cited as [9] as well as [4, 8] and the original idea by [7]. See also, references cited as [3, 5, 10, 12] for more on the rational approach to decumulation planning.
- For those readers (and users) who are interested in computing values of δ for situations in which the individual already has some pre-existing annuity income π, see the work cited as [9]. In particular, the technical appendix in that article contains an elaborate **R** script that solves for δ, when the retiree already has some pre-existing annuity income π, per the following equation:

$$U_x(F(1+\delta), \pi) = U_x(0, \pi + F/a_1). \tag{12.14}$$

- This chapter has attempted to tiptoe around the mathematics (and in particular the calculus of variations) required to derive the **R** scripts from first principles. An extended or advanced chapter on *pensionization* would solve for an optimal dynamic annuitization strategy, such as the work cited as [6], as well as the article cited as [11], which addresses whether or not utility might be reduced (and not increased) from excess *pensionization*. After all, although pensions do provide longevity insurance, per [2] or [1], it's possible to have too much of a good thing.

Questions and Problems

12.1 Compute the contribution rate, s^*, for a copper-plated pension plan (CPP versus GPP) that replaces 35% of your *consumable* income. In other words, if your real *disposable* income is \$100, and the contribution rate is s^*, the CPP would provide you with $(0.35) \times \$100 \times (1 - s^*)$ for your entire life, starting at retirement age R. Assume that you enter the system at age $x = 25$, contribute for 40 years until age $R = 65$, and the plan provides a pension annuity until death, which is modeled as a Gompertz variable with ($m = 88, b = 10$). Provide s^* numbers for $r = 1\%$ and $r = 4\%$. Note that wage growth g is zero.

12.2 Building on the CPP described in the prior question, i.e. a plan that replaces 35% of your consumable income, now assume wage growth $g > 0\%$ per year. In other words, at retirement your wage is $\$100 \times (1+g)^{R-x}$, and the CPP replaces 35% of that final wage times $(1 - s^*)$. Remember (again) that your consumable income is *net* of the CPP contributions. Compute s^* values for $r = 1\%$ and $r = 4\%$.

12.3 Assume (hypothetically) that you are $x = 65$-years-old, have $F = \$100$ in liquid wealth, and are entitled to a pension annuity of $\pi = \$50$. What level of longevity risk-aversion γ will lead to a wealth depletion time (WDT) of exactly $\tau = 20$ years, that is you live on your pension (only) if you get to age $(x + \tau) = 85$. For this question, assume that $r = \rho = 4\%$ and then do it again for $r = \rho = 1\%$. Explain the difference.

12.4 Assume that you are $x = 40$-years-old, plan to retire at age $R = 70$, and haven't yet saved anything for retirement, so that $F_{40} = \$0$. You are trying to create a personal gold-plated pension plan and trying to figure out how much to contribute, s^*, so that you will have flat and constant consumption until age $D = 95$. Assume that $r = 4\%$. Now, what would that contribution rate be, if you become part of a collective (DB) pension plan in which the average participant lives to age $D = 90$. If you earn $w = \$100{,}000$ per year, how much more would you be able to consume (per year) if you joined such a program? Assume no growth, so that $g = 0\%$, for simplicity.

12.5 Solve the above question (12.4), assuming that your wage grows (in real terms) by $\rho = 1\%$. How do the solution and answer change?

References

1. Blake, D. (1999). Annuity markets: Problems and solutions. *Geneva Papers on Risk and Insurance, 24*(3), 358–375.
2. Bodie, Z. (1990). Pensions as retirement income insurance. *Journal of Economic Literature, 28*, 28–49.
3. Brown, J. R., Mitchell, O. S., Poterba, J. M., & Warshawsky, M. J. (2001). *The role of annuity markets in financing retirement*. Cambridge: MIT Press.
4. Cannon, E., & Tonks, I. (2008). *Annuity markets*. New York: Oxford University Press.
5. Edwards, R. D. (2013). The cost of uncertain life-span. *Journal of Population Economics, 26*, 1485–1522.
6. Huang, H., Milevsky, M. A., & Young, V. R. (2017). Optimal purchasing of deferred income annuities when payout yields are mean-reverting. *Review of Finance, 21*(1), 327–361.
7. Kotlikof, L. J., & Spivak, A. (1981). The family as an incomplete annuity market. *Journal of Political Economy, 89*(2), 372–391.
8. Milevsky, M. A. (2020). Swimming with Wealthy sharks: Longevity, volatility and the value of risk pooling. *Journal of Pension Economics and Finance, 19*(2), 217–246. https://doi.org/10.1017/S1474747219000040
9. Milevsky, M. A., & Huang, H. (2018). The utility value of longevity risk pooling: Analytic insights. *North American Actuarial Journal, 22*(4), 574–590.
10. Poterba, J. M., Venti, S., & Wise, D. (2011). The composition and drawdown of wealth in retirement. *Journal of Economic Perspectives, 25*(4), 95–118.

11. Reichling, F., & Smetters, K. (2015). Optimal annuitization with stochastic mortality and correlated mortality cost. *American Economic Review, 11*, 3273–3320.
12. Sheshinski, E. (2007). *The economic theory of annuities*. Princeton: Princeton University Press.
13. Yaari, M. E. (1965). Uncertain lifetime, life insurance and the theory of the consumer. *The Review of Economic Studies, 32*(2), 137–150.

Chapter 13
Biological (and Other) Ages

This chapter examines the implications of *mortality heterogeneity*, that is the dispersion of longevity prospects within the population. It begins by discussing the extended Gompertz–Makeham model, as well as the *compensation* law of mortality, linking moments of the remaining lifetime random variable. It then introduces non-chronological measures of age, such as biological age and (especially) longevity risk-adjusted age to illustrate its dispersion. This chapter illustrates how true age can differ around the world and even within countries, based on wealth and income. The main computational implication of this chapter is that the *human longevity* random variable T_x, depends on (much) more than just chronological age x. Such heterogeneity must be accounted for in any *intelligent drawdown* methodology or *pensionization* scheme.

13.1 Functions Used and Defined

13.1.1 Sample of Native R Functions Used

- `which.min(.)` selects the argument with the smallest value.

13.1.2 User-Defined R Functions

- `GMSP(x,t,lam,m,b)` is the Gompertz–Makeham (GM) survival probability.
- `GMPDF(x,t,lam,m,b)` is the probability density function of the GM variable.
- `GMLE(x,lam,m,b)` computes life expectancy under a GM variable.

M. A. Milevsky, *Retirement Income Recipes in R*, Use R!,
https://doi.org/10.1007/978-3-030-51434-1_13

- `CLAM(b,x star,lam star)` maps b into m via compensation law.
- `LRAG(x,x star,g hat,g,lam hat,lam,lam star),` risk-adjusted age.

13.2 A Quick Refresher on Gompertz and Makeham

It's been a few chapters since I introduced (and discussed) actuarial models for longevity uncertainty, so allow me to quickly recap the main points and equations. Recall that to this point in the book, the working-horse model for mortality has been the Gompertz law. It postulates that mortality hazard rates, denoted by λ_x, increase exponentially (at the rate of $g = 1/b$) over your adult life, until the last possible age x to which you can live, denoted by ω. This could also be expressed as: *log* mortality hazard rates increase linearly in age, with a slope of $g = 1/b$. Stated differently—and you should be able to do the math to prove this yourself—mortality hazard rates λ_x double every: $\ln[2]b \approx 0.693 \times b$ years under the Gompertz law. So, if you are currently $x = 50$-years-old and $\lambda_{50} = 1\%$, assuming $b = 10$, then at the age of (approximately) $x = 57$, your hazard rate will be 2%. Seven years later (roughly at age 64) your hazard rate will be 4%, etc. Make sure you understand the "doubling" aspect of the Gompertz assumption. Perhaps I didn't emphasize this fact enough in Chap. 8, so look back at (8.6) and solve for z in the equation: $\lambda_{x+z}/\lambda_x = 2$, where $\lambda_{x+z} = (1/b)e^{(x+z-m)/b}$ and $\lambda_x = (1/b)e^{(x-m)/b}$ as shown in Chap. 8.

Moving on, you might recall that towards the end of Chap. 8, I mentioned (in Sect. 8.10) that a certain actuary by the name of William Makeham (in 1860) helped promote and then extend the original work of Benjamin Gompertz (in 1825) [7]. In particular, Mr. Makeham added a constant λ to the hazard rate λ_x, to account for accidental (and other) deaths that weren't necessarily age dependent and affected all ages equally. This constant wasn't just a theoretical addition on Mr. Makeham's part, but an extra parameter and degree of freedom that helped *fit the mortality data.* I'll get back to real-world data in a moment, but from this point onward I'll refer to the Gompertz–Makeham (GM) law of mortality as:

$$\lambda_x = \lambda + \frac{1}{b}e^{(x-m)/b}, \tag{13.1}$$

where (m, b) are the usual mode and dispersion coefficients. I should warn that by adding Makeham's constant λ, the moments (such as the mean and variance) of the remaining lifetime random variable T_0 can't be approximated by the neat expressions in Eq. (8.9). In fact, m itself is no longer the modal value of the random variable T_x. Nevertheless, and out of habit, I will continue to refer to the pair (m, b) as the mode and dispersion coefficients of the GM specification. And, by subtracting λ from both side of Eq. (13.1) and taking (natural) logarithms, the GM law can also be written as follows:

$$\ln[\lambda_x - \lambda] = \overbrace{-\ln[b] - m/b}^{\ln[h_0]} + \overbrace{(1/b)}^{g} x. \tag{13.2}$$

Similar to Eq. (8.6), the constants $\ln[h_0] = -(\ln[b] + m/b)$ and $g = 1/b$ are introduced for convenience and reasons that will become evident in the next section.

Intuitively, one can think of λ_x as the *total* hazard rate and $(\lambda_x - \lambda)$ as the *biological* hazard rate, because it only includes aging-related causes of death. Now, from a computational point of view, the survival probability under a GM law is

$$\Pr[T_x \geq t] = e^{-\int_x^{x+t} \lambda_s ds} = \exp\{-\lambda t + e^{(x-m)/b}(1 - e^{t/b})\}. \tag{13.3}$$

Please compare this with Eq. (8.7) in Chap. 8, which is the basis for the much-used `TPXG(.)` function in **R**. The only difference between Eqs. (8.7) and (13.3) is the extra $e^{-\lambda t}$ which reduces the survival probability, by accounting for non-age dependent deaths. So, although it's quite easy to modify `TPXG(.)` and add the Makeham constant λ, here is an explicit script for $\Pr[T_x \geq t]$, in **R**:

```
#Gompertz Makeham Survival Probability
GMSP<-function(x,t,lam,m,b){
exp(-lam*t+exp((x-m)/b)*(1-exp(t/b)))
}
```

Once again the current (assumed) age is denoted by `x`, the survival time is denoted by `t`, and the *three* mortality parameters are `(lam,m,b)`. Here are a few numerical examples of $\Pr[T_{50} \geq 40]$, that is surviving from age 50 to age 90, under $m = 88$ and $b = 10$. The only parameter I am modifying here is the λ, a.k.a. Makeham's constant.

```
# Age, Time, Makeham, Mode, Dispersion.
GMSP(50,40,1/1000,88,10)
[1] 0.2896645
GMSP(50,40,5/1000,88,10)
[1] 0.2468358
GMSP(50,40,9/1000,88,10)
[1] 0.2103396
```

Notice that as the accidental death rate increases from *one* in a thousand (per year), to *five* in a thousand to *nine* in a thousand, the conditional survival probability (to age 90) declines from 28.96 to 21.03%. For the record, and compared to real-world parameters, those are very large values of λ. So, although the *biological* parameters (m, b) haven't changed, a higher accident rate λ will (obviously) reduce the chances of surviving. And, needless to say, when $\lambda = 0$ in the GM formulas, we are back to the based G-world. For example:

```
# The Gompertz Survival Probability
TPXG(50,40,88,10)
```

```
[1] 0.3014859
# The Gompertz Makeham Survival Probability
GMSP(50,40,0,88,10)
[1] 0.3014859
```

Now, as I stated earlier (and one of the reasons I ignored this in Chap. 8) Mr. Makeham's constant λ is quite small, and on the order of 10^{-5}, which isn't as noticeable a difference, but adding this third parameter does improve the *goodness of fit*. Just as importantly, the magnitude of λ differs across countries, which is something I'll get back to in the next section. To summarize, the two main parameters under a GM law of mortality are (m, b) and they do most of the heavy lifting (so to speak) in determining the shape and location of T_x, but from here onwards I'll keep track of Makeham's λ as well.

As far as the probability density function (PDF) of the GM random variable, denoted by $f_x(t)$, I will simply remind readers that it's the derivative of the cumulative distribution function (CDF), $F_x(t) := 1 - \Pr[T_x \geq t]$. And, based on Eq. (13.3), it follows that:

$$f_x(t) := \frac{d}{dt}F_x(t) = -\frac{d}{dt}\mathrm{e}^{-\int_x^{x+t}\lambda_s ds} = \Pr[T_x \geq t]\,\frac{d}{dt}\int_x^{x+t}\lambda_s ds, \tag{13.4}$$

which, according to the fundamental theorem of calculus, applied to the very last integral in Eq. (13.4), results in the following expression for the PDF of the remaining lifetime random variable T_x.

$$f_x(t) = \overbrace{\exp\{-\lambda t + e^{(x-m)/b}(1 - e^{t/b})\}}^{\Pr[T_x \geq t]} \times \overbrace{\left(\lambda + \frac{1}{b}e^{(x+t-m)/b}\right)}^{\lambda_{x+t}} \tag{13.5}$$

Remember that x is the current (chronological) age, t is time, and (λ, m, b) are now the three parameters that determine the shape of the density function. And, although I have done my best to "minimize" the calculus (especially at the very beginning of the chapter), Eq. (13.5) provides a very convenient expression that can be used for visualizing *when you will die* according to the Gompertz–Makeham (GM) law. First, I will create a user-defined function in **R**, which maps (x, t, λ, m, b) into the relevant density value, so that I can then plot the entire function.

```
# The Gompertz Makeham Probability Density Function
GMPDF<-function(x,t,lam,m,b){
exp(-lam*t+exp((x-m)/b)*(1-exp(t/b)))
*(lam+(1/b)*exp((x+t-m)/b))}
```

This can easily be identified as Eq. (13.5), where the first line in the code is the survival probability $\Pr[T_x \geq t]$, and the second line is the hazard rate function λ_{x+t}. Test the code to ensure you get `GMPDF(60,10,1/250,88,10)=0.01776789`,

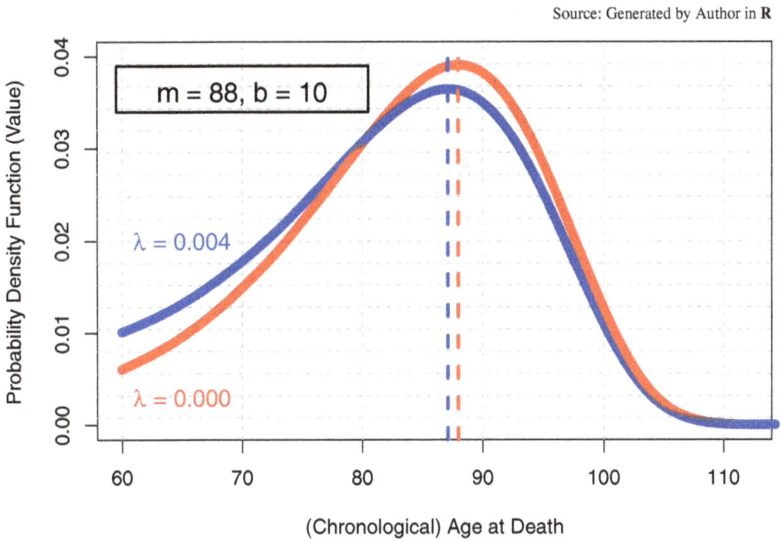

Fig. 13.1 Gompertz–Makeham density: the visual impact of lambda

before you move on. Intuitively, and (very) loosely speaking, that number (approximately 1.7%) is the probability of dying at age $x = 70$, conditional on being alive at age $x = 60$. The Makeham constant is: $\lambda = 1/250 = 0.004$ and the Gompertz parameters are $(m = 88, b = 10)$. Among other things, this function can also be used to (numerically) compute the *modal* value T_x. See the following script, which leverages the built-in minimizer in **R**.

```
# The (negative) PDF of GM, when lambda=0.0
gm.mode<-function(t){-GMPDF(60,t,0,88,10)}
round(optimize(gm.mode,c(0,60))$minimum+60,digits=4)
[1] 88
# The (negative) PDF of GM when lambda=0.004
gm.mode<-function(t){-GMPDF(60,t,1/250,88,10)}
round(optimize(gm.mode,c(0,60))$minimum+60,digits=4)
[1] 87.1472
```

The first part computes the largest value of $f_0(t)$, when $\lambda = 0$, and adds the value to $x = 60$. We know (analytically) that it is: $m = 88$. The second part repeats the same procedure when $\lambda = 1/250$. Notice that the modal value (that is the age at which one is most likely to die) declines to 87.15 from 88, due to the (extra deaths caused by the) λ term. Figure 13.1 plots the two density functions and superimposes vertical lines at the two modal (maximum density) values.

Notice that the (qualitative) shape of the two density curves is quite similar. The elevated (fatter) left-tail of the $\lambda = 0.004$ density is due to the greater number of (accidental) deaths soon-after age $x = 60$.

Finally, while the above discussion (and vertical line) centered on the modal value, that is the age at which death is most likely, the expected age at death ($E[T_x]+x$) is computed via the usual methods that were first described around equation (8.8) in Chap. 8, as well as the (derivations) in Chap. 10.

$$E[T_x] = \int_0^{\infty} f_x(t)dt = \int_0^{\infty} \Pr[T_x \geq t]\, dt = \frac{b\Gamma(-b\lambda, \eta)}{\eta^{-b\lambda} e^{-\eta}}, \tag{13.6}$$

where $\Gamma(.,.)$ is the incomplete Gamma function, and $\eta = e^{(x-m)/b}$, a.k.a. the standardized *Euler age*. Both of these were introduced and used to derive a closed-form expression for the annuity valuation expression, towards the end of Chap. 10. For our purposes here I am simply interested in obtaining some numerical values for $E[T_x]$, so readers can see the impact of λ on the remaining life expectancy. So, here is an **R** representation of Eq. (13.6), replacing η with its explicit value.

```
# Gompertz Makeham Life Expectancy
GMLE<-function(x,lam,m,b){
b*G(-lam*b,exp((x-m)/b))/exp((m-x)*lam-exp((x-m)/b))}
```

Recall that the above script makes use of another user-defined function `G(.)`, which was coded-up, defined, and explained in Chap. 9, when I introduced the lifetime ruin probability. It is the incomplete Gamma function. Finally, here are some values of $E[T_{65}]$ under ($m = 88$, $b = 10$) values, but different values of Makeham's λ.

```
# Age, Makeham, Mode, Dispersion.
GMLE(60,0,88,10)+60
[1] 84.258
GMLE(60,1/2500,88,10)+60
[1] 84.12115
GMLE(60,1/250,88,10)+60
[1] 82.93856
```

As you already knew from prior discussions of the *human longevity* random variable T_x, the *mean* is a few years under the *modal* value. Moreover, increasing the value of λ from zero (pure Gompertz) to 1/2500 and then 1/250 removes no more than a year or two from $E[T_{60}]$. Of course, changing the value of m itself, or even b, will have (much) greater impact on the remaining lifetime random variable T_x. For example, see what happens when $\lambda = 20 \times 10^{-5}$, a typical value, but m is varied from $m = 75$ to $m = 90$. The difference in life expectancy, $E[T_{60}]$ is over 10 years.

```
GMLE(60,20*10^(-5),75,10)+60
[1] 74.14982
GMLE(60,20*10^(-5),80,10)+60
[1] 77.74945
GMLE(60,20*10^(-5),90,10)+60
[1] 85.90368
```

This then brings us to the next question (and section of this chapter). As you know, I used ($m = 88, b = 10$) values for most of the numerical examples in this book. But should everyone—*the healthy and sick, rich and poor*—use the same GM parameters in their own retirement income recipes? How do these numbers vary by gender, country of origin, and wealth? Are there any important patterns or relationships between λ, m, and b around the world?

13.3 Mortality and Longevity Around the World

It should be obvious to you by now that the mortality hazard rate λ_x depends on much *more* than (chronological) age x or gender. Most developed countries have (much) higher life expectancy and lower mortality rates, compared to non-developed countries. In our language, the appropriate (m, b) values depend on where you live. Tables 13.1 and 13.2 are based on raw data from the Human Mortality Database (discussed in Chap. 7). The exact procedure for estimating (λ, m, b) is explained in the papers referenced as [13] and [14] and is also discussed briefly in the final section of this chapter. Here I present a subset of country values to give an indication of the dispersion of longevity around the world. Focus on the last column, the expected age at death, which you should confirm using the `GMLE(.)` function.

There are a number of important items worth emphasizing in these tables, some more obvious than others. First, regardless of the country, females have a higher

Table 13.1 Male: longevity around the world: best GM parameters

Country	Makeham λ	Gompertz: m	Gompertz: b	Hazard λ_{55}	$E[T_{55}]+55$
Australia	63×10^{-5}	86.78	9.16	0.442%	82.4
Canada	32×10^{-5}	86.23	9.73	0.492%	81.9
Lithuania	1×10^{-5}	75.75	14.01	1.744%	74.7
Russia	212×10^{-5}	74.18	13.99	2.161%	73.1
USA	53×10^{-5}	84.36	10.94	0.738%	80.3
UK	59×10^{-5}	85.69	9.55	0.526%	81.4

Data source: HMD 2011, using period mortality rates. Parameter estimates by author

Table 13.2 Female: longevity around the world: best GM parameters

Country	Makeham λ	Gompertz: m	Gompertz: b	Hazard λ_{55}	$E[T_{55}]+55$
Australia	30×10^{-5}	90.40	9.00	0.273%	85.8
Canada	16×10^{-5}	89.91	9.57	0.318%	85.3
Lithuania	38×10^{-5}	85.70	10.45	0.596%	81.4
Russia	153×10^{-5}	84.15	9.67	0.716%	79.7
USA	37×10^{-5}	88.19	10.24	0.458%	83.6
UK	26×10^{-5}	88.85	9.38	0.347%	84.3

Data source: HMD 2011, using period mortality rates. Parameter estimates by author (period) life expectancy $E[T_{55}]$, compared to males. You should be well aware of this gap from the discussion of Canadian cohort life tables back in Chap. 7. Here you see it's a global phenomenon. Second, *averaging* the numbers across all countries, the global modal value is approximately $m = 88$ years, and the dispersion value is roughly $b = 10$ years, but there is quite a bit of variation. For example, a Canadian male who is $x = 55$-years-old can expect to live until the age of $82.4 = E[T_{55}]+55$, whereas a Russian male at the same age can only expect to live to age 73.1. Although these are all period (technically using death rates in the year 2011, and not cohort) expectations, it's a gap of over 10 years, and that's at the age of 55.

Evidently, the *human longevity* random variable really does depend on where you live, in addition to age and gender. Now, this will not come as a surprise to specialists in actuarial science, demography, or pension policy, but might be news to students and non-specialists. And yet, oddly enough, age 65 is consistently used as the canonical *age* of retirement around the world, in many languages, and over many decades. Now sure, every country has its own eligibility ages and rules, and in some (countries and) professions you can draw your pension at earlier ages than others. Nevertheless, it seems that *chronological age 65* is given too much importance in retirement policy. The number of times you have circled the sun—the definition of chronological age—has become an *anchor* that simply isn't very relevant. Stated differently and closer to home, the Gompertz $m = 88$ and $b = 10$ parameters I used in most of the book are the beginning of a proper discussion about longevity risk, not the end. Again, a 65-year-old today (in 2020) is healthier (think cohorts), compared to a 65-year-old in the year 1980. Moreover, if longevity prospects depend on the country in which you live, could they also depend on the *county* within a country? Perhaps human longevity depends on how long your parents lived (genetics) as well as lifestyle, but these factors can be proxied by country and county.

My point—and at the risk of digressing—is as follows. Perhaps legislated retirement ages should depend on your longevity prospects? Perhaps consumers with lower $E[T_x]$ should be entitled to retire—that is withdraw funds or start a defined benefit pension—earlier. But those who are lucky enough to have higher $E[T_x]$, should wait a little bit longer. This idea has actually been promoted by a number of (academic) pension economists and is gaining currency among policymakers as well. Here is the bottom line—in case you didn't sense this already—the most important determinant of $E[T_x]$, as you get into your retirement years, might not be chronological age x. Per Table 13.1, a typical (a.k.a. average) 55-year-old Russian male experiences a hazard rate of $\lambda_{55} = 2.161\%$. In contrast, a 55-year-old Canadian male experiences (a much lower) hazard rate of $\lambda_{55} = 0.492\%$. Conversely, a 55-year-old Canadian male will live 9 years more, on average, compared to the Russian male. Assume you are asked to set an *intelligent drawdown* rate for a retiree, but you could only ask them one question. Would it be their chronological age? Or would it be the country in which they live?

So, perhaps true age should be defined based on mortality rate? In that scheme, a 55-year-old Russian would have a true age that is older than a 55-year-old Canadian.

Now yes, this might sound odd at first—what formula would one use to compute true age?—and I'll get back to this idea in section (13.7). In the meantime, though, there is another interesting factoid lurking in the tables.

13.4 The Compensation Law of Mortality

Although six countries aren't enough to draw any conclusions, please compare the estimated Gompertz mode and dispersion parameters for Lithuanian males ($m = 74.7, b = 14.01$) versus Australian males ($m = 82.4, b = 9.16$). Notice that (in Lithuania) the estimated m value is smaller than in Australia, but the b value is higher. Compare both of those countries to the relevant numbers in the US row. The m value isn't as high as in Australia, but it isn't as low as in Lithuania. The US pair sits somewhere in between the other two, and Fig. 13.2 illustrates this graphically. Stated statistically, there appears to be a *negative* correlation between the dispersion of your remaining lifetime random variable and the modal value. This relationship is often called the *compensation law of mortality.*

The (blue) line within Fig. 13.2, that weaves its way from the upper-left corner to the bottom-right, is the output of a function that maps b values into m values. It satisfies the following expression:

$$m = x^* - b \ln[b\lambda^*], \tag{13.7}$$

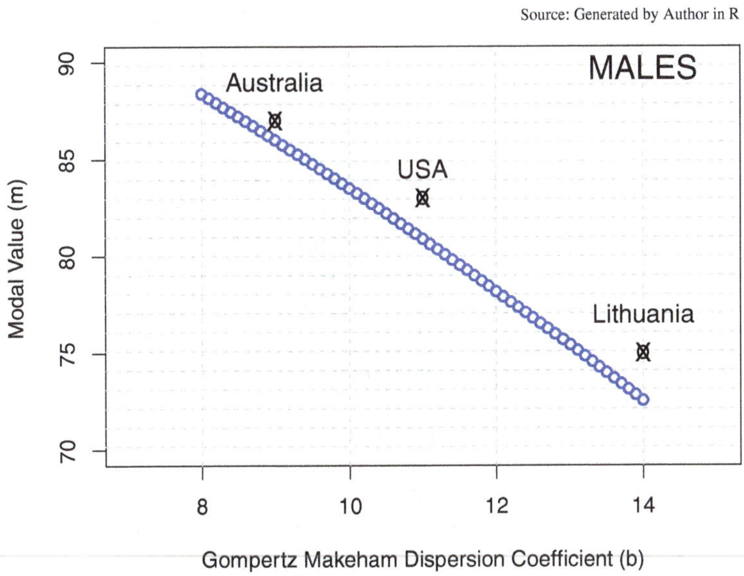

Fig. 13.2 Gompertz–Makeham modal values m versus dispersion b

where x^* and λ^* are two free parameters that pin down the *compensation* law of mortality. As you can see from the figure, the m value is nearly linear in b. Now, obviously the line (or more precisely, the curve) doesn't provide a perfect—or even a good—fit to all the country points around the world. But again, it serves as a reasonable approximation to the natural relationship between the m parameter and (reasonable value of the) b parameter in the world of Gompertz. Now, we don't really need a special function in **R** to implement equation (13.7) and draw the curve in Fig. 13.2, but given its centrality in the next few sections, here it is in **R**,

```
CLAM<-function(b,x_star,lam_star){
x_star-b*(log(b*lam_star))}
```

The user-defined function *CLAM* takes as input the Gompertz–Makeham dispersion coefficient b, as well as the (new) parameter pair (x^*, λ^*). It then maps these three numbers into the appropriate values of m. I'll get back (very soon) to the exact meaning and interpretation of x^* and λ^*, but the former is measured in years (like chronological age x) and the latter is a hazard rate of sorts, similar to λ_x. For now, here are some numerical examples.

When $b = 10$ years, $x^* = 100$ years, and $\lambda^* = 1/3$, the value of `CLAM(10,100,1/3)=87.96` years, which isn't far from the $m = 88$ used in most of the book. In contrast, if you happen to be in a country (or county) where $b = 14$ years (think Russia), which is a higher dispersion coefficient, then `CLAM(14,100,1/3)=78.43` years. Now, this number isn't exactly the Russian value of m in Table 13.1, but it's close enough to be useful. In the other direction, if we happen to be in a country (or county) where the dispersion of longevity is (much lower) at $b = 8$ years, for example, then `CLAM (8,100,1/3)=92.15`. This number is higher by almost 4 years, relative to the $m = 88$ number. To be very clear, different values of x^* and λ^* in the `CLAM(.)` equation will change the results. For example, if $x^* = 105$ (instead of 100) and $\lambda^* = 1/3$, then `CLAM(10,105,1/3)=92.96` years. It's a difference, but not very large. A subtle point that emerges from *compensation* laws of mortality is that death doesn't have as much freedom as you might think. If nature (genetics, environment, or luck) endows you with a large (m) value of life, then your dispersion coefficient b will be smaller. And, vice versa, if you are unfortunate enough to be facing a low modal (m) value of life, then your dispersion—a.k.a. uncertainty, variance, and standard deviation of life—is higher as well. In some sense it's the exact opposite of the classical relationship between *risk and return* in capital markets. You face lower returns (life) and higher risk (in life).

Remember that similar to the much-discussed *Gompertz* law of mortality, the *compensation* law of mortality is a *theory* about the rate at which people die as a function of chronological age. The latter law isn't as widely known (or as successful as) the former law, but like all theories its objective is to fit data and make predictions. And, while observed death rates are generally supportive of the *Gompertz + Makeham* theory over adult ages, *compensation* is more controversial and doesn't fit the (country) data as well. Nevertheless—like all conceptual models—the *compensation* law is a simplified way of *thinking* about the parameters driving mortality.

13.5 Mortality Plateaus

The as of yet unanswered question is: what exactly do the x^* and λ^* represent? To answer this question and shed (more) light on the *compensation* law, please reexamine the basic Gompertz–Makeham equation (13.1) at the very beginning of this chapter. I'll reproduce a version of it here, albeit with a minor addition.

$$\ln[\lambda_x - \lambda] = \begin{cases} \ln[h_0] + gx, & x < x^* \\ \ln[\lambda^*], & x \geq x^*. \end{cases} \tag{13.8}$$

The left-hand side (after subtracting Makeham's constant λ) is the so-called biological hazard rate, but expressed using the (h_0, g) parameters instead of (m, b). Remember that I actually started the discussion of continuous laws of mortality, back in Sect. 8.4, using the (h_0, g) formulation, and it's quite easy to transition between the two. Look back at Eq. (13.1) for a refresher. Notice that: $g = 1/b$, which is a (biological) mortality growth rate, and $\ln[h_0] = \ln[g] - gm$. I like to think of (m, b) as the probabilistic formulation and (h_0, g) as the demographic formulation. It's really six of one versus half-a-dozen of the other, but for the discussion that follows I would rather talk in dozens. The other (more important) tweak in Eq. (13.8) is the *restriction* on the right-hand side, to ages $x \leq x^*$. Technically, after age x^*, the log of the biological hazard rate is now forced to equal λ^*. Stated differently, at some very advanced age x^*, the biological hazard rate $(\lambda_x - \lambda)$ reaches a *plateau* and converges to a constant value: e^{λ^*}. Or, back to the (m, b) formulation, $\ln[\lambda_{x^*} - \lambda] = \ln[1/b] + (x^* - m)/b$, which also preempts equation (13.5).

Figure 13.3 should help you visualize both the previously discussed mortality (i.) compensation effect and (ii.) plateaus, underpinning equation (13.8). The thick middle line is: $\ln[\lambda_x - \lambda]$ and has a slope of g and an intercept of $\ln[h_0]$. That line (again) is the natural logarithm of the biological hazard rate. It's the upper branch in Eq. (13.8). But, if-and-when retirees hit the age of x^*, their biological hazard rate hits λ^* and stays there until they die. The dashed lines in Fig. 13.3 represent hazard rates for sub-groups within the (human) population that are healthier (lower lines) and less healthy (upper lines), but they all converge together at age x^*.

This also implies that if someone reaches age x^*, they actually stop aging! In other words, their hazard rate stops increasing. Warning: This doesn't mean people stop dying, which will continue at very high rates until age ω, by which point everyone is dead. Rather, the constant (biological) hazard rate implies that after reaching age x^*, remaining lifetimes $\{E[T_x], x \geq x^*\}$ are exponentially distributed. They no longer obey the Gompertz–Makeham law. Now, to be transparent and honest, this rather odd sounding mortality plateau is yet another *theory* about old-age

Source: Generated by Author in **R**

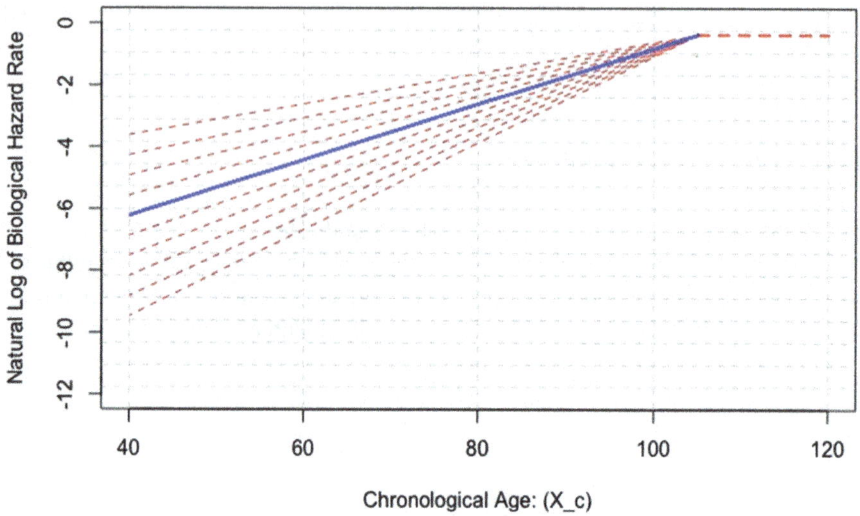

Fig. 13.3 Compensation laws and mortality plateaus: visualizing x^* and λ^*

patterns of *human longevity*. In fact, it's quite controversial among demographers and gerontologists. Even within the community of researchers who do believe in some universal mortality plateau, there is quite a bit of debate about the exact age x^* at which it comes into effect in humans (and even rodents). Some scientists claim x^* is in the mid-to-late 90s, while others believe it kicks in during the post-centenarian years. Yet others claim that (x^*, λ^*) vary by personal circumstances and there are no universal (global) values. Alas, one of the problems with testing this particular theory is the current absence of (reliable) data on mortality for centenarians.

Lest readers worry I have deviated far beyond recipes, the point of this discussion was to shed light on the two (rather mysterious) parameters (x^*, λ^*) in Eq. (13.7). It governed the natural relationship between Gompertz m and b, which do have much to say about human longevity and retirement income planning. In sum, x^* is slightly north of age 100, and $\ln[\lambda^*] = -1$, or $\lambda^* = 1/e$, per the apex of the various dashed lines in Fig. 13.3.

13.6 Human Longevity: Rich vs. Poor

The pattern described in Fig. 13.3, that is the negative relationship between initial mortality rates h_0 and mortality growth rates g, is observed beyond geographic regions around the world. In fact, when mortality rates are collected based on income, a similar pattern is observed. While I'm weary of going too far down the socio-demographic rabbit hole, in this section I would like to remind readers

Table 13.3 U.S. death rates per thousand, based on income percentile

	Male: $1000q_x$			Female: $1000q_x$		
Income group	Age = 40	Age = 50	Age = 60	Age = 40	Age = 50	Age = 60
Lowest (1st pct.)	5.8	12.5	22.1	4.3	8.0	12.8
25th percentile	2.0	4.5	10.9	1.2	2.7	5.9
Median (50th pct.)	1.2	2.9	7.3	0.8	2.0	4.5
75th percentile	0.8	1.8	4.9	0.5	1.3	3.5
Highest (100th pct.)	0.6	1.1	2.8	0.3	0.8	2.2

Data source: Journal of the American Medical Association (JAMA)
See articles referenced as [2] and [13] for details and methodology

and emphasize that picking suitable values of (λ, m, b) depends on more than just country of origin. In fact, wealth and income are just as important. Table 13.3 provides a summary of data collected a few years ago in the USA and published in the *Journal of the American Medical Association* (which from here on the JAMA dataset). The details are explained in the article cited as [2], which is one of the most comprehensive attempts (ever) to measure the relationship between household income and mortality rates, based on administrative tax fillings.

In particular, Table 13.3 displays death rates (q_x) for males and females in the USA as a function of various ages and income percentile. These represent realized mortality rates per 1000 people during the period 2001–2014. Like all 2-year death rates, the numbers listed are the ratio of observed deaths at a given age (say age 50) divided by the total number of people alive at that age (say 50). These rates aren't actuarial projections and are based on over 1.4 billion person-year observations and close to 6.7 million deaths. Again, the methodology is described in [2] and the entire dataset of mortality rates as a function of *income percentile* was made available as part of the JAMA article. They collected (lagged 2-year income) death rates for ages $x = 40$ to $x = 63$, after which they employed a *Gompertz* model to project q_x at later ages.

The death rates in Table 13.3 contain a number of insights that echo takeaways from Tables 13.1 and 13.2. Let's begin with mortality rates for median income levels. At the age of 40, a total of 1.2 per 1000 (median income) males died, whereas for (median income) females the rate was only 0.8 per 1000 individuals.

Stated differently, the 1-year death rate for (median income) males at the age of 40 is 50% higher than it is for females, which naturally leads to a lower life expectancy for (median income) males. This is to be expected. Continuing along the same row, at the age of 50 the male mortality rate is now higher at 2.9 per 1000 and for females it is 2.0, where I have dispensed with the phrases 1-year and median income for the sake of brevity. At the age of 60, the rates are 7.3 (males) and 4.5 (females), respectively. This is simply the effect of aging and the exponential growth in death (mortality) rates per the Gompertz law. Notice how the excess of male-to-female mortality shrinks from 150% (=1.2/0.8) at the age of 40, to 145% (=2.9/2.0) at the age of 50. This isn't quite a downward trend (at least in the table), since at the

Table 13.4 U.S. longevity by income percentile: best-fitting GM parameters

Income group	Makeham λ	Gompertz: m	Gompertz: b	Hazard λ_{55}	$E[T_{55}]+55$
Male.					
Lowest (1st)	1×10^{-5}	77.47	16.59	1.653%	76.89
Median (50th)	26×10^{-5}	87.23	10.12	0.478%	82.82
Highest (100th)	22×10^{-5}	93.42	8.79	0.183%	88.75
Female.					
Lowest (1st)	34×10^{-5}	85.95	17.12	1.050%	82.83
Median (50th)	15×10^{-5}	91.27	10.10	0.317%	86.49
Highest (100th)	7×10^{-5}	96.06	9.07	0.140%	91.26

Data source: JAMA, with thanks to Ariel Sosnovsky. $E[T_x]$ computed using `GMLE(.)`

age of 60 the excess death is back to 162% (=7.3/4.5), but is yet another hint of a *compensation* law.

For a U.S. male in the lowest-income percentile, the death rate q_{50} at the age of 50 is over four times higher at 12.5 deaths per 1000, versus 2.9 at the median income. In stark contrast, a 50-year-old male at the highest-income percentile experiences a mortality rate of only 1.1 per 1000. This is less than half the median (income) rate. Stated differently, the range in mortality rates between the 1st percentile and 100th percentile is (12.5/1.1) or over eleven to one. To those who haven't seen such numbers before they might seem extreme, but they are by no means original or novel. But, back to the topic of *compensation* laws of mortality. Notice how the ratio of death rates between the lowest-income percentile (top of the table) and the highest-income percentile (bottom of the table) shrinks or declines over age x. For example, for males at the age of 40 the ratio of worst-to-best is 9.67 (=5.8/0.6), whereas at the age of 60 the ratio falls to 7.89 (=22.1/2.8). The same decline (in relative rates) is observed for females. At age 40 the ratio of worst-to-best is 14 (=4.2/0.3), but by age 60 it shrinks to a multiple of 5.82 (12.8/2.2). Disparate mortality rates converge with age as illustrated in Fig. 13.3. And finally, Table 13.4 displays the best-fitting Gompertz–Makeham parameters, for different income levels, similar to tables for individual countries. Notice the over 10-year gap in the expected remaining lifetime $E[T_{55}]$, between the highest- and lowest-income percentiles in the USA. Alas, this is *mortality heterogeneity*, even within a country.

13.7 A Longevity Risk Adjustment to Your Age

Whether it be the location or size of your wallet, it's quite clear that chronological age x isn't enough information to project *human longevity*. Indeed, you might be $x = 55$-years-old, but your mortality hazard rate λ_x (or death rate q_{55}) might be higher or lower, depending on (1) what country you live in, (2) your wealth and income, in addition to (3) your overall state of health. Simply put, the number of

Source: Generated by Author in **R**

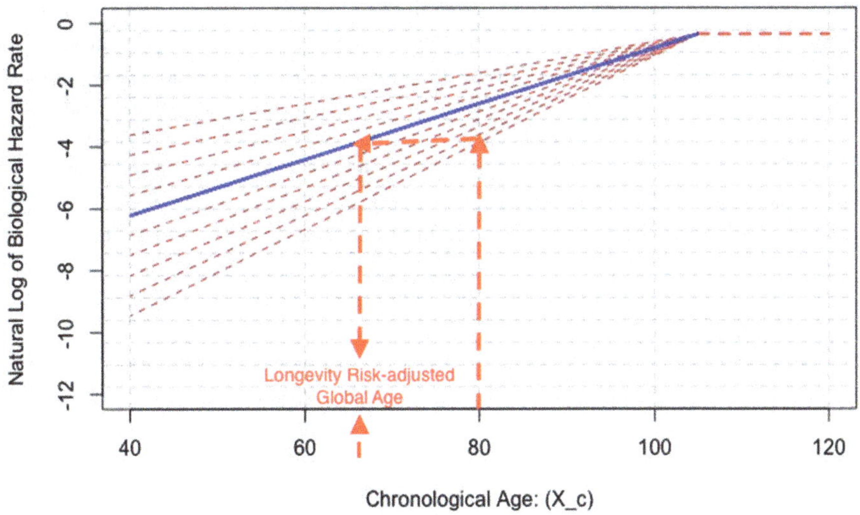

Fig. 13.4 Longevity risk-adjusted age: from chronological x to $x(1+\beta)$

times you have circled the sun doesn't mean as much as you think. So, although Benjamin Gompertz (in 1825) [7] was correct in asserting that mortality rates double between x and $(x + b\ln[2])$, your *current* mortality rate depends on much more than chronological age x. This then raises the following question: *can one redefine age to account for longevity risk?* Now, I explored alternative measures of aging, such as *biological age*, in the article cited as [14]. So in this section I would simply like to give a brief overview on how to adjust ages for *relative* longevity risk. Figure 13.4 is a graphical illustration of the adjustment. I'm solving for age $x(1+\beta)$, whose hazard rate using global average parameters is equal to the hazard rate when this person's chronological age is x. The parameter β does the risk adjustment. A $\beta < 0$ makes you "younger" and $\beta > 0$ makes you "older." Formally, I solve for β in the equation.

$$\lambda_{x(1+\beta)}(\hat{\lambda}, \hat{h}_0, \hat{g}) = \lambda_x(\lambda, h_0, g) \tag{13.9}$$

The parameters $\hat{\lambda}$, $\hat{h}_0$, and $\hat{g}$ are the global averages of all the country-specific λ, h_0, and g values. Now, after quite a bit of manipulation, all of which is carefully described in the article cited as [14], the longevity risk-adjusted age: $x(1+\beta)$ can be expressed as:

$$x(1+\beta) = x^* + \ln\left[e^{g(x-x^*)} - (\hat{\lambda} - \lambda)/\lambda^*\right]/\hat{g}. \tag{13.10}$$

This expression will collapse to: $\beta = (1 - g/\hat{g})(x^* - x)/x$ when the Makeham constants $\hat{\lambda} = \lambda$, i.e. the *local* accidental death rate is equal to the *global* rate. In fact, considering that $(\hat{\lambda} - \lambda)/\lambda^*$ is much smaller than $e^{g(x-x^*)}$ (because λ^* is much greater than λ or $\hat{\lambda}$), the contribution of $(\hat{\lambda} - \lambda)/\lambda^*$ can be safely ignored and $\beta \approx (1 - g/\hat{g})(x^* - x)/x$, regardless of the specific values of the Makeham constant. And, since by definition $(x^* - x)/x$ is always positive, it should be easy to see the impact of the local g relative to the global $\hat{g}$, on the required longevity risk adjustment β. If $g < \hat{g}$, and you are aging more slowly, then $\beta > 0$ and you are *older* than your chronological age. Vice versa, if $g > \hat{g}$, and you (or more specifically your country) are aging faster than the global average, then $\beta < 0$ and $x(1+\beta) < x$. Congratulations: Your longevity risk-adjusted age is lower than your chronological age.

The relevant script in **R**, based on the full equation (13.10). The function solves for the longevity risk-adjusted age $x(1 + \beta)$, as opposed to the longevity-risk adjustment β, but one can easily convert from the former to the latter. Also, be mindful (and careful) of the difference between `lam hat`, which is the global average accidental death rate $\hat{\lambda}$, and `lam star`, which is the biological mortality plateau. And, don't confuse either of those two with plain old λ, which is your own (local, unique) Makeham accidental constant.

```
LRAG<-function(x,x_star,g_hat,g,lam_hat,lam,lam_star){
x_star+(1/g_hat)*
log(exp(g*(x-x_star))-(lam_hat-lam)/lam_star)}
```

Here are some numerical examples that should help develop a better intuition for (what I defined as) your longevity risk-adjusted age $x(1 + \beta)$. Assume that you are $x = 55$-years-old (chronologically) and that the global (population) average mortality growth rate is $g = 1/b = 0.10$. Let's examine two situations. In the first, your $g > 10\%$ and in the second $g < 10\%$. Here are the results.

```
# You are aging FASTER than average.
LRAG(55,100,0.1,0.11,25*10^(-5),1*10^(-5),exp(-1))
[1] 49.53378
# You are aging SLOWER than average.
LRAG(55,100,0.1,0.09,25*10^(-5),1*10^(-5),exp(-1))
[1] 59.11836
```

In the first case, your longevity risk-adjusted age drops from $x = 55$ to $x = 49.5$, per Eq. (13.10). Why? Because your unique (personal) hazard rate is lower than the population average. How do I know it's lower? Because $g > \hat{g}$ is higher. You are aging faster than average (meaning your chronological age is higher than the average person with the same hazard rate)—which might sound awful and to your detriment—but according to the compensation law it's good news. This implies that you are on one of the lower lines (in Fig. 13.4) and your age is adjusted downwards.

In contrast, in the second example with $g = 9\% < \hat{g} = 10\%$, you are aging more slowly than average. This might sound like good news, but the slope of your

Source: Author in **R**.

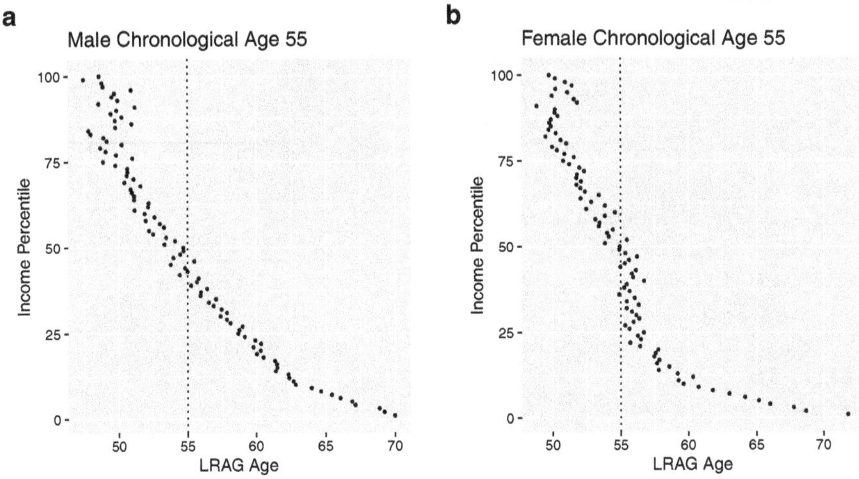

Fig. 13.5 Longevity risk-adjusted age, based on income percentiles in the USA

line (again, see Fig. 13.4) is lower than average, placing your (log, biological) hazard rate line above average. Ergo, you are older. In fact, your longevity risk-adjusted age is $59.11 = 55(1 + \beta)$, and you are $\beta = 7.48\%$ older (than you think).

Now, I fully admit that this is a different way of thinking about and presenting mortality information. After all, this is just another way of saying that your life expectancy is higher/lower depending on what line you "live on" in Fig. 13.4. That said, I do think that presenting and discussing personal longevity prospects as a risk-adjusted age has some incremental (behavioral) benefits. So, if this idea appeals to you, please see the article cited as [14] for more details and information. Here I simply present a summary Fig. 13.5 of the longevity risk-adjusted age, applied to the above-noted JAMA data on income percentiles in the USA. Notice how the adjusted age, $55(1 + \beta)$, ranges from 50 to as high as 70, at the lowest income levels. Alas, poverty makes you older—via higher mortality rates.

13.8 The Estimation Algorithm

The longevity risk-adjusted age is based on the (x^*, λ^*) plateau, as well as the Makeham constant λ and mortality growth rate g, for both *local* and *global* groups. In this section I provide a high-level **R**-script that can be used to estimate the *local* parameter pair (λ, g), which can then be used to compute global values. Although `LRAG(.)` doesn't require the m value, it's a by-product of the estimation procedure.

```
x<-35:95
# Minimum and Maximum Regression Age
qx<-HMD2011$ABC[36:96]
lambda_max<-min(qx)*10^5-1
# Accidental must be less than Biological Hazard Rate
gap<-c()
for (i in 1:lambda_max){
lambda<-i*10^(-5)
# Start from lowest lambda value and increase.
y<-log(log(1/(1-qx))-lambda)
# This is the canonical Gompertz regression
fit<-lm(y~x)
gap[i]<-sigma(fit)}
# Vector of all regression standard errors
lambda_makeham<-which.min(gap)*10^(-5)
# This is the error minimizing value.
y<-log(log(1/(1-qx))-lambda_makeham)
# Final pick for the regression.
fit<-lm(y~x)
g<-as.numeric(fit$coefficients[2])
lnh<-as.numeric(fit$coefficients[1]-log((exp(g)-1)/g))
lnh;g;lambda_makeham*10^5
summary(fit)
```

This procedure is described in much greater detail within the article referenced as [14], but the essence is to start with a country (or income percentile) qx vector from the HMD (or JAMA dataset). The procedure then starts with a very low value of λ, which is the accidental death rate, and then estimates a regression of the (transformed) death rate q_x on the chronological age x, estimating the mortality growth rate (slope) g and the log initial mortality rate (intercept) $\ln[h_0]$. The procedure then computes the standard error, for the given λ, and repeats the process with a slightly larger value of λ. The algorithm continues until the largest possible value of λ, bounded by the smallest value of q_x. Finally, the procedure selects or picks the value of λ with the smallest standard error, which together with the relevant $(\ln[h_0], g)$ is declared the best-fitting Gompertz–Makeham parameters for that particular sub-group.

This is then repeated for all countries (or income percentiles), creating a large set of unique $\{\lambda, \ln[h_0], g\}$ values. After this is done, a second regression procedure is estimated to obtain the best-fitting *compensation* line, per Fig. 13.6. The arrow pointing to $L = \ln[\lambda^*]$ is the value of the mortality plateau, and the slope of that line is the estimated x^*. For more on *why*, see [14].

Source: Generated by Author in **R**

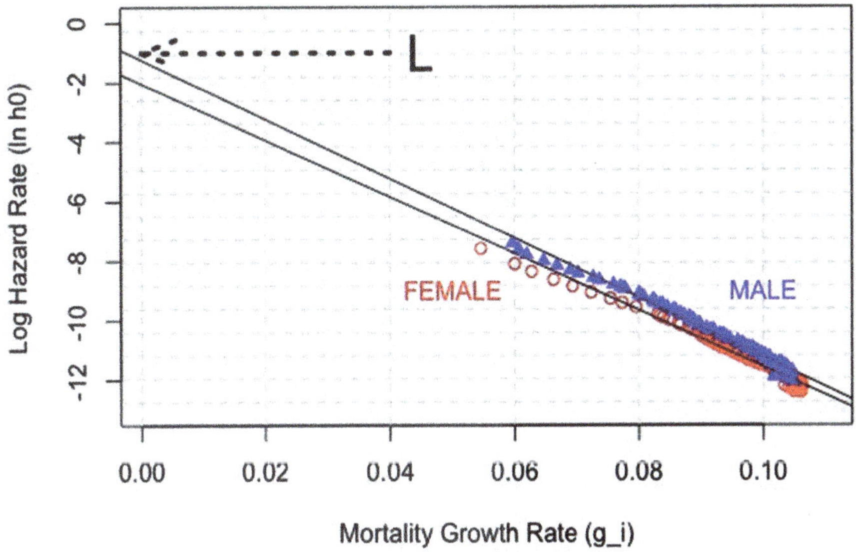

Fig. 13.6 Mortality plateau using $\ln[h_0]$ and g. Point $L = \ln[\lambda^*]$

13.9 Final Comments

- I am sympathetic to the view of some readers who might feel this chapter went far afield from the book's mandate to provide recipes for retirement income planning. Nevertheless, the fact is that mortality *heterogeneity* and the *compensation* law of mortality have important implications for the valuation, pricing, and utility of annuities—among other implications. I elaborated on this idea in the article cited as [13], but the main takeaway is that retirees with greater longevity uncertainty—that is higher b—are more likely to appreciate the risk pooling benefits of life annuities. In other words, although retirees who aren't expected to live very long might think that they won't benefit from (additional) annuity income, their higher standard deviation of life increases their subjective utility from annuities.
- For more on the subject of mortality plateaus, and whether or not they exist in humans (versus rodents), please see the articles cited as [1, 4, 5]. See also the recently published article cited as [16] for more on the actuarial implications of the compensation law of mortality. That article makes the argument that there isn't as much freedom as one thinks (two free parameters) in the Gompertz model, if indeed there is a compensating effect. In fact, taken to the extreme, a

jump in mortality (during a virus, for example) which increases the entire **Term Structure of Mortality** might be associated with a reduction in the slope g or an increase in the dispersion coefficient b.

- For more on the concept of biological age, as well as heterogenous mortality and how it affects life-cycle models in economics, see [9–11, 19]. In particular, see references [3, 6, 8, 12, 15] for the various models use to analyze heterogeneity and well as the economic implications.
- For more on adjusting the definition of age (to account for inflation) and other measures, see the work by Shoven and Goda [18] as well as the recent book by Sanderson and Scherbov [17]. Finally, for an interesting discussion of subjective versus objective age, see [20].

Questions and Problems

13.1 Create a series of four (4) plots of the probability density function (PDF) of Gompertz–Makeham, using the `par(mfrow=c(2,2))` command, for $x = 60$. Use the parameter values $\lambda = 3 \times 10^{-5}$, and $m = 75$, $m = 85$, and $b = 8$, $b = 12$. Compute $E[T_x]$ for all four combinations, using `GMLE(.)`, and discuss the impact of m and b on life expectancy.

13.2 Derive an expression for the number of (calendar) years it takes your mortality rate to triple under a pure Gompertz law (i.e. assuming the Makeham constant $\lambda = 0$), assuming $b = 1/g = 10$.

13.3 Using the *compensation* law of mortality, and the `CLAM(.)` function, please compute the range of possible value of m, assuming that $b \in [8, 12]$, that $x^* \in [95, 105]$ and that $\ln[\lambda^*] \in [-2, 0]$. In other words, what are highest and lowest possible values of m?

13.4 Please download 1-year death rates from the HMD, for the period 2011 in Australia and Lithuania (male or female) and use the algorithm in section #13.8 to estimate the best-fitting Gompertz–Makeham values of $(\lambda, \ln[h_0], g)$. Convert the numbers from the *demographic* reference frame (h, g) to the *probabilistic* reference frame using (m, b). Finally, compare your estimates to those in Table 13.1 or Table 13.2.

13.5 Assuming that $x^* = 100$ and that $\ln[\lambda^*] = -1$, which recall are the assumed coordinates of the mortality plateau, use the `LRAG(.)` function to compute the longevity risk-adjusted age of an $x = 55$-year-old Russian versus Australian. Please average the two corresponding (i.e. the Russian and the Australian) values of λ and g, to obtain the required (average) $\hat{\lambda}$ and $\hat{g}$, which you need for the formula. Who is "older" the 55-year-old Russian or the 55-year-old Australian? Explain.

References

1. Barbi, E., Lagona, F., Marsili, M., Vaupel, J. W., & Wachter, K. W. (2018). The plateau of human mortality: Demography of longevity pioneers. *Science, 360*, 1459–1461.
2. Chetty, R., Stepner, M., Abraham, S., Lin, S., Scuderi, B., Turner, N., et al. (2016). The association between income and life expectancy in the United States, 2001–2014. *Journal of the American Medical Association, 315*(16), 1750–1766.
3. Deaton, A. (2016). On death and money: History, facts and explanations. *Journal of the American Medical Association, 315*(16), 1703–1705.
4. Gavrilov, L. A., & Gavrilova, N. S. (1991). *The biology of lifespan: A quantitative approach*. Reading: Harwood Academic Publishers.
5. Gavrilov, L. A., & Gavrilova, N. S. (2001). The reliability theory of aging and longevity. *Journal of Theoretical Biology, 213*(4), 527–545.
6. Goldman, D. P., & Orszag, P. R. (2014). The growing gap in life expectancy: Using the future elderly model to estimate implications for social security and medicare. *American Economic Review, 104*(5), 230–233.
7. Gompertz, B. (1825). On the nature of the function expressive of the law of human mortality and on a new mode of determining the value of life contingencies. *Philosophical Transactions of the Royal Society of London, 115*, 513–583.
8. Holzman, R., Alonso-Garcia, J., Labit-Hardy, H., & Villegas, A. M. (2017). NDC schemes and heterogeneity in longevity: Proposals for redesign. *ARC Centre of excellence in population ageing research, working Paper No. 2017/18*.
9. Huang, H., Milevsky, M. A., & Salisbury, T. S. (2017). Retirement spending and biological age. *Journal of Economic Dynamics and Control, 84*, 58–76.
10. Jylhava, J., Pederson, N. L., & Hagg, S. (2017). Biological age predictors. *EBioMedicine, 10*, 29–36.
11. Meyricke, R., & Sherris, M. (2013). The determinants of mortality heterogeneity and implications for pricing annuities. *Insurance: Mathematics and Economics, 53*, 379–387.
12. Milligan, K., & Schirle, T. (2018). The evolution of longevity: Evidence from Canada. *National bureau of economic research, working paper # 24929*.
13. Milevsky, M. A. (2020). Swimming with wealth sharks: Longevity, volatility and the value of risk pooling. *Journal of Pension Economics and Finance, 19*(2), 217–246. https://doi.org/10.1017/S1474747219000040
14. Milevsky, M. A. (2020). Calibrating Gompertz in reverse: What is your longevity risk-adjusted global age? *Insurance: Mathematics and Economics, 92*, 147–161.
15. Peltzman, S. (2009). Mortality inequality. *Journal of Economic Perspectives, 23*(4), 175–190.
16. Richards, S. J. (2020). A Hermite-spline model of post-retirement mortality. *Scandinavian Actuarial Journal, 2020*(2), 110–127.
17. Sanderson, W. C., & Scherbov, S. (2019). *Prospective longevity: A new vision for population aging*. Cambridge, Massachusetts: Harvard University Press.
18. Shoven J. B., & Goda, G. S. (2008). Adjusting government policies for age inflation. *National bureau of economic research, working paper #13476*.
19. Su, S., & Sherris, M. (2012). Heterogeneity of Australian population mortality and implications for a viable life annuity market. *Insurance: Mathematics and Economics, 51*, 322–332.
20. Ye, Z., & Post, T. (2020). What age do you feel? Subjective age identity and economic behaviors. *Journal of Economic Behavior and Organization, 173*, 322–341.

Chapter 14
Exotic Annuities for Longevity Risk

This chapter motivates—and offers recipes for valuing—a unique type of life annuity that is contingent on the performance of a stock market index or portfolio. It is christened a *ruin-contingent life annuity* (RCLA), a contingent claim that is also the foundation of all variable annuities (VAs) with guaranteed withdrawal benefits. Like an advanced life delayed annuity (ALDA), the RCLA begins making payments at a later date, but it is only triggered when an underlying reference portfolio hits zero, a.k.a. ruin. This chapter explains why an RCLA might be a desirable financial instrument for retirees and compares its (cheaper) theoretical value to (more expensive) life annuities.

14.1 Functions Used and Defined

14.1.1 Sample of Native R Functions Used

- No new **R** functions introduced in this chapter.

14.1.2 User-Defined R Functions

- `RCLA(x,m,b,xi,sigma,r,N)` values a ruin-contingent life annuity.

M. A. Milevsky, *Retirement Income Recipes in R*, Use R!,
https://doi.org/10.1007/978-3-030-51434-1_14

14.2 Motivation for Considering Exotics

Here is where we stand, going into the penultimate chapter of the book. First, the *portfolio longevity* random variable L_ξ, formally defined in Chap. 5, depends on (projected, forecasted) investment returns, as well the withdrawal rate: ξ. And, a very bad sequence of investment returns—similar to what was experienced in the first quarter of the year 2020—can have a dramatic (and non-linear) impact on portfolio longevity, as discussed in Chap. 6. This is the main reason for introducing *intelligent drawdown* schemes, that is avoiding a fixed ξ altogether, as argued in Chap. 11. Likewise, the randomness of portfolio longevity L_ξ (a.k.a. the dispersion of outcomes in a systematic withdrawal plan) illustrates the benefit of pension annuities (or just plain life annuities), discussed in Chap. 12. In addition to the behavioral (forced savings) component, once you actually reach your retirement years they provide income for life, regardless of how long you live. This then brings us to the second random variable at the core of this book, T_x.

Per the discussion in Chap. 13, the parameters governing *human longevity* depend on more than chronological age x. That random variable depends on your biology, genetics, country, and county of residence, as well as your wealth and income. This then implies that the variation in life expectancy for a typical $x = 55$-year-old can be as high as 20 years, depending on these background factors. Using the language of the Gompertz law of mortality from Chap. 8, the underlying (m, b) parameters, which are the mode and dispersion coefficients, are personal. Or, stated bluntly, healthy 55-year-olds are described by higher m values, and less-healthy 55-year-olds should use a lower m, in their retirement income recipes. Likewise, we learned from Chap. 13 that higher m values are associated with lower b values, and vice versa, which followed from the *compensation* law of mortality. All of this came under the label of *mortality heterogeneity*.

Practically speaking, it implies that valuing life annuities (a.k.a. defined benefit pensions) is more complicated than plugging some `(x,v,m,b)` parameters into the `GILA(.)` function. So, what (m, b) should be used? Yes, for most of the book I assumed (with ample warning) that $(m = 88, b = 10)$, but the true values—and especially the m parameter—can vary by 10–15 years. Note that this isn't only a philosophical question around valuation ("what is my pension worth?"). It's a pricing problem as well. Namely, how much should an insurance company charge (and you pay) for a life annuity? Do they assume a high value of m, for example, 90 years? Or should they assume a low value, perhaps 75 years? Clearly, if they want to be safe and charge enough to cover the risk, cover their capital and set aside ample reserves, they have to assume (the worst, from their perspective) and price the annuity using a high m. This of course makes the annuity less appealing (i.e. too expensive, lower utility) for those with lower m values, who might then decide to forgo the life annuity all together. Taken to the extreme, the insurance company might then be "left" with the very healthy (large m) buyers, which induces an even higher value of m in their pricing, etc.

Here is the bottom line: *Life annuities are great at hedging longevity risk, but they can get very expensive.* In fact, the current economic environment where interest rates and bond yields are abnormally low makes these things worse. To remind you of how expensive pensions can become depending on parameter "assumption," here is a numerical example using the familiar `GILA(.)` function.

```
expensive<-1000*12*GILA(65,0.01,92,8); expensive
[1] 247122.5
cheap<-1000*12*GILA(65,0.04,84,12); cheap
[1] 141831.1
(expensive-cheap)/cheap
[1] 0.742371
```

Notice that when $m = 92$ years (great health, good country, nice income), and a correspondingly lower dispersion coefficient $b = 8$, the cost of a $1000 monthly pension annuity is $247,123, when interest rates are at 1%. In contrast, the unhealthy $m = 84$, with corresponding $b = 12$ and $r = 4\%$, would only have to pay $141,831 up-front for the same pension annuity. The difference of over 74% is due to both longevity prospects and interest rates. None of this should come as a surprise, and these numbers were reported (and emphasized) in Chap. 10, as well as the early Chap. 2, using the very basic `RGOA(.)` function. My point is that true life annuities are wonderful, but can be (very) expensive. Indeed, full *pensionization* is great in theory, but might be terribly impractical in the real world. So, this chapter is about alternative annuity-like products, a.k.a. exotic annuities, that are cheaper. Of course, you get what you pay for in capital markets so there are downsides to these as well. In due time I'll discuss the good, the bad, and the ugly.

14.3 The Retirement Risk that Really Worries Me

At the risk of flogging a dead horse, here it is again. The two greatest sources of financial and economic risk in the *retirement income* phase are related to (1) the uncertainty of human longevity (a.k.a. your true age) and (2) stochastic portfolio returns and sequence of risk, which impacts portfolio longevity. Of course, retirees face other **Non-quantifiable Uncertainties**, such as the unpredictable cost of healthcare, personal inflation rates, family members with unexpected needs (during a virus), or income taxes (once a virus has been defeated). Now, some of these other sources of uncertainty are smaller in scale, more predictable in magnitude, or can be directly traced to T_x and L_ξ. If by chance your investment portfolio happens to (get lucky and) earn extraordinarily high returns, you will likely have more than enough money to cover your obligations and costs. Likewise, if your personal longevity or lifespan is much shorter than average, then as ghastly as it sounds, with hindsight you didn't need that much financial capital. With many other

Source: Generated by Author

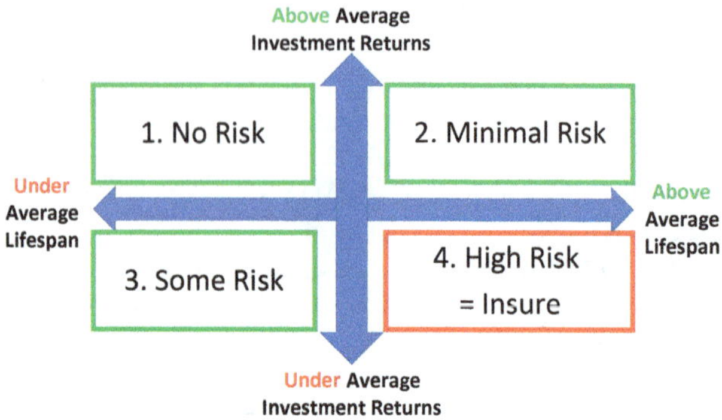

Fig. 14.1 The four quadrants of quantifiable risk in retirement

non-quantifiable uncertainties, there really is not much I (and my scripts) can do about it, sadly.

Conceptually, this two-dimensional space or continuum can be envisioned in a graphical manner. The human longevity and financial market vectors (or lines) partition a square into four distinct quadrants. Look carefully at Fig. 14.1. The east side represents above-average longevity and the west side represents the opposite, namely an early death. Living to exactly your average lifespan $E[T_x]$ places you directly in the middle, but due to the large standard deviation of life $SD[T_x]$, you always end up on either side of the vertical line. Now, focusing on the portfolio performance, the north represents your investments achieving above-average returns and the south is, as the word suggests, under-average performance. Using the notation and language of Chap. 5 and letting $\tilde{v}$ denote a random rate of return over the first few decades of retirement, the north region is where $\tilde{v} > E[\tilde{v}]$ and the south region is where $\tilde{v} < E[\tilde{v}]$.

Most financial plans are geared or calibrated to the intersection of these two lines, which represent an average life (e.g. 85 years) and average returns after fees and inflation (e.g. 2.5% real). Of course, realized numbers will be all over the chart or the two-dimensional plane in the figure. A financial mathematician would describe the two dimensions as being orthogonal to each other or statistically independent uncertainties. But, and here is the important point, from a risk management perspective both of these *risks should be insured.* Basically, there are four broad scenarios that can take place over the course of your retirement, each with approximately a one-quarter chance of happening. And, more relevantly, each with a very different economic implication.

14.3.1 Four Economic Outcomes

I'll go through each one of these four quadrants in Fig. 14.1 separately, and you will eventually see how they relate to exotic annuity options and longevity insurance. The northeast quadrant represents a prosperous retirement in which you live (much) longer than average, so $T_x > E[T_x]$, and realized portfolio returns are well above average: $\tilde{v} > E[\tilde{v}]$. I would (vigorously) argue that your retirement risk exposure or the negative implications of this *state of nature* are minimal. Hence, there is no need to insure or protect against this outcome. It's a blessing in two dimensions. Yes, an unexpectedly long retirement, $T_x > E[T_x]$ is expensive, but strong investment returns should be able to sustain spending, withdrawals, and drawdowns.

In the second quadrant, to the northwest, the portfolio has performed well above the expected average, so $\tilde{v} > E[\tilde{v}]$, but your lifespan was under average, so $T_x < E[T_x]$. Of course, this knowledge is only gained in hindsight after the fact. And, while I obviously can't describe the northwest outcome as a blessing in any dimension, the fact is that it isn't (or wasn't, in hindsight) a costly retirement scenario. Therefore, it doesn't require insurance protection. The money lasted for as long as you did, or $L_\xi > T_x$. The limited years of your income needs were met.

Moving to the southwest region, the portfolios haven't performed as well as expected. Using our language, $\tilde{v} < E[\tilde{v}]$, and at the same time $T_x < E[T_x]$. Poor returns *might have* resulted in some financial stress, but the reduced longevity (i.e. you died early, so to speak) means that the actuarial present value of this outcome won't be as costly. To be clear, the third quadrant does lead to some risk for the sustainability of retirement income, but it's relatively manageable.

Ok. We now get to the main point of this entire exercise. The most stressful retirement quadrant is in the southeast. This fourth quadrant represents the unpleasant outcome in which your lifespan T_x was above average—with the associated higher costs of retirement—but market returns weren't enough to support these longer periods of withdrawals. It is represented by the red box (for those of you seeing this in color). In my opinion this is an outcome asking for a longevity insurance solution. It's the rationale for exotic annuities.

14.3.2 Protect Against the Worst Quadrant

Up to this point in the discussion of life annuities and the `GILA(.)` function, I focused on one dimension, longevity. Pure life annuity products, whether they are *immediate* or *deferred*, offer protection against the entire right side of Fig. 14.1, the north as well as the south. Likewise, although I only discussed put options briefly at the end of Chap. 6, those sorts of strategies would protect the east as well as the west of Fig. 14.1.

But both of these conventional and well-understood products, stand-alone puts and stand-alone life annuities (are more expensive, and) generate unnecessary overprotection. Yes, they are both simpler, more transparent, and easier to explain, but might not be as efficient. My point is: *be surgical with your longevity insurance.*

As you read the next few sections you might ponder and ask yourself: *why?* Well, keep in mind Fig. 14.1. The value proposition of market-contingent longevity insurance, which I'll describe in just a moment, resides in the unique combination of two-dimensional protection embedded in its DNA. Such a product will implicitly protect against two distinct risks, each of which on its own would likely be more expensive.

14.4 Introducing Ruin-Contingent Life Annuities (RCLA)

Imagine the following variation of the deferred life annuity, `GDLA(.)`, a.k.a. a_1. I use the word *imagine* because this product doesn't quite exist (yet), but is the basis for—and embedded within—more complex variable annuities (VA). Recall from the discussion in Chap. 10, that in contrast to an *immediate* life annuity, the *deferred* version doesn't begin payments until some later date and age. For example, you might currently be $x = 50$ and a deferred life annuity could start 30 years later, at age $y = 80$. As I mentioned, I purchased one of those. If-and-when I get to the age of 80, the insurance company on the other side of this wager—or perhaps better described as a financial hedge—will provide me with an income annuity for the rest of my life. To be clear, the trigger for this payout is *staying alive.* That's it. There are no other qualifications, criteria, or requirements. From the perspective of Fig. 14.1, the protection pays off in two (2) of the four (4) quadrants, the entire east side, which is a few years after I reach my life expectancy. However, as I argued in the prior section, an even better and cheaper annuity would be one in which the payment is made (to me) if my portfolio declines during the 20–25 years between purchase and the income start date, *and* I am alive. Alas, that is precisely the security I would like you to imagine; a *deferred* annuity that is triggered, not at some pre-specified age $(x + \tau)$, but at a *random* portfolio ruin time L_ξ. Let's think about how this financial innovation might work.

Now, to make this a viable (mass market) product the *ruin-contingent life annuity* (RCLA) would have to be based on a transparent index, which I'll label the reference portfolio index (RPI). It would be quite difficult (although not inconceivable) to have an insurance company insure the performance of my own personal (unique, small) portfolio. The underlying RPI would be initiated at an artificial level of \$100, for example, and consist of a broad portfolio of stocks (for example, the SP500 index). However at the end of each month the RPI would be adjusted for total investment returns (plus or minus), *and* by a fixed cash outflow (minus) that reduces the value of the RPI. The payments could be constant in nominal terms or real terms.

The idealized (imaginary) product that I will value and provide an **R** script for will assume inflation-adjusted cash-flows and all numbers will be real (not nominal). To be clear, the exotic *deferred* income annuity I am calling an RCLA begins payments if-and-when the RPI hits zero. Or, using the language of this book, it starts

Source: Generated by Author

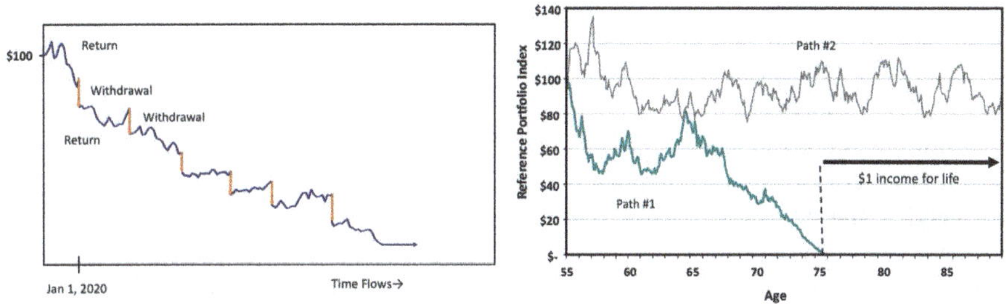

Fig. 14.2 Sample paths for the ruin-contingent life Annuity

paying at the end of portfolio longevity L_ξ, a.k.a. ruin time. Figure 14.2 provides an example of a possible sample path for the RPI and should hopefully make this concept clear. Basically, you walk into your favorite insurance company and ask for a $\xi = 1\%$ or $\xi = 3\%$ or $\xi = 5\%$ RCLA. The choice is yours to make, but you will pay a premium commensurate with the risk. A higher ξ is more expensive because L_ξ is shorter and the income for life starts earlier.

Here is a numerical example that should help explain the mechanics of the RPI, as well as the *stochastic* annuity start date. Assume that the SP500 index is at a level of \$100 on January 1st, 2020. This is the starting value of the reference portfolio whose longevity L_ξ will trigger the life annuity payment. Now, let's say you purchase an RCLA with a $\xi = 7\%$ withdrawal rate. (The exact price or premium for the RCLA is something I'll get to in the next section.) You could have selected a $\xi = 5\%$ or $\xi = 3\%$, etc., but settled on the $\xi = 7\%$, for whatever personal reasons. Moving on, during that first month of January 2020 assume the inflation-adjusted total return of the SP500 was 2%. This means that the level of a *vintage* 2020 reference portfolio index on the first day of February 2020 would be $\$100(1.02) - (7/12) = \$101.42$. Why? It is the annual withdrawal amount of \$7, divided by 12 to create the monthly withdrawal. Then, markets continue to evolve in February, March, April, etc., and the same calculation algorithm continues each month. The RPI (kind of) mimics the behavior of your retirement income portfolio. And, if the RPI hits zero (a.k.a. ruin) the insurance company commences a \$1 life annuity payments, as long as they were still **alive.** Again, Fig. 14.2 illustrates how the unique path of the RPI triggers the lifetime income payment. Under simulated path #1, the income starts at the age of 75. Under path #2 where the RPI never hits zero, the buyer (in January 2020) would receive nothing. Think of this as buying home insurance, car insurance, or any property insurance—but never putting in a claim. With an RCLA, the \$1 life annuity begins when your portfolio dies.

14.5 Some (Advanced) Valuation Theory

Echoing the notation and terminology around equation (9.6) in Chap. 9, I will use $\tilde{F}_t = \tilde{F}_t(\xi)$ to denote the level/value of the reference portfolio index. It is meant to mimic your retirement income portfolio, where the initial withdrawal rate is set at ξ percent of: $\tilde{F}_0 = F_0$. This means that $\tilde{F}_t$ is the so-called *state variable* underlying the payout from this type of *exotic option*. Note that from the point of view of the insurance company selling the RCLA, it can be (perfectly) hedged, no different from a conventional put option that was discussed at the end of Chap. 6. Therefore, from here on, I use the phrase *discounted value* to denote the company's *hedging cost*. I use these two terms interchangeably, knowing full-well that real-world companies must bake-in (to the recipes) profit margins, reserve requirements, and other regulatory capital that will increase the *market cost*. Note that what makes hedging possible for the insurance company is (1) the *law of large numbers* plus (2) the ability to **Delta Hedge** the embedded put option. In other words, the assumption here is the insurance company is selling many such RCLA policies, no different than the assumption they sell many life annuities. This way the cash outflows due to mortality become deterministic, leaving only cash-flows due to market fluctuations, which are no different from any other exotic (path dependent) put option. Likewise, the *discounted value* that I'm about to compute for this exotic option will differ from the personal *utility value*. Think back to the so-called δ at the end of Chap. 12, which captures how much an individual retiree would be willing to pay for such a product. To those who are familiar with the language of modern option pricing, I am computing the expected **Risk Neutral** payout.

To appreciate the valuation of an RCLA, I'll do a bit of a refresher and begin with the RCLA's close cousin, the *deferred* life annuity, denoted by GTLA, a.k.a. the *Advanced Life Delayed Annuity* (ALDA). The user-defined **R** function GTLA$(x, x+\tau, r, m, b)$ values a life annuity that pays \$1 per annum, where x denotes the purchase age, r denotes the risk-free discount rate, and $(x+\tau)$ is the starting age. Consistent with prior chapters, this annuity factor (generic a) can be written and expressed as

$$a := E\left[\int_{\tau}^{\infty} 1_{\{T_x>t\}} e^{-rt} dt\right] = \int_{\tau}^{\infty} ({}_t p_x) e^{-rt} dt, \tag{14.1}$$

where T_x is the remaining lifetime random variable (of a person age x) and $({}_t p_x)$ denotes the conditional probability of survival to age $(x+t)$. Remember that in the above expression τ is deterministic and denotes the deferral period before the insurance company begins making lifetime payments to the annuitant. The expectation embedded within Eq. (14.1) is taken with respect to the physical (real-world) measure underlying the distribution of T_x. Again, due to the *law of large numbers* we can eliminate all *idiosyncratic* mortality risk, so technically it's also the risk-neutral measure. But, in the event the mortality hazard rate $\tilde{\lambda}_t$ is stochastic, one would have to add a *mortality risk premium* to the annuity factor. (And yes, I do realize I'm veering too far into the chemistry versus the cooking.)

Rather, the only thing I would like to point out here is that under *any* continuous law of mortality that can be specified by a deterministic function $\lambda_t > 0$, the expectation in Eq. (14.1) can be rewritten as:

$$a := \int_{\tau}^{\infty} e^{-\int_0^t \lambda_s\, ds} e^{-rt}\, dt = \int_{\tau}^{\infty} e^{-\int_0^t (\lambda_s + r) ds} dt. \tag{14.2}$$

And, while virtually all the numerical examples in this chapter (and book) are based on the Gompertz–Makeham representation in which $\lambda_t = \lambda + (1/b)\exp\{(x + t - m)/b)\}$, the methodology described in this section can be used with *any* analytic form. Moving on, at the end of Chap. 10, and specifically in the derivation leading up to Eq. (10.15), I demonstrated how the *deferred* annuity factor can be written and expressed as:

$$a = \frac{b\Gamma(-(r+\lambda)b, \exp\{\frac{x-m+\tau}{b}\})}{\exp\left\{(m-x)(r+\lambda) - \exp\left\{\frac{x-m}{b}\right\}\right\}}, \tag{14.3}$$

where, once again, $\Gamma(\alpha, \beta)$ denotes the incomplete Gamma function. This is all well-known by now. But the reason I'm repeating this yet again is that the above expression can only be applied when τ is fixed and known in advance, that is the life annuity is *deferred* to age $(x+\tau)$. In contrast, the *ruin-contingent life annuity* begins payment when the reference portfolio index $\tilde{F}_t$ hits zero, which is an unknown. In fact, it would be tempting (but quite wrong) to let $\tau = E[L_\xi]$ and use that value in Eq. (14.3). See Jensen's inequality, for example.

So, it's time to (do a wee bit of chemistry and) delve into the stochastic properties of the state variable $\tilde{F}_t$, which triggers the payment. As I noted earlier and originally explained in Eq. (9.6), the dynamics of the reference portfolio satisfy

$$d\tilde{F}_t = \left(\mu\tilde{F}_t - \xi F_0\right) dt + \sigma\tilde{F}_t dB_t, \qquad \tilde{F}_0 = F_0. \tag{14.4}$$

The (new) parameter μ (mu) denotes the drift rate, which in Chap. 9 was actually $(\nu - \sigma^2/2)$ and σ denotes the diffusion coefficient. The constant ξF_0 is the fixed annual withdrawal amount. For the record, when $\xi = 0$ the process $\tilde{F}_t$ collapses to a so-called geometric Brownian motion (GBM), which is Eq. (9.4). That process can never access zero in finite time. So technically, positive values of ξ reduce the *drift* rate, making zero accessible in finite time. More relevant to us, the greater the value of ξ, the greater is the probability of ruin, all else being equal. Continuing with the formalities, I'll define the ruin time (a.k.a. the longevity of the portfolio) using the usual letter: L_ξ, which satisfies

$$L_\xi := \inf\left\{t;\, \tilde{F}_t \le 0 \mid \tilde{F}_0 = F_0\right\}. \tag{14.5}$$

Now, as I mentioned (many times) in Chaps. 5, 6 as well as Chap. 9, there is a possibility that $L_\xi = \infty$, which in the context of the RCLA means that the reference portfolio could possibly never hit zero. Of course, the insurance element is concerned with the opposite, namely that L_ξ is finite. I should remind readers that the lifetime ruin probability φ, defined and computed in Chap. 9, is actually: $\Pr[T_x \geq L_\xi]$. From that perspective, in this chapter I am interested in pricing and valuing a security that pays \$1 during the *time gap* between L_ξ and T_x, assuming it happens to be positive.

No different than any other generic life annuity, the ruin-contingent life annuity (RCLA) is acquired with a lump-sum premium now, even though the \$1 income payments do not commence until a random time: L_ξ. Again, if the portfolio never hits zero—or the annuitant dies prior to the RPI hitting zero—the RCLA expires worthless. Thus, the defining structure of the RCLA is similar to the annuity factor in Eq. (14.1), albeit with a stochastic upper *and* lower bound. Formally:

$$\texttt{RCLA} = E\left[\int_{L_\xi}^{L_\xi \vee T_x} e^{-rt} dt\right], \tag{14.6}$$

where the expression at the upper bound of integration $L_\xi \vee T_x$ represents the *latter* of the two random times. In words, both T_x and L_ξ are stochastic and unknown at time $t = 0$. But, if it happens that $T_x > L_\xi$, the annuity will pay from time L_ξ to time T_x. But, if $T_x < L_\xi$, and the retiree died prior to the ruin time, then the integral is from L_ξ to L_ξ, which is zero. In terms of currency, remember that each RCLA unit entitles the annuitant to (only) \$1 of income, which is how `GILA(.)`, `GTLA(.)`, and `GDLA(.)` are cooked. Therefore, if you think of an RCLA as insuring a fixed ξF_0 withdrawal plan, buying ξF_0 of these would generate ξF_0 dollars, if-and-when the portfolio is ruined.

Next, in order to derive a valuation expression (or formula) for the RCLA defined by Eq. (14.6), I'll do the following. First, I simplify notation by writing the standard *deferred* annuity factor as a function $H(\tau)$, where τ is the deferral time, so that $H(0)$ is recognized as an immediate annuity (previously written in short-form using a).

$$H(\tau) = \int_{\tau}^{\infty} ({}_t p_x)\, e^{-rt}\, dt = E\left[\int_{\tau}^{\tau \vee T_x} e^{-rt} dt \mid \tau\right] \tag{14.7}$$

This then leads us to the most important equation in this section, which is the expression for the *discounted value* of an RCLA.

$$E[H(L_\xi)] = E\left[E\Big[\int_{L_\xi}^{L_\xi \vee T_x} e^{-rt} dt \mid L_\xi\Big]\right] = E\left[\int_{L_\xi}^{L_\xi \vee T_x} e^{-rt} dt\right] \tag{14.8}$$

The left-hand side is the expectation we want to compute to get the RCLA. The double expectation in the middle of Eq. (14.8) is the short-cut used to compute the overall expectation in two steps. The internal one is known, the outer one is to be computed. At risk of flogging an entire stable of dead horses, from the perspective of the insurance company, any idiosyncratic longevity risk is diversified away.

Finally, in one last bit of "deep chemistry," using technical arguments explained in the paper referenced as [14], the central and key expectation we are after, $E[H(L_\xi)]$ is a **Martingale** in t. So, by the **Markov property**, it can be represented in the form $h(t \wedge L_\xi, \tilde{F}_t)$, where $h(t, z)$ is a new function that will be solved for. Then, alluding back to the brief mention in Sect. 9.6 and applying Ito's lemma leads to (something called) the **Kolmogorov** backward partial differential equation (PDE) for the expectation $E[H(L_\xi)]$ and the value of the RCLA.

$$\frac{\partial h(t,z)}{\partial t} + (\mu z - \xi F_0)\frac{\partial h(t,z)}{\partial z} + \frac{1}{2}\left(\sigma^2 z^2\right)\frac{\partial^2 h(t,z)}{\partial z^2} = 0 \tag{14.9}$$

for $z > 0$ and $t > 0$. In this equation—which I admit to some readers might look rather odd—the expression $\partial h(t,z)/\partial t$ is the first derivative of the (to be solved for) function $h(t,z)$ with respect to the time variable t. The expression $\partial h(t,z)/\partial z$ is the first derivative of $h(t,z)$ with respect to the space variable z, and $\partial^2 h(t,z)/\partial z^2$ is the second derivative of $h(t,z)$ with respect to the space variable z. The bottom line is that the value of the *ruin-contingent life annuity* is equal to $h(0, F_0)$, which is simply the function $h(t,z)$ evaluated at time $t = 0$, and the initial portfolio value $z = F_0 = \$100$.

Now, back to cooking, in the next section I will use a simulation-based approach to solve the integral in Eq. (14.8) and leave the numerical solution of the PDE as an exercise for the enterprising students. However, for those who are interested in the PDE route to RCLA, I should note the following. Equation (14.9) is quite similar to the (very) famous Black–Scholes–Merton (BSM) PDE which is used in option pricing, but upon closer inspection differs from BSM in a number of critical places. For example, the presence of the constant ξF_0 multiplying the "space" derivative $\partial h(t,z)/\partial z$ doesn't appear in the BSM version. Also, the **Boundary Conditions** that are a critical part of any solution scheme for PDEs are different from the linear ones used in valuing put and call options, for example. In the case of RCLA, two of the boundary conditions are: $h(t,z) \to 0$ when $t \to \infty$ or when $z \to \infty$. Why? Well, intuitively, the RCLA is worthless in situations where the underlying index (or portfolio) never gets ruined, that is $L_\xi = \infty$, and/or only gets ruined after the annuitants have all died. Also, another boundary condition for the PDE is that $f(t,0) = H(t)$, defined by Eq. (14.7). The intuition here is that if-and-when the underlying index hits zero at some future time τ, the live annuitant will be entitled to lifetime income whose actuarially discounted value is the annuity factor $F(\tau)$. These facts can also be confirmed in the **R** script (using simulation techniques) which I am about to describe. And again, for those who are interested in taking the PDE route, I refer readers to [14].

14.6 The R for RCLA

The following script values an RCLA by simulating and averaging N values of the *deferred* life annuity GDLA(.), where the deferral period is the *stochastic* portfolio longevity. The script assumes monthly withdrawals up to a maximum age of $\omega = 110$.

```
RCLA<-function(x,m,b,xi,sigma,r,N){
  mnths<-12*(110-x)
  path<-matrix(nrow=N,ncol=mnths)
  PLV<-c()
  for (i in 1:N){
    k2<-sigma/sqrt(12)
    k1<-r/12-(0.5)*k2^2
    return<-exp(rnorm(mnths,k1,k2))
    path[i,1]<-1
    for (j in 2:mnths){
      path[i,j]<-path[i,j-1]*return[j]-xi/12
      if (path[i,j]<=0) {break}
      }
    PLV[i]=GDLA(x,x+(j-2)/12,r,m,b)}
  mean(PLV)
}
```

Here are a number of important facts to remember about the above script. As noted earlier, because I am *valuing* an embedded option, the assumed growth rate, for the purposes of computing portfolio longevity L_ξ, is assumed to be the risk-free valuation rate and not the expected return from the portfolio. Please refer back to the discussion around Eq. (9.5) in Chap. 9, to understand how and why the drift $(\nu + \sigma^2/2)$ is replaced with the risk-free rate r, which implies that: $(\nu = r - \sigma^2/2)$ in continuous time. So, when discretizing and transitioning to monthly returns, the *mean* of the normally distributed return becomes: $(r - (0.5)\sigma^2)/12$. Stated using the language and terminology of option pricing, the portfolio longevity variable L_ξ is simulated using the *risk neutral*, not the *real-world* measure. For more information on the methodology, see the paper cited as [14]. To ensure your algorithm is working correctly, here are some numerical example of the value of a ruin-contingent life annuity (RCLA). Remember that these are simulated (not analytic) values, so your numbers will differ (slightly) from mine.

```
# (x,m,b,xi,sigma,valuation_rate,N)
RCLA(65,88,10,0.05,0.30,0.01,50000)
[1] 5.640901
RCLA(65,88,10,0.04,0.30,0.01,50000)
[1] 4.569608
```

```
RCLA(65,88,10,0.03,0.30,0.01,50000)
[1] 3.391947
```

The following table offers a more comprehensive list of values, which should help readers develop some intuition for the `RCLA(.)` concept. Start with the upper-left corner value, where $x = 55$, the investment volatility is $\sigma = 15\%$, and the withdrawal rate $\xi = 3\%$. In that case, the value of the ruin-contingent life annuity is \$3.093 per dollar of income. So, if you start with a \$1 million portfolio and drawdown \$30,000 per year, you can purchase an *exotic* longevity insurance policy that pays 30000× one RCLA unit or approximately \$92,790. This may seem like a very large sum of money to pay for insurance, but remember that it will protect you against *running out of money* while you are still alive. If-and-when your portfolio hits zero, the RCLA will continue to seamlessly pay the \$30,000 per year for the rest of your life.

Now, in contrast to the early retiree who begins $\xi = 3\%$ withdrawals at the age of $x = 55$, let us examine the price of the RCLA for the retiree at age $x = 65$. That number is (only) \$1.028 per \$1 of lifetime income, which means that price of protecting the entire \$30,000 withdrawal is (only) \$30,840. The price is (much) cheaper because you are 10 years older. So, even if the portfolio is ruined during your lifetime and the insurance company must pay you for the rest of your life, that period will be shorter. Hence, it's cheaper to insure. Notice that as you increase the withdrawal rate ξ and/or the volatility of the underlying portfolio σ, the cost of the ruin-contingent life annuity increases. Why? Because portfolio ruin is more likely (recall the discussion in Chap. 9), so the insurance is more expensive. For example, if your portfolio volatility is $\sigma = 30\%$ and you are withdrawing at the (familiar) rate of $\xi = 4\%$ from a \$1 million portfolio, then the insurance premium or cost is now $8.951 \times \$40{,}000 = \$358{,}040$ at the age of $x = 55$ and $4.570 \times \$40{,}000 = \$182{,}800$, if purchased at the age of $x = 65$. This high cost for protection might be yet another way of arguing that $\xi = 4\%$ is an imprudent and very high withdrawal rate from a portfolio. Remember, though, that all of the above numbers assume not only the usual Gompertz ($m = 88$, $b = 10$) parameters, but also a risk-free (valuation) rate of $r = 1\%$, which increases the cost of protection.

14.7 Final Comments

- The original RCLA was introduced and priced together with my two (long time) co-authors T.S. Salisbury and H. Huang, and most of the latter part of this chapter borrows heavily from our work together. In particular, see [13] as well as [14] and [9] for more. Likewise, see the articles [8] and especially [11] which argue for the utility value of *deferred* life annuities that begin payments at some advanced age.

- An RCLA is embedded inside every variable annuity with a guaranteed lifetime withdrawal benefit (GLWB), which means that the relative value of the GLWB, which depends on the specified withdrawal rate ξ, as well as the (lowest allowed) age x, and the (highest allowed) volatility σ. For some early and widely cited references on the valuation of GLWBs, see [1, 2, 5, 7, 10] and [16].
- For more on some alternative (exotic) annuity designs, see the references cited as [3, 12, 17]. For more on systematic longevity risk see references [4, 6]. References cited as [15, 19] discuss other exotic annuities and reference [18] discuss the economic implications of longevity on workplace pensions.

Questions and Problems

14.1 Per the discussion around the partial differential equation (14.9), create an **R** script that solves for the value of the RCLA using the numerical scheme which is described in great detail in the reference cited as [14]. This course assumes you have experience solving a PDE. If not, skip right ahead to the next problem.

14.2 Using the **R** script for the `RCLA(.)` value, confirm the values listed in Table 14.1 and compute the relevant numbers at the age of $x = 60$ and $\sigma = 25$, and confirm they all sit in between the values listed in the table.

14.3 Modify the `RCLA(.)` code so that it assumes *weekly* and not monthly withdrawals and then recompute the numbers in Table 14.1. Are the RCLA values higher or lower when the withdrawals are taken out weekly versus monthly? Is there a consistent pattern? Explain intuitively why this might be the case.

14.4 Modify the `RCLA(.)` code to value a modified version that begins paying \$1 for life, as soon as the underlying reference index, which I denoted by $\tilde{F}_t$, loses 80% of its value. In other words, the payoff is not triggered by *ruin*, but by *very bad markets*. Please generate numbers similar to Table 14.1, and compare results. How much *more* expensive is such a product? Why?

Table 14.1 The value of a ruin-contingent life Annuity (RCLA)

	Initial withdrawal rate from the portfolio				
Initial purchase age	$\xi = 3\%$	$\xi = 4\%$	$\xi = 5\%$	$\xi = 6\%$	$\xi = \infty$
			Low volatility $\sigma = 15\%$		
Age $x = 55$	\$3.093	\$5.398	\$7.623	\$9.590	\$24.456
Age $x = 65$	\$1.028	\$2.131	\$3.446	\$4.713	\$17.879
			High volatility $\sigma = 30\%$		
Age $x = 55$	\$7.118	\$8.951	\$10.463	\$11.850	\$24.456
Age $x = 65$	\$3.392	\$4.570	\$5.641	\$6.620	\$17.879

Note: $N = 50{,}000$ with $v = 1\%$, and Gompertz $m = 88$, $b = 10$

14.5 Finally, please modify (or create a new) **R** script that prices the following variant of an RCLA. Namely, assume that you have $\tilde{F}_0 = \$100$ and are withdrawing at the rate of $\xi \tilde{F}_0$. But, if at the end of the year the portfolio value $\tilde{F}_t$ exceeds the original F_0, the withdrawal amount is **ratcheted** up and increased to $\xi \tilde{F}_t$. So, for example, if $\tilde{F}_1 = \$200$, by some lucky chance, then from that point onward the withdrawal amount is doubled, but never reduced. What is the value of an RCLA that pays off \$1 if-and-when this enhanced index is ruined?

References

1. Bacinello, A. R., Millossovich, P., Olivieri, A., & Pitacco, E. (2011). Variable annuities: A unifying valuation approach. *Insurance: Mathematics and Economics, 49*(3), 285–297.
2. Bauer, D., Kling, A., & Russ, J. (2008). A universal pricing framework for guaranteed minimum benefits in variable annuities. *ASTIN Bulletin: The Journal of the IAA, 38*(2), 621–651.
3. Brautigam, M., Guillen, M., & Nielsen, J. P. (2017). Facing up to longevity with old actuarial methods: a comparison of pooled funds and income tontines. *The Geneva Papers on Risk and Insurance-Issues and Practice, 42*(3), 406–422.
4. Boon, L. N., Briere, M., & Werker, B. J. (2019). Systematic longevity risk: to bear or to insure? *Journal of Pension Economics and Finance, 19*, 409–441.
5. Chen, Z., Vetzal, K., & Forsyth, P. A. (2008). The effect of modeling parameters on the value of GMWB guarantees. *Insurance: Mathematics and Economics, 43*(1), 165–173.
6. Cocco, J. F., & Gomes, F. J. (2012). Longevity risk, retirement savings and financial innovation. *Journal of Financial Economics, 103*(3), 507–529.
7. Dai, M., Kuen Kwok, Y., & Zong, J. (2008). Guaranteed minimum withdrawal benefit in variable annuities. *Mathematical Finance: An International Journal of Mathematics, Statistics and Financial Economics, 18*(4), 595–611.
8. Denuit, M., Haberman, S., & Renshaw, A. E. (2015). Longevity-contingent deferred life annuities. *Journal of Pension Economics and Finance, 14*(3), 315–327.
9. Fard, F. A., & Rong, N. (2014). Pricing and managing risks of ruin contingent life annuities under regime switching variance gamma process. *Annals of Finance, 10*(2), 315–332.
10. Fonseca, J. D., & Ziveyi, J. (2017). Valuing variable annuity guarantees on multiple assets. *Scandinavian Actuarial Journal, 2017*(3), 209–230.
11. Gong, G., & Webb, A. (2010). Evaluating the Advanced life deferred annuity: An annuity people might actually buy. *Insurance: Mathematics and Economics, 46*(1), 210–221.
12. Horneff, V., Maurer, R., Mitchell, O. S., & Rogalla, R. (2015). Optimal life cycle portfolio choice with variable annuities offering liquidity and investment downside protection. *Insurance: Mathematics and Economics, 63*, 91–107.
13. Huang, H., Milevsky, M. A., & Salisbury, T. S. (2009). A different perspective on retirement income sustainability: The blueprint for a ruin contingent life annuity (RCLA). *The Journal of Wealth Management, 11*(4), 89–96.
14. Huang, H., Milevsky, M. A., & Salisbury, T. S. (2014). Valuation and hedging of the ruin-contingent life annuity (RCLA). *Journal of Risk and Insurance, 81*(2), 367–395.
15. Marshall, C., Hardy, M., & Saunders, D. (2010). Valuation of a guaranteed minimum income benefit. *North American Actuarial Journal, 14*(1), 38–58.
16. Milevsky, M. A., & Salisbury, T. S. (2006). Financial valuation of guaranteed minimum withdrawal benefits. *Insurance: Mathematics and Economics, 38*(1), 21–38.

17. Milevsky, M. A., & Salisbury, T. S. (2015). Optimal retirement income tontines. *Insurance: Mathematics and Economics, 64*, 91–105.
18. Mitchell, O. S., & Piggott, J. (2016). Workplace-linked pensions for an aging demographic. *Handbook of the Economics of Population Aging, 1*, 865–904. North-Holland.
19. Pitacco, E. (2016). Guarantee structures in life annuities: A comparative analysis. *The Geneva Papers on Risk and Insurance-Issues and Practice, 41*(1), 78–97.

Chapter 15
Very Last Thoughts

This chapter very briefly discusses some of the topics that were **not** covered in this book, but that nevertheless are important for *retirement income* planning. References to relevant research work are noted where appropriate and interested readers are directed to those sources for further information.

15.1 Annuity Puzzles

A substantial portion of this recipe book has been focused on the valuation and/or benefits of life annuities, see in particular Chaps. 10 and 12. The general topic of annuities, both variable and fixed, has been a primary research focus of mine for over two decades now. I published my first paper on *annuities* in the year 1998, cited as [16], which argued for the benefits of annuities using a *probabilistic* framework, but also showed why you shouldn't buy them too early in life. The term *pensionize*—as an alternative to the word annuitize—was coined in my mass market book with A. Macqueen, originally published in 2010, revised in 2015, and cited as [17]. But alas, not everyone *likes* annuities as much we (academics) do, and the jaundiced group includes both financial advisors and the public. The benefits of longevity insurance, risk-pooling, and guaranteed income for life are difficult to argue with, and yet the aversion to (and bias against) these insurance products is widespread. *Why?* Well, the reasons for this aversion might be due to (1) product illiquidity, (2) bequest motives, (3) distrust of insurance companies, (4) anti-selection costs, and (5) most certainly the confusion surrounding the exact definition of an annuity. The widespread dislike of annuities is now a formal field of academic study (you can actually write a Ph.D. thesis on the topic) known as *The Annuity Puzzle.*

For more on this, start with article [1] and then [2, 3, 6, 9, 13, 19]. In particular, [20] makes the compelling argument that (the fear of) unexpected medical expenses

M. A. Milevsky, *Retirement Income Recipes in R*, Use R!,
https://doi.org/10.1007/978-3-030-51434-1_15

can be a (very) large and rational impediment to *pensionization*. This gets to the topic of long-term care, which I'll return to in a moment.

15.2 Consumption Puzzles

While on the topic of (so-called) puzzles, another fact that is hard to explain or justify within the conventional life-cycle model—the economic backbone of this book—is the observation that retirees do not consume their retirement wealth *fast enough*. So, while Chap. 11 introduced an *intelligent drawdown* scheme that is expected to deplete wealth during the retirement years, few people do in fact spend down (that) quickly. Oddly enough, a large number of retirees spend nothing more than the interest plus dividends generated by their financial capital, and many end up dying with the same wealth they started with, when they retired. Of course, not everyone behaves in this puzzling way, and the COVID-19 recession (depression) might change that behavior—or reinforce it—in a permanent manner. Nevertheless, for additional research on this *consumption puzzle*, linked to the above-noted *annuity puzzle*, start with the articles cited as [15], as well as [18]. Interestingly, the recent article [11] argues that overly optimistic longevity projections are to blame. Namely, many retirees (erroneously) believe they will live much longer than their true life horizon, which I denoted by: T_x. So, they spend (much) less. Of course, if retirees truly think they will live *that* long, why don't these same (overly) optimistic consumers buy (more) life annuities? I guess the *puzzles* continue. A recent movement to covert Defined Contribution (DC) pension balances into stream of income might help individuals better optimize their consumption plans. See [10] for more.

15.3 Long-Term Care (LTC) Insurance

One *retirement risk* that I didn't address in the book is the growing (concern and) need for long-term care, including nursing homes and assisted living facilities. The cost (or blessing) of longevity is amplified by the inability to care for yourself towards the end of the life-cycle. In one way or another we all need some form of assistance for that *stage of our lives*. And, the insurance industry has created a variety of long-term care policies that pay off if-and-when you are unable to perform the normal activities of daily living. See, for example, the article cited as [22] for a review and discussion of how such LTC products work and would be triggered. Interestingly, these products are (also) not as popular as *classical life-cycle theory* would suggest, and there is a growing body of research that tries to (1) develop more advanced utility-based models that can explain the aversion to LTC insurance and/or (2) focus on the flaws and problems with existing products, and how they can be improved. For more on LTC from the perspective of life-cycle economics, see the articles cited as [5], as well as [7] more generally about the demand for insurance. It's quite possible that given the rather subjective triggers within these LTC policies—*Can you really not dress or bathe yourself?*—consumers justifiably fear insurance companies will renege, decline, or simply deny these claims. This obviously reduces the demand for these products. See the work by Richard Thaler and Amos Tversky, cited as [21] for more on this concern as a possible justification for the reduced demand for (any type of) insurance whose payoff is *probabilistic* or subject to default.

15.4 Drawdowns with Income Taxes

Looking back with hindsight, one of the topics that didn't receive as much attention as it should in this recipe book is the complex subject of *income taxes*, and in particular the impact on intelligent drawdown strategies. Needless to say, almost every retiree is subject to some form of explicit (or implicit) income tax, which distorts and impedes attempts to *smooth consumption* towards the end of the life-cycle. The complexities that arise from income taxes take on many forms. In practice financial capital is held in different accounts that are taxed differently. For example, some accounts (a.k.a. "buckets") are fully *taxable*, some accounts are *tax deferred* (similar to RRSPs in Canada, or 401k's in the USA), and some accounts are *tax-free* (such as TFSAs in Canada or ROTH accounts in the USA). There are other accounts (or buckets) inside life insurance policies that are tax-deferred and possibly tax-free to the beneficiary, upon the death of the insured. Likewise, some pension annuity benefits are tax-free, others are taxable. Annuity taxation depends on the buckets in which the annuities are placed, etc.

What this all means is that in addition to deciding how much to withdraw in every year of retirement—a.k.a. the drawdown problem—the retiree must decide from which of the many accounts to actually make these withdrawals. This is a *devilishly* difficult mathematical problem, especially when you consider that income taxes are a non-linear function of income. Add to that the uncertainty of future tax rates themselves—as well as the stochasticity of investment returns—and it's no wonder Professor (and economics Nobel Laureate) Bill Sharpe labeled this "one of the most difficult financial problems" he has ever tried to solve. (So, I didn't try.)

But, for those readers who are interested in pursuing and/or reading more about this embryonic area of research, namely the overlap of retirement income optimization and tax uncertainty, see the articles cited as [4, 8, 14] and [12] and the references therein.

In conclusion, if indeed there is a sequel or second edition of this recipe book, properly modifying the *intelligent drawdown* algorithm to account for the various income tax buckets in conjunction with pension benefit entitlements, will be at the very top of my list. In the meantime, I trust there is enough *meat* (or tofu) in the current version to keep you *cooking*.

References

1. Alexandrova, M., & Gatzert, N. (2019). What do we know about annuitization decisions? *Risk Management and Insurance Review, 22*(1), 57–100.
2. Benartzi, S., Previtero, A., & Thaler, R. H. (2011). Annuitization puzzles. *Journal of Economic Perspectives, 25*(4), 143–64.
3. Boyer, M. M., Box-Couillard, S., & Michaud, P. C. (2019, in press). Demand for annuities: Price sensitivity, risk perceptions, and knowledge. *Journal of Economic Behavior and Organization*. https://doi.org/10.1016/j.jebo.2019.03.022
4. Brown, D. C., Cederburg, S., & O'Doherty, M. S. (2017). Tax uncertainty and retirement savings diversification. *Journal of Financial Economics, 126*(3), 689–712.
5. Brown, J. R., & Finkelstein, A. (2007). Why is the market for long-term care insurance so small? *Journal of Public Economics, 91*(10), 1967–1991.
6. Brown, J. R., Kling, J. R., Mullainathan, S., & M. V. Wrobel (2008). Why don't people insure late-life consumption? A framing explanation of the under-annuitization puzzle. *American Economic Review, 98*(2), 304–309.
7. Cohen, A., & Einav, L. (2007). Estimating risk preferences from deductible choice. *American Economic Review, 97*(3), 745–788.
8. DiLellio, J. A., & Ostrov, D. N. (2017). Optimal strategies for traditional versus Roth IRA/401(k) consumption during retirement. *Decision Sciences, 48*(2), 356–384.
9. Finkelstein, A., & Poterba, J. (2004). Adverse selection in insurance markets: Policyholder evidence from the U.K. annuity market. *Journal of Political Economy, 112*(1), 183–208.
10. Goda, G. S., Manchester, C. F., & Sojourner, A. J. (2014). What will my account really be worth? Experimental evidence on how retirement income projections affect saving. *Journal of Public Economics, 119*, 80–92.
11. Heimer, R. Z., Myrseth, K. O. R., & Schoenle, R. S. (2019). YOLO: Mortality beliefs and household finance puzzles. *Journal of Finance, 74*(6), 2957–2996.
12. Huang, H., & Milevsky, M. A. (2016). Longevity risk and retirement income tax efficiency: A location spending rate puzzle. *Insurance: Mathematics and Economics, 71*, 50–62.
13. Inkman, J., Lopes, P., & Michaelides, A. (2010). How deep is the annuity market participation puzzle. *The Review of Financial Studies, 24*(1), 279–317.
14. Lachance, M. E. (2013). Roth versus traditional accounts in a life-cycle model with tax risk. *Journal of Pension Economics and Finance, 12*(1), 28–61.
15. Love, D. A., Palumbo, M. G., & Smith, P. A. (2009). The trajectory of wealth in retirement. *Journal of Public Economics, 93*(1–2), 191–208.
16. Milevsky, M. A. (1998). Optimal asset allocation towards the end of the life cycle: to annuitize or not to annuitize? *Journal of Risk and Insurance, 65*(3), 401–426.
17. Milevsky, M. A., & Macqueen, A. C. (2015). *Pensionize your nest egg: How to use product allocation to create a guaranteed income for life*. Toronto: Wiley.
18. Poterba, J. M., Venti, S., & Wise, D. (2011). The composition and drawdown of wealth in retirement. *Journal of Economic Perspectives, 25*(4), 95–118.
19. Ramsay, C. M., & Oguledo, V. I. (2018). Annuity puzzle and an outline of its solution. *North American Actuarial Journal, 22*(4), 623–645. https://doi.org/10.1080/10920277.2018.1470936
20. Reichling, F., & Smetters, K. (2015). Optimal annuitization with stochastic mortality and correlated mortality cost. *American Economic Review, 11*, 3273–3320.
21. Wakker, P., Thaler, R., & Tversky, A. (1997). Probabilistic insurance. *Journal of Risk and Uncertainty, 15*(1), 7–28.
22. Wu, S., Bateman, H., & Stevens, R. (2016). *Optimal portfolio choice with health-contingent income products: The value of life care annuities*. Available at SSRN: https://ssrn.com/abstract=2817208 or http://dx.doi.org/10.2139/ssrn.2817208

Glossary of User Defined R-Functions

`RGOA(g,v,N)`. This function is an abbreviation for regular growth ordinary annuity, which is a type of present value factor for growing cash-flows.

`SMCR(x,f,w,g,v,R,D)`. Computes an optimal smooth consumption rate, as a function of financial and demographic parameters.

`OLCF(x,x0,f0,w0,g,v,R,D)`. Computes the optimal amount of financial capital that should be accumulated at any age, using financial and demographic parameters.

`FCMW(x,x0,g,v,R,D)`. Computes the optimal amount of financial capital that should be accumulated at any age, expressed as a wage multiple.

`PL(v,c,F)`. Computes portfolio longevity (PL), in units of years, assuming a given amount of initial wealth and fixed withdrawals under a constant fixed return.

`DTRJ(t,v,c,F)`. Computes the deterministic trajectory of a retirement portfolio using the life-cycle parameters.

`PLSM(F,c,nu,sigma,N)`. Computes a vector of random portfolio longevity (PL) values, assuming normally distributed investment returns.

`PLSM.SR(F,c,nu,sigma,N)`. Simulates and retains portfolio investment returns as well as the portfolio longevity values associated with those returns. This function is a generalized version of the `PLSM` function.

`SPQR(x,y,qx)`. Computes the survival rate (a.k.a. probability) to a given age, conditional on a current age and given the 1-year death rate vector.

`TPXG(x,t,m,b)`. Computes survival probabilities based on the Gompertz law.

`GRAN(N,x,m,b)`. Generates *random* lifetimes, based on the Gompertz law.

`LTLD(z)`. Creates a cohort life table (CLT) from a dataset of random lifetimes.

`G(a,c)`. Computes the incomplete Gamma function.

`a(v,x,m,b)`. Computes a Gompertz random lifetime present value.

`LRPG(v,xi,x,m,b)`. Computes the lifetime ruin probability (LRP) at a given age, under fixed investment rates, and an initial withdrawal rate with a Gompertz lifetime.

M. A. Milevsky, *Retirement Income Recipes in R*, Use R!,
https://doi.org/10.1007/978-3-030-51434-1

VARPHI.SM(N,x,m,b,xi,nu,sigma). Using simulation techniques, it approximates the lifetime ruin probability when investment returns are random (lognormal), under a Gompertz remaining lifetime.

VARPHI.MM(.). Computes the lifetime ruin probability using moment-matching techniques.

IRR(v). Computes internal rates of return.

GILA(x,v,m,b). Gompertz *immediate* life annuity.

GTLA(x,tau,v,m,b). Gompertz *temporary* life annuity.

GDLA(x,y,v,m,b). Gompertz *deferred* life annuity (a.k.a. ALDA, DIA, QLAC).

IDDR(Fx,pi,x,m,b,r,rho,gam). Computes a "rational" amount of consumption (a.k.a. drawdown or portfolio spending), as a function of current age, financial capital, assumed returns, the Gompertz parameters, as well as the amount of pre-existing pension income, longevity risk aversion, and a subjective discount rate.

WDT.PSI(psi,x,m,b,r,rho,gam). Computes the wealth depletion time (WDT).

PSI.OPT(tau,x,m,b,r,rho,gam). Optimal *pensionization* based on WDT.

DLTA(x,m,b,v,gam). Computes the utility-based value of a pension annuity.

UGHG(x,h0,g,v,gam). The same as DLTA, but using (h_0, g).

GMSP(x,t,lam,m,b). Is the Gompertz–Makeham (GM) survival probability.

GMPDF(x,t,lam,m,b). Is the probability density function of the GM variable.

GMLE(x,lam,m,b). Computes life expectancy under a GM variable.

CLAM(b,x star,lam star). Applies compensation law of mortality to map b into m.

LRAG(x,x star,g hat,g,lam hat,lam,lam star). Computes long evity risk-adjusted global age.

RCLA(x,m,b,xi,sigma,r,N). Values a ruin-contingent life annuity.

Printed in the USA
CPSIA information can be obtained
at www.ICGtesting.com
CBHW071009060924
14193CB00004B/112

9 783030 514334